# HTTP Programming Recipes for Java Bots

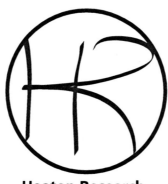

**Heaton Research**

# HTTP Programming Recipes for Java Bots

by Jeff Heaton

Heaton Research, Inc.
St. Louis

HTTP Programming Recipes for Java Bots, First Edition

First printing

Publisher: Heaton Research, Inc

Author: Jeff Heaton

Editor: Mary McKinnis

Cover Art: Carrie Spear

```
ISBN's for all Editions:
0-9773206-6-9, Softcover
0-9773206-8-5, Adobe PDF e-book
```

# SOFTWARE LICENSE AGREEMENT: TERMS AND CONDITIONS

## WARRANTY

Heaton Research, Inc. warrants the enclosed media to be free of physical defects for a period of ninety (90) days after purchase. The Software is not available from Heaton Research, Inc. in any other form or media than that enclosed herein or posted to www.heatonresearch.com. If you discover a defect in the media during this warranty period, you may obtain a replacement of identical format at no charge by sending the defective media, postage prepaid, with proof of purchase to:

```
Heaton Research, Inc.
Customer Support Department
1734 Clarkson Rd #107
Chesterfield, MO 63017-4976


Web: www.heatonresearch.com
E-Mail: support@heatonresearch.com
```

After the 90-day period, you can obtain replacement media of identical format by sending us the defective disk, proof of purchase, and a check or money order for $10, payable to Heaton Research, Inc..

## DISCLAIMER

Heaton Research, Inc. makes no warranty or representation, either expressed or implied, with respect to the Software or its contents, quality, performance, merchantability, or fitness for a particular purpose. In no event will Heaton Research, Inc., its distributors, or dealers be liable to you or any other party for direct, indirect, special, incidental, consequential, or other damages arising out of the use of or inability to use the Software or its contents even if advised of the possibility of such damage. In the event that the Software includes an online update feature, Heaton Research, Inc. further disclaims any obligation to provide this feature for any specific duration other than the initial posting.

The exclusion of implied warranties is not permitted by some states. Therefore, the above exclusion may not apply to you. This warranty provides you with specific legal rights; there may be other rights that you may have that vary from state to state. The pricing of the book with the Software by Heaton Research, Inc. reflects the allocation of risk and limitations on liability contained in this agreement of Terms and Conditions.

## SHAREWARE DISTRIBUTION

This Software may contain various programs that are distributed as shareware. Copyright laws apply to both shareware and ordinary commercial software, and the copyright Owner(s) retains all rights. If you try a shareware program and continue using it, you are expected to register it. Individual programs differ on details of trial periods, registration, and payment. Please observe the requirements stated in appropriate files.

*This book is dedicated,*
*with love, to Tracy.*

## Acknowledgments

There are several people who I would like to acknowledge. First, I would like to thank the many people who have given me suggestions and comments on my other books over the years.

I would like to thank Mary McKinnis for editing the book. I would also like to thank Mary McKinnis for trying out the book examples and offering many helpful suggestions.

I would like to thank Carrie Spear for the cover, as well as layout and formatting suggestions.

# Contents at a Glance

# Contents

# Table of Figures

# Table of Listings

# Table of Tables

# INTRODUCTION

Java provides a rich set of classes to allow for programmatic access to the web. Using these classes HTTP and HTTPS programs can be created that automate tasks performed by human users of the web. These programs are called bots. Chapters 1 and 2 introduce you to HTTP programming.

Chapter 1 of this book begins by examining the structure of HTTP requests. If you are to create programs that make use of the HTTP protocol it is important to understand the structure of the HTTP protocol. This chapter explains what packets are exchanged between web servers and web browsers, as well as the makeup of these packets.

Chapter 2 shows how to monitor the packets being transferred between a web server and web browser. Using a program, called a Network Analyzer, you can quickly see what HTTP packets are being exchanged. To create a successful bot, your bot must exchange the same packets with the web server that a user would. A Network Analyzer can help quickly create a bot by showing you

From Chapter 3 and beyond this book is structured as a set of recipes. You are provided with short concise programming examples for many common HTTP programming tasks. Most of the chapters are organized into two parts. The first part introduces the topic of the chapter. The second part is a collection of recipes. These recipes are meant to be starting points for your own programs that will require similar functionality.

Chapter 3 shows how to execute simple HTTP requests. A simple HTTP request is one that accesses only a single web page. All data that is needed will be on that page and no additional information must be passed to the web server.

Chapter 4 goes beyond simple requests and shows how to make use of other features of the HTTP protocol. HTTP server and client headers are introduced. Additionally, you will be shown how to access data from basic HTML files.

Chapter 5 shows how to use HTTPS. HTTPS is the more secure version of HTTP. Use of HTTPS is generally automatic in Java. However, you will be shown some of the HTTPS specific features that Java provides, and how to use them. You will also be introduced to HTTP authentication, which is a means by which the web server can prompt the user for an id and password.

Chapter 6 shows how to access data from a variety of HTML sources. An HTML parser is developed that will be used with most of the remaining recipes in this book. You are shown how to use this parser to extract data from forms, lists, tables and other structures. Recipes are provided that will serve as a good starting point for any of these HTML constructs.

Chapter 7 shows how to interact with HTML forms. HTML forms are very important to web sites that need to interact with the user. This chapter will show how to construct the appropriate response to an HTML form. You are shown how each of the control types of the form interacts with the web server.

Chapter 8 shows how to handle cookies and sessions. You will see that the web server can track who is logged on and maintain a session using either cookies or a URL variable. A useful class will be developed that will handle cookie processing in Java.

Chapter 9 explains the effects that JavaScript can have on a bot. JavaScript allows programs to be executed by the web browser. This can complicate matters for bots. The bot programmer must understand how JavaScript helps to shape the content of HTTP packets being produced by the browser. The bot must provide these same packets if it is to work properly.

Chapter 10 explains the effects that AJAX can have on a bot. AJAX is based on XML and JavaScript. It has many of the same effects on a bot program as JavaScript does. However, most AJAX web sites are designed to communicate with the web server using XML. This can make creating a bot for an AJAX website easier.

Chapter 11 introduces web services. Web services have replaced many of the functions previously performed by bots. Sites that make use of web services provide access to their data through XML. This makes it considerably easier to access their data than writing a traditional bot. Additionally, you can use web services in conjunction with regular bot programming. This produces a hybrid bot.

Chapter 12 shows how to create bots that make use of RSS feeds. RSS is an XML format that allows quick access to the newest content on a web site. Bots can be constructed to automatically access RSS information from a web site.

Chapter 13 introduces the Heaton Research Spider. The Heaton Research Spider is an open source implementation of a Java spider. There is also a C# version of the Heaton Research Spider. A spider is a program that is designed to access a large number of web pages. The spider does this by continuously visiting the links of web pages, and then pages found at those links. A web spider visits sites much as a biological spider crawls its web.

The remaining chapters of the chapters of this book do not include recipes. Chapters 14 and 15 explain how the Heaton Research Spider works. Chapter 16 explains how to create well behaved bots.

Chapter 14 explains the internals of the Heaton Research Spider. The Heaton Research Spider is open source. Because of this you can modify it to suit your needs. Chapter 14 discusses the internal structure of the Heaton Research Spider. By default the Heaton Research Spider uses computer memory to track the list of visited URLs. This chapter explains how this memory based URL tracking works. The next chapter explains how to use an SQL database instead of computer memory.

Chapter 15 explains how the Heaton Research Spider makes use of databases. The Heaton Research Spider can use databases to track the URLs that it has visited. This allows the spider to access a much larger volume of URLs than when using computer memory to track the URL list.

The book ends with Chapter 16 which discusses how to create "Well Behaved Bots". Bots are not welcome on all web sites. Some web sites publish files that outline how bots are to access their site. It is very important to respect the wishes of the web master when creating a bot.

# CHAPTER 1: THE STRUCTURE OF HTTP REQUESTS

- Understanding the Structure of Surfing
- Using the HTTP Recipes Web Site
- Understanding HTTP Requests

This book will show how to create HTTP programs in Java. HTTP programming allows programs to be constructed that retrieve information from web sites in much the same way as a human user surfs the web. These programs are called bots. This book will present many useful recipes for commonly performed HTTP programming tasks. Using these recipes a wide array of bots can be constructed.

To create HTTP programs with Java an understanding of the structure of HTTP requests is required. This chapter will introduce this structure. Understanding this structure will allow the programmer to create programs that surf the web just as a user does.

## The HTTP Recipes Examples Site

The Java bots created in this book are only half of the HTTP communication protocol. These bots must communicate with a web server. For example, a typical HTTP bot may access a popular online bookseller and obtain a price for a certain book. I could write an example bot that accesses Amazon.com and obtains this price. However, there are several problems with this.

- Amazon may prohibit bot access of their site
- Amazon may modify their site and break my bot

Both issues are important. If the examples in this book were all written to use real-world web sites, a major site redesign to these sites could leave many of the book examples non-functional. One minor change to one of these sites, and the related examples in the book would immediately become out of date.

Additionally, some sites do not allow access by bots. There are two main ways to stop bot access to a web site.

- Lawyers
- Technology

Some sites specify in their Terms of Service (TOS) agreement that their site may not be accessed programmatically with a bot. From a technical standpoint, they may do nothing to actually prevent bots from accessing their site. They just reserve the right to take legal action for accessing their site programmatically. If you have any questions about the legality of accessing a particular site, always contact a lawyer. Such information is beyond the scope of this book.

Because of these reasons, the book examples all make use of a special demonstration site owned by Heaton Research. The pages, used by the book's bots, on the special web site will never change. This special web site contains many pages and applications that simulate many of the real-world web sites that bots may be written for. This web site can be accessed at the following URL:

`http://www.httprecipes.com/`

If accessed with a browser, the recipe site will appear as Figure 1.1.

**Figure 1.1: The HTTP Recipes Web Site**

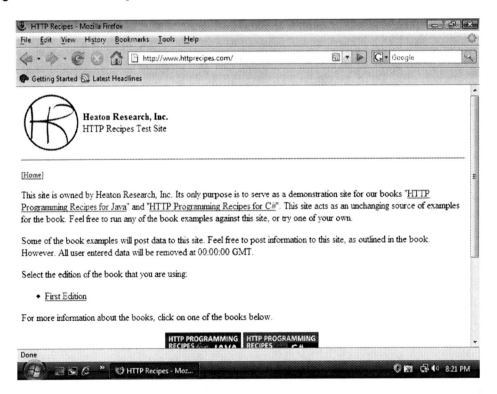

As can be seen from Figure 1.1, the first thing the web site presents the surfer with is the edition of this book. If future editions of this book are released, in the years to come, the examples on this site for a particular edition will not change. New areas will be added for new editions. Since this is the first edition of the book, choose the first edition.

The homepage for the first edition of this book is shown in Figure 1.2.

**Figure 1.2: The Homepage for this Book**

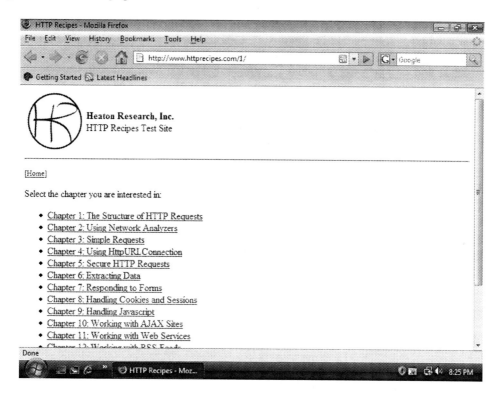

From this page links are provided to all of the chapters from this book. Some of the examples will require access the site using a web browser. Other examples will use bots to access this site. Some examples may be a combination of both.

The examples site will be put to use in the following sections.

## The Structure of Surfing

As a user uses the web browser there is considerable network activity occurring to support the browsing experience. The Hyper Text Transport Protocol (HTTP) is what allows this to happen. HTTP specifies how web browsers and web servers manage the flurry of requests and responses that occur while a web user is surfing the web. Once it understood how web browsers and servers communicate, the built in HTTP classes, provided by Java, can be used to obtain information from a web server programmatically.

If you already understand the structure of HTTP requests between web servers and web browsers, you may be able to skip this chapter and proceed directly to Chapter 2, "Analyzing Sites", or Chapter 3, "Simple HTTP Requests". Chapter 2 expands on Chapter 1 by showing how to use a "network analyzer" to examine, first hand, the information exchanged between a web server and web browser. A network analyzer can be very valuable when attempting to program a bot to access a very complex web site. However, if you are already familiar with using network analyzers, you may proceed directly to Chapter 3, which begins with Java HTTP programming.

The first thing to understand about web browsing is that it is made up of a series of HTTP requests and responses. The web browser sends a request to the server, and the server responds. This is a one sided communication. The opposite never occurs. The web server will never request something of the web browser.

The HTTP protocol begins when the browser requests the first page from a web server. It continues as additional pages from that site are requested. To see how this works, the next section will examine the requests that are sent between the web server and web browser.

## Examining HTTP Requests

In this section the requests that pass between the web server and web browser will be examined. The first step is to examine the HTTP requests for a typical web page. This page will be covered in the next section. Understanding how a single page is transmitted is key to seeing how that page fits into a typical surfing session.

### A Typical Web Page

A typical web page is displayed on the browser by placing text and images via requests. One of the first things to understand about HTTP requests is that at the heart of each request is a Uniform Resource Locater (URL). The URL tells the web server which file should be sent. The URL could point to an actual file, such as a Hyper Text Markup Language (HTML), or it could point to an image file, such as a GIF or JPEG.

URLs are what the web user types into a browser to access a web page. Chapter 3, "Simple HTTP Requests", will explain what each part of the URL is for. For now, they simply identify a resource, somewhere on the Internet, that is being requested.

The "typical webpage" for this example is at the following URL:

`http://www.httprecipes.com/1/1/typical.php`

The actual contents of the "typical webpage" are shown in Figure 1.3.

## Figure 1.3: A Typical Webpage

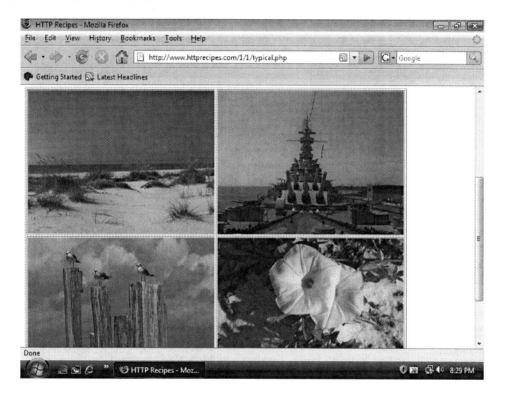

As can be seen in Figure 1.3, four pictures are displayed in the middle of the page. There are actually a total of five pictures, if the Heaton Research logo is counted. When a web page such as this is opened, the HTML, as well as all images must be downloaded.

The first HTTP request is always for the URL that was typed into the browser. This URL is usually an HTML page. The HTML page is a single HTTP request. The text of this HTML file is all that will be transferred on this HTTP request.

It is important to note that only one physical file is transferred per HTTP request. The HTML page will be downloaded and examined for other embedded files that are required to display the web page. Listing 1.1 shows the HTML of the "typical web page".

**Listing 1.1: HTML for the Typical Web Page**

```
<!DOCTYPE HTML PUBLIC "-//W3C//DTD HTML 4.01 Transitional//EN">

<HTML>
<HEAD>
     <TITLE>HTTP Recipes</TITLE>
     <meta http-equiv="Content-Type" content="text/html;
charset=UTF-8">
     <meta http-equiv="Cache-Control" content="no-cache">
</HEAD>

<BODY>

<table border="0"><tr><td>
<a href="http://www.httprecipes.com/"><img src="/images/logo.gif"
alt="Heaton Research Logo" border="0"></a>
</td><td valign="top">Heaton Research, Inc.<br>
HTTP Recipes Test Site
</td></tr>
</table>
<hr><p><small>[<a href="/">Home</a>:<a href="/1/">
First Edition</a>:<a href="/1/1/">Chaper 1</a>]</small></p>
<h1>Typical Web Page</h1>
<p>Vacation pictures.</p>
<table border=1>
<tr><td><img src="beach.jpg" height="240" width="320" alt="Beach">
</td><td><img src="ship.jpg" height="240" width="320"
alt="Battleship"></td></tr>
<tr><td><img src="birds.jpg" height="240" width="320" alt="Birds">
</td><td><img src="flower.jpg" height="240" width="320"
alt="Beach Flowers"></td></tr>
</table>
<hr>
<p>Copyright 2006 by
<a href="http://www.heatonresearch.com/">Heaton Research, Inc.
</a></p>
</BODY>
</HTML>
```

As can be seen from the above listing, there are a total of five **<img>** HTML tags. The following five tags are found:

- <img src="/images/logo.gif" alt="Heaton Research Logo" border="0">
- <img src="beach.jpg" height="240" width="320" alt="Beach">
- <img src="ship.jpg" height="240" width="320" alt="Battleship">
- <img src="birds.jpg" height="240" width="320" alt="Birds">
- <img src="flower.jpg" height="240" width="320" alt="Beach Flowers">

Once the HTML has been downloaded, it is scanned for **<img>** tags. These **<img>** tags will cause other requests to be generated to download the images. The above tags are converted to the following five URL's:

- http://www.heatonresearch/images/logo.gif
- http://www.heatonresearch/1/1/beach.jpg
- http://www.heatonresearch/1/1/ship.jpg
- http://www.heatonresearch/1/1/birds.jpg
- http://www.heatonresearch/1/1/flower.jpg

As can be seen from the above list, the requests are given in fully qualified form. The URL for the file **beach.jpg** is given in the form:

**http://www.httprecipes.com/1/1/beach.jpg**

The URL would not be in the form "**beach.jpg**" as it is represented in the HTML file. Since the web server has no idea what page is currently being browsed, a web browser must fully qualify every request that is sent.

### A Typical Surfing Session

Once the user is browsing the "typical web page," examined in the last section, they will not likely stay there long. The typical web user will "surf," and visit a large number of pages. The typical web page example contains five different pages that the user may choose to surf to. All of these pages are linked to with anchor tags **<a>**. The following anchor tags are found in Listing 1.1:

- <a href="http://www.httprecipes.com/">
- <a href="/">
- <a href="/1/">
- <a href="/1/1/">
- <a href="http://www.heatonresearch.com/">

Just as was done with the `<img>` tags, the above URLs must be converted into their fully qualified form. The above list, when converted into fully qualified form, will give the following five URL's:

- http://www.httprecipes.com/
- http://www.httprecipes.com/
- http://www.httprecipes.com/1/
- http://www.httprecipes.com/1/1/
- http://www.heatonresearch.com/

As can be seen, some of the `<a>` tags convert to the same target. For example, two of the tags will open the URL **http://www.httprecipes.com/**.

When a user chooses one of the links, the URL is moved to the address line of the browser. The new URL will be handled as if the user had specifically requested the page by typing the URL into the address line of the browser. This process repeats as the user selects more and more pages.

So far HTTP requests have only been discussed as abstract concepts. The actual make up of an HTTP request has not yet been discussed. This will be covered in the next section where the structure of an HTTP request will be examined.

## HTTP Requests and Responses

In the last section HTTP requests generated during a typical surfing session were examined. Now these requests will be examined in detail. First, the different types of requests will be discussed. There are a total of three standard HTTP requests that are commonly used:

- GET
- POST
- HEAD

The **GET** request is the most common request. Any time the user enters a URL into a web browser, a **GET** request is issued. Additionally, each hyperlink followed, or image downloaded is also a **GET** request.

The **POST** request is usually the response to an HTML form. Whenever a form is filled out and submitted, a **POST** request is being issued.

The **HEAD** request is rarely used. It allows only the HTTP headers to be requested. The actual contents of the "file" requested will not be sent. A web browser will not generate the **HEAD** request; however, some search engines make use of it to determine if a URL is still valid. Because the **HEAD** request is not generated by a web browser and is of little real use to a bot, this book will not discuss it further.

The response from the web server, to the **GET** and **POST** requests is the same. In both cases, the response will be an HTML file, image, or some other form of data. What is returned depends on what the web server is programmed to return for the request it has received. The usual response to a **POST** will be a HTML page that displays the result of the form. For example, the response to a **POST** from an order form might be a HTML page that contains the user's order number.

In the next few sections how the **GET** and **POST** requests work will be explained in greater detail.

## GET Requests

Choosing between **GET** and **POST** usually comes down to how much data must pass to the web site. **GET** allows only a limited amount of data to be passed to the web server. **POST** allows a nearly infinite amount of data to be passed to the web server. However, if you are writing an HTTP program to communicate with an existing web site, the choice is not yours. You must conform to what that site expects. Therefore, most HTTP applications will need to support a mix of **GET** and **POST** requests.

The **GET** request is good for when little, or no, additional information must be sent to the web server with a request. For example, the following URL, if sent with a **GET** request, will pass no data to the web server.

```
http://www.httprecipes.com/1/test.php
```

The above URL simply requests the **test.php** page and does not pass any arguments on to the page. However, several arguments may need to be passed. What if the bot needed to pass two arguments named "**first**" and "**last**"? The following URL would do this:

```
http://www.httprecipes.com/1/test.php?first=Jeff&last=Heaton
```

This would pass two arguments to the **test.php** page. As can be seen, passing arguments with a **GET** request requires them to be appended onto the URL. The question mark (?) indicates that the arguments have started. Each argument is the name of the argument, followed by an equal sign (=), followed by the value of the argument. Each argument is separated from the other arguments using an ampersand (&) symbol.

If there are a large number of arguments to pass, **GET** can be cumbersome. In such cases, the **POST** request should be considered. Of course, as previously stated, if using an existing web site, the bot must conform to what request type is already being used.

Figure 1.4 shows the results of the above URL.

### Figure 1.4: Result of GET Request

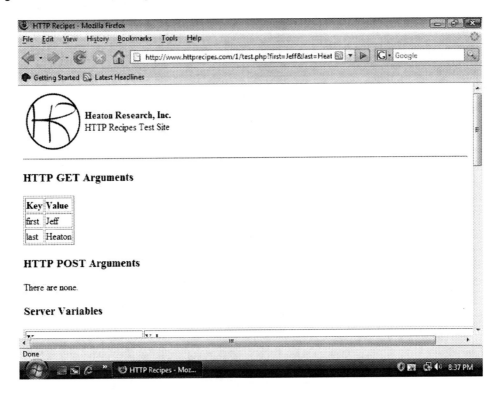

As can be seen, the two arguments showed up as URL arguments in the URL address input area.

## POST Requests

**GET** request are limited by size. All arguments must fit on the URL. **POST** requests have no such limitation. This is possible because the data that sent with a **POST** request will be transmitted separately from the URL.

To use an HTTP post, there will usually be an HTML page with a form. Figure 1.5 shows such a form.

**Figure 1.5: An HTML Form**

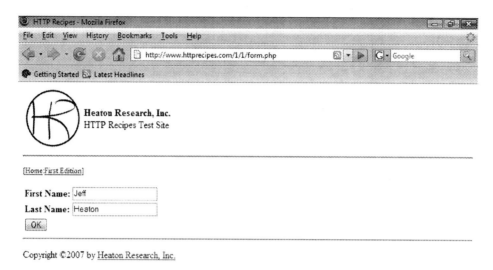

The arguments used by the form will be specified in the HTML. Listing 1.2 shows the HTML that was used to produce Figure 1.5.

**Listing 1.2: The HTML Form**

```
<!DOCTYPE HTML PUBLIC "-//W3C//DTD HTML 4.01 Transitional//EN">

<HTML>
<HEAD>
     <TITLE>HTTP Recipes</TITLE>
     <meta http-equiv="Content-Type" content="text/html;
charset=UTF-8">
     <meta http-equiv="Cache-Control" content="no-cache">
</HEAD>

<BODY>

<table border="0"><tr><td>
<a href="http://www.httprecipes.com/">
<img src="/images/logo.gif" alt="Heaton Research Logo" bor-
der="0"></a>
```

```
</td><td valign="top">Heaton Research, Inc.<br>
HTTP Recipes Test Site
</td></tr>
</table>
<hr><p><small>[<a href="/">Home</a>:
<a href="/1/">First Edition</a>]</small></p>
<table border="0">
<form method="post" action="/1/test.php">
<tr><td><b>First Name:</b></td><td><input name="first"></td></tr>

<tr><td><b>Last Name:</b></td><td><input name="last"></td></tr>
<tr><td colspan="2"><input type="submit" value="OK"></td></tr>
</form>
</table>

<hr>
<p>Copyright 2006 by <a href="http://www.heatonresearch.com/">
Heaton Research, Inc.</a></p>
</BODY>
</HTML>
```

As can be seen from the above form, there are two **<input>** tags that both accept text from the user. These will be picked up as posted variables when the **POST** request is sent to the web server. The result of the POST request is shown in Figure 1.6.

**Figure 1.6: Result of the POST Request**

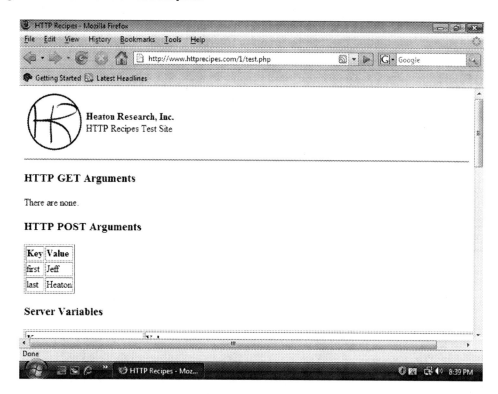

Notice how Figure 1.6 is different than Figure 1.5? The arguments are displayed as **POST** arguments, rather than HTTP GET arguments. Additionally, the request type is **POST**.

So far, only the data passed in HTTP requests and responses has been examined. There are also headers that contain useful information. The headers will be examined in the next section.

# HTTP Headers

HTTP headers are additional information that is transferred along with both HTTP requests and responses. HTTP requests and responses will return different headers. In the following sections both HTTP request and response headers will be examined.

HTTP headers provide many important elements of the browsing experience. For example, HTTP headers allow browsers to know length and type of data they are displaying. They also allow pages to be secure and can prompt for user and password information. Some of the specific types of information that can be found in the HTTP headers are summarized here:

- User authentication
- Data type
- Data length
- Cookies to maintain state

This book covers each of these uses for headers. HTTP request headers will be examined first.

## HTTP Request Headers

HTTP request headers are sent as part of the HTTP request. These headers tell the web server nearly everything about the request. The **GET** request is made up entirely of headers. The **POST** request contains an extra block of data, immediately after the headers that contain the posted arguments.

Listing 1.3 shows a typical HTTP request.

### Listing 1.3: Typical Request Headers

```
GET /1/1/typical.php HTTP/1.1
Accept: */*
Accept-Language: en
Accept-Encoding: gzip, deflate
User-Agent: Mozilla/5.0 (Macintosh; U; PPC Mac OS X; en)
AppleWebKit/418 (KHTML, like Gecko) Safari/417.9.3
Connection: keep-alive
Host: www.httprecipes.com
```

There are really two parts to the headers: the first line and then the rest of the header lines. The first line, which begins with the request type, is the most important line in the header block, and it has a slightly different format than the other header lines. The request type can be **GET**, **POST**, **HEAD**, or one of the other less frequently used headers. Browsers will always use **GET** or **POST**. Following the request type is the file that is being requested. In the above request, the following URL is being requested:

**http://www.httprecipes.com/1/1/typical.php**

The above URL is not represented exactly in URL form in the request header. The "**Host**" header line in the header names the web server that contains the file. The request shows the remainder of the URL, which in this case is **/1/1/typical.php**. Finally, the third thing that the first line provides is the version of the HTTP protocol being used. As of the writing of this book there are only two versions currently in widespread use:

- HTTP/1.1
- HTTP/1.0

This book only deals with HTTP 1.1. Because this book is about writing programs to connect to web servers, it will be assumed that HTTP 1.1 is being used, which is what Java uses when the Java HTTP classes are used.

The lines after the first line make up the actual HTTP headers. Their format is colon delimited. The header name is to the left of the colon and the header value is to the right. It is valid to have two of the same header name in the same request.

The headers give a variety of information. Examining the headers shows type of browser as well as the operating system and other information. In the headers listed above, in Listing 1.3, the Safari browser was being used on the Macintosh platform. Safari is the built in browser for the Macintosh platform.

The headers finally terminate with a blank line. If the request had been a **POST**, any posted data would follow the blank line. Even when there is no posted data, as is the case with a **GET**, the blank line is still required.

A web server should respond to every HTTP request from a web browser. The web server's response is discussed in the next section.

## HTTP Response Headers

When the web server responds to a HTTP request, HTTP response header lines are sent. The HTTP response headers look very similar to the HTTP request headers. Listing 1.4 shows the contents of typical HTTP response headers.

### Listing 1.4: Typical Response Headers

```
HTTP/1.1 200 OK
Date: Sun, 02 Jul 2006 22:28:58 GMT
Server: Apache/2.0.40 (Red Hat Linux)
Last-Modified: Sat, 29 Jan 2005 04:13:19 GMT
ETag: "824319-509-c6d5c0"
Accept-Ranges: bytes
Content-Length: 1289
Connection: close
Content-Type: text/html
```

As can be seen from the above listing, at first glance, response headers look nearly the same as request headers. However, look at the first line.

Although the first line is space delimited as in the request, the information is different. The first line of HTTP response headers contains the HTTP version and status information about the response. The HTTP version is reported as 1.1, and the status code, **200**, means "OK," there was no error. Also, this is where the famous error code **404** (page not found) comes from.

Error codes can be grouped according to the digit in their hundreds position:

- 1xx: Informational - Request received, continuing process
- 2xx: Success - The action was successfully received, understood, and accepted
- 3xx: Redirection - Further action must be taken in order to complete the request
- 4xx: Client Error - The request contains bad syntax or cannot be fulfilled
- 5xx: Server Error - The server failed to fulfill an apparently valid request

Immediately following the headers will be a blank line, just as was the case with HTTP requests. Following the blank line delimiter will be the data that was requested. It will be of the length specified in the **Content-Length header**. The **Content-Length** header in Listing 1.4 indicates a length of 1,289 bytes. For a list of HTTP codes, refer to Appendix G, "HTTP Response Codes."

## Recipes

In this chapter, the structure of HTTP requests and responses was examined. As shown in Listing 1.3 and 1.4, the structure of HTTP is not terribly complex. As a result, it is relatively easy to create a web server. This is what the two recipes in this chapter will deal with. The first Recipe, 1.1, will show how to create a really simple web server. Next, Recipe 1.2 will show how to extend the simple web server to use HTML and image files, just as a regular web server would.

The recipes in this chapter make use of Java sockets. Sockets are the lowest level that an application programmer will usually get to the Internet connection. The socket level allows a web server to be created. After this chapter, all Java recipes will make use of the Java HTTP classes. If desired, HTTP programming could be performed at the socket level; however, using the Java HTTP classes will get the needed functionality, without the complexity of dealing directly with sockets.

### Recipe #1.1: A Simple Web Server

The first recipe is a "Hello World" program of sorts. Recipe 1.1 is a web server. Its purpose is to show how to serve web pages from your program. This very simple program only serves one web page. This page simply says "Hello World".

When this program is launched the port that web server will listen at must be specified. Normally web servers listen at port **80**. However, there may already be a web server running at port **80**. If this is the case a higher port number such as **8080** or **8081** should be used. The server is started as follows:

```
SimpleWebServer 8080
```

This will start the web server on port **8080**. The above command simply shows the abstract format to call this recipe, with the appropriate parameters. For exact information on how to run this recipe refer to Appendix B, C, or D, depending on the operating system you are using. If something already has that port in use then a **BindingException** error message will be shown, as seen in Listing 1.5.

### Listing 1.5: Port Already in Use

```
java.net.BindException: Address already in use
      at java.net.PlainSocketImpl.socketBind(Native Method)
      at java.net.PlainSocketImpl.bind(PlainSocketImpl.java:359)
      at java.net.ServerSocket.bind(ServerSocket.java:319)
      at java.net.ServerSocket.<init>(ServerSocket.java:185)
      at java.net.ServerSocket.<init>(ServerSocket.java:97)
      at com.heatonresearch.httprecipes.ch1.recipe2.WebServer.
<init>(WebServer.java:51)
      at com.heatonresearch.httprecipes.ch1.recipe2.WebServer.
main(WebServer.java:290)
```

If the web server is started properly, and no error occurs, there should be no output. The web server is now waiting for a connection. Connecting to the web server is easy. Use any web browser and access the following URL:

**http://localhost:8080/**

No matter what request is sent to this web server, it will produce a page that says Hello World. The output from Recipe 1.1 is shown in Figure 1.7.

**Figure 1.7: Hello World**

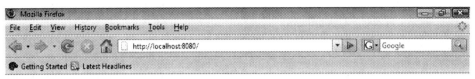

Now that the program has been demonstrated, it is time to take a look at what was necessary to implement this program. Recipe 1.1 is shown in Listing 1.6.

**Listing 1.6: Simple Web Server (SimpleWebServer.java)**

```java
package com.heatonresearch.httprecipes.ch1.recipe1;

import java.io.*;
import java.net.*;

public class SimpleWebServer
{
  /*
   * The server socket.
   */
  private ServerSocket serverSocket;

  /**
   * Construct the web server to listen on the specified
   * port.
   *
```

```java
 * @param port The port to use for the server.
 * @throws IOException Thrown if any sort of error occurs.
 */
public SimpleWebServer(int port) throws IOException
{
  serverSocket = new ServerSocket(port);
}


/**
 * The run method endlessly waits for connections.
 * As each connection is opened (from web browsers)
 * the connection is passed off to handleClientSession.
 */
public void run()
{
  for (;;)
  {
    try
    {
      Socket clientSocket = serverSocket.accept();
      handleClientSession(clientSocket);
    } catch (IOException e)
    {
      e.printStackTrace();
    }
  }
}


/**
 * Handle a client session. This method displays the incoming
 * HTTP request and responds with a "Hello World" response.
 *
 * @param url The URL to download.
 * @return The contents of the URL that were downloaded.
 * @throws IOException Thrown if any sort of error occurs.
 */
private void handleClientSession(Socket socket)
throws IOException
{
  // setup to read from the socket in lines
  InputStream is = socket.getInputStream();
  InputStreamReader inputStreamReader =
    new InputStreamReader(is);
  BufferedReader in = new BufferedReader(inputStreamReader);

  // setup to write to socket in lines
```

```java
OutputStream os = socket.getOutputStream();
PrintStream out = new PrintStream(os);

// read in the first line
System.out.println("**New Request**");
String first = in.readLine();
System.out.println(first);

// read in headers and post data
String line;
do
{
  line = in.readLine();
  if(line!=null)
  System.out.println(line);
} while (line!=null && line.trim().length() > 0);

// write the HTTP response
out.println("HTTP/1.1 200 OK");
out.println("");
out.println("<html>");
out.println("<head><title>Simple Web Server</title></head>");
out.println("<body>");
out.println("<h1>Hello World</h1>");
out.println("<//body>");
out.println("</html>");

// close everything up
out.close();
in.close();
socket.close();

}

/**
 * Read in the arguments and start the server.
 *
 * @param args Web server port.
 */
public static void main(String args[])
{
  try
  {
    if (args.length < 1)
    {
      System.out.println("Usage:\njava SimpleWebServer [port]");
```

```
    } else
    {
      int port;
      try
      {
        port = Integer.parseInt(args[0]);
        SimpleWebServer server = new SimpleWebServer(port);
        server.run();
      } catch (NumberFormatException e)
      {
        System.out.println("Invalid port number");
      }

    }
  } catch (IOException e)
  {
    e.printStackTrace();
  }
  }
}
```

Java supports two primary types of sockets: server sockets and client sockets. Server sockets are implemented using the **ServerSocket** class. Client sockets are implemented using the **Socket** class. This program begins by creating a server socket. This is done with the following line of code in the **WebServer** constructor:

```
serverSocket = new ServerSocket(port);
```

Once the server connection has been opened, the program must wait for connections. This is done using the **accept** function of the **ServerSocket** object. This is done in the **run** method. The **run** method begins by entering an endless loop, as seen here:

```
for (;;)
{
```

This command causes the web server to wait endlessly for connections. The server does not include a mechanism for shutting itself down. To shut down the server simply, press **ctrl-c** or close the web server's window.

Next, the **accept** function is called to accept a connection. If no connection is available, then the **accept** function blocks (or waits), until a connection is available. Because of this, the **accept** call is often put inside of a thread. This would allow the rest of the program to continue executing while the thread waits for a connection. However, for this simple example, everything will be done in a single thread.

```
try
{
  Socket clientSocket = serverSocket.accept();
```

When a connection is made, a **Socket** object is returned. This object is passed onto the **handleClientSession** method to fulfill the request.

```
handleClientSession(clientSocket);
```

A **catch** block is also provided to handle any exceptions. If an exception occurs, it will be displayed to the console, and the server will continue to run.

```
} catch (IOException e)
{
  e.printStackTrace();
}
```

Once a connection is established, the **handleClientSession** method is called. This method begins by obtaining an **InputStream** to the socket. The **InputStream** is passed into an **InputStreamReader**, and then to a **BufferedReader**. This allows the **readLine** function to read the socket as a series of lines.

```
// Setup to read from the socket in lines.
InputStream is = socket.getInputStream();
InputStreamReader inputStreamReader = new InputStreamReader(is);
BufferedReader in = new BufferedReader(inputStreamReader);
```

Next, an **OutputStream** for the socket is created. The **OutputStream** will allow a socket to be written to. The **OutputStream** object is used to construct a **PrintStream** object. Using a **PrintStream** object will allow the **println** method to write lines of text to the **OutputStream**.

```
// Setup to write to socket in lines.
OutputStream os = socket.getOutputStream();
PrintStream out = new PrintStream(os);
```

Now that the streams are setup, it is time to begin reading from the socket. As was discussed earlier in the chapter, the first line of an HTTP request has a special format. Because of this, the first line is read separately. It is then printed out.

```
// Read in the first line.
System.out.println("**New Request**");
String first = in.readLine();
System.out.println(first);
```

Once the first line has been read in, the headers can be read. The headers are read until a blank line is found. As was discussed earlier in this chapter, a blank line indicates the end of HTTP headers.

```
// Read in headers and post data.
String line;
do
{
```

```
  line = in.readLine();
  System.out.println(line);
} while (line.trim().length() > 0);
```

Once the first blank line is hit, the program is done reading the HTTP headers. Because this server only supports **GET** requests, the program is also done reading the HTTP request. Now it is time to write the HTTP response. The following lines of code write a simple HTML message that says "Hello World" to the browser.

```
// Write the HTTP response.
out.println("HTTP/1.1 200 OK");
out.println("");
out.println("<html>");
out.println("<head><title>Simple Web Server</title></head>");
out.println("<body>");
out.println("<h1>Hello World</h1>");
out.println("<//body>");
out.println("</html>");
```

Now that the message has been written, it is time to close the streams. The following lines of code do this.

```
// Close everything up.
out.close();
in.close();
socket.close();
```

The above recipe showed how to create a simple web server. In addition to this basic functionality, this recipe can be expanded to be a custom web server that will respond to different requests. For example, a web server could be constructed to give information about how a process is running or other status information collected by the computer.

Most web servers simply present files to the browser. However, Recipe 1.1 generated its response internally. This can be a very useful technique to display status information for your web server. The next recipe, Recipe 1.2, shows how to create a web server that will allow access to files.

### Recipe #1.2: File Based Web Server

This recipe shows how to create a very common sort of web server. This web sever exposes a directory tree to the Internet. This directory tree is called the "HTTP root", or "web root". Files placed into this directory will be accessed by web browsers. A default file, named **index.html**, should be placed into this directory. This file is displayed when the user browses to the directory. The **index.html** file usually has links to the other files in that directory, and serves as a starting point.

This web server requires only two configuration arguments. Both of these are specified in the command line. The two parameters are:

- HTTP Port
- HTTP Root Directory

For example, to start the web server using port **8080** and the directory **c:\httproot\** as the root directory, the following command is used.

```
WebServer 8080 c:\httproot\
```

The above command simply shows the abstract format to call this recipe, with the appropriate parameters. For exact information on how to run this recipe refer to Appendix B, C, or D, depending on the operating system you are using. The web server featured in this recipe is an expanded version of the server featured in Recipe 1.1. Because of this the details will not be repeated that are the same between the two web servers; therefore, Recipe 1.1 should be reviewed for additional information.

Now the construction of the web server will be examined. Listing 1.7 shows the source code necessary for the file based web server.

### Listing 1.7: File Based Web Server (WebServer.java)

```java
package com.heatonresearch.httprecipes.ch1.recipe2;

import java.io.*;
import java.net.*;
import java.util.*;

public class WebServer
{
  /*
   * The server socket.
   */
  private ServerSocket serverSocket;

  /*
   * The directory to contain HTML and image files.
   */
  private String httproot;

  /**
   * Construct the web server to listen on the specified
   * port.
   *
   * @param port The port to use for the server.
   * @param httproot The root directory for HTML and image files.
   * @throws IOException Thrown if any sort of error occurs.
   */
```

```java
public WebServer(int port, String httproot) throws IOException
{
  serverSocket = new ServerSocket(port);
  this.httproot = httproot;
}

/**
 * The run method endlessly waits for connections.
 * As each connection is opened(from web browsers)
 * the connection is passed off to handleClientSession.
 */
public void run()
{
  for (;;)
  {
    try
    {
      Socket clientSocket = serverSocket.accept();
      handleClientSession(clientSocket);
    } catch (IOException e)
    {
      e.printStackTrace();
    }
  }
}

/**
 * Add a slash to the end of a path, if there is not a slash
 * there already.  This method adds the correct type of slash,
 * depending on the operating system.
 *
 * @param path The path to add a slash to.
 * @return The path with a slash added.
 */
private String addSlash(String path)
{
  path = path.trim();
  if (path.endsWith("" + File.separatorChar))
    return path;
  else
    return path + File.separatorChar;
}

/**
 * Handle a client session. This method displays the incoming
 * HTTP request and passes the response off to either sendFile
```

```java
 * or error.
 *
 * @param socket The client socket.
 * @throws IOException Thrown if any sort of error occurs.
 */
private void handleClientSession(Socket socket)
throws IOException
{
  // setup to read from the socket in lines
  InputStream is = socket.getInputStream();
  InputStreamReader inputStreamReader =
    new InputStreamReader(is);
  BufferedReader in = new BufferedReader(inputStreamReader);

  // setup to write to socket in lines
  OutputStream os = socket.getOutputStream();

  // read in the first line
  System.out.println("**New Request**");
  String first = in.readLine();
  System.out.println(first);

  // read in headers and post data
  String line;
  do
  {
    line = in.readLine();
    System.out.println(line);
  } while (line!=null && line.trim().length() > 0);

  // write the HTTP response
  StringTokenizer tok = new StringTokenizer(first);
  String verb = (String) tok.nextElement();
  String path = (String) tok.nextElement();


  if (verb.equalsIgnoreCase("GET"))
    sendFile(os, path);
  else
    error(os, 500, "Unsupported command");

  // close everything up
  os.close();
  in.close();
  socket.close();
}
```

```java
/**
 * Determine the correct "content type" based on the file
 * extension.
 *
 * @param path The file being transfered.
 * @return The correct content type for this file.
 * @throws IOException Thrown if any sort of error occurs.
 */
private String getContent(String path)
{
  path = path.toLowerCase();
  if (path.endsWith(".jpg") || path.endsWith(".jpeg"))
    return "image/jpeg";
  else if (path.endsWith(".gif"))
    return "image/gif";
  else if (path.endsWith(".png"))
    return "image/png";
  else
    return "text/html";
}

/**
 * Send a disk file.  The path passed in is from the URL, this
 * URL is translated into a local disk file, which is then
 * transfered.
 *
 * @param out The output stream.
 * @param path The file requested from the URL.
 * @throws IOException Thrown if any sort of error occurs.
 */
private void sendFile(OutputStream out, String path)
  throws IOException
{
  // parse the file by /'s and build a local file
  StringTokenizer tok = new StringTokenizer(path, "/", true);
  System.out.println(path);
  String physicalPath = addSlash(httproot);

  while (tok.hasMoreElements())
  {
    String e = (String) tok.nextElement();
    if (!e.trim().equalsIgnoreCase(File.separator))
    {
      if (e.equals("..") || e.equals("."))
      {
```

```
        error(out, 500, "Invalid request");
        return;
      }
      physicalPath += e;
    } else
      physicalPath = addSlash(physicalPath);


  }

  // if there is no file specified, default
  // to index.html

  if (physicalPath.endsWith(File.separator))
  {
    physicalPath = physicalPath + "index.html";
  }

  // open the file and send it if it exists
  File file = new File(physicalPath);
  if (file.exists())
  {
    // send the file
    FileInputStream fis = new FileInputStream(file);
    byte buffer[] = new byte[(int) file.length()];
    fis.read(buffer);
    fis.close();
    this.transmit(out, 200, "OK", buffer,
      getContent(physicalPath));
  }
  // file does not exist, so send file not found
  else
  {
    this.error(out, 404, "File Not Found");
  }
}


/**
 * Transmit a HTTP response.  All responses are handled by
 * this method.
 *
 * @param out The output stream.
 * @param code The response code, i.e. 404 for not found.
 * @param message The message, usually OK or error message.
 * @param body The data to be transfered.
 * @param content The content type.
```

```java
 * @throws IOException Thrown if any sort of error occurs.
 */
private void transmit(OutputStream out,
  int code,
  String message,
  byte body[],
  String content)
throws IOException
{
  StringBuilder headers = new StringBuilder();
  headers.append("HTTP/1.1 ");
  headers.append(code);
  headers.append(' ');
  headers.append(message);
  headers.append("\n");
  headers.append("Content-Length: " + body.length + "\n");
  headers.append("Server: Heaton Research Example Server\n");
  headers.append("Connection: close\n");
  headers.append("Content-Type: " + content + "\n");
  headers.append("\n");
  out.write(headers.toString().getBytes());
  out.write(body);

}


/**
 * Display an error to the web browser.
 *
 * @param out The output stream.
 * @param code The response code, i.e. 404 for not found.
 * @param message The error that occurred.
 * @throws IOException Thrown if any sort of error occurs.
 */
private void error(OutputStream out, int code, String message)
    throws IOException
{
  StringBuilder body = new StringBuilder();
  body.append("<html><head><title>");
  body.append(code + ":" + message);
  body.append(
    "</title></head><body><p>An error occurred.</p><h1>");
  body.append(code);
  body.append("</h1><p>");
  body.append(message);
  body.append("</p></body></html>");
  transmit(out, code, message,
```

```
        body.toString().getBytes(), "text/html");
  }


  /**
   * Read in the arguments and start the server.
   *
   * @param args Web server port and http root directory.
   */
  public static void main(String args[])
  {
    try
    {
      if (args.length < 2)
      {
        System.out.println(
          "Usage:\njava WebServer [port] [http root path]");
      } else
      {
        int port;
        try
        {
          port = Integer.parseInt(args[0]);
          WebServer server = new WebServer(port, args[1]);
          server.run();
        } catch (NumberFormatException e)
        {
          System.out.println("Invalid port number");
        }

      }
    } catch (IOException e)
    {
      e.printStackTrace();
    }
  }
}
```

The **main** function, the constructor, and the **run** method are all nearly the same as those in Recipe 1.1. The only difference is the support of the additional command line argument for the "HTTP root" path. For more information on these three methods, review Recipe 1.1.

The **handleClientSession** method begins the same as Recipe 1.1; however, once the connection is established, this recipe becomes more complex.

```
// Write the HTTP response.
StringTokenizer tok = new StringTokenizer(first);
```

```
String verb = (String) tok.nextElement();
String path = (String) tok.nextElement();
String version = (String) tok.nextElement();

if (verb.equalsIgnoreCase("GET"))
sendFile(os, path);
else
error(os, 500, "Unsupported command");
```

As can be seen above, the first line of the HTTP request is parsed. The first line of a HTTP request will be something like the following form.

```
GET /index.html HTTP/1.1
```

As previously discussed in this chapter, there are three parts of this line, separated by spaces. Using a **StringTokenizer**, this string can be broken into the three parts. The verb is checked to see if it is a request other than **GET**. If the request is not a **GET** request, then an error is displayed. Otherwise, the path is sent onto the **sendFile** method.

The next few sections will discuss the major methods provided in this recipe.

### The Send File Method

The **sendFile** method is used to send a file to the web browser. This consists of a two step process:

- Figure out the local path to the file
- Read in and transmit the file

An HTTP request will request a file path such as **/images/logo.gif**. This must be translated to a local path such as **c:\httproot\images\logo.gif**. This transformation is the first thing that the **sendFile** method does.

First a **StringTokenizer** is created to break up the path using slashes (/) as delimiters. This is done using the following lines of code:

```
// Parse the file by /'s and build a local file.
StringTokenizer tok = new StringTokenizer(path, "/", true);
System.out.println(path);
String physicalPath = addSlash(httproot);
```

The **physicalPath** variable will hold the path to the file to be transferred. A slash is added, using the **addSlash** function. The **physicalPath** is now ready to have subdirectories or files concatenated to it. The **sendFile** method will then parse the HTTP path and concatenate any sub directories followed by the file requested to the **physicalPath** variable. The following lines of code begin this loop:

```
while (tok.hasMoreElements())
{
```

```
String e = (String) tok.nextElement();
if (!e.trim().equalsIgnoreCase(File.separator))
{
```

As the elements of the file are parsed, the program must look out for the previous directory code of "..". If ".." is allowed to be part of the path, a malicious user could use ".." to access the parent HTTP root directory. This would be a security risk. Therefore, if the string ".." is located inside of the URL, an error is displayed.

```
if (e.equals("..") || e.equals("."))
{
  error(out, 500, "Invalid request");
  return;
}
```

For each section, the sub directory, or file, is concatenated to the **physicalPath** variable. Additionally, a slash is added for each of the sub directory levels.

```
    physicalPath += e;
    } else
  physicalPath = addSlash(physicalPath);
}
```

Now, that the entire path has been parsed, it is time to check for a default file. If the path specified by the user is a directory only, the default file **index.html** needs to be specified as shown below:

```
// If there is no file specified, default
// to index.html.

if (physicalPath.endsWith(File.separator))
  physicalPath = physicalPath + "index.html";
```

Once the path is complete, there are really only two possibilities that will occur. Either the file will be transmitted to the user or a **404** error will be generated. The error code **404**, which is the most famous of HTTP error codes, means that the file was not found.

Next the file that is to be transmitted must be read. The following lines of code will read the file.

```
// Open the file and send it if it exists.
File file = new File(physicalPath);
if (file.exists())
{
  // Send the file.
  FileInputStream fis = new FileInputStream(file);
  byte buffer[] = new byte[(int) file.length()];
  fis.read(buffer);
  fis.close();
```

```
   this.transmit(out, 200, "OK", buffer, getContent(physicalPath));
}
```

As can be seen from the above lines of code, the file is read into an array of bytes. Once the file has been read, the **transmit** method is called. The **transmit** method actually transmits the data to the web browser.

If the file can not be found, an error is sent to the web browser.

```
// File does not exist, so send file not found.
else
   this.error(out, 404, "File Not Found");
```

Notice the last parameter sent to the **transmit** method. It is the content type. This tells the web browser what type of data the file contains. The next section explains how this is determined.

### The Get Content Function

Since the **transmit** method needs to know what type of data is being transferred, the **getContent** function should be called to determine the content type. The content type will be a string such as **image/gif** for a GIF image or **text/html** for an HTML file. This type is determined by the file extension, as shown in the following lines of code:

```
path = path.toLowerCase();
if (path.endsWith(".jpg") || path.endsWith(".jpeg"))
   return "image/jpeg";
else if (path.endsWith(".gif"))
   return "image/gif";
else if (path.endsWith(".png"))
   return "image/png";
else
   return "text/html";
```

The **getContent** function can be called to quickly determine the content type based on the filename. Content types themselves will be discussed in greater detail in Chapter 4, "Beyond Simple Requests."

### The Error Method

When an error occurs, the **error** method is called. The **error** method accepts three arguments:

- The output stream
- The error code
- The error message

The **error** method works by constructing an HTML page that displays the error. This code can be seen here:

```
StringBuilder body = new StringBuilder();
body.append("<html><head><title>");
body.append(code + ":" + message);
body.append("</title></head><body><p>An error occured.</p><h1>");
body.append(code);
body.append("</h1><p>");
body.append(message);
body.append("</p></body></html>");
```

This HTML page is then converted into an array of bytes. Next, this array of bytes, along with the **code** and **message**, is passed to the **transmit** method. Finally, the **transmit** method will send this data to the web browser.

```
transmit(out, code, message, body.toString().getBytes(),
"text/html");
```

The **error** method is handy because it can be called from several different locations when an error occurs.

### The Transmit Method

Both the **error** and **sendFile** methods use the **transmit** method to actually send the page to the web browser. This is very convenient because the **transmit** method properly handles all of the HTTP headers, and thus saves both the **error** and **sendFile** methods from both having to implement this functionality.

First, the HTTP headers are constructed. The HTTP headers are constructed into a **StringBuilder**, as seen here:

```
StringBuilder headers = new StringBuilder();
headers.append("HTTP/1.1 ");
headers.append(code);
headers.append(' ');
headers.append(message);
headers.append("\n");
headers.append("Content-Length: " + body.length + "\n");
headers.append("Server: Heaton Research Example Server\n");
headers.append("Connection: close\n");
headers.append("Content-Type: " + content + "\n");
headers.append("\n");
```

Once the headers have been constructed, both the header and body can be transmitted. This is done using the following two commands. These commands make use of the **OutputStream** and write the necessary data.

```
out.write(headers.toString().getBytes());
out.write(body);
```

As can be seen, Recipe 1.2 implements a very simple, yet functional, web server. This web server is far from being "industrial strength", but it would serve as a great starting point for any sort of application that would require a built-in web server.

## Summary

This book is about how to write programs that browse the web, just as a human does. Such programs are called bots. To create bots, it is important to review how web browsing works at a technical level, to form a foundation for the rest of the book. In this chapter, the general structure of web browsing and HTTP requests were explored. The two recipes in this chapter were both web servers.

The first web server did nothing more than display the text "Hello World" to any request; however, the second example implemented a full file based web server. Both of these recipes focused on socket programming and web servers. Socket programming uses the **Socket** and **ServerSocket** classes provided by Java. Although socket programming is touched on, most of this book will focus on creating applications that access web servers. These applications will mainly use the Java HTTP classes to access a web server, rather than direct sockets.

The next chapter will show how to use certain tools to examine the interaction between a web browser and server. These tools will be very helpful, when you create programs of your own to access web servers. They will allow the programmer to understand exactly what information the desired web server expects.

# CHAPTER 2: EXAMINING HTTP TRAFFIC

- Using WireShark
- Using Network Analyzers for Debugging
- Analyzing Cookies
- Analyzing Forms

The goal of most bot programs is to access data that a web user could access with a web browser. The advantage is that a bot is an automated program and can access a large amount of data quickly. Creating bots can be challenging. If the data that is to be accessed is on a single public web page, the task is easy. However, usually a bot must navigate through a series of pages to find the data it needs.

Why would a bot need to navigate through several pages to access a piece of data? Perhaps the most common reason is that some web sites require a user to log into the web server before they are allowed to get to the data they would like to view. Your bank would surely require you to log into the bank web site, prior to viewing your bank balances. To access such a site, the bot must be able to send the web server the same data in exactly the same format as a regular browser session with a human user.

These more complex bots can be difficult to debug manually. Fortunately, by using a program called a "Network Analyzer", manual debugging is not necessary. Network analyzers are also frequently referred to as "Packet Sniffers".

## Using a Network Analyzer

A network analyzer is a program that allows TCP/IP traffic between the web server and a web browser to be monitored. With a network analyzer, a typical web browser accessing the desired web server can be monitored. This shows exactly what information is transmitted.

The network analyzer is useful during all of the bot's development phases. Initially, the network analyzer can be used to analyze a typical session with the desired web server. This shows the HTTP requests and responses the bot must support. Once the bot is created, the network analyzer is used again during the debugging process and then to verify the final product.

### Using a Network Analyzer to Design a Bot

The first step in designing a bot is to analyze the HTTP requests and responses that flow between the web browser and web server. The bot will need to emulate these requests in order to obtain the desired data from the web server.

Sometimes this flow of requests and responses are difficult to determine. Just viewing the source of the HTML pages and trying to understand what is going on can be a lengthy task. For sites that use techniques such as AJAX, the requests can become quite complex.

To analyze HTTP requests and properly design the bot, the network analyzer should be started and begin recording network traffic. This will be discussed later in this chapter. The web browser should then be launched and the web browser started. It is a good idea to clear the browser's cache at this point. The procedure for clearing the cache varies with each browser; this option is usually located under the Internet configuration. Cached files may cause some information to be hidden from the network analyzer.

Once the web browser is launched, the desired web site should be accessed. While on the desired web site, use the site as a regular user would. The objective while using the analyzer is to get to the data that the bot should access. Take as direct a path to the desired data as possible. The simpler the path, the easier it will be to emulate. As the web site is navigated, the network analyzer will record the progress. The analyzer will capture every request made by the web browser. In order to access this site, the bot must provide the same requests to the web server.

### Using a Network Analyzer to Debug a Bot

Creating a bot for some sites can be tricky. For example, a site may use complex messages to communicate with the web server. If the bot does not exactly reproduce these requests, it will not function properly. If the bot is not functioning properly, then a network analyzer should be used to debug the bot.

The technique that I normally use is to run the network analyzer while my bot runs. The network analyzer can track the HTTP requests issued by the bot just as easily as it can track the requests issued by a real user on a web browser.

If the web server is not communicating properly with the bot, then one of the HTTP requests must be different than what a regular web browser would issue. The packets captured from the bot's session with the desired web site should then be compared to the packets captured from a regular browser session with the desired web site.

The next section will show how to use a Network Analyzer. There are many different Network Analyzers available. The one that will be used for this book is WireShark. WireShark is a free open source network analyzer that runs on a wide variety of operating systems.

## Understanding WireShark

WireShark is one of the most popular network analyzers available. WireShark was once known by the name Ethereal, but due to copyright issues changed their name to WireShark. WireShark can be downloaded from the following web site:

`http://www.wireshark.org/`

WireShark supports a wide variety of operating systems. To use WireShark, choose the version for the operating system, then download and install that version.

## Preparing the Browser

Most web browsers are configured to display a home page when the browser is first started. This home page will have an undesirable effect when attempting to analyze packets sent by the web browser. The homepage will cause a flurry of network packets to be sent when the web browser is first opened. This amounts to extra data being captured that has nothing to do with the web site being analyzed. To avoid this, set the web browser's home page to "blank". This can easily be done using the browser preferences menu in Firefox, which is shown in Figure 2.1

### Figure 2.1: Firefox Preferences

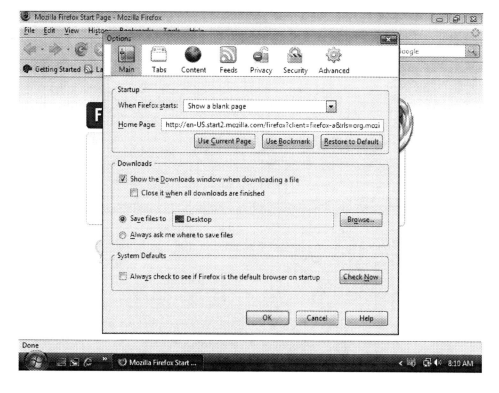

As seen in Figure 2.1, Firefox can be configured to use a blank homepage by clicking the "Show a Blank Page" button.

To set the home page to blank in Internet Explorer use the "Internet Options" menu. This option is located under the tools menu.

Now that the browser is set up, WireShark can be started. When WireShark is started, it will appear similar to Figure 2.2

**Figure 2.2: WireShark**

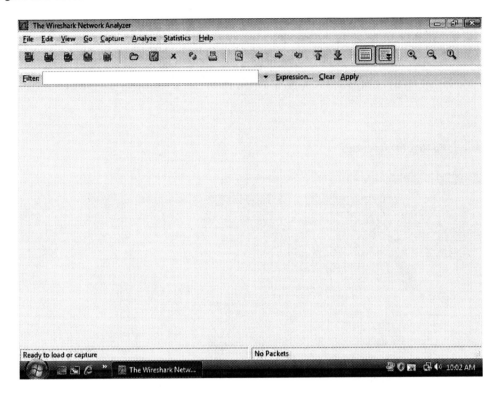

Now that WireShark has been started, it is time to use it to monitor HTTP traffic. This will be covered in the next sections.

### Select an Interface

Before packets can be captured with WireShark, WireShark must be told what interface the packets should be captured from. This will most likely be the Ethernet card. However, if a dial-up modem connection is being used, then it should be specified as the interface. Select the "Interfaces..." option of the "Capture" menu. WireShark will now appear as the image in Figure 2.3.

**Figure 2.3: Select an Interface**

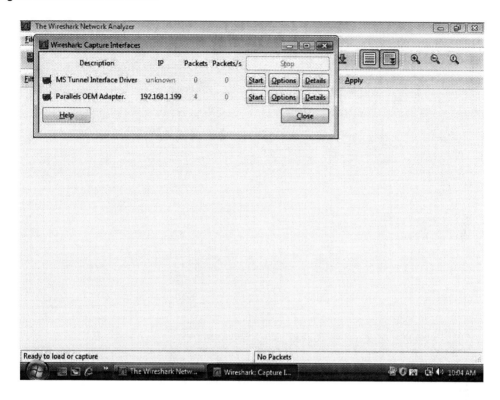

Once the correct interface is found, notice its "Capture" button next to the interface. As mentioned previously, the browser's home page should be set to blank and the browser's cache cleared. Once these steps have been preformed the "Capture" button can be pressed. This will begin the process of capturing packets.

## Capturing Packets

Once the "Capture" button has been pressed, packet capture will begin. Capturing packets is the main task usually performed by a network analyzer. The term "capture" may be a bit misleading. The packets are left "as is" and are not taken out of the network stream. Rather the packets are "spied" upon.

These packets will contain the HTTP requests and responses being transferred between the web browser and the desired web server. While capturing packets, NetShark will appear as the image in Figure 2.4.

**Figure 2.4: Capturing Packets**

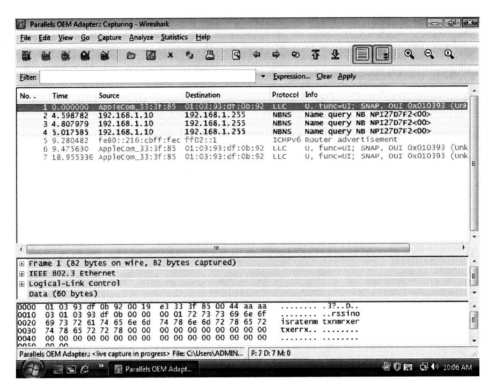

Now that packets are being captured the browser should be started. Proceed to the following URL:

`http://www.httprecipes.com/`

Once the web page has completely displayed, close the web browser. Now select Wire-Shark. WireShark will now appear as the image in Figure 2.5.

## Figure 2.5: Captured Packets

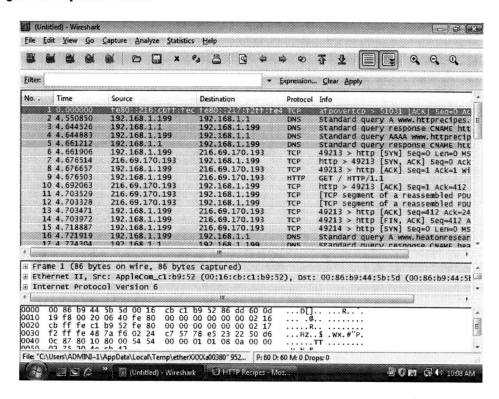

As can be seen from Figure 2.5 there are quite a few packets! Almost all of them are of no importance to creating a bot. Sift through the unimportant packets using a filter.

### Filtering Packets

Look at Figure 2.5. Notice the "Protocol" column? This column contains a few packets of the type HTTP. These are the packets that are of interest. We will filter out all other packets. To create a filter, click on the "Expression…" button. This will display the image in Figure 2.6.

**Figure 2.6: Filter Options**

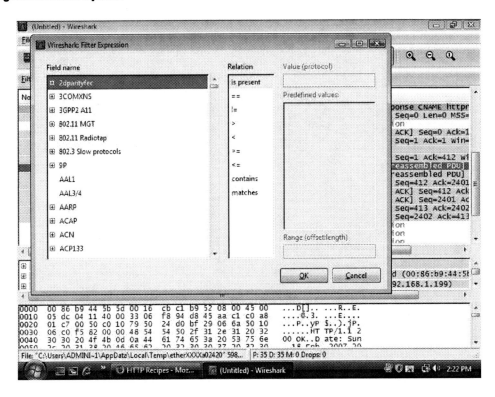

From this window choose HTTP for the "Field Name" list, and "is present" from the "Relation" list. Once these two are chosen, click "OK". This will return you to the packet list screen, seen in Figure 2.5.

At this point all of the packets are still visible. This is because no filtering has yet taken place. To use the filter, click the "Apply" button near the "Expression" button that was clicked to create the filter. Once the filter is applied, there will be considerably fewer packets. Figure 2.7 shows the filtered packet list.

**Figure 2.7: Filtered to Only HTTP Packets**

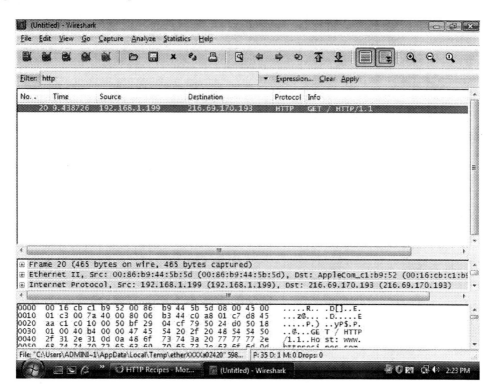

## Examining a HTTP Request

We will now examine an HTTP request in greater detail. Click on the first row, as seen in Figure 2.7. The middle pane should be resized to be larger so that the HTTP headers can be seen. This will result in Figure 2.8 appearing.

### Figure 2.8: The Parts of an HTTP Request Packet

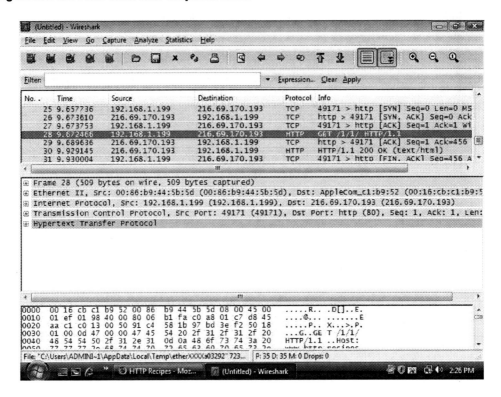

As can seen in Figure 2.8 the packet is broken into the following sections:

- Frame 9
- Ethernet II
- Internet Protocol (IP)
- Transmission Control Protocol (TCP)
- Hypertext Transfer Protocol (HTTP)

Of these, the only one that is important is the HTTP part of the packet. Clicking the plus (+) next to this section will expand it. After expanding, the HTTP part of the packet is seen as in Figure 2.9.

**Figure 2.9: An HTTP Request**

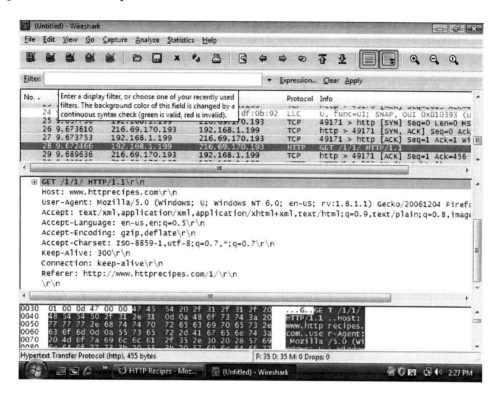

The HTTP headers for this **GET** request can be seen in Figure 2.9. As the book progresses, many of these HTTP headers will be explained. For example, consider the **User-Agent** header. This tells the web server what sort of browser is being used. For this example, Firefox running on Microsoft Windows was used.

### Examining an HTTP Response.

HTTP responses can also be examined using WireShark. Figure 2.10 shows the response packet from the logo GIF file.

**Figure 2.10: An HTTP Response**

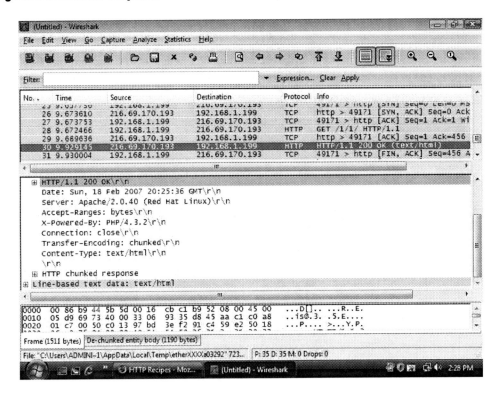

As seen in Figure 2.10 there are a different set of headers that come back from the server. For example there is a header named **Server**, which tells what version of a web server I am running the HTTP Recipes site from. As seen in Figure 2.10, the HTTP recipes site is running Apache 2.0.

### Reassembled PDU

Sometimes the packet will not arrive in one piece. Instead, the packet arrives as several Protocol Data Units (PDU). WireShark will try to reassemble these units back into a single packet. Such a packet is called a reassembled PDU. This packet can be seen on the second row of Figure 2.5. Selecting the reassembled PDU produces Figure 2.11.

**Figure 2.11: A Reassembled PDU**

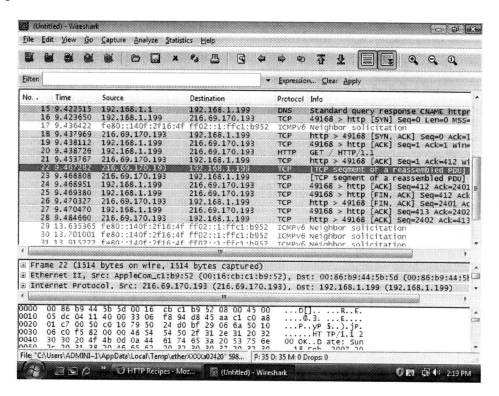

When working with a reassembled PDU, the display will not be as nice as a regular packet. The headers of the response are in the bottom pane of Figure 2.11.

## Recipes

This chapter includes two recipes. These two recipes demonstrate how to examine two very important request items for bots:

- Cookies
- Forms

Cookies and forms are used by many websites. This book has an entire chapter devoted to each. Chapter 7, "Responding to Forms" discusses HTML forms. Chapter 8, "Handling Sessions and Cookies" discusses cookies. For now how to examine cookies in a request will be explained.

### Recipe #2.1: Examining Cookies

Cookies are used to maintain a state in a web server. A web server can attach a cookie to a response so that it can identify that browser when the web server sees another request from this web browser. Cookies will be discussed in much greater detail in Chapter 8, "Handling Sessions and Cookies". For now we will simply examine a cookie in the network analyzer.

To see cookies in action, visit a web site that makes use of cookies. The following page, on the HTTP Recipes site, uses cookies:

`http://www.httprecipes.com/1/2/cookies.php`

The contents of this page are shown in Figure 2.12.

### Figure 2.12: Ready to Create a Cookie

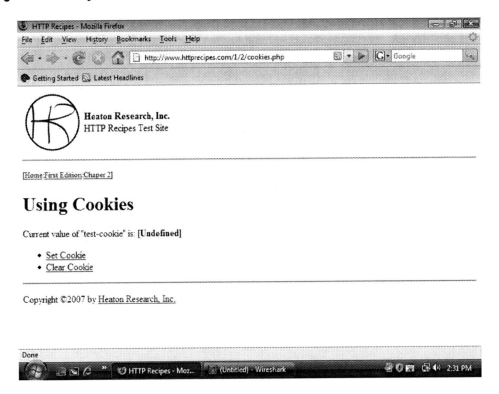

When the page is first accessed, there will be no cookie, so the cookie will show the value of "Undefined". When the "Set Cookie" button is clicked, the cookie's value can be set to any value.

Cookies always have a name. This cookie is named `test-cookie`. Remember this name! It will allow you to locate the correct packet in the network monitor.

Before clicking anything, start WireShark. If the cookie was already set, ensure you click "Clear Cookie" before continuing. Begin capturing packets and return to the web browser. Once back at the web browser, select "Set Cookie". Enter a value for the cookie, such as "Hello", and you will be taken back to the page shown in Figure 2.12. However, this time, the value previously set to the cookie to should be displayed.

Select WireShark and stop capturing packets. Filter to just HTTP packets in WireShark and look for the HTTP response just after the `POST 1/2/cookies-set.php` request. Figure 2.13 shows this.

**Figure 2.13: Cookie as Part of a HTTP Response**

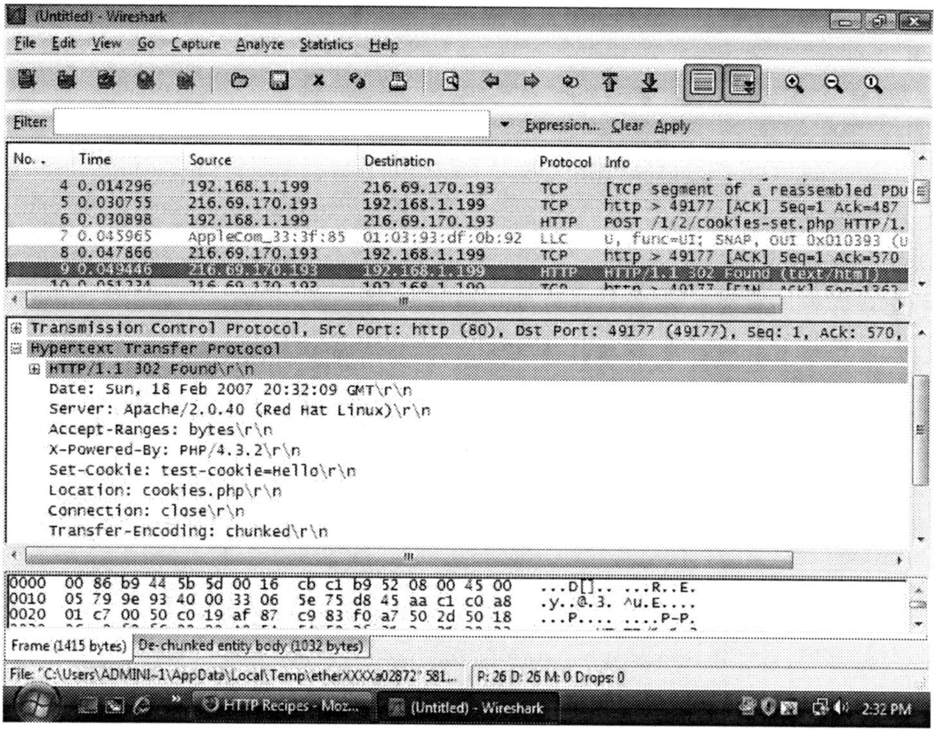

Notice the cookie? It is created by the **Set-Cookie** HTTP tag. Once the server has set a cookie, the browser must echo this cookie with each request. Look at the next request, which is **GET /1/2/cookies.php**. This request can be seen in Figure 2.14.

**Figure 2.14: Cookie as Part of a HTTP Request**

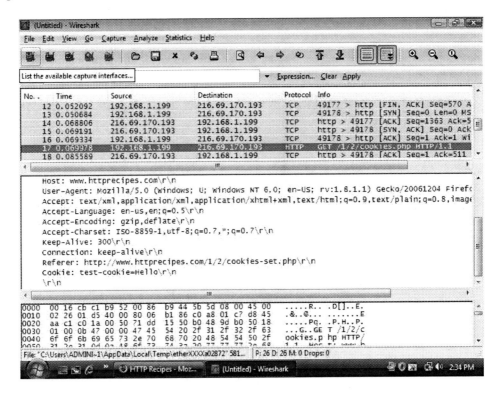

Notice the **Cookie** header in the request above. This will be sent by the web browser now that the server has requested it. This tag now allows the server to identify this particular web browser.

Tracking cookie usage can be very important when writing a bot. Using a network analyzer can assist in seeing how a web server is making use of cookies.

### Recipe #2.2: Examining Forms

Forms are another key element of most web sites. Using the network analyzer, it can quickly be determined how a web server makes use of forms. Forms will be covered in much greater detail in Chapter 7. For now, capturing forms with a network analyzer will be covered.

To demonstrate HTML forms, the following URL from the HTTP Recipes site will be used:

`http://www.httprecipes.com/1/2/forms.php`

Figure 2.15 shows the contents of this URL.

**Figure 2.15: An HTML Form**

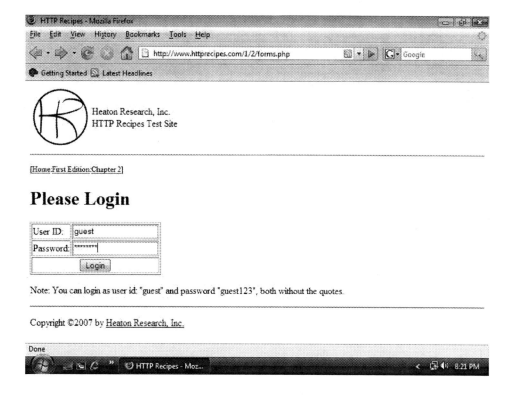

This form allows a user name and password to be entered. Turn on packet capturing in WireShark to see what happens when this form is submitted. Fill in the correct user name and password and click the "Login" button. This should allow a login to the web site.

Once logged in, stop capturing packets. Examine the HTTP request, labeled **POST /1/2/forms2.php**, this will reveal Figure 2.16.

**Figure 2.16: An HTTP Form Request**

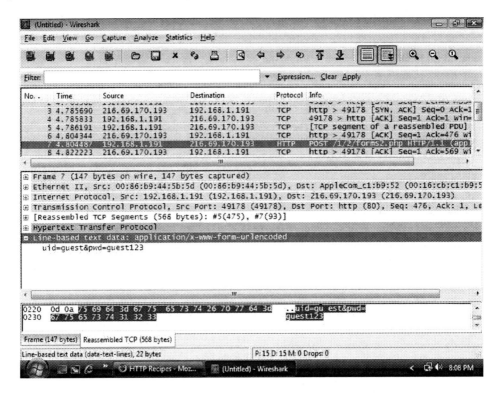

As seen in the above figure, the form data is communicated in the following line:

```
uid=guest&pwd=guest123
```

This is the format in which a web browser sends form data back to the web server. When a bot is created to respond to forms, data must be sent in this format.

## Summary

In this chapter, network analyzers were demonstrated. A network analyzer shows exactly what data is being exchanged between a web server and a web browser. There are many different network analyzers to choose from. The network analyzer that will be used by this book is WireShark. WireShark was formerly known as Ethereal.

Cookies allow a web browser to maintain a state. Values can be attached to a web browser, which the web browser will return with each request. Chapter 8 will cover cookies in much greater detail. Using a network analyzer, it can be quickly determined how a web server uses cookies.

Forms allow a web browser to receive input from the user. Forms are a very important part of most web sites. Chapter 7, "Responding to Forms" discusses forms in much greater detail. Using a network analyzer, it can quickly be determined how a web server is making use of HTML forms.

Now that HTTP packets have been covered, it is time to begin writing HTTP applications. The next chapter will show how to create HTTP programs, or bots, that can perform simple requests of web sites.

# CHAPTER 3: SIMPLE REQUESTS

- Using the URL Class
- Downloading a Page
- Downloading an Image
- Parsing Data

The purpose of the HTTP protocol is to exchange information between an HTTP server and an HTTP client. Usually the HTTP client is a user with a web browser; however, this is not always the case. Sometimes, the HTTP client is actually a program using the web. Java provides many classes that allow Java programs to make use of web pages. In this chapter, these classes will be introduced.

The concept of a web page is very important. Information that you would like to access, using HTTP, will be on a specific web page. The web browsing experience is based on many different web pages. For example, every time a link is clicked, the browser usually moves to a new web page. Likewise, the information you would like to access, using HTTP programming, is on such a page.

Each of these pages has a unique address, which is used to identify that page. This address is the Uniform Resource Locater (URL). The quickest way to find the URL of your "page of interest", is to navigate directly to that page with a web browser. The web browser's address line will show the address of the desired page.

As seen in Figure 3.1, the browser is currently at the URL address of `http://www.httprecipes.com/1/3/time.php`. If you wanted to collect data from this web page, you would use this URL.

**Figure 3.1: The Address of a Web Page**

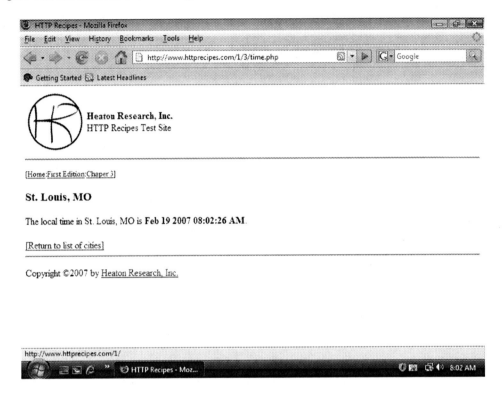

## Constructing URLs

Java expresses URLs using the **URL** class. The **URL** class allows the program to take a simple text string, such as **http://www.httprecipes.com/**, and transform it into a **URL** object that Java can deal with. The following code segment demonstrates this.

```
try
{
  URL u = new URL("http://www.httprecipes.com/");
} catch (MalformedURLException e)
{
  e.printStackTrace();
}
```

As you can see, a **URL** object can be constructed simply by passing a **String**, containing the desired URL, to the constructor of the **URL** class. You should also notice that a **catch** block is required. This is because the **MalformedURLException** exception can be thrown. The **MalformedURLException** will be thrown if an invalid URL is provided.

For example, the following would throw the **MalformedURLException**.

```
try
{
  URL u = new URL("http;//www.httprecipes.com/");
} catch (MalformedURLException e)
{
  e.printStackTrace();
}
```

The **MalformedURLException** would be thrown because the "http" protocol specified ends with a semicolon instead of a colon.

## What is a URL

In the last section I showed how to construct a **URL** object. You also saw that a **MalformedURLException** would be thrown if an invalid URL is specified. To understand what an invalid URL is, you should first understand the format of a good URL. URLs follow the following format:

```
URL Scheme://Host/Path?Query
```

As seen above, the URL is made up of the following three components:

- Scheme
- Host
- Path
- Query

In the next few sections, each of these components will be discussed. We will start with the URL scheme.

### URL Scheme

The scheme is the protocol that will be used to transfer data. For the purposes of this book, we will be dealing with the "http" and "https" schemes. Many of the more common schemes are listed in Table 3.1.

**Table 3.1: Common HTML Schemes**

| Scheme | Name |
| --- | --- |
| http | HTTP resources |
| https | HTTP over SSL |
| ftp | File Transfer Protocol |
| mailto | E-mail address |
| ldap | Lightweight Directory Access Protocol lookups |
| file | Resources available on the local computer or over a local file sharing network |
| news | Usenet newsgroups |
| gopher | The Gopher protocol |
| telnet | The TELNET protocol |
| data | URL scheme for inserting small pieces of content in place |

Following the URL scheme, the URL's host is specified. The URL host will be discussed in the next section.

## URL Host

The host specifies to which server the HTTP request is to be directed. There are several different formats in which the URL host can be represented. First, it can be in the typical domain form, such as:

`www.httprecipes.com`

Second, it can be expressed as an IP address, such as:

`127.0.0.1`

Finally, it can be expressed as a symbol that is resolved in the "**hosts**" file on the computer, such as:

`localhost`

Following the URL host is the URL path and query. The URL path and query will be discussed in the next section.

## URL Path and Query

The path specifies which file to retrieve, or which script to run on the server. The "query" specifies parameters to be passed to the URL. The query immediately follows the path delimited by a question mark. The following URL specifies only a path:

`http://www.httprecipes.com/1/1/cities.php`

The above URL specifies a path of "`/1/1/cities.php`".

Parameters can be passed using the query portion of the URL. The following URL demonstrates this idea.

`http://www.httprecipes.com/1/1/city.php?city=2`

The above URL passes one parameter using the query string. A parameter named "city" is passed to the query string. The parameter "city" has the value of "2". It is also possible to pass multiple parameters. If you would like to pass multiple parameters, they should be separated by the ampersand symbol (&). The following URL makes use of the ampersand to pass in two parameters. These two parameters are named "city" and "zip code".

`http://www.httprecipes.com/1/1/city.php?city=2&zipcode=63017`

So far the URLs we have examined all contain standard ASCII (American Standard Code for Information Interchange) letters and numbers. In the next section, you will see how to encode special characters into the URL.

## Encoding Special Characters into a URL

URLs can contain a wide variety of characters; however, there are only certain characters that you can put directly into a URL. For example, you cannot put a space into a URL. If you wanted to pass the value "John Smith" to the variable "name", you could not construct a URL such as:

`http://www.httprecipes.com/1/test.php?name=John Smith`

The above URL is invalid because spaces are not allowed in a URL. To put a space into a URL, express the URL as follows:

`http://www.httprecipes.com/1/test.php?name=John%20Smith`

As you can see, the above URL contains the characters "%20" where the space is. This is because a space is ASCII code 32. The decimal number "32" is "20" in hexadecimal. Any ASCII code, from 0 (hexadecimal 0) to 255 (hexadecimal FF) can be represented this way.

The space character, however, is special. It also has a second way that it can be represented. Spaces can be represented with the plus (+) character. Therefore, it would also be valid to represent the above URL as:

`http://www.httprecipes.com/1/test.php?name=John+Smith`

Of course, this means the only way to represent a "+" symbol itself in a URL is to use the hexadecimal ASCII code "%2B".

Now that you understand how to construct a URL, it is time to see how to use them. This will be covered in the next section.

# Reading from URLs

Java allows you to read data from URLs. This forms the basis of HTTP programming in Java. In this chapter you will see how to construct simple requests from web sites. What is meant by a simple request? A simple request is a request where you only request data from a URL. It can get much more complex than that. As you progress through the book you will learn more complex HTTP programming topics such as:

- HTTPS
- Posting Data
- Cookies
- Authentication
- Content Types

For now, we will focus on simply getting data from a URL, and leave the more complex operations for later. There are three basic steps that you will need to carry out to read data from a URL. These steps are summarized as follows:

- Create a **URL** Object
- Open a Stream
- Read Data from the Stream

We will begin by examining the Java **URL** class.

## The URL Class

Java provides a class to hold URLs. Even though a URL is actually a **String**, it is convenient to have a class to handle the URL. The **URL** class offers several advantages over storing URLs as strings. There are methods to:

- Determine if URL is valid
- Extract information, such as host or schema
- Open a connection to the URL

To create a **URL** object, simply pass the URL string to the constructor of the **URL** class, as follows:

```
URL url = new URL("http://www.httprecipes.com");
```

This will create a new **URL** object that is ready to be used. However, it can throw a checked exception, named **MalformedURLException**. As mentioned previously, to properly handle the exception you should use the following code.

```
try
{
  URL url = new URL("http://www.httprecipes.com");
}
catch(MalformedURLException e)
{
  System.out.println("This URL is not valid.");
}
```

The **MalformedURLException** will be thrown if the provided URL is invalid. For example, a URL such as the following would throw the exception:

**http:////www.httprecipes.com/**

The above URL would throw the exception, because the URL has four slashes (////), which is not valid. It is important to remember that the **URL** class only checks to see if the URL is valid. It does NOT check to see if the URL actually exists on the Internet. Existence of the URL will not be verified until a connection is made. The next section discusses how to open a connection.

### Opening the Stream

Java uses streams to access files and perform other I/O operations. When you access the URL, you will be given an **InputStream**. This **InputStream** is used to download the contents of the URL. The **URL** class makes it easy to open a stream for the URL. To open a stream, you simply use the **openStream** function, provided by the **URL** class. The following code shows how this is done.

```
try
{
  URL url = new URL("http://www.httprecipes.com");
  InputStream is = url.openStream();
}
catch(MalformedURLException e)
{
  System.out.println("Invalid URL");
}
catch(IOException e)
{
  System.out.println("Could not connect to URL");
}
```

As you can see, the above code is very similar to the code from the last section. However, an additional line follows the URL declaration. This line calls the **openStream** function, and receives an **InputStream** object. You will see what to do with this object in the next section.

The above code also has to deal with an additional exception. The **IOException** can be thrown by the **openStream** function, so it is necessary to catch the exception. Remember from the last section that the constructor of the **URL** class does not check to see if a URL actually exists? This is where that is checked. If the URL does not exist, or if there is any trouble connecting to the web server that holds that URL, then an **IOException** will be thrown.

Now that you have constructed the **URL** object and opened a connection, you are ready to download the data from that URL.

## Downloading the Contents

Downloading the contents of a web page uses the same procedure you would use to read data from any input stream. Just as if you were reading from a disk file, you will use the **read** function of the stream. The following block of code reads the contents of the URL and stores it into a **StringBuilder**.

```
try
{
  URL u = new URL("http://www.httprecipes.com");
  InputStream is = u.openInputStream();

  StringBuilder result = new StringBuilder();
  byte buffer[] = new byte[BUFFER_SIZE];

  InputStream s = u.openStream();
  int size = 0;

do
{
  size = s.read(buffer);
  if (size != -1)
    result.append(new String(buffer, 0, size));
} while (size != -1);

System.out.println( result.toString() );
}

catch(MalformedURLException e)
{
  System.out.println("Invalid URL");
```

```
}
catch(IOException e)
{
  System.out.println("Could not connect to URL");
}
```

As you can see, the above code is a continuation of what we have already seen. Just as in the previous code segments, the **URL** object is first created. Next a stream is opened to the URL. Finally, a while loop is used to loop through and read from the stream, until there is nothing more to read.

When reading from a stream, it is best to read the data in blocks, rather than one byte at a time. To accomplish this, a buffer, of size 8,192, is used. The choice for 8,192 is purely arbitrary. It is 8 kilobytes. Many web pages are under 8k, so they will be read in one block. Once the **read** function returns -1 we know there is no data left to read.

## Recipes

This chapter showed you how to use some of the basic HTTP functionality built into Java. You have seen how you can use the **URL** class to open a stream to a web page. You have also seen how to read the contents of the web page into a **StringBuilder**. The recipes for this chapter will build upon this.

There are five recipes for this chapter. All of these recipes provide you with reusable code that demonstrates the basic HTTP programming learned in this chapter. These recipes will demonstrate the following functionality:

- Download the contents of a web page
- Extract data from a web page
- Pass parameters to a web page
- Parse time and date information

We will begin with recipe 3.1, which demonstrates how to download the contents of a web page.

### Recipe #3.1: Downloading the Contents of a Web Page

This recipe is the culmination of the example code given, up to this point, in this chapter. Recipe 3.1 accesses a URL and downloads the contents into a **StringBuilder**. The **StringBuilder** is then converted into a string and displayed.

This is shown in Listing 3.1.

### Listing 3.1: Download a Web Page (GetPage.java)

```
package com.heatonresearch.httprecipes.ch3.recipe1;

import java.io.*;
```

```java
import java.net.*;

public class GetPage
{
  /**
   * The size of the download buffer.
   */
  public static int BUFFER_SIZE = 8192;

  /**
   * This method downloads the specified URL into a Java
   * String. This is a very simple method, that you can
   * reused anytime you need to quickly grab all data from
   * a specific URL.
   *
   * @param url The URL to download.
   * @return The contents of the URL that was downloaded.
   * @throws IOException Thrown if any sort of error occurs.
   */
  public String downloadPage(URL url) throws IOException
  {
    StringBuilder result = new StringBuilder();
    byte buffer[] = new byte[BUFFER_SIZE];

    InputStream s = url.openStream();
    int size = 0;

    do
    {
      size = s.read(buffer);
      if (size != -1)
        result.append(new String(buffer, 0, size));
    } while (size != -1);

    return result.toString();
  }

  /**
   * Run the example.
   *
   * @param page The page to download.
   */
  public void go(String page)
  {
    try
    {
```

```java
    URL u = new URL(page);
    String str = downloadPage(u);
    System.out.println(str);

  } catch (MalformedURLException e)
  {
    e.printStackTrace();
  } catch (IOException e)
  {
    e.printStackTrace();
  }
}

/**
 * Typical Java main method, create an object, and then
 * call that object's go method.
 *
 * @param args Website to access.
 */
public static void main(String args[])
{
  GetPage module = new GetPage();
  String page;
  if (args.length == 0)
    page = "http://www.httprecipes.com/1/3/time.php";
  else
    page = args[0];
  module.go(page);
}
}
```

The above example can be run in two ways. If you run the example without any parameters (by simply typing "java GetSite"), it will download from the following URL, which is hardcoded in the recipe:

**http://www.httprecipes.com/1/3/time.php**

If you run the program with arguments it will download the specified URL. For example, to download the contents of the homepage of the recipes site, you would use the following command:

GetSite http://www.httprecipes.com

The above command simply shows the abstract format to call this recipe, with the appropriate parameters. For exact information on how to run this recipe refer to Appendix B, C, or D, depending on the operating system you are using.

After running the above command, the contents of **http://www.httprecipes.com** will now be displayed to the console, instead of **http://www.httprecipes.com/1/3/time.php**.

This recipe provides one very useful function. The **downloadPage** function, shown here:

```
public String downloadPage(URL url) throws IOException
```

This function accepts a **URL**, and downloads the contents of that web page. The contents are returned as a string. The implementation of the **downloadPage** function is somewhat simple, and follows the code already discussed in this chapter.

This recipe can be applied to any real-world site that contains data on a single page for which you wish to download the HTML.

Once you have the web page downloaded into a string, you may be wondering what you can do with the data. As you will see from the next recipe, you can extract information from that page.

## Recipe #3.2: Extract Simple Information from a Web Page

If you need to extract simple information from a web page, this recipe can serve as a good foundation for a more complex program. This recipe downloads the contents of a web page and extracts a piece of information from that page. For many tasks, this recipe will be all that is needed. This is particularly true, if you can get to the data directly from a URL and do not need to log in, or pass through any intermediary pages.

This recipe will download the current time for the city of St. Louis, MO. To do this it will use the following URL:

**http://www.httprecipes.com/1/3/time.php**

The above URL is one of the examples on the HTTP recipes web site. The contents of this page are shown in Listing 3.2. The piece of data that we would like to extract from Figure 3.2 is the current date and time. Figure 3.2 shows exactly what the web page looks like to a user. For exact information on how to run this recipe refer to Appendix B, C, or D, depending on the operating system you are using.

**Figure 3.2: The Current Time**

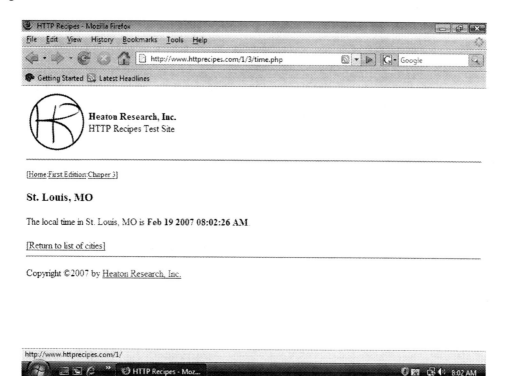

But to know how to extract this date and time, we need to see what this page looks like to the computer. To do this, we must examine the HTML source. While viewing the above URL in a web browser, select "View Source". This will show you Listing 3.2.

**Listing 3.2: HTML Source for the Current Time**

```
<!DOCTYPE HTML PUBLIC "-//W3C//DTD HTML 4.01 Transitional//EN">

<HTML>
<HEAD>
     <TITLE>HTTP Recipes</TITLE>
     <meta http-equiv="Content-Type" content="text/html;
charset=UTF-8">
     <meta http-equiv="Cache-Control" content="no-cache">
</HEAD>

<BODY>

<table border="0"><tr><td>
<a href="http://www.httprecipes.com/">
<img src="/images/logo.gif" alt="Heaton Research Logo" bor-
```

```
der="0"></a>
</td><td valign="top">Heaton Research, Inc.<br>
HTTP Recipes Test Site
</td></tr>
</table>
<hr><p><small>[<a href="/">Home</a>:<a href="/1/">First Edition</
a>
:<a href="/1/3/">Chaper 3</a>]</small></p>


<h3>St. Louis, MO</h3>
The local time in St. Louis, MO is <b>Jun 27 2006 05:58:38 PM</b>.

<br><br><a href="cities.php">[Return to list of cities]</a><br>

<hr>
<p>Copyright 2006 by <a href="http://www.heatonresearch.com/">
Heaton Research, Inc.</a></p>
</BODY>
</HTML>
```

Look at the above listing and see if you can find the time and date for St. Louis? Did you find it? It is the line about two-thirds of the way down that starts with the text "The local time in St. Louis, MO is". To extract this data we need to look at the two HTML tags that enclose it. For this web page, the time and date are enclosed in the **** and **** tags.

The following example, shown in Listing 3.3, will download this data, and extract the date and time information.

### Listing 3.3: Get the Time in St. Louis (GetTime.java)

```java
package com.heatonresearch.httprecipes.ch3.recipe2;

import java.io.*;
import java.net.*;

public class GetTime
{
  /**
   * The size of the download buffer.
   */
  public static int BUFFER_SIZE = 8192;

  /**
   * This method downloads the specified URL into a Java
   * String. This is a very simple method, that you can
   * reused anytime you need to quickly grab all data from
```

```
 * a specific URL.
 *
 * @param url The URL to download.
 * @return The contents of the URL that was downloaded.
 * @throws IOException Thrown if any sort of error occurs.
 */
public String downloadPage(URL url) throws IOException
{
  StringBuilder result = new StringBuilder();
  byte buffer[] = new byte[BUFFER_SIZE];

  InputStream s = url.openStream();
  int size = 0;

  do
  {
    size = s.read(buffer);
    if (size != -1)
      result.append(new String(buffer, 0, size));
  } while (size != -1);

  return result.toString();
}


/**
 * Extract a string of text from between the two specified
 * tokens.  The case of the two tokens must match.
 *
 * @param url The URL to download.
 * @param token1 The text, or tag, that comes before the
 * desired text.
 * @param token2 The text, or tag, that comes after the
 * desired text.
 * @param count Which occurrence of token1 to use, 1 for
 * the first.
 * @return The contents of the URL that was downloaded.
 */
public String extract(String str, String token1,
  String token2, int count)
{
  int location1, location2;

  location1 = location2 = 0;
  do
  {
    location1 = str.indexOf(token1, location1);
```

```java
      if (location1 == -1)
        return null;

      count--;
    } while (count > 0);

    location2 = str.indexOf(token2, location1 + 1);
    if (location2 == -1)
      return null;

    return str.substring(location1 + token1.length(), location2);
  }

  /**
   * Run the example.
   */
  public void go()
  {
    try
    {
      URL u = new URL("http://www.httprecipes.com/1/3/time.php");
      String str = downloadPage(u);

      System.out.println(extract(str, "<b>", "</b>", 1));

    } catch (MalformedURLException e)
    {
      e.printStackTrace();
    } catch (IOException e)
    {
      e.printStackTrace();
    }
  }

  /**
   * Typical Java main method, create an object, and then
   * call that object's go method.
   *
   * @param args Not used.
   */
  public static void main(String args[])
  {
    GetTime module = new GetTime();
    module.go();
  }
}
```

The main portion of this program is contained in a method named **go**. The following three lines do the main work performed by the **go** method.

```
URL u = new URL("http://www.httprecipes.com/1/3/time.php");
String str = downloadPage(u);
System.out.println(extract(str, "<b>", "</b>", 1));
```

First, a **URL** object is constructed with the URL that we are to download from. This **URL** object is then passed to the **downloadPage** function.

Using the **downloadPage** function from the last recipe, we can download the above HTML into a string. Now that the above data is in a string, you may ask - what is the easiest way to extract the date and time? Any Java string parsing method can be used to do this. However, this recipe provides one very useful function to do this, named **extract**. The contents of the **extract** function is shown here:

```
int location1, location2;

location1 = location2 = 0;
do
{
  location1 = str.indexOf(token1, location1);

  if (location1 == -1)
    return null;

  count--;
} while (count > 0);

location2 = str.indexOf(token2, location1 + 1);
if (location2 == -1)
  return null;

return str.substring(location1 + token1.length(), location2);
```

As you can see from above, the **extract** function is passed the string to parse, including the beginning and ending tags. The **extract** function will then scan the specified string, and find the beginning tag. In this case, the beginning tag is **<b>**. Once the beginning tag is found, the **extract** function will return all text found until the ending tag is found.

It is important to note that the beginning and ending text need not be HTML tags. You can use any beginning and ending text you wish with the **extract** function.

You might also notice that the **extract** function accepts a number as its last parameter. In this case, the number passed was one. This number specifies which instance of the beginning text to locate. In this example there was only one **<b>** to find. What if there were several? Passing in a two would have located the text at the second instance of the **<b>** tag.

The **extract** function is not part of Java. It is a useful function that I developed to help with string parsing. The extract function returns some text that is bounded by two token strings. Now, let's take a look at how it works.

The **extract** function begins by declaring two **int** variables. Additionally the parameters **token1** and **token2** are passed in. The parameter **token1** holds the text, which is usually an HTML tag that occurs at the beginning of the desired text. The parameter **token2** holds the text, which is usually an HTML tag that occurs at the end of the desired text.

```
int location1, location2;

location1 = location2 = 0;
```

These two variables will hold the location of the beginning and ending text. To begin with, they are both set to zero. Next, the function will begin looking for instances of **token1**. This is done with a **do/while** loop.

```
do
{
  location1 = str.indexOf(token1, location1);

  if (location1 == -1)
    return null;
```

As you can see **location1** is set to the location of **token1**. The search begins at **location1**. Since **location1** begins with the value of zero, this search also begins at the beginning of the string. If no instance of **token1** is found, the **null** is returned to let the caller know that the string could not be extracted.

Each time an instance of **token1** is found, the variable **count** is decreased by one. This is shown here:

```
  count--;
} while (count > 0);
```

Once the final instance of **token1** has been found, it is time to locate the ending token. This is done with the following lines of code:

```
location2 = str.indexOf(token2, location1 + 1);
if (location2 == -1)
  return null;

return str.substring(location1 + token1.length(),location2);
```

The above code locates **token2** using **indexOf**. If the second token is not found, then **null** is returned to indicate an error. Otherwise **substring** is called to return the text between the two tokens. It is important to remember to add the length of **token1** to **location1**. If you do not add this to **location1**, you will extract **token1** along with the desired text.

This recipe can be applied to any real-world site that contains data on a single page that you wish to extract. Although this recipe extracted information from the web page, it did not do anything with it. The next recipe will actually process the downloaded data.

## Recipe #3.3: Parsing Dates and Times

This recipe shows how to extract data from several pages. It also shows how to parse date and time information. This recipe will download the date and time for several US cities. It will extract this data from the following URL:

**http://www.httprecipes.com/1/3/cities.php**

Figure 3.3 shows this web page.

### Figure 3.3: Cities for which to Display Time

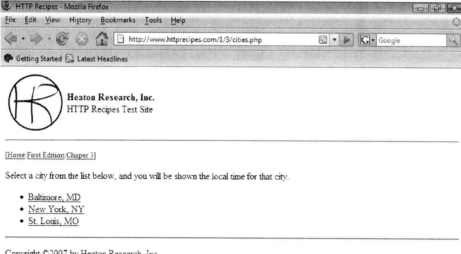

As you can see from the above list, there are three USA cities, which you may choose to find the time. To find the time for each city you would have to click on the link and view that city's page. This would be a total of four pages to access - first the city list page, and then a page for each of the three cities. For exact information on how to run this recipe refer to Appendix B, C, or D, depending on the operating system you are using.

This recipe will access the city list page, obtain the URL for each city, and then obtain the time for that city. Now, let's examine Listing 3.4 - the HTML that makes up the city list page.

### Listing 3.4: The HTML for the Cities List

```
<!DOCTYPE HTML PUBLIC "-//W3C//DTD HTML 4.01 Transitional//EN">

<HTML>
<HEAD>
      <TITLE>HTTP Recipes</TITLE>
      <meta http-equiv="Content-Type" content="text/html;
charset=UTF-8">
      <meta http-equiv="Cache-Control" content="no-cache">
</HEAD>

<BODY>

<table border="0"><tr><td>
<a href="http://www.httprecipes.com/">
<img src="/images/logo.gif" alt="Heaton Research Logo" bor-
der="0"></a>
</td><td valign="top">Heaton Research, Inc.<br>
HTTP Recipes Test Site
</td></tr>
</table>
<hr><p><small>[<a href="/">Home</a>:<a href="/1/">First Edition
</a>:
<a href="/1/3/">Chaper 3</a>]</small></p>

<p>Select a city from the list below, and you will be
shown the local time for that city.<br>
<ul>
<li><a href="city.php?city=2">Baltimore, MD</a>
<li><a href="city.php?city=3">New York, NY</a>
<li><a href="city.php?city=1">St. Louis, MO</a></ul>

<hr>
<p>Copyright 2006 by <a href="http://www.heatonresearch.com/">
Heaton Research, Inc.</a></p>
</BODY>
</HTML>
```

Do you see the cities in the above HTML? Find the **<li>** tags and you will find the cities. Each of these city lines link to the **city.php** page. For example, to display Baltimore's time, you would access the following URL:

**http://www.httprecipes.com/1/3/city.php?city=2**

This recipe will access the city list page to obtain a list of cities. Then that list will be used to build a second list that will contain the times for each of those cities. You can see Recipe 3.3 in Listing 3.5.

**Listing 3.5: Get the Time for Select Cities (GetCityTime.java)**

```java
package com.heatonresearch.httprecipes.ch3.recipe3;

import java.io.*;
import java.net.*;
import java.text.*;
import java.util.*;

public class GetCityTime
{
  // the size of a buffer
  public static int BUFFER_SIZE = 8192;

  /**
   * This method downloads the specified URL into a Java
   * String. This is a very simple method, that you can
   * reused anytime you need to quickly grab all data from
   * a specific URL.
   *
   * @param url The URL to download.
   * @return The contents of the URL that was downloaded.
   * @throws IOException Thrown if any sort of error occurs.
   */
  public String downloadPage(URL url) throws IOException
  {
    StringBuilder result = new StringBuilder();
    byte buffer[] = new byte[BUFFER_SIZE];

    InputStream s = url.openStream();
    int size = 0;

    do
    {
      size = s.read(buffer);
      if (size != -1)
        result.append(new String(buffer, 0, size));
```

```
  } while (size != -1);

  return result.toString();
}

/**
 * Extract a string of text from between the two specified
 * tokens.  The  case of the two tokens must match.
 *
 * @param url The URL to download.
 * @param token1 The text, or tag, that comes before the
 * desired text.
 * @param token2 The text, or tag, that comes after the
 * desired text.
 * @param count Which occurrence of token1 to use, 1 for
 * the first.
 * @return The contents of the URL that was downloaded.
 */
public String extract(String str, String token1,
  String token2, int count)
{
  int location1, location2;

  location1 = location2 = 0;
  do
  {
    location1 = str.indexOf(token1, location1 + 1);

    if (location1 == -1)
      return null;

    count--;
  } while (count > 0);

  location2 = str.indexOf(token2, location1 + 1);
  if (location2 == -1)
    return null;

  return str.substring(location1 + token1.length(), location2);
}

/**
 * Get the time for the specified city.
 */
public Date getCityTime(int city) throws IOException,
  ParseException
```

```
    {
      URL u =
new URL("http://www.httprecipes.com/1/3/city.php?city=" + city);
      String str = downloadPage(u);

      SimpleDateFormat sdf = new SimpleDateFormat(
        "MMM dd yyyy hh:mm:ss aa");
      Date date = sdf.parse(extract(str, "<b>", "</b>", 1));
      return date;
    }

  /**
    * Run the example.
    */
  public void go()
  {
    try
    {
      URL u =
        new URL("http://www.httprecipes.com/1/3/cities.php");
      String str = downloadPage(u);
      int count = 1;
      boolean done = false;

      while (!done)
      {
        String line = extract(str, "<li>", "</a>", count);

        if (line != null)
        {
          int cityNum = Integer.parseInt(
            extract(line, "=", "\"", 2));
          int i = line.indexOf(">");
          String cityName = line.substring(i + 1);
          Date cityTime = getCityTime(cityNum);
          SimpleDateFormat sdf = new SimpleDateFormat(
            "hh:mm:ss aa");
          String time = sdf.format(cityTime);
          System.out.println(count + " " + cityName + "\t"
            + time);
        } else
          done = true;
        count++;
      }

    } catch (Exception e)
```

```
      {
        e.printStackTrace();
      }
    }

  /**
   * Typical Java main method, create an object, and then
   * call that object's go method.
   *
   * @param args Not used.
   */
  public static void main(String args[])
  {
    GetCityTime module = new GetCityTime();
    module.go();
  }
}
```

This recipe uses the same **extract** and **downloadPage** functions as do the previous examples. However, the main **go** method is different. We will begin by examining the **go** method to see how the list of cities is downloaded.

First, a **URL** object is constructed for the city list URL, and the entire contents are downloaded.

```
URL u = new UR("http://www.httprecipes.com/1/3/cities.php");
String str = downloadPage(u);
```

After the entire contents of the city list page have been downloaded, we must parse through the HTML and find each of the cities. To begin, a **count** variable is created, which holds the current city number. Secondly, a **done** variable is created and initialized to **false**. This is demonstrated in the following lines of code:

```
int count = 1;
boolean done = false;

while (!done)
{
  String line = extract(str, "<li>", "</a>", count);
```

To extract each city, the beginning and ending tokens to search between must be identified. If you examine Listing 3.4, you will see that each city is on a line between the tokens **<li>** and **</a>**.

```
<li><a href="city.php?city=2">Baltimore, MD</a>
```

Calling the **extract** function with these two tokens will return Baltimore as follows:

```
<a href="city.php?city=2">Baltimore, MD
```

The above value will be copied into the **line** variable that is then parsed.

```
if (line != null)
{
  int cityNum = Integer.parseInt(extract(line, "=", "\"", 2));
  int i = line.indexOf(">");
  String cityName = line.substring(i + 1);
  Date cityTime = getCityTime(cityNum);
```

Next, we will parse out the city number by extracting what is between the **=** and the quote character. Given the line extracted (shown above), the extract function should return a "2" for Baltimore. Finally, we parse the city and state by searching for a **>** symbol. Extracting everything to the right of the **>** symbol will give us "Baltimore, MD". We now have the city's number, as well as its name and state.

We now can pass the city's number into the **getCityTime** function. The **getCityTime** function performs the same operation as the last recipe; that is, it will access the URL for the city for which we are seeking the time. The time will be returned as a string. For more information about how the **getCityTime** function works, review Recipe 3.2.

Now that we have the city time, we will format it using **SimpleDateFormat** as shown below:

```
SimpleDateFormat sdf = new SimpleDateFormat("hh:mm:ss aa");
String time = sdf.format(cityTime);
System.out.println(count + " " + cityName + "\t" + time);
} else
  done = true;
count++;
}
```

You may notice in the above code, that in this program, the time is formatted to exclude the date. This allows us to display each of the cities, and what the current time is, without displaying the date.

This recipe can be revised and applied to any real-world site that contains a list that leads to multiple other pages that you wish to extract data from.

## Recipe #3.4: Downloading a Binary File

The last two recipes for this chapter will demonstrate how to download data from a web site directly to a disk file. The first recipe will download to a binary file while the second will show how to download to a text file. A binary file download will make an exact copy of what was at the URL. The binary download is best used with a non-text resource, such as an image, sound or application file. Text files must be treated differently and will be discussed in detail in recipe 3.5.

To demonstrate downloading to a binary file, this recipe will download an image from the HTTP recipes site. This image can be seen on the web page at the following URL:

`http://www.httprecipes.com/1/3/sea.php`

The contents of this page are shown in Figure 3.4.

**Figure 3.4: An Image to Download**

If you examine the HTML source for this page you will find that the actual image is located at the following URL:

`http://www.httprecipes.com/1/3/sea.jpg`

Now let's examine how to download an image by downloading a binary file. The example recipe, Recipe 3.4, is shown below in Listing 3.6.

**Listing 3.6: Download a Binary File (DownloadBinary.java)**

```
package com.heatonresearch.httprecipes.ch3.recipe4;
```

```java
import java.io.*;
import java.net.*;

public class DownloadBinary
{
  // the size of a buffer
  public static int BUFFER_SIZE = 8192;


  /**
   * This method downloads the specified URL into a Java
   * String. This is a very simple method, that you can
   * reused anytime you need to quickly grab all data from
   * a specific URL.
   *
   * @param url The URL to download.
   * @return The contents of the URL that was downloaded.
   * @throws IOException Thrown if any sort of error occurs.
   */
  public String downloadPage(URL url) throws IOException
  {
    StringBuilder result = new StringBuilder();
    byte buffer[] = new byte[BUFFER_SIZE];

    InputStream s = url.openStream();
    int size = 0;

    do
    {
      size = s.read(buffer);
      if (size != -1)
        result.append(new String(buffer, 0, size));
    } while (size != -1);

    return result.toString();
  }

  public void saveBinaryPage(String filename, String page)
    throws IOException
  {
    OutputStream os = new FileOutputStream(filename);
    os.write(page.getBytes());
    os.close();
  }
```

```java
/**
 * Download a binary file from the Internet.
 *
 * @param page The web URL to download.
 * @param filename The local file to save to.
 */
public void download(String page, String filename)
{
  try
  {
    URL u = new URL(page);
    String str = downloadPage(u);
    saveBinaryPage(filename, str);

  } catch (MalformedURLException e)
  {
    e.printStackTrace();
  } catch (IOException e)
  {
    e.printStackTrace();
  }
}

/**
 * Typical Java main method, create an object, and then
 * start that object.
 *
 * @param args URL to download, and local file.
 */
public static void main(String args[])
{
  try
  {
    if (args.length != 2)
    {
      DownloadBinary d = new DownloadBinary();
      d.download("http://www.httprecipes.com/1/3/sea.jpg",
        "./sea2.jpg");
    } else
    {
      DownloadBinary d = new DownloadBinary();
      d.download(args[0], args[1]);
    }
  } catch (Exception e)
  {
    e.printStackTrace();
```

```
    }
  }
}
```

This recipe is very similar to Recipe 3.1. However, in this recipe, you must specify a URL and a file to save that URL to. For example, to download the Heaton Research logo, you would use the following command:

```
DownloadBinary http://www.httprecipes.com/images/logo.gif
./logo.gif
```

The above arguments will download the image shown above to a file named **logo.jpg**. The above command simply shows the abstract format to call this recipe. For exact information on how to run this recipe refer to Appendix B, C, or D, depending on the operating system you are using.

As mentioned, this recipe is very similar to Recipe 3.1. It even uses the same **downloadPage** function as Recipe 3.1; however, an extra method is added named **saveBinaryPage**. This method is shown here.

```
public void saveBinaryPage(String filename, String page) throws
IOException
```

As you can see, this method accepts a **filename** and a **page**. The specified page content will be saved to the local file specified by **filename**. The variable, **page,** contains the actual contents of the page, as returned by the **downloadPage** function.

Saving the string to a binary file is very easy. The following lines of code do this.

```
OutputStream os = new FileOutputStream(filename);
os.write(page.getBytes());
os.close();
```

It is very simple. The stream is opened to a disk file, the contents of the string are written to the file, and the file is closed. This recipe could be applied to any real-world site where you need to download images, or other binary files to disk.

In this recipe, you learned how to download a binary file. Binary files are exact copies of what is downloaded from the URL. In the next recipe you will see how to download a text file.

### Recipe #3.5: Downloading a Text File

This recipe will download a web page to a text file. But why is a text file treated differently than a binary file? They are treated differently because different operating systems end lines differently. Table 3.2 summarizes how the different operating systems store text file line breaks.

**Table 3.2: How Operating Systems End Lines**

| Operating System | ASCII Codes | Java |
|---|---|---|
| UNIX | #10 | "\n" |
| Windows | #13 #10 | "\r\n" |
| Mac OSX | #10 | "\n" |
| Mac Classic | #13 | "\r" |

To properly download a text file, the program must make sure that the line breaks are compatible with the current operating system. Since Java can be run on a variety of operating systems, this is especially important.

To use this recipe to download the index page of the HTTP recipes site, you would use the following command:

```
DownloadText http://www.httprecipes.com/ ./contents.txt
```

The above command simply shows the abstract format to call this recipe, with the appropriate parameters. For exact information on how to run this recipe refer to Appendix B, C, or D, depending on the operating system you are using. The above arguments will download the HTML text to a file named **contents.txt**.

Listing 3.7 shows how this is done.

**Listing 3.7: Download a Text File (DownloadText.java)**

```java
package com.heatonresearch.httprecipes.ch3.recipe5;

import java.io.*;
import java.net.*;

public class DownloadText
{

  /**
   * Download the specified text page.
   *
   * @param page The URL to download from.
   * @param filename The local file to save to.
   */
  public void download(String page, String filename)
  {
    try
    {
      URL u = new URL(page);
```

```
      InputStream is = u.openStream();
      OutputStream os = new FileOutputStream(filename);
      downloadText(is, os);
      is.close();
      os.close();

   } catch (MalformedURLException e)
   {
     e.printStackTrace();
   } catch (IOException e)
   {
     e.printStackTrace();
   }
}


/**
 * Download a text file, and convert the line breaks for
 * whatever the current operating system is.
 *
 * @param is The input stream to read from.
 * @param os The output stream to write to..
 */
private void downloadText(InputStream is, OutputStream os)
  throws IOException
{
  byte lineSep[] =
    System.getProperty("line.separator").getBytes();
  int ch = 0;
  boolean inLineBreak = false;
  boolean hadLF = false;
  boolean hadCR = false;

  do
  {
    ch = is.read();
    if (ch != -1)
    {
      if ((ch == '\r') || (ch == '\n'))
      {
        inLineBreak = true;
        if (ch == '\r')
        {
          if (hadCR)
            os.write(lineSep);
          else
            hadCR = true;
```

```java
        } else
        {
          if (hadLF)
            os.write(lineSep);
          else
            hadLF = true;
        }
      } else
      {
        if (inLineBreak)
        {
          os.write(lineSep);
          hadCR = hadLF = inLineBreak = false;
        }
        os.write(ch);
      }
    }
  } while (ch != -1);
}


/**
 * Typical Java main method, create an object, and then
 * pass the parameters on if provided, otherwise default.
 *
 * @param args URL to download, and local file.
 */
public static void main(String args[])
{
  try
  {
    if (args.length != 2)
    {
      DownloadText d = new DownloadText();
      d.download(
      "http://www.httprecipes.com/1/3/text.php", "./text.html");
    } else
    {
      DownloadText d = new DownloadText();
      d.download(args[0], args[1]);
    }
  } catch (Exception e)
  {
    e.printStackTrace();
  }
}
}
```

This recipe works differently than Recipe 3.4 in that the text file is not first loaded to a string. Rather, the text file is read from the input stream as it is written to the output stream. A method is provided, called **downloadText**, which accepts an input stream and an output stream. The input stream should be from the URL, and the output stream should be to a disk file. This method is shown here:

```
private void downloadText(InputStream is, OutputStream os) throws
IOException
{
```

The first thing that the **downloadText** method must do is obtain the line separator for the current operating system. This can be done with a call to **System.getProperty**, as shown here:

```
byte lineSep[] = System.getProperty("line.separator").getBytes();
```

Next, several variables are declared. First, the variable **ch** is used to hold the current character, which was just read in from the **InputStream**. Next, a **boolean** named **inLineBreak** is used to hold whether the **InputStream** is currently inside of a line break. The next two variables, **hadLF** and **hadCR**, are set if the line break was caused by a line feed (char code 10) or a carriage return (char code 13). These lines are shown here:

```
int ch = 0;
boolean inLineBreak = false;
boolean hadLF = false;
boolean hadCR = false;
```

Next, a **do/while** loop is used to read each character in, and process it.

```
do
{
  ch = is.read();
```

Each character is then checked to see if it is a line break character.

```
if (ch != -1)
{
  if ((ch == '\r') || (ch == '\n'))
  {
```

The above code checks to see if the character returned is -1, which indicates we have reached the end and there are no more characters to read. Otherwise, we check to see if the character returned was a line break character.

```
inLineBreak = true;
if (ch == '\r')
{
  if (hadCR)
    os.write(lineSep);
  else
    hadCR = true;
```

```
  } else
  {
  if (hadLF)
    os.write(lineSep);
  else
    hadLF = true;
  }
} else
{
```

If the character was a carriage return, then we check to see if there already was a carriage return, then we write a line separator. If the character was not a carriage return, then we do not write a line separator. Line feed is handled the same way. This causes each combination of line ending characters to be written to the operating system's standard for line breaks.

If the character was not a line break, then it is handled with the following lines of code.

```
if (inLineBreak)
{
  os.write(lineSep);
  hadCR = hadLF = inLineBreak = false;
}
  os.write(ch);
}
```

If we were in a line break, then an operating system line break is written; otherwise, we write the character to the output stream.

Finally, we check to see if the character read was -1. If the character read was -1, this indicates there are no more characters to read.

```
} while (ch != -1);
```

The algorithm is useful because it allows you to adjust incoming text to exactly how the operating system would like it to be represented.

## Summary

In this chapter you learned how to perform basic HTTP operations with Java. You saw how you can access a URL and download the contents of that URL.

Java contains a **URL** class. This class allows you to open connections to a URL. By calling the **openStream** function on a **URL** object, you are given an **InputStream** object that you can use to access the contents of the URL. Once you have an **InputStream,** you can read from the URL essentially the same as if you were reading from a file.

You were shown that downloading to a binary file means making an exact copy of the incoming data and is preferred when downloading images, audio, and other binary data. Downloading a text file requires you to translate the incoming line breaks to the correct format for your operating system.

In this chapter you saw how to use the **URL** and **InputStream** classes to access web pages. This is fine for simple requests; however for more complex requests you will need to use the **HttpURLConnection** class. This class will be introduced in the next chapter.

# CHAPTER 4: BEYOND SIMPLE REQUESTS

- The HttpURLConnection Class
- Reading HTTP Response Headers
- Setting HTTP Request Headers
- Managing HTTP Timeouts

The connection between a bot and a web server is very important. In the previous chapters this link was established using either a **Socket** object or an **InputStream** object, obtained from a call to the **openStream** function of a **URL** class. There is a third way to open a connection to a web server—you can use the **HttpURLConnection** object. In summary, the three ways to open a connection to a web server are:

- **Socket**
- **InputStream** from **URL.openStream**
- **HttpURLConnection**

The **HttpURLConnection** class allows much more flexibility than just using an **InputStream** object. It is also much simpler to use than a socket.

## Introducing HttpURLConnection

The **HttpURLConnection** class provides many additional options that you do not have access to with only an **InputStream**. The **HttpURLConnection** class provides access to the following operations:

- Reading data from the URL
- Posting data to the URL
- Setting client headers
- Reading server headers
- Setting socket parameters

Using the **HttpURLConnection** class is easy enough. It is created using a **URL** object, much like the **InputStream**. The following code creates an **HttpURLConnection** class:

```
URL u = new URL("http://www.httprecipes.com");
HttpURLConnection http = (HttpURLConnection)u.openConnection();
```

Once you have the **HttpURLConnection** object, you can easily get an **InputStream** to the web site. This will allow you to download the contents of the web site, just as you did in Chapter 3, "Simple HTTP Requests". The following line of code obtains an **InputStream** from the **HttpURLConnection** object created above.

```
InputStream is = http.getInputStream();
```

In addition to the **InputStream**, each **HttpURLConnection** object also has an **OutputStream**, if requested. The following code requests an **OutputStream** for the **HttpURLConnection** object.

```
OutputStream os = http.getOutputStream();
```

If you use the **OutputStream** to send data to the web server, then the HTTP request will be a **POST** request. If you do not make use of the **OutputStream**, the request will be a **GET**. **POST** requests are usually used when the user responds to a form. Chapter 7, "Responding to Forms," will show you how to use forms and **POST** requests.

## HTTP Request Headers

Setting the values of HTTP request headers is another common task of an **HttpURLConnection** object. The web browser sends browser headers, or HTTP request headers, to the web server. These headers are most commonly used for the following purposes:

- Identifying the type of web browser
- Transmitting any cookies
- Facilitating HTTP authentication

There are other things that can be accomplished with HTTP request headers; however, these are the most common. HTTP authentication will be covered in Chapter 5, "Secure HTTP Requests," and cookies will be covered in Chapter 8, "Handling Sessions and Cookies". Setting the type of browser will be covered later in this section.

### Setting HTTP Request Headers

The **HttpURLConnection** class provides several functions and methods that can be used to access the HTTP request headers. These functions and methods are shown in Table 4.1.

**Table 4.1: HTTP Request Header Methods and Functions**

| Method or Function Name | Purpose |
|---|---|
| addRequestProperty(String key, String value) | Adds a general request property specified by a key-value pair. |
| getRequestProperties() | Returns an unmodifiable Map of general request properties for this connection. |
| getRequestProperty(String key) | Returns the value of the named general request property for this connection. |
| setRequestProperty(String key, String value) | Sets the general request property. |

Usually the only method from the above list that you will use will be the **setRequestProperty** method. The others are useful when you need to query what values have already been set. If there is already a header with the specified name, then **setRequestHeader** will overwrite it. The **addRequestProperty** can be used to add more than one of the same request header with the same name. Usually, you do not want to do this. Adding more that one header of the same name is useful when dealing with cookies - which are discussed in Chapter 8, "Handling Cookies and Sessions".

## Identifying the Browser Type

One of the HTTP request headers identifies the browser type that the user is using. Many web sites take this header in to account. For example, some web sites are only designed to work with certain versions of Microsoft Internet Explorer. To make use of such sites, you need to change how **HttpURLConnection** reports the browser type.

The browser type can be determined from the **user-agent** HTTP request header. You can easily set the value of this, or any, HTTP request header using the **setRequestProperty**. For example, to identify the bot as a browser of type "My Bot", you would use the following command:

```
http.setRequestProperty("user-agent","My Bot");
```

The **user-agent** header is often used to identify the bot. For example, each of the major search engines use spiders to find pages for their search engines. These search engine companies use **user-agent** headers to identify them as a search engine spider, and not a human user.

When you write a bot of your own, you have some decisions to make with the **user-agent** header. You can either identify the bot, as seen above, or you can emulate one of the common browsers. If a web site requires a version of Internet Explorer, you will have to emulate Internet Explorer.

Table 4.2 shows the header used by most major browsers to identify them. As you can see, this header also communicates what operating system the user is running as well.

**Table 4.2: Identities of Several Major Browsers**

| Browser | User-Agent Header |
|---|---|
| Firefox 1.5 (PC) | Mozilla/5.0(PC) (Windows; U; Windows NT 5.1; en-US; rv:1.8.0.4) Gecko/20060508 Firefox/1.5.0.4 |
| Internet Explorer 6.0 (PC) | Mozilla/4.0(PC) (compatible; MSIE 6.0; Windows NT 5.1; SV1; .NET CLR 1.1.4322) |
| Safari v2 (Mac) | Mozilla/5.0 (Macintosh; U; PPC Mac OS X; en) AppleWebKit/418.8 (KHTML, like Gecko) Safari/419.3 |
| Firefox v1.5 (Mac) | Mozilla/5.0 (Macintosh; U; PPC Mac OS X Mach-O; en-US; rv:1.8.0.4) Gecko/20060508 Firefox/1.5.0.4 |
| Internet Explorer 5.1 (Mac) | Mozilla/4.0 (compatible; MSIE 5.14; Mac_PowerPC) |
| Java(PC/Mac) | Java/1.5.0_06 |

You will also notice from the above list, I have Java listed as a browser. This is what Java will report to a web site, if you do not override the **user-agent**. It is usually better to override this value with something else.

## Server Headers

The server headers contain many useful pieces of information. Server headers are commonly used for:

- Determining the type of data at a URL
- Determining the cookies in use
- Determining the web server software in use
- Determining the size of the content at this URL

For the bots that you create, you will most commonly use server headers to determine the type of data at a URL and to support cookies.

### Reading Server Headers

Once you retrieve the contents of a URL back from the server, there are headers available to the program. The web server provided this second set of headers. The **HttpURLConnection** class provides several functions and methods to access these server response headers. These functions and methods are listed in Table 4.3.

**Table 4.3: HTTP Response Header Methods and Functions**

| Method or Function Name | Purpose |
|---|---|
| getHeaderField() | Returns the value for the nth header field. |
| getHeaderField(String name) | Returns the value of the named header field. |
| getHeaderFieldDate(String name, long Default) | Returns the value of the named field parsed as date. |
| getHeaderFieldInt(String name, int Default) | Returns the value of the named field parsed as a number. |
| getHeaderFieldKey(int n) | Returns the key for the nth header field. |
| getHeaderFields() | Returns an unmodifiable Map of the header fields. |

As you can see from the above methods, you can read the headers in a variety of formats. To read headers as a **String**, use the **getHeaderField** function. To read headers as an **int**, use the **getHeaderFieldInt** function. To read the headers as a **Date**, use the **getHeaderFieldDate** function.

## MIME Types

One very important HTTP response header is the content type. The **content-type** header tells the web browser what type of data the URL is attached to. For example, to determine the type of content at a URL, you would use the following line of code:

```
String type = http.getHeaderField("content-type");
```

This type information is called a Multipurpose Internet Mail Extensions (MIME) type. The "Mail" in MIME is largely historical. MIME types were originally developed for email attachments, long before there was a World Wide Web (WWW). However, they are now applied to many different Internet applications, such as web browsers and servers.

A MIME type consists of two identifiers separated by a slash (/). For example **text/html** is a mime type that identifies a resource as an HTML document. The first part of the type, in this case **text**, identifies the family of the type. The second identifies the exact type, within that family. Plain text files are also part of the **text** family, and have the type **text/plain**.

**Table 4.4: MIME Families**

| Method/Function Name | Purpose |
|---|---|
| application | Application, or raw binary data. |
| audio | Sounds and music. |
| example | Used only for example types. |
| image | Images. |
| message | Mail messages. |
| model | Compound type document. |
| multipart | Another compound type documents. |
| text | Text formats. |
| video | Video formats. |

There are many different MIME types under each of these families. However, there is only a handful that you will commonly see. Table 4.5 summarizes these.

**Table 4.5: Common MIME Types**

| MIME Type | Purpose |
|---|---|
| image/gif | GIF image files. |
| image/jpeg | JPEG image files. |
| image/png | PNG image files. |
| image/tiff | TIFF image files. |
| text/html | HTML text files. |
| text/plain | Unformatted text files. |

Often, the program will only need to look at the family. For example, if you wanted to download `text` and binary files differently, you would simply look at the family part of the MIME type. If it is determined that `text` is the family, you may download the URL as a text file. Any other family would require downloading the information as a binary file. The difference between a binary file and a text file is that binary files are copied exactly to the hard drive, whereas text file's line endings are reformatted properly for the resident operating system.

## Calling Sequence

As you have seen in this chapter, there is a variety of operations that can be performed on an **HttpURLConnection** object. You can set request headers, read response headers, **POST** data and read response data. Please note, however, that there is a very specific order that these operations must follow. For example, you can't set a request header, after you are already reading the response. If you are reading the web server's reply, the request was already sent. Therefore, all request information must be set before you begin working with the response. The general order that you should follow is shown here:

- Step 1: Set any HTTP request headers.
- Step 2: POST data, if this is a POST request.
- Step 3: Read HTTP response headers.
- Step 4: Read HTTP response data.

If you ever face a bug where it seems the request headers are being ignored, check to see if you are not already calling a method related to the response before setting the header. All headers must be set before the request is sent.

# Other Useful Options

In addition to headers, there are other useful options that the **HttpURLConnection** class provides. Although there are a number of options in the **HttpURLConnection** class that are used only for very rare or obscure situations, in this section we will examine the two most common options used in the **HttpURLConnection** class. The two most frequently used are "timeouts" and "redirect following". The next two sections will cover these options.

## Timeout

When you request that the **HttpURLConnection** class process a URL, certain operations can timeout. The **HttpURLConnection** class will wait a certain amount of milliseconds, before it times out. There is a default value of time; however, you can adjust this time to be longer or shorter to suit your needs. There are two different timeouts supported by Java:

- Timeout while connecting to the web host.
- Timeout while transferring data with the web host.

To control the timeout value while connecting to the host, you should use the **setConnectionTimeout** on the **HttpURLConnection** class. Likewise, you can call the **getConnectionTimeout** to determine the current connection timeout. The timeout is measured in milliseconds. For instance, to set the connection timeout to one second you would use the following line of code:

```
http.setConnectionTimeout(1000);
```

To control the timeout value while reading data from the host, you should use the **setReadTimeout** on the **HttpURLConnection** class. Likewise, you can call the **getReadTimeout** to determine the current read timeout. This timeout is also measured in milliseconds. To set the read timeout to one second you would use the following line of code:

```
http.setReadTimeout(1000);
```

Please note that timeouts were added in J2SE 5.0. If you are using an earlier version, these methods and functions will not be available.

## Redirect Following

One very handy feature in HTTP is "redirect following". Many web sites make use of the HTTP redirect internally, so you will likely encounter redirects when writing a bot. The HTTP redirect allows the server to redirect the web browser to a new URL.

To see an HTTP redirect in action, enter the following URL into your web browser. You would expect the browser to take you to the URL you entered.

**http://www.httprecipes.com/1/4/redirect.php**

However, you do not end up on the above URL. You actually end up at the root of the "Recipe Site" at the following URL:

**http://www.httprecipes.com/**

This was due to an HTTP redirect. By default, the **HttpURLConnection** class will follow all such redirects automatically and often, you do not need to even be concerned with them. Web browsers will always follow redirects automatically. However, if you would like to handle the redirects yourself, you can disable auto following. The following line of code would do this:

```
http.setInstanceFollowRedirects(false);
```

Additionally, you can call a static method and disable auto following for all instances of **HttpURLConnection**. The following line of code would do this:

```
HttpURLConnection.setFollowRedirects(false);
```

If you disable redirection following, you may manually follow the redirects by looking at the **location** response header.

# Recipes

This chapter includes four recipes. These four recipes will demonstrate the following:

- Scanning a URL for headers
- Searching a range of IP addresses for web sites
- Downloading a binary or text file
- Monitoring a site to see that it stays up

These recipes will introduce you to some of the things that can be done with the **HttpURLConnection** class.

## Recipe #4.1: Scan URL

Sometimes it is helpful to examine the headers for a particular URL. Recipe 4.1 shows how to use the **HttpURLConnection** class to access the headers for a particular URL. This program is shown in Listing 4.1.

### Listing 4.1: Scan a URL for HTTP Response Headers (ScanURL.java)

```java
package com.heatonresearch.httprecipes.ch4.recipe1;

import java.io.IOException;
import java.net.*;


public class ScanURL
{
  /**
   * Scan the URL and display headers.
   *
   * @param u The URL to scan.
   * @throws IOException Error scanning URL.
   */
  public void scan(String u) throws IOException
  {
    URL url = new URL(u);
    HttpURLConnection http =
      (HttpURLConnection) url.openConnection();
    int count = 0;
    String key, value;

    do
    {
      key = http.getHeaderFieldKey(count);
      value = http.getHeaderField(count);
      count++;
      if (value != null)
```

```java
    {
      if (key == null)
        System.out.println(value);
      else
        System.out.println(key + ": " + value);
    }
  } while (value != null);
}

/**
 * Typical Java main method, create an object, and then
 * start the object passing arguments. If insufficient
 * arguments are provided, then display startup
 * instructions.
 *
 * @param args Program arguments.
 */
public static void main(String args[])
{
  try
  {
    if (args.length != 1)
    {
      System.out.println("Usage: \njava ScanURL [URL to Scan]");
    } else
    {
      ScanURL d = new ScanURL();
      d.scan(args[0]);
    }
  } catch (Exception e)
  {
    e.printStackTrace();
  }
}
}
```

This program is designed to accept one parameter, which is the URL that you would like to scan. For example, to scan the web site **http://www.httprecipes.com/** you would use the following command.

```
ScanURL http://www.httprecipes.com/
```

Issuing the above command would cause the program to access the web site and then display all HTTP server headers that were returned. The above command simply shows the abstract format to call this recipe, with the appropriate parameters. For exact information on how to run this recipe refer to Appendix B, C, or D, depending on the operating system you are using.

All of the work performed by this program is done inside of the **scan** method. The first thing that the scan method does is to create a new **URL** object and then create an **HttpURLConnection** object from there. The following lines of code do this:

```
URL url = new URL(u);
HttpURLConnection http = (HttpURLConnection)
url.openConnection();
```

Once the connection has been established, a few local variables are created to keep track of the headers being displayed. The **key** variable will hold the name of each header found. The **value** variable will hold the value of that header. The **count** variable keeps a count of which header we are on.

```
int count = 0;
String key, value;
```

Next, a **do/while** loop will be used to loop through each of the headers.

```
do
{
  key = http.getHeaderFieldKey(count);
  value = http.getHeaderField(count);
```

We know that we have reached the end of the headers when we find a header that has a **null** value. However; a **null** key is acceptable, the first header always had a **null** key, because, as you recall from Chapter 1 and 2, the first header is always in a different format.

```
count++;
if (value != null)
{
```

If there is no key value, then just display the value. If both are present, then display both. You will never have a key, but no value.

```
if (key == null)
  System.out.println(value);
else
  System.out.println(key + ": " + value);
```

The loop continues until a **value** with the value of **null** is found.

```
  }
} while (value != null);
```

This process will continue until all headers have been displayed.

### Recipe #4.2: Scan for Sites

You can also use the **HttpURLConnection** class to determine if there is an active web server at a specific URL. Recipe 4.2 shows how to loop through a series of IP addresses to find any web servers. To use this program, you must specify an IP address prefix. An example of this would be **192.168.1**. Specifying this prefix would visit 256 IP addresses. It would visit from **192.168.1.0** to **192.168.1.255**.

This recipe shows how to decrease the timeout for connection. Because almost all of the IP addresses will not have web servers, it takes a while for this example to run. This is because; by default Java will wait several minutes to connect to a web server.

Because of this the connection timeout is taken down to only a few seconds. For a more thorough scan the timeout can be increased. Listing 4.2 shows the site scanner:

### Listing 4.2: Scan for Web Sites (ScanSites.java)

```java
package com.heatonresearch.httprecipes.ch4.recipe2;

import java.io.*;
import java.net.*;
import java.util.*;

public class ScanSites
{
  // the size of a buffer
  public static int BUFFER_SIZE = 8192;

  /**
   * This method downloads the specified URL into a Java
   * String. This is a very simple method, that you can
   * reused anytime you need to quickly grab all data from
   * a specific URL.
   *
   * @param url The URL to download.
   * @param timeout The number of milliseconds to wait for
   * connection.
   * @return The contents of the URL that was downloaded.
   * @throws IOException Thrown if any sort of error occurs.
   */
  public String downloadPage(URL url, int timeout)
    throws IOException
  {
    StringBuilder result = new StringBuilder();
    byte buffer[] = new byte[BUFFER_SIZE];

    URLConnection http = url.openConnection();
```

```
  http.setConnectTimeout(100);
  InputStream s = http.getInputStream();
  int size = 0;

  do
  {
    size = s.read(buffer);
    if (size != -1)
      result.append(new String(buffer, 0, size));
  } while (size != -1);

  return result.toString();
}


/**
 * Extract a string of text from between the two specified
 * tokens.  The case of the two tokens need not match.
 *
 * @param url The URL to download.
 * @param token1 The text, or tag, that comes before the
 * desired text.
 * @param token2 The text, or tag, that comes after the
 * desired text.
 * @param count Which occurrence of token1 to use, 1 for
 * the first.
 * @return The contents of the URL that was downloaded.
 */
public String extractNoCase(String str, String token1,
  String token2,
    int count)
{
  int location1, location2;

  // convert everything to lower case
  String searchStr = str.toLowerCase();
  token1 = token1.toLowerCase();
  token2 = token2.toLowerCase();

  // now search
  location1 = location2 = 0;


  do
  {
    location1 = searchStr.indexOf(token1, location1 + 1);
```

```java
    if (location1 == -1)
      return null;

    count--;
  } while (count > 0);

  // return the result from the original string that has mixed
  // case
  location2 = str.indexOf(token2, location1 + 1);
  if (location2 == -1)
    return null;

  return str.substring(location1 + token1.length(), location2);
}


/**
 * Scan the specified IP address and return the title of
 * the web page found there, or null if no connection can
 * be made.
 *
 * @param ip The IP address to scan.
 * @return The title of the web page, or null if no website.
 */
private String scanIP(String ip)
{
  try
  {
    System.out.println("Scanning: " + ip);
    String page = downloadPage(new URL("http://" + ip), 1000);
    String title = extractNoCase(page, "<title>",
      "</title>", 0);
    if (title == null)
      title = "[Untitled site]";
    return title;
  } catch (IOException e)
  {
    return null;
  }
}
```

```java
/**
 * Scan a range of 256 IP addressed.  Provide the prefix
 * of the IP address, without the final fourth.  For
 * example "192.168.1".
 *
 * @param ip The IP address prefix(i.e. 192.168.1)
 */
public void scan(String ip)
{
  if (!ip.endsWith("."))
  {
    ip += ".";
  }

  // create a list to hold sites found
  List<String> list = new ArrayList<String>();

  // scan through IP addresses ending in 0 - 255
  for (int i = 1; i < 255; i++)
  {
    String address = ip + i;
    String title = scanIP(address);
    if (title != null)
      list.add(address + ":" + title);
  }

  // now display the list of sites found
  System.out.println();
  System.out.println("Sites found:");
  if (list.size() > 0)
  {
    for (String site : list)
    {
      System.out.println(site);
    }
  } else
  {
    System.out.println("No sites found");
  }
}
```

```java
/**
 * Typical Java main method, create an object, and then
 * start the object passing arguments. If insufficient
 * arguments are provided, then display startup
 * instructions.
 *
 * @param args Program arguments.
 */
public static void main(String args[])
{
  try
  {
    if (args.length != 1)
    {
      System.out.println(
        "Usage: ScanSites [IP prefix, i.e. 192.168.1]");
    } else
    {
      ScanSites d = new ScanSites();
      d.scan(args[0]);
    }
  } catch (Exception e)
  {
    e.printStackTrace();
  }
}
}
```

To run this program, you must specify the IP prefix. For example, to scan the IP prefix **192.168.1** you would use the following command:

```
ScanSites http://www.httprecipes.com/
```

The above command simply shows the abstract format to call this recipe, with the appropriate parameters. For exact information on how to run this recipe refer to Appendix B, C, or D, depending on the operating system you are using. You may find more sites on your home network than you knew existed. For example, I found that my laser printer has a web site. Logging into my printer's built in web site shows me how much toner is still available. You can see the results of my scan in Figure 4.1.

**Figure 4.1: Scan for Sites**

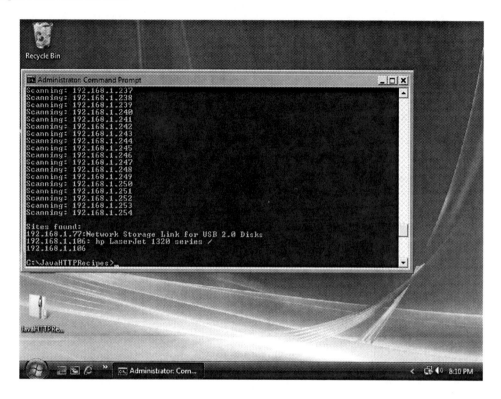

First the IP prefix is checked to see if it ends with a period ".". If it does not end this way, then a period is appended. This is because we need the IP prefix in the form:

```
192.168.1.
```

not

```
192.168.1
```

We will be appending a count from 0 to 255 to the end, so the trailing period is completely necessary.

```
if (!ip.endsWith("."))
{
  ip += ".";
}
```

Next, an array is created to hold a list of the sites that are located. The sites located are not displayed until the end of the scan.

```
// Create a list to hold sites found.
List<String> list = new ArrayList<String>();
```

Now we are ready to scan. A **for** loop is used to count from 0 to 255.

```
// Scan through IP addresses ending in 0 - 255.
for (int i = 0; i <= 255; i++)
{
  String address = ip + i;
  String title = scanIP(address);
  if (title != null)
    list.add(address + ":" + title);
}
```

For each IP address, the **scanIP** function is called. If a valid site exists at that address, the title (from the HTML) is returned. If no valid site is found, then the value **null** is returned. The **scanIP** function is covered in detail later in this section.

Once the loop completes, we display what sites were found. The code to do this is shown below:

```
// Now display the list of sites found.
System.out.println();
System.out.println("Sites found:");
if (list.size() > 0)
{
  for (String site : list)
  {
    System.out.println(site);
  }
```

The user is informed if there are no sites to display.

```
} else
{
  System.out.println("No sites found");
}
```

As you saw above, for each IP address, the **scanIP** method was called. I will now show you how the **scanIP** function is constructed.

The **scanIP** function begins by displaying the IP address that is currently being scanned. The **downloadPage** method is called to retrieve the HTML at the URL formed from the IP address. The following lines of code do this.

```
try
{
  System.out.println("Scanning: " + ip);
  String page = downloadPage(new URL("http://" + ip),1000);
```

The **downloadPage** function is the one we created in Chapter 3; however, you will notice an additional parameter. The second parameter specifies a 1,000-millisecond timeout. If a connection is not made in one second, which is 1,000 milliseconds, the connection will abort and throw an exception.

Next the **extractNoCase** function is called to extract the text between the **<title>** and **</title>** tags. The **extractNoCase** is a special version of the extract function introduced in Chapter 3. The **extractNoCase** version of extract does not care about the case of the tags. For example, **<title>** and **<Title>** would be considered the same. If no title is found, then the site is listed as an "Untitled Site".

```
String title = extractNoCase(page, "<title>", "</title>", 0);
if (title == null)
title = "[Untitled site]";
return title;
```

If an exception occurs, then a value of **null** is returned, indicating that a site could not be found.

```
} catch (IOException e)
{
  return null;
}
```

This recipe makes use of the **extractNoCase** which is a new version of **extract** function. Both of these functions can be seen in Listing 4.2. They are both slight modifications of the functions introduced in Chapter 3. For more information on these functions, see Chapter 3.

### Recipe #4.3: Download Binary or Text

Downloading a file from a URL is a common task for a bot. However, different procedures must be followed depending on the type of file being downloaded. If the file is binary, such as an image, then an exact copy of the file must be made on the local computer. If the file is text, then the line breaks must be properly formatted for the current operating system.

Chapter 3 introduced two recipes for downloading files from a URL. One version would download a text file; the other would download a binary file. As you saw earlier in this chapter, the content-type header tells what type of file will be downloaded. Recipe 4.3 contains a more sophisticated URL downloader, than that in Chapter 3. It first determines the type of file and then downloads it in the appropriate way. Listing 4.3 shows this new URL downloader.

### Listing 4.3: Download Text or Binary (DownloadURL.java)

```
package com.heatonresearch.httprecipes.ch4.recipe3;

import java.net.*;
import java.io.*;
```

```java
public class DownloadURL
{
  public static int BUFFER_SIZE = 8192;

  /**
   * Download either a text or binary file from a URL.
   * The URL's headers will be scanned to determine the
   * type of tile.
   *
   * @param remoteURL The URL to download from.
   * @param localFile The local file to save to.
   * @throws IOException Exception while downloading.
   */
  public void download(URL remoteURL, File localFile)
    throws IOException
  {
    HttpURLConnection http =
      (HttpURLConnection) remoteURL.openConnection();
    HttpURLConnection.setFollowRedirects(true);
    InputStream is = http.getInputStream();
    OutputStream os = new FileOutputStream(localFile);
    String type =
      http.getHeaderField("Content-Type").toLowerCase().trim();
    if (type.startsWith("text"))
      downloadText(is, os);
    else
      downloadBinary(is, os);
    is.close();
    os.close();
    http.disconnect();
  }


  /**
   * Overloaded version of download that accepts strings,
   * rather than URL objects.
   *
   * @param remoteURL The URL to download from.
   * @param localFile The local file to save to.
   * @throws IOException Exception while downloading.
   */
  public void download(String remoteURL, String localFile)
    throws IOException
  {
```

```java
   download(new URL(remoteURL), new File(localFile));
}



/**
 * Download a text file.  This is done by converting the line
 * ending characters to the correct type for the
 * operating system that is being used.
 *
 * @param is The input stream, which is the URL.
 * @param os The output stream, a local file.
 * @throws IOException Exception while downloading.
 */
private void downloadText(InputStream is, OutputStream os)
  throws IOException
{
  byte lineSep[] =
    System.getProperty("line.separator").getBytes();
  int ch = 0;
  boolean inLineBreak = false;
  boolean hadLF = false;
  boolean hadCR = false;

  do
  {
    ch = is.read();
    if (ch != -1)
    {
      if ((ch == '\r') || (ch == '\n'))
      {
        inLineBreak = true;
        if (ch == '\r')
        {
          if (hadCR)
            os.write(lineSep);
          else
            hadCR = true;
        } else
        {
          if (hadLF)
            os.write(lineSep);
          else
            hadLF = true;
        }
      } else
      {
```

```java
            if (inLineBreak)
            {
              os.write(lineSep);
              hadCR = hadLF = inLineBreak = false;
            }
            os.write(ch);
          }
        }
    } while (ch != -1);
}

/**
 * Download a binary file.  This means make an exact
 * copy of the incoming stream.
 *
 * @param is The input stream, which is the URL.
 * @param os The output stream, a local file.
 * @throws IOException Exception while downloading.
 */
private void downloadBinary(InputStream is, OutputStream os)
    throws IOException
{
  byte buffer[] = new byte[BUFFER_SIZE];

  int size = 0;

  do
  {
    size = is.read(buffer);
    if (size != -1)
      os.write(buffer, 0, size);
  } while (size != -1);
}

/**
 * Typical Java main method, create an object, and then
 * start the object passing arguments. If insufficient
 * arguments are provided, then display startup
 * instructions.
 *
 * @param args Program arguments.
 */
public static void main(String args[])
{
  try
  {
```

```
      if (args.length != 2)
      {
        System.out.println(
"Usage: \njava DownloadURL [URL to Download] [Output File]");
      } else
      {
        DownloadURL d = new DownloadURL();
        d.download(args[0], args[1]);
      }
    } catch (Exception e)
    {
      e.printStackTrace();
    }
  }
}
```

To run this program you must specify the URL to download and the local file. For example, to download the contents of **http://www.httprecipes.com** to the file **local.html**, you would use the following command:

```
DownloadURL http://www.httprecipes.com/ local.html
```

The above command simply shows the abstract format to call this recipe, with the appropriate parameters. For exact information on how to run this recipe refer to Appendix B, C, or D, depending on the operating system you are using. This program makes use of the following two methods that were first introduced in Chapter 3.

- downloadText
- downloadBinary

These two methods are exactly the same as the ones used in Chapter 3; therefore, they will not be discussed again here. If you would like more information about these two functions, refer to Chapter 3.

The example presented here connects to the specified URL and determines the type of that URL. Once the type is determined, the URL is downloaded by calling the appropriate download method, either **downloadText** or **downloadBinary**.

To begin, the **downloadURL** method creates an **HttpURLConnection** object to the specified URL. Then, an **InputStream** is created to receive the contents of the URL and an **OutputStream** is created to write the downloaded data to a file.

```
HttpURLConnection http = (HttpURLConnection) remoteURL.openConnec-
tion();

InputStream is = http.getInputStream();
OutputStream os = new FileOutputStream(localFile);
```

Next, the **content-type** header is checked to determine what type of file it is. If it starts with "text", then the file is in the "text family", and it will be downloaded as a text file. Otherwise, the file is downloaded as a binary file.

```
String type = http.getHeaderField("Content-Type").toLowerCase().
trim();
if (type.startsWith("text"))
downloadText(is, os);
else
downloadBinary(is, os);
```

Once the file has been downloaded, the objects are closed, and the HTTP connection disconnected.

```
is.close();
os.close();
http.disconnect();
```

This recipe can be used anywhere you need to download the contents of a URL. It frees the programmer of having to determine the type of file downloaded.

### Recipe #4.4: Site Monitor

Bots are great at performing repetitive tasks. Probably one of the most repetitive tasks in the world, is checking to see if a web server is still up. If a person were to perform this task, they would sit at a computer with a stopwatch. Every minute, the user would click the refresh button on the browser, and make sure that the web site still loaded.

Recipe 4.4 will show how to accomplish this same task, using a bot. This program will attempt to connect to a web server every minute. As soon as the web server stops responding, the program displays a message alerting the user that the web server is down. This program is shown in Listing 4.4.

### Listing 4.4: Monitor Site (MonitorSite.java)

```
package com.heatonresearch.httprecipes.ch4.recipe4;

import java.util.*;
import java.net.*;
import java.io.*;

public class MonitorSite
{

  /**
   * Scan a URL every minute to make sure it is still up.
   * @param url The URL to monitor.
   */
  public void monitor(URL url)
```

```java
{
  while (true)
  {
    System.out.println(
      "Checking " + url + " at " + (new Date()));

    // try to connect
    try
    {
      URLConnection http = url.openConnection();
      http.connect();
      System.out.println("The site is up.");
    } catch (IOException e1)
    {
      System.out.println("The site is down!!!");
    }

    // now wait for a minute before checking again
    try
    {
      Thread.sleep(60000);
    } catch (InterruptedException e)
    {
    }
  }
}

/**
 * Typical Java main method, create an object, and then
 * start the object passing arguments. If insufficient
 * arguments are provided, then display startup
 * instructions.
 *
 * @param args Program arguments.
 */
public static void main(String args[])
{
  try
  {
    if (args.length != 1)
    {
      System.out.println("Usage: MonitorSite [URL to Monitor]");
    } else
    {
      MonitorSite d = new MonitorSite();
      d.monitor(new URL(args[0]));
```

```
        }
      } catch (Exception e)
      {
        e.printStackTrace();
      }
    }
}
```

To run this program, you must specify the URL to monitor. For example, to monitor the web site at **http://www.httprecipes.com** you would use the following command:

```
MonitorSite http://www.httprecipes.com/
```

The above command simply shows the abstract format to call this recipe, with the appropriate parameters. For exact information on how to run this recipe refer to Appendix B, C, or D, depending on the operating system you are using. The program begins by entering an endless loop. (Because of this, in order to exit this program, you must press **ctrl-c** or close its window.)

```
while (true)
{
System.out.println("Checking " + url + " at " + (new Date()));
```

The program then attempts to connect to the web server by calling the **openConnection** method of the **URL** class.

```
// Try to connect.
try
{
  URLConnection http = url.openConnection();
  http.connect();
```

If the site responds, then a message is displayed to indicate that the site is still up. If an exception is thrown, it is reported that the site is down.

```
  System.out.println("The site is up.");
} catch (IOException e1)
{
  System.out.println("The site is down!!!");
}
```

The program will now wait for a minute before checking again. To do this, the **sleep** method of the **Thread** class is called.

```
// now wait for a minute before checking again
try
{
  Thread.sleep(60000);
} catch (InterruptedException e)
{
}
```

The **InterruptedException** is meaningless to our program because it is not multithreaded. As a result, the **InterruptedException** is ignored. However; we must include the **catch** block because **InterruptedException** is a checked exception, and Java requires that all checked exceptions be caught.

This program is a very simple web site monitoring utility. A more "industrial strength" version would perform some additional operations, such as:

- E-Mailing on failure
- Paging on failure
- Tracking multiple sites

As it is written, this recipe implements only the basic functionality.

## Summary

This chapter showed how to use the **HttpURLConnection** class. This class adds much more functionality than was provided by using only an **InputStream**, as was done in Chapter 3.

Using the **HttpURLConnection** allows access to both the HTTP request and response headers. Accessing these headers provides you with useful information about the HTTP transaction. These headers give such information as the type of document, the web server being used, the web browser being used and other important information.

The **HttpURLConnection** class also allows you to specify the connection and read timeouts. The connection timeout specifies the amount of time that the **HttpURLConnection** object will wait for a connection. The read timeout specifies the amount of time that must pass before the read is terminated.

This chapter presented four recipes. The first recipe showed how to scan a site and see the headers. The second recipe showed how to scan a range of IP addresses for web sites. The third recipe will download either a text or binary file. The fourth recipe will monitor a web site to make sure it does not go down.

So far we have only made use of the HTTP protocol. The HTTP protocol is not secure, because it does not encrypt data being transmitted. For non-sensitive information this is fine. However, when you must pass sensitive information, the HTTPS protocol is usually used. The next chapter will discuss the HTTPS protocol.

# CHAPTER 5: SECURE HTTP REQUESTS

- HTTP Security
- Using HTTPS
- Using HTTP Authentication
- Understanding Base-64

The HTTP protocol, as it was originally designed, is completely unencrypted. Everything transmitted by the HTTP protocol is transmitted in plain text. There is no way for a web server to be sure who is requesting data. Likewise, there is no way for a web browser to be sure what web server it is requesting data from. This presents a security risk because a third party could intercept packets that are being exchanged between your browser and the web server. If these packets are encrypted then it is less of a problem if they are intercepted.

Several mechanisms were added to HTTP to create security. Many web sites make use of these secure mechanisms of HTTP. If your bot program is to access data on a site using the secure mechanisms of HTTP, you will need to know how to support them.

There are two primary mechanisms that provide HTTP with security. These two mechanisms, which will be discussed in this chapter, are listed here:

- HTTPS
- HTTP Authentication

This chapter will show you how to support both secure mechanisms of HTTP in your Java programs.

## Using HTTPS in Java

HTTPS is implemented as a protocol just like HTTP. Whereas an HTTP URL starts with "http", an HTTPS protocol starts with "https". For example, the following URL specifies a secure page on the HTTP Recipe Site:

```
https://www.httprecipes.com/1/5/https.php
```

It is important to understand that a URL that starts with "https" is not just a secure version of the same URL beginning with an "http". Consider the following URL:

```
http://www.httprecipes.com/1/5/https.php
```

The two URLs you see in this section are exactly the same, except that one is HTTP and the other HTTPS. You might think that entering the second URL would simply take you to an unencrypted version of the **https.php** page. It does not. If you enter the second URL into a web browser, you will get a page not found, or the 404, error.

This is because the file **https.php** does not exist on the "HTTP Recipes" site's unencrypted server. This is the important distinction. There are two web servers running at **www.httprecipes.com**. There is an unencrypted HTTP server running at port **80**. There is also an encrypted HTTPS server running at port **443**. These two servers do not share the same set of HTML files. In the case of the HTTP Recipes site, Chapter 5 is hosted on the HTTPS server, and the rest of the chapters on the HTTP server.

Hypertext Transfer Protocol Secure (HTTPS) uses sockets just like HTTP. However, it uses a special sort of socket called a secure socket. Secure sockets are implemented using the Secure Socket Layer (SSL). SSL, which is supported by Java, provides two very important security mechanisms, which are listed here.

- Encrypted packets
- Server verification

Web servers commonly use both of these mechanisms. These two mechanisms will be discussed in the next two sections.

### Understanding Encrypted Packets

The aspect that most users associate with HTTPS, is data encryption. When you use an HTTPS site, you normally see a small "lock symbol" near the bottom of your browser. Once you see the lock, you know that your data is being encrypted, and you are using a secure site.

Data encryption is very important. When you enter a credit card number into a web site, you want to be sure that only that web site gains access to your credit card number. Because TCP/IP traffic can travel through a number of different hosts before it finally reaches your intended web server, you do not want a malicious user intercepting your credit card number somewhere between you and the web server.

By encrypting the packets being exchanged between you and the web server, the problem of your packets getting intercepted is decreased. If someone does intercept your packet, it will be encrypted.

### Understanding Server Verification

Encryption is not the only benefit provided by HTTPS. Server verification is another important benefit. Consider what happens when you access the following URL:

```
https://www.httprecipes.com/1/5/https.php
```

The web browser takes apart the URL and finds the **hostname**. In this case, the host name is **www.httprecipes.com**. This is a domain name, which the web browser then looks up in a Domain Name System (DNS) server. As of the writing of this book, the IP address for **www.httprecipes.com** is **216.69.170.193**. But how do you know that the IP address **216.69.170.193** is really the HTTP Recipes site? IP addresses sometimes change when the web master switches hosting companies, or for other reasons. Someone could have hijacked the **www.httprecipes.com** DNS entry and pointed it to a malicious web server running on a different IP address.

HTTPS solves this problem. Part of the SSL protocol, upon which HTTPS is based, verifies that the IP address returned by DNS is the actual address of the site. Every website that uses HTTPS must be issued a SSL certificate. Usually these certificates are issued by Verisign (**http://www.verisign.com**). When a web server is granted a certificate, the company that issues the certificate verifies the IP address that the certificate is issued to matches the domain name.

When you access **https://www.httprecipes.com**, your web browser looks up the returned IP address of **216.69.170.193** with the company that issued the HTTP Recipes site our SSL certificate. If these IP addresses do not match, then your browser will warn you.

Most certificate issuers provide "seals" that web masters can place on their web sites to show that their identity has been verified. Figure 5.1 shows the seal on the HTTP Recipes site:

**Figure 5.1: HTTPS Verification Seal**

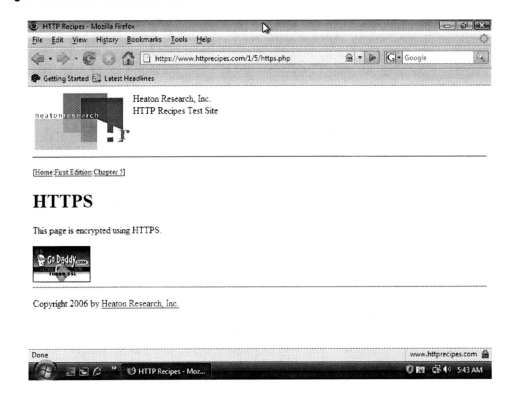

You can click the site's seal and be taken to the certificate issuer's web site. This will display the certificate. The SSL certificate for HTTP Recipes can be seen in Figure 5.2.

**Figure 5.2: The HTTP Recipes Certificate**

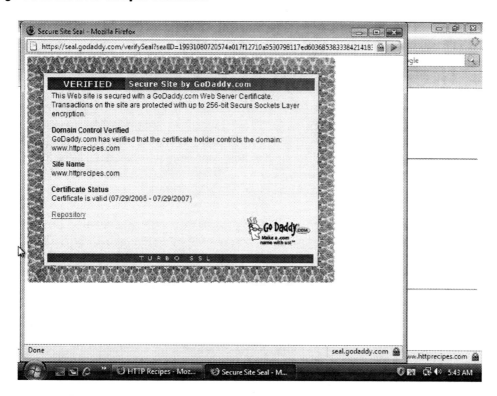

Now that you understand what HTTPS is and how it is used, the next section will show you how to write Java programs that make use of HTTPS.

## Using HTTPS in Java

Java provides methods that make it simple to connect to an HTTPS web site. The following code would open an **HttpURLConnection** to an HTTPS server:

```
try
{
  URL u = new URL("https://www.httprecipes.com/1/5/https.php");
  HttpURLConnection http = (HttpURLConnection)u.openConnection();
// Now do something with the connection.
}
catch(MalformedURLException e)
{
  System.out.println("Invalid URL");
}
catch(IOException e)
{
  System.out.println("Error connecting: " + e.getMessage() );
}
```

Does something seem familiar about this code? It is exactly the same code used to access an HTTP URL that was introduced in Chapter 4 with the https URL instead. Java supports HTTPS transparently. Simply pass an "https" based URL to any of the code used in this book, and HTTPS will be supported.

## Understanding the HttpsURLConnection Class

So far every application in this book has made use of either a direct **InputStream** or the **HttpURLConnection** class. There is also an **HttpsURLConnection** class, which is used for HTTPS sites. The **HttpsURLConnection** class subclasses the **HttpURLConnection** class. Because of this, your code does not need to be aware of if it receives an **HttpsURLConnection** or an **HttpURLConnection** object from your call to the **openConnection** function of a **URL** object.

In some rare cases, you may want to make use of the **HttpsURLConnection** class directly. It does offer some additional functionality, not provided by the **HttpURLConnection** class. If you would like to make use of the **HttpsURLConnection** class, simply cast the result of the **openConnection** function. The following code opens a connection to a HTTPS site and retrieves an **HttpsURLConnection** class:

```
try
{
  URL u = new URL("https://www.httprecipes.com/1/5/https.php");
  HttpsURLConnection http = u.openConnection();
// Now do something with the connection.
}
catch(MalformedURLException e)
{
  System.out.println("Invalid URL");
}
catch(IOException e)
{
  System.out.println("Error connecting: " + e.getMessage() );
}
```

As you can see from above, the result of the **openConnection** function is typecast to an **HttpsURLConnection**. You should be careful, though. The above code will only work with HTTPS URLs. If you use an HTTP URL with the above code, you will get a **ClassCastException** thrown. This is because the **openConnection** function would return an **HttpURLConnection**, which cannot be typecast to an **HttpsURLConnection**.

Code that was designed to work with HTTP can almost always work just as well with HTTPS; however, the opposite is not true.

Using the **HttpsURLConnection** class directly gives you some additional information about the connection that would not be available with **HttpURLConnection**. For example, you can determine the cipher suite used by the server. In addition, you can get a list of all certificates used by the web server. Usually this information is unimportant to a bot. However, if you find that you need access to this data, you have the ability to use an **HttpsURLConnection** object.

## Understanding HTTP Authentication

As you saw earlier in this chapter, HTTPS allows you to determine that the web server you are connecting to, is who it claims to be. HTTP authentication provides the other side of this verification. HTTP authentication allows the server to determine that the web user is who they say that they are.

HTTP authentication is not tied to HTTPS. It can be used with either HTTP or HTTPS. To access a page protected by HTTP authentication, a web user must enter both a user id and password. If a user id and password are not provided, or if it is incorrect, the user will receive an HTTP error.

Most websites do not use HTTP authentication; instead, many websites use their own authentication. This works by displaying a form to the user and prompting for identifying information, usually an id and password.

### HTTP Authentication in Action

You have probably seen sites that make use of HTTP authentication. Sites that use HTTP authentication popup a window that prompts you for a user id and password. HTTP authentication always pops up a second window. If you are being prompted for a user id and password on the actual webpage, then the site is doing its own authentication. To see HTTP authentication in action, visit the following URL:

**https://www.httprecipes.com/1/5/auth.php**

This URL will display the page show in Figure 5.3.

**Figure 5.3: Ready to Enter a Protected Area**

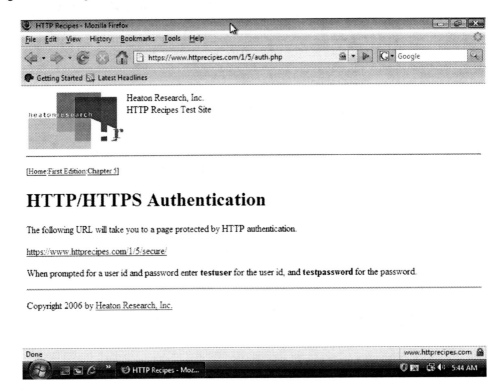

Click the URL displayed on the page, and you will be taken to the secure area. Note the user id and password prompts displayed on the page. When you enter the secure area you will see a popup that prompts you for your user id and password. This page is shown in Figure 5.4.

**Figure 5.4: Enter your ID and Password**

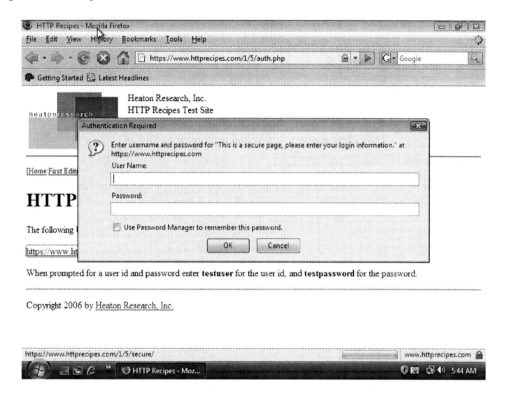

If you enter the correct user id and password you will be taken to the secure area. If you enter an invalid user id and password then you will be prompted several more times. Eventually, the browser will take you to an error page, if you fail to enter the correct user id and password. For this site, the correct user id is "testuser" and the password is "testpassword".

## Supporting HTTP Authentication in Java

Most websites will use their own authentication, and not rely on HTTP authentication. Chapter 7, "Accessing Forms", will show how to access sites that make use of their own authentication. However, if the site that you would like to access makes use of HTTP authentication, then you must support that as well.

The Java HTTP classes do not directly support HTTP authentication. To make use of HTTP authentication, you will have to add a special HTTP request header named **Authorization**, to the HTTP request. This header must also be encrypted into a "base-64" number system. Recipe 5.2 demonstrates adding this header, and using HTTP authentication.

## Recipes

This chapter includes two recipes. These two recipes will demonstrate the following:

- Determining if a URL uses HTTPS
- Using HTTP authentication

The first recipe will introduce you to some of the things that can be done with the **HttpsURLConnection** class. The second recipe shows how to access a site that uses HTTP authentication.

### Recipe #5.1: Is a URL HTTPS

This recipe is a fairly simple example of using the **HttpsURLConnection** class. This example simply checks a URL connection to see if it is HTTPS or not. I use this code when I need to be sure that a connection is being made over a secure link. Unless you care about examining HTTPS certificate chains and cipher suites directly, this is probably the only use you will have for the **HttpsURLConnection** object.

As previously mentioned, you will not normally use the **HttpsURLConnection** class directly. Because **HttpsURLConnection** is a subclass of **HttpURLConnection**, you will normally just use what the **URL** object returns, and not be concerned if you are reading with HTTP and HTTPS. Only when you care about the specifics of HTTPS will you need to use **HttpsURLConnection**.

This program is fairly short, so it is implemented entirely in the **main** method. This HTTPS checker program is shown below in Listing 5.1.

### Listing 5.1: Is a Connection HTTPS (IsHTTPS.java)

```java
package com.heatonresearch.httprecipes.ch5.recipe1;

import java.io.*;
import java.net.*;

import javax.net.ssl.*;

public class IsHTTPS
{

  /**
   * Typical Java main method, create an object, and then
   * start the object passing arguments. If insufficient
   * arguments are provided, then display startup
   * instructions.
   *
   * @param args Program arguments.
   */
```

```java
public static void main(String args[])
{
  String strURL = "";

  // obtain a URL to use
  if (args.length < 1)
  {
    strURL = "https://www.httprecipes.com/1/5/secure/";
  } else
  {
    strURL = args[0];
  }

  URL url;
  try
  {
    url = new URL(strURL);
    URLConnection conn = url.openConnection();
    conn.connect();

    // see what type of object was returned
    if (conn instanceof HttpsURLConnection)
    {
      System.out.println("Valid HTTPS URL");
    } else if (conn instanceof HttpURLConnection)
    {
      System.out.println("Valid HTTP URL");
    } else
    {
      System.out.println("Unknown protocol URL");
    }

  } catch (MalformedURLException e)
  {
    System.out.println("Invalid URL");
  } catch (IOException e)
  {
    System.out.println("Error connecting to URL");
  }
}

}
```

This program can be passed a URL to access on the command line; or, if no URL is provided, the program will default to the following URL:

`https://www.httprecipes.com/1/5/secure/`

You can also specify a URL. For example, to run this recipe with the URL of **http://www.httprecipes.com/**, you would use the following command:

```
IsHTTPS http://www.httprecipes.com
```

The above command simply shows the abstract format to call this recipe, with the appropriate parameters. For exact information on how to run this recipe refer to Appendix B, C, or D, depending on the operating system you are using. This program begins by obtaining a URL. The URL is either provided from the command line, or defaults to a page on the HTTP Recipes site. The following lines of code do this.

```
String strURL = "";

// Obtain a URL to use.
if (args.length < 1)
{
  strURL = "https://www.httprecipes.com/1/5/secure/";
} else
{
  strURL = args[0];
}
```

Next, a **URL** object is created for the specified URL. A connection is then opened with a call to the **openConnection** function on the **URL** object.

```
URL url;
try
{
  url = new URL(strURL);
  URLConnection conn = url.openConnection();
```

Once the connection **URL** has been obtained, a connection is made. This will throw an **IOException** if the website is not accepting connections.

```
conn.connect();
```

Next, the program will check to see what type of object was returned. If an **HttpsURLConnection** object is returned, the connection is using HTTPS. If an **HttpURLConnection** object is returned, the connection is using HTTP. If it is neither of these two, then the program reports that it does not know what sort of a connection is being used.

```
// See what type of object was returned.
if (conn instanceof HttpsURLConnection)
{
  System.out.println("Valid HTTPS URL");
} else if (conn instanceof HttpURLConnection)
{
  System.out.println("Valid HTTP URL");
} else
```

```
{
System.out.println("Unknown protocol URL");
}
```

If an invalid URL was provided, then a **MalformedURLException** will be thrown.

```
} catch (MalformedURLException e)
{
  System.out.println("Invalid URL");
```

If any other sort of error occurs while connecting to the URL, an **IOException** will be thrown.

```
} catch (IOException e)
{
  System.out.println("Error connecting to URL");
}
```

This recipe will be rarely used; however, it demonstrates one practical purpose of using the **HttpsURLConnection** object directly.

### Recipe #5.2: HTTP Authentication

The next recipe is very useful if you need to retrieve data from a site that requires HTTP authentication. First, the code downloads the contents of a URL and then saves it to a local file. This recipe can be used either in whole are in part.

Used in its entirety, this recipe provides a method, named **download**. This method requires the URL to download, the local file to save to, and the user id and password. The **download** method will then download the contents. If the user id or password is invalid, an exception will be thrown.

If your application doesn't call for downloading directly to a file, you could use part of this recipe. Perhaps your application needs only to parse data at an HTTP authenticated site. If this is the case, you should copy the **addAuthHeaders** method. This method requires an **HttpURLConnection** object, and a user id and password. The **addAuthHeaders** method then adds the correct HTTP request header for the specified user id and password.

I have used this recipe in both ways for several bots that required HTTP authenticated access. The program is shown in Listing 5.2.

**Listing 5.2: Download Authenticated URL (AuthDownloadURL.java)**

```java
package com.heatonresearch.httprecipes.ch5.recipe2;

import java.net.*;
import java.io.*;

public class AuthDownloadURL
{
  public static int BUFFER_SIZE = 8192;

  /**
   * Download either a text or binary file from a URL.
   * The URL's headers will be scanned to determine the
   * type of tile.
   *
   * @param remoteURL The URL to download from.
   * @param localFile The local file to save to.
   * @throws IOException Exception while downloading.
   */
  public void download(URL remoteURL, File localFile,
    String uid, String pwd)
      throws IOException
  {
    HttpURLConnection http = (
      HttpURLConnection) remoteURL.openConnection();
    addAuthHeader(http, uid, pwd);
    InputStream is = http.getInputStream();
    OutputStream os = new FileOutputStream(localFile);
    String type =
      http.getHeaderField("Content-Type").toLowerCase().trim();
    if (type.startsWith("text"))
      downloadText(is, os);
    else
      downloadBinary(is, os);
    is.close();
    os.close();
    http.disconnect();
  }

  /**
   * Add HTTP authntication headers to the specified
   * HttpURLConnection
   * object.
   * @param http The HTTP connection.
   * @param uid The user id.
   * @param pwd The password.
```

```java
    */
  private void addAuthHeader(HttpURLConnection http, String uid,
String pwd)
  {
    String hdr = uid + ":" + pwd;
    String encode = base64Encode(hdr);
    http.addRequestProperty("Authorization", "Basic " + encode);
  }

  /**
   * Encodes a string in base64.
   *
   * @param s The string to encode.
   * @return The encoded string.
   */
  static public String base64Encode(String s)
  {
    ByteArrayOutputStream bout = new ByteArrayOutputStream();

    Base64OutputStream out = new Base64OutputStream(bout);
    try
    {
      out.write(s.getBytes());
      out.flush();
    } catch (IOException e)
    {
    }

    return bout.toString();
  }

  /**
   * Overloaded version of download that accepts strings,
   * rather than URL objects.
   *
   * @param remoteURL The URL to download from.
   * @param localFile The local file to save to.
   * @throws IOException Exception while downloading.
   */
  public void download(String remoteURL, String localFile,
      String uid,
      String pwd) throws IOException
  {
    download(new URL(remoteURL), new File(localFile), uid, pwd);
  }
```

```java
/**
 * Download a text file, which means convert the line
 * ending characters to the correct type for the
 * operating system that is being used.
 *
 * @param is The input stream, which is the URL.
 * @param os The output stream, a local file.
 * @throws IOException Exception while downloading.
 */
private void downloadText(InputStream is, OutputStream os)
  throws IOException
{
  byte lineSep[] =
    System.getProperty("line.separator").getBytes();
  int ch = 0;
  boolean inLineBreak = false;
  boolean hadLF = false;
  boolean hadCR = false;

  do
  {
    ch = is.read();
    if (ch != -1)
    {
      if ((ch == '\r') || (ch == '\n'))
      {
        inLineBreak = true;
        if (ch == '\r')
        {
          if (hadCR)
            os.write(lineSep);
          else
            hadCR = true;
        } else
        {
          if (hadLF)
            os.write(lineSep);
          else
            hadLF = true;
        }
      } else
      {
        if (inLineBreak)
        {
          os.write(lineSep);
          hadCR = hadLF = inLineBreak = false;
```

```
      }
        os.write(ch);
      }
    }
  } while (ch != -1);
}

/**
 * Download a binary file.  Which means make an exact
 * copy of the incoming stream.
 *
 * @param is The input stream, which is the URL.
 * @param os The output stream, a local file.
 * @throws IOException Exception while downloading.
 */
private void downloadBinary(InputStream is, OutputStream os)
    throws IOException
{
  byte buffer[] = new byte[BUFFER_SIZE];

  int size = 0;

  do
  {
    size = is.read(buffer);
    if (size != -1)
      os.write(buffer, 0, size);
  } while (size != -1);
}

/**
 * Typical Java main method, create an object, and then
 * start the object passing arguments. If insufficient
 * arguments are provided, then display startup
 * instructions.
 *
 * @param args Program arguments.
 */
public static void main(String args[])
{
  try
  {
    AuthDownloadURL d = new AuthDownloadURL();

    if (args.length != 4)
    {
```

```
        d.download("https://www.httprecipes.com/1/5/secure/",
            "./test.html",
            "testuser",
            "testpassword");
    } else
    {

        d.download(args[0], args[1], args[2], args[3]);
    }
  } catch (Exception e)
  {
    e.printStackTrace();
  }
 }
}
```

This program can be passed a URL, local filename, user id and password on the command line. If no parameters are provided, the program will default to the following URL:

```
https://www.httprecipes.com/1/5/secure/
```

The program will also default to a local file of **test.html**, a user id of **testuser**, and a password of **testpassword**.

You can also specify a URL. For example, to run this recipe with the URL of **http://www.httprecipes.com/**, a local file of **index.html**, a user id of **user** and a password of **password**, you would use the following command:

```
AuthDownloadURL http://www.httprecipes.com ./index.html user password
```

The above command simply shows the abstract format to call this recipe, with the appropriate parameters. For exact information on how to run this recipe refer to Appendix B, C, or D, depending on the operating system you are using. This recipe is very similar to Recipe 4.3, except that it can download from an HTTP authenticated site as well as a regular site. Only the new code relating to HTTP authentication will be discussed here. If you would like to review how this recipe actually downloads a binary or text file, refer to Recipe 4.3. The downloading code is the same in both recipes.

To access an HTTP authenticated site, the program makes use of a method called **addAuthHeader**. This method adds the **Authorization** header to the **HttpURLConnection** object. This process is shown here.

```
String hdr = uid + ":" + pwd;
```

First the **addAuthHeader** method builds the header. This header is very simple, it is just the user id delimited by a colon (:) followed by the password.

```
String encode = base64Encode(hdr);
http.addRequestProperty("Authorization", "Basic " + encode);
```

Of course, it would be a bad idea to send the password as plain text. So both the user id and password are encoded into base-64. It is very easy to encode/decode from base-64, so this is not a very strong security system. However, it does keep someone casually examining packets from determining the password.

When HTTP Authentication is combined with HTTPS, it is quite effective. HTTP Authentication requires an id and password, and HTTPS encrypts the entire packet, password included, thus preventing someone from examining the password. Base-64 is just another number system, like decimal (base 10) or hexadecimal (base 16). To convert to base-64, this program uses the function **base64Encode**. This method will now be examined.

The **base64Encode** method begins by creating a **ByteArrayOutputStream** that holds the base-64 encoded data.

```
ByteArrayOutputStream bout = new ByteArrayOutputStream();
```

Next, a **Base64OutputStream** class is created. This recipe also provides this class. The **Base64OutputStream** class receives an output stream argument to which it writes the base-64 encoded data. You then call the **write** method of the **Base64OutputStream** object, and give it the data you want encoded. This is shown below:

```
Base64OutputStream out = new Base64OutputStream(bout);
try
{
  out.write(s.getBytes());
  out.flush();
```

As you can see, the above lines of code create the **Base64OutputStream** object, and then write the string to it. The stream is then flushed, ensuring all data is encoded and is not being buffered.

It is unlikely that an exception will occur, since this is a completely "in memory" operation. However, if an exception does occur, the following line of code will catch it:

```
} catch (IOException e)
{
}
```

Finally, we return the converted base-64 string.

```
return bout.toString();
```

The **Base64OutputStream** class described above is shown below in Listing 5.3.

**Listing 5.3: Base-64 Output Stream (Base64OutputStream.java)**

```java
package com.heatonresearch.httprecipes.ch5.recipe2;

import java.io.*;

class Base64OutputStream extends FilterOutputStream
{

  /**
   * The constructor.
   *
   * @param out The stream used to write to.
   */
  public Base64OutputStream(OutputStream out)
  {
    super(out);
  }

  /**
   * Write a byte to be encoded.
   *
   * @param c The character to be written.
   * @exception java.io.IOException
   */
  public void write(int c) throws IOException
  {
    buffer[index] = c;
    index++;
    if (index == 3)
    {
      super.write(toBase64[(buffer[0] & 0xfc) >> 2]);
      super.write(toBase64[((buffer[0] & 0x03) << 4)
          | ((buffer[1] & 0xf0) >> 4)]);
      super.write(toBase64[((buffer[1] & 0x0f) << 2)
          | ((buffer[2] & 0xc0) >> 6)]);
      super.write(toBase64[buffer[2] & 0x3f]);

      index = 0;
    }
  }
}
```

```
/**
 * Ensure all bytes are written.
 *
 * @exception java.io.IOException
 */
public void flush() throws IOException
{
  if (index == 1)
  {
    super.write(toBase64[(buffer[2] & 0x3f) >> 2]);
    super.write(toBase64[(buffer[0] & 0x03) << 4]);
    super.write('=');
    super.write('=');
  } else if (index == 2)
  {
    super.write(toBase64[(buffer[0] & 0xfc) >> 2]);
    super.write(toBase64[((buffer[0] & 0x03) << 4)
        | ((buffer[1] & 0xf0) >> 4)]);
    super.write(toBase64[(buffer[1] & 0x0f) << 2]);
    super.write('=');
  }
}

/**
 * Allowable characters for base-64.
 */
private static char[] toBase64 = { 'A', 'B', 'C', 'D', 'E', 'F',
'G', 'H',
    'I', 'J', 'K', 'L', 'M', 'N', 'O', 'P', 'Q', 'R', 'S', 'T',
'U', 'V',
    'W', 'X', 'Y', 'Z', 'a', 'b', 'c', 'd', 'e', 'f', 'g', 'h',
'i', 'j',
    'k', 'l', 'm', 'n', 'o', 'p', 'q', 'r', 's', 't', 'u', 'v',
'w', 'x',
    'y', 'z', '0', '1', '2', '3', '4', '5', '6', '7', '8', '9',
'+', '/' };

/**
 * Current index.
 */
private int index = 0;

/**
 * Outbound buffer.
 */
private int buffer[] = new int[3];
}
```

To convert to base-64, this program makes use of an array that holds the entire base-64 alphabet. For the normal number system, base 10, this alphabet would be "0", "1", "2", "3", "4", "5", "6", "7", "8", and "9". For hexadecimal (base 16) the alphabet would be "0", "1", "2", "3", "4", "5", "6", "7", "8", "9", "A", "B", "C", "D", "E" and "F".

Base-64's alphabet has so many elements that both upper and lower case letters are needed to represent different numerical digits. The alphabet representation used by base-64 shown in Listing 5.3 above is stored in the **toBase64** variable.

The majority of the encryption work is done by the **write** method. Base-64 conversion requires the input data to be broken up into 3-byte chunks.

```
buffer[index] = c;
index++;
if (index == 3)
{
```

Once we have three bytes, then we write the base-64 version of the number. This is accomplished by taking the 24 bits gathered, 6 bits at a time. This results in four digits, as shown here:

```
  super.write(toBase64[(buffer[0] & 0xfc) >> 2]);
  super.write(toBase64[((buffer[0] & 0x03) << 4)
  | ((buffer[1] & 0xf0) >> 4)]);
  super.write(toBase64[((buffer[1] & 0x0f) << 2)
  | ((buffer[2] & 0xc0) >> 6)]);
  super.write(toBase64[buffer[2] & 0x3f]);
  index = 0;
}
```

Each **write** statement segments one of the groups of 6-bits, and writes that digit.

The **flush** method is needed because the data to be converted may not end exactly on a 3-byte boundary. The **flush** method works like the write method, in that it fills the remaining buffer with zeroes and writes the final digits of the conversion.

This is a very useful recipe that can be applied anytime you must access an HTTP authenticated web page. The **addAuthHeader** method can be used to add HTTP authentication support to programs of your own.

## Summary

This chapter showed you how to make use of HTTP security mechanisms. HTTP has two built-in security mechanisms. First, HTTP supports encryption through HTTPS. Secondly, HTTP provides authentication, which requires users to identify themselves.

HTTP encryption is supported through HTTPS. Any website that you access that makes use of HTTPS will begin with the prefix `https://`. HTTPS encrypts the data so that it cannot be intercepted. Support for HTTPS is built into Java. You are only required to use an HTTPS URL where you would normally use an HTTP URL. HTTPS encryption prevents a third party from examining packets being exchanged between your browser and the web server.

HTTP authentication allows the web server to prompt the user for a user id and password. The web server then can determine the identity of the user accessing it. Most web sites do not use HTTP authentication, rather they use their own HTML forms to authenticate. However, some sites make use of HTTP authentication, and to access these sites with a bot, you will have to support HTTP authentication.

Java contains no support for HTTP authentication. Therefore, to support HTTP authentication, you must add the header yourself. Additionally, the authentication header must be encrypted. Base-64 is used to encrypt this header.

This chapter provided two recipes. The first determines if a URL is using HTTPS. The second recipe downloads data from an HTTP authenticated site.

Up to this point, the chapters have shown you how to access data. In the next chapter we will begin to learn what to do with HTTP data once you have retrieved it. Chapter 6 will show how to parse HTML and extract data from forms, lists, tables and other HTML constructs.

# CHAPTER 6: EXTRACTING DATA

- Parsing HTML
- Extracting from forms
- Extracting lists, images and hyperlinks
- Extracting data form multiple pages

The previous chapters showed how to extract simple data items from web pages. This chapter will expand upon this. This chapter will focus on how to extract more complex data structures from HTML messages. Of course HTML is not the only format to extract from. Later chapters will discuss non-HTML formats, such as XML.

This chapter will present several recipes for extracting data from a variety of different HTML forms.

- Extracting data spread across many HTML pages
- Extracting images
- Extracting hyperlinks
- Extracting data form HTML forms
- Extracting data form HTML lists
- Extracting data from HTML tables

Extracting data from these types of HTML structures is more complex than the simple data extracted in previous chapters. To extract this data we will need an HTML parser. There are three options for obtaining an HTML parser.

- Use the HTML parser built into Java Swing
- Use a third-party HTML parser
- Write your own HTML parser

Java includes a full-featured HTML parser, which is built into Swing. I've used this parser for a number of projects. However, it has some limitations. The Swing HTML parser has some issues with heavy multithreading. This can be a problem with certain spiders and bots that must access a large number of HTML pages and make use of heavy multithreading.

Additionally, the swing HTML parser expects HTML to be properly formatted and well defined. All HTML tags are defined as symbolic constants, and making tags unknown to the Swing parser more difficult to process. In an ideal world all web sites would have beautifully formatted and syntactically correct HTML. And in this world, the Swing parser would be great. However, I've worked with several cases where a poorly formatted site causes great confusion for the Swing Parser.

There are also several third-party HTML parsers available. However, it is really not too complex to create a simple lightweight HTML parser. The idea of this book is to present many small examples of HTTP programming that the reader can implement in their own programs. As a result, we will create our own HTML parser.

Implementing a HTML parser is not terribly complex. The HTML parser presented in this chapter is implemented in three classes. Before getting to the recipes for this chapter we will first examine the HTML parser. This HTML parser will be used by all of the recipes in this chapter. The HTML parser is presented in the next few sections. If you are not interested in how to implement an HTML parser, you can easily skip to the recipes section of this chapter. You do not need to know how the HTML parser was implemented in order to make use of it.

# Peekable InputStream

To properly parse any data, let alone HTML, it is very convenient to have a peekable stream. A peekable stream is a regular Java **InputStream**, except that you can peek several characters ahead, before actually reading these characters. First we will examine why it is so convenient to use **PeekableInputStream**.

Consider parsing the following the following line of HTML.

```
<b>Hello World</b>
```

The first thing we would like to know is are we parsing an HTML tag or HTML text. Using the **PeekableInputStream** we can look at the first character and determine if we are staring with a tag or text. Once we know that we are parsing text, we can begin reading the actual text characters.

The **PeekableInputStream** class is also very useful for HTML comments. Consider the following HTML comment:

```
<!--HTML Comment-->
```

To determine if something is an HTML comment you must look at the first four characters of the tag. Using the **PeekableInputStream** we can examine the next four characters and see if we are about to read a comment.

## Using PeekableInputStream

Using the **PeekableInputStream** is very simple. The usage of **PeekableInputStream** closely follows the usage of the Java class **InputStream**. To use **PeekableInputStream** you must already have an **InputStream**. You will then attach the **PeekableInputStream** to the existing **InputStream**. The following code demonstrates this.

```
InputStream is = new FileInputStream("./SomeFile.txt");
PeekableInputStream peek = new PeekableInputStream(is);
```

Now that you have created the **PeekableInputStream**, we can read from it just like a normal **InputStream**.

```
int i = peek.read();
```

However, we can now peek as well.

```
int i = peek.peek();
```

The above code will peek at the next byte to be read by the underlying **InputStream**. When you next call the **read** function, you will get the same byte as was returned by the **peek** function. Multiple calls to the **peek** function will always return the same byte, because you are only peeking at the byte, not actually reading it.

It is also possible to peek several bytes into the future by passing a parameter to the **peek** function. The following code would **peek** three bytes into file, and return the third byte to be read.

```
int i = peek.peek(2);
```

Remember, the **peek** function is zero based, so passing two returns the third byte.

### Implementing Peekable InputStream

In the last section you saw how to use the **PeekableInputStream** class. The **PeekableInputStream** class is not provided by Java. It will have to be implemented. This section will show you how to implement the **PeekableInputStream**. The **PeekableInputStream** class is shown in Listing 6.1.

#### Listing 6.1: The Peekable InputStream (PeekableInputStream.java)

```java
package com.heatonresearch.httprecipes.html;

import java.io.*;

public class PeekableInputStream extends InputStream
{

  /**
   * The underlying stream.
   */
  private InputStream stream;

  /**
   * Bytes that have been peeked at.
   */
  private byte peekBytes[];
```

```java
/**
 * How many bytes have been peeked at.
 */
private int peekLength;

/**
 * The constructor accepts an InputStream to setup the
 * object.
 *
 * @param is
 *            The InputStream to parse.
 */
public PeekableInputStream(InputStream is)
{
  this.stream = is;
  this.peekBytes = new byte[10];
  this.peekLength = 0;
}

/**
 * Peek at the next character from the stream.
 *
 * @return The next character.
 * @throws IOException
 *             If an I/O exception occurs.
 */
public int peek() throws IOException
{
  return peek(0);
}

/**
 * Peek at a specified depth.
 *
 * @param depth
 *            The depth to check.
 * @return The character peeked at.
 * @throws IOException
 *             If an I/O exception occurs.
 */
public int peek(int depth) throws IOException
{
  // does the size of the peek buffer need to be extended?
  if (this.peekBytes.length <= depth)
  {
```

```
    byte temp[] = new byte[depth + 10];
    for (int i = 0; i < this.peekBytes.length; i++)
    {
      temp[i] = this.peekBytes[i];
    }
    this.peekBytes = temp;
  }

  // does more data need to be read?
  if (depth >= this.peekLength)
  {
    int offset = this.peekLength;
    int length = (depth - this.peekLength) + 1;
    int lengthRead = this.stream.read(this.peekBytes,
      offset, length);

    if (lengthRead == -1)
    {
      return -1;
    }

    this.peekLength = depth + 1;
  }

  return this.peekBytes[depth];
}

/*
 * Read a single byte from the stream. @throws IOException
 * If an I/O exception occurs. @return The character that
 * was read from the stream.
 */
@Override
public int read() throws IOException
{
  if (this.peekLength == 0)
  {
    return this.stream.read();
  }

  int result = this.peekBytes[0];
  this.peekLength--;
  for (int i = 0; i < this.peekLength; i++)
  {
    this.peekBytes[i] = this.peekBytes[i + 1];
  }
```

```
    return result;
  }


}
```

The **PeekableInputStream** class makes use of three **private** instance variables to hold its current state. These three variables are shown here.

```
private InputStream stream;
private byte peekBytes[];
private int peekLength;
```

The first variable, named **stream**, holds the underlying **InputStream**. The second variable, named **peekBytes**, holds the bytes that have been "peeked" from the file, yet have not bee actually read by a call to the **read** function of the **PeekableInputStream** class. The third variable, named **peekLength**, keeps track of how much of the **peekBytes** variable array contains actual data.

The **read** function must be implemented, because the **PeekableInputStream** class is derived from **InputStream** class. This function begins by checking the **peekLenth** variable. If no bytes have been peeked, then the **read** function can simply call the **read** function for the underlying **InputStream**.

```
if (peekLength == 0)
  return stream.read();
```

If there is data in the **peekBytes** buffer, then return the first value in that array.

```
int result = peekBytes[0];
```

Next, move the rest of the array in to fill the value that was just read.

```
for (int i = 0; i < peekLength; i++)
{
  peekBytes[i] = peekBytes[i + 1];
}
```

Finally, decrease the **peekLength** variable to reflect the data that has been read, and return the **result**.

```
peekLength--;

return result;
```

Usually you will not directly use the **PeekableInputStream** class when parsing HTML. HTML parsing is done by the **ParseHTML** class, which is discussed in the next section.

## Parsing HTML

The **ParseHTML** class does HTML parsing. This class is used by all of the recipes in this chapter. Additionally, many recipes through the remainder of the book will use the **ParseHTML** class. I will begin by showing you how to use the **ParseHTML** class. A later section will show you how the **ParseHTML** class was implemented.

### Using ParseHTML

It is very easy to use the **ParseHTML** class. The following code fragment demonstrates how to make use of the **ParseHTML** class.

```
InputStream is = url.openStream();
ParseHTML parse = new ParseHTML(is);

int ch;
while ((ch = parse.read()) != -1)
{
  if (ch == 0)
  {
    HTMLTag tag = parse.getTag();
    System.out.println("Read HTML tag: " + tag);
  }
  else
  {
    System.out.println("Read HTML text character: "
      + ((char)ch) );
  }
}
```

As you can see from the above code an **InputStream** is acquired from a URL. This **InputStream** is used to construct a **ParseHTML** object. The **ParseHTML** class can parse HTML from any **InputStream** object.

Next the code enters a loop calling **parse.read()**. Once **parse.read()** returns a negative one value, there is nothing more to parse, and the program ends. If **parse.read()** returns a zero, then an HTML tag was encountered. You can call **parse.getTag()** to determine which tag was encountered.

If neither a negative one or zero is returned, then a regular character has been found in the HTML. This process continues until there is nothing else to read from the HTML file. This is only a basic example of using **ParseHTML**. The recipes for this chapter will expand on this greatly.

### Implementing ParseHTML

In this section we will examine how the **ParseHTML** class is implemented. The **ParseHTML** class makes use of the **PeekableInputStream** class, which was discussed in the last section. The **ParseHTML** class is shown in Listing 6.2.

### Listing 6.2: Parsing HTML (ParseHTML.java)

```java
package com.heatonresearch.httprecipes.html;

import java.io.*;
import java.util.*;

public class ParseHTML
{

  /*
   * A mapping of certain HTML encoded values(i.e.  )
   * to their actual character values.
   */
  private static Map<String, Character> charMap;

  /**
   * The stream that we are parsing from.
   */
  private PeekableInputStream source;

  /**
   * The current HTML tag. Access this property if the read
   * function returns 0.
   */
  private HTMLTag tag = new HTMLTag();

  private String lockedEndTag;

  /**
   * The constructor should be passed an InputStream that we
   * will parse from.
   *
   * @param is
   *            An InputStream to parse from.
   */
  public ParseHTML(InputStream is)
  {
    this.source = new PeekableInputStream(is);

    if (charMap == null)
```

```
  {
    charMap = new HashMap<String, Character>();
    charMap.put("nbsp", ' ');
    charMap.put("lt", '<');
    charMap.put("gt", '>');
    charMap.put("amp", '&');
    charMap.put("quot", '\"');
    charMap.put("bull", (char) 149);
    charMap.put("trade", (char) 129);
  }
}

/**
 * Return the last tag found, this is normally called just
 * after the read function returns a zero.
 *
 * @return The last HTML tag found.
 */
public HTMLTag getTag()
{
  return this.tag;
}

/**
 * Read a single character from the HTML source, if this
 * function returns zero(0) then you should call getTag to
 * see what tag was found. Otherwise the value returned is
 * simply the next character found.
 *
 * @return The character read, or zero if there is an HTML
 *         tag. If zero is returned, then call getTag to
 *         get the next tag.
 *
 * @throws IOException
 *             If an error occurs while reading.
 */
public int read() throws IOException
{
  // handle locked end tag
  if (this.lockedEndTag != null)
  {
    if (peekEndTag(this.lockedEndTag))
    {
      this.lockedEndTag = null;
    } else
    {
```

```java
        return this.source.read();
      }
    }

    // look for next tag
    if (this.source.peek() == '<')
    {
      parseTag();
      if (!this.tag.isEnding()
          && (this.tag.getName().equalsIgnoreCase("script")
          || this.tag.getName().equalsIgnoreCase("style")))
      {
        this.lockedEndTag = this.tag.getName().toLowerCase();
      }
      return 0;
    } else if (this.source.peek() == '&')
    {
      return parseSpecialCharacter();
    } else
    {
      return (this.source.read());
    }
  }

  /**
   * Convert the HTML document back to a string.
   */
  @Override
  public String toString()
  {
    try
    {
      StringBuilder result = new StringBuilder();

      int ch = 0;
      StringBuilder text = new StringBuilder();
      do
      {
        ch = read();
        if (ch == 0)
        {
          if (text.length() > 0)
          {
            System.out.println("Text:" + text.toString());
            text.setLength(0);
          }
```

```java
      System.out.println("Tag:" + getTag());
    } else if (ch != -1)
    {
      text.append((char) ch);
    }
  } while (ch != -1);
  if (text.length() > 0)
  {
    System.out.println("Text:" + text.toString().trim());
  }
  return result.toString();
} catch (IOException e)
{
  return "[IO Error]";
}
}
}

/**
 * Parse any special characters(i.e.  );
 *
 * @return The character that was parsed.
 * @throws IOException
 *             If a read error occurs
 */
private char parseSpecialCharacter() throws IOException
{
  char result = (char) this.source.read();
  int advanceBy = 0;

  // is there a special character?
  if (result == '&')
  {
    int ch = 0;
    StringBuilder buffer = new StringBuilder();

    // loop through and read special character
    do
    {
      ch = this.source.peek(advanceBy++);
      if ((ch != '&') && (ch != ';')
        && !Character.isWhitespace(ch))
      {
        buffer.append((char) ch);
      }

    } while ((ch != ';') && (ch != -1) &&
```

```java
            !Character.isWhitespace(ch));

      String b = buffer.toString().trim().toLowerCase();

      // did we find a special character?
      if (b.length() > 0)
      {
        if (b.charAt(0) == '#')
        {
          try
          {
            result = (char) Integer.parseInt(b.substring(1));
          } catch (NumberFormatException e)
          {
            advanceBy = 0;
          }
        } else
        {
          if (charMap.containsKey(b))
          {
            result = charMap.get(b);
          } else
          {
            advanceBy = 0;
          }
        }
      } else
      {
        advanceBy = 0;
      }
    }

    while (advanceBy > 0)
    {
      read();
      advanceBy--;
    }

    return result;
  }

  /**
   * Check to see if the ending tag is present.
   * @param name The type of end tag being saught.
   * @return True if the ending tag was found.
   * @throws IOException Thrown if an IO error occurs.
   */
```

```java
private boolean peekEndTag(String name) throws IOException
{
  int i = 0;

  // pass any whitespace
  while ((this.source.peek(i) != -1)
      && Character.isWhitespace(this.source.peek(i)))
  {
    i++;
  }

  // is a tag beginning
  if (this.source.peek(i) != '<')
  {
    return false;
  } else
  {
    i++;
  }

  // pass any whitespace
  while ((this.source.peek(i) != -1)
      && Character.isWhitespace(this.source.peek(i)))
  {
    i++;
  }

  // is it an end tag
  if (this.source.peek(i) != '/')
  {
    return false;
  } else
  {
    i++;
  }

  // pass any whitespace
  while ((this.source.peek(i) != -1)
      && Character.isWhitespace(this.source.peek(i)))
  {
    i++;
  }

  // does the name match
  for (int j = 0; j < name.length(); j++)
  {
```

```java
      if (Character.toLowerCase(this.source.peek(i)) != Character
          .toLowerCase(name.charAt(j)))
      {
        return false;
      }
      i++;
  }

  return true;
}

/**
 * Remove any whitespace characters that are next in the
 * InputStream.
 *
 * @throws IOException
 *             If an I/O exception occurs.
 */
protected void eatWhitespace() throws IOException
{
  while (Character.isWhitespace((char) this.source.peek()))
  {
    this.source.read();
  }
}

/**
 * Parse an attribute name, if one is present.
 *
 * @throws IOException
 *             If an I/O exception occurs.
 */
protected String parseAttributeName() throws IOException
{
  eatWhitespace();

  if ("\"\'".indexOf(this.source.peek()) == -1)
  {
    StringBuilder buffer = new StringBuilder();
    while (!Character.isWhitespace(this.source.peek())
        && (this.source.peek() != '=') &&
        (this.source.peek() != '>')
        && (this.source.peek() != -1))
    {
      int ch = parseSpecialCharacter();
      buffer.append((char) ch);
```

```java
      }
      return buffer.toString();
    } else
    {
      return (parseString());
    }
  }

  /**
   * Called to parse a double or single quote string.
   *
   * @return The string parsed.
   * @throws IOException
   *                 If an I/O exception occurs.
   */
  protected String parseString() throws IOException
  {
    StringBuilder result = new StringBuilder();
    eatWhitespace();
    if ("\"\'".indexOf(this.source.peek()) != -1)
    {
      int delim = this.source.read();
      while ((this.source.peek() != delim) &&
             (this.source.peek() != -1))
      {
        if (result.length() > 1000)
        {
          break;
        }
        int ch = parseSpecialCharacter();
        if ((ch == 13) || (ch == 10))
        {
          continue;
        }
        result.append((char) ch);
      }
      if ("\"\'".indexOf(this.source.peek()) != -1)
      {
        this.source.read();
      }
    } else
    {
      while (!Character.isWhitespace(this.source.peek())
          && (this.source.peek() != -1) &&
             (this.source.peek() != '>'))
      {
```

```
        result.append(parseSpecialCharacter());
      }
    }

  return result.toString();
}

/**
 * Called when a tag is detected. This method will parse
 * the tag.
 *
 * @throws IOException
 *              If an I/O exception occurs.
 */
protected void parseTag() throws IOException
{
  this.tag.clear();
  StringBuilder tagName = new StringBuilder();

  this.source.read();

  // Is it a comment?
  if ((this.source.peek(0) == '!') &&
      (this.source.peek(1) == '-')
      && (this.source.peek(2) == '-'))
  {
    while (this.source.peek() != -1)
    {
      if ((this.source.peek(0) == '-') &&
          (this.source.peek(1) == '-')
          && (this.source.peek(2) == '>'))
      {
        break;
      }
      if (this.source.peek() != '\r')
      {
        tagName.append((char) this.source.peek());
      }
      this.source.read();
    }
    tagName.append("--");
    this.source.read();
    this.source.read();
    this.source.read();
    return;
  }
```

```java
    // Find the tag name
    while (this.source.peek() != -1)
    {
      if (Character.isWhitespace((char) this.source.peek())
          || (this.source.peek() == '>'))
      {
        break;
      }
      tagName.append((char) this.source.read());
    }

    eatWhitespace();
    this.tag.setName(tagName.toString());

    // get the attributes

    while ((this.source.peek() != '>') &&
           (this.source.peek() != -1))
    {
      String attributeName = parseAttributeName();
      String attributeValue = null;

      if (attributeName.equals("/"))
      {
        eatWhitespace();
        if (this.source.peek() == '>')
        {
          this.tag.setEnding(true);
          break;
        }
      }

      // is there a value?
      eatWhitespace();
      if (this.source.peek() == '=')
      {
        this.source.read();
        attributeValue = parseString();
      }

      this.tag.setAttribute(attributeName, attributeValue);
    }
    this.source.read();
  }

}
```

The **ParseHTML** class makes use of three instance variables to track HTML parsing. These variables are shown here.

```
private PeekableInputStream source;
private HTMLTag tag;
private static Map<String, Character> charMap;
```

As you can see, all three variables are private. The **source** variable holds the **PeekableInputStream** that is being parsed. The **tag** variable holds the last HTML tag found by the parser. The **charMap** variable holds a mapping between HTML encoded characters, such as ** **, and their character code.

We will now examine each of the functions in the next section.

### The Constructor

The **ParseHTML** class's constructor was two responsibilities. The first is to create a new **PeekableInputStream** objct based on the **InputStream** that was passed to the constructor. The second is to initialize the **charMap** variable, if it has not already been initialized.

```
source = new PeekableInputStream(is);

if (charMap == null)
{
  charMap = new HashMap<String, Character>();
  charMap.put("nbsp", ' ');
  charMap.put("lt", '<');
  charMap.put("gt", '>');
  charMap.put("amp", '&');
  charMap.put("quot", '\"');
}
```

In HTML encoding there are two ways to store several of the more common characters. For example the double quote character can be stored by its ASCII character value as **&#34;** or as **&quot;**. The ASCII character codes are easy to parse, as you simply extract their numeric values and convert them to characters.

As you can see from the above code, each of the special characters are loaded into a **Map**, which will allow the **parseSepcialCharacter** method, which will be discussed later, to quickly access them.

### Removing White Space with eatWhiteSpace

HTML documents generally have quite a bit of extra white space. This white space has nothing to do with the display, and is useless to the computer. However, the white space makes the HTML source code easier to read for a human. White space is the extra spaces, carriage returns and tabs placed in an HTML document.

The **peek** function of the **PeekableInputStream** is very handy for eliminating white space. By peeking ahead, and seeing if the next character is white space or not, you can decide if you need to remove it.

```
while (Character.isWhitespace((char) source.peek()))
{
  source.read();
}
```

As you can see, from the above code, white space characters are read, and thus removed, one by one, until **peek** finds a non-white space character.

## Parse a String with parseString

Strings occur often inside of HTML documents, particularly when used with HTML attributes. For example, consider the following HTML tags, all of which have the same meaning.

```
<img src="/images/logo.gif">
<img src='/images/logo.gif'>
<img src=/images/logo.gif>
```

The first line is the most common. It uses double quotes to delineate the string value. The second uses single quotes. Though not the preferred method, the third uses no delimiter at all. All three methods are common in HTML, so the **ParseHTML** class uses a function, named **parseString** that handles all three.

First, the **parseString** method creates a **StringBuilder** to hold the parsed string. Next the **parseString** method checks to see if there is a leading delimiter, which could be either a single or double quote.

```
StringBuilder result = new StringBuilder();
if ("\"\'".indexOf(source.peek()) != -1)
{
```

To read in the delimited string, characters are read in until we reach the end of the string, or the end of the file. The **parseSpecialCharacter** function is used to convert any special HTML characters.

```
int delim = source.read();
while (source.peek() != delim && source.peek() != -1)
{
  result.append(this.parseSpecialCharacter());
}
```

Next, read the ending delimiter, if present. If end of file was found first, the ending delimiter might not be present.

```
if ("\"\'".indexOf(source.peek()) != -1)
  source.read();
```

If a leading delimiter is not found, then the string is parsed up to the first white space character.

```
}
else
{
  while ( ! Character.isWhitespace(source.peek())
    && source.peek() != -1)
  {
    result.append(this.parseSpecialCharacter());
  }
}
```

Because there is no delimiter, the only choice is to parse until the first white space character. This means that the string can contain no embedded white space characters.

```
return result.toString();
```

Finally, the parsed string is returned.

### Parse a Tag with parseTag

The **parseTag** method is called whenever an HTML tag is encountered. This method will parse the tag, as well as any HTML attributes of the tag. The **parseTag** method first creates a **StringBuilder** object to hold the tag name, as well as a new **HTMLTag** object that will hold the tag and attributes. A call to the **read** function moves past the opening less-than symbol for the tag.

```
StringBuilder tagName = new StringBuilder();
tag = new HTMLTag();

source.read();
```

Next, the **parseTag** method checks to see if this tag is an HTML comment. If it is an HTML comment, this tag will be ignored. HTML comments begin with the **< ! - -** symbols.

```
// Is it a comment?
if ((source.peek(0) == '!') && (source.peek(1) == '-')
&& (source.peek(2) == '-'))
{
```

If the tag is an HTML comment, then enter a **while** loop to read the rest of the comment.

```
while (source.peek() != -1)
{
  if ((source.peek(0) == '-') && (source.peek(1) == '-')
    && (source.peek(2) == '>'))
    break;
  if (source.peek() != '\r')
```

```
    tagName.append((char) source.peek());

  source.read();
}
```

Once the end of the comment tag has been found, append the last characters of the comment and return.

```
  tagName.append("--");
  source.read();
  source.read();
  source.read();
  return;
}
```

If the tag is not a comment, the proceed with extracting the name of the tag. Enter a **while** loop that looks for the first non-white space character, or an tag ending greater then symbol.

```
// Find the tag name
while (source.peek() != -1)
{
  if (Character.isWhitespace((char) source.peek())
    || (source.peek() == '>'))
    break;
  tagName.append((char) source.read());
}
```

If a tag has no attributes, then a greater than symbol will be found, which will end the tag. If the tag has attributes, then a white space character will follow the tag name, followed by the attributes.

Now prepare to read the attributes, if there are any. First remove any white space, and then record the tag name.

```
eatWhitespace();
tag.setName(tagName.toString());
```

Enter a **while** loop to read all attributes. If there are no attributes this loop will end immediately, as it will find a tag ending greater than symbol.

If an attribute is found, call the **parseAttributeName** function to read the name of the attribute. The **parseAttributeName** function will be covered in the next section.

```
// get the attributes
while (source.peek() != '>' && source.peek() != -1)
{
  String attributeName = parseAttributeName();
  String attributeValue = null;
```

Once the attribute name has been read, we must check to see if there is an attribute value. If there is an attribute value the next character will be an equal sign. If an equal sign is present, then read the attribute value.

```
// is there a value?
eatWhitespace();
if (source.peek() == '=')
{
  source.read();
  attributeValue = parseString();
}
```

Once the attribute has been read the attribute value is set. If there is no attribute value, then the attribute will be set to **null**.

```
    tag.setAttribute(attributeName, attributeValue);
}
sourcc.read();
```

Once the tag name, and all attributes have been read, call **source.read()** to read past the ending greater than sign.

### Parse an Attribute Name with parseAttributeName

The **parseAttributeName** function is called to parse the name of an attribute. This function begins by checking to see if there is a single or double quote around the attribute name. As an example of a HTML tag that has an attribute with a double quote, consider the following tag.

```
<!DOCTYPE HTML PUBLIC "-//W3C//DTD HTML 4.01 Transitional//EN">
```

The above tag contains two name-only attributes: **HTML** and **PUBLIC**. Additionally, it contains a third double quote-delineated attribute.

The **parseAttributeName** function uses the **peek** function to determine if the attribute name is enclosed in either single or double quotes. If the name is not quoted, then create a **StringBuilder** object to hold the attribute name.

```
eatWhitespace();

if ("\"\'".indexOf(source.peek()) == -1)
{
  StringBuilder buffer = new StringBuilder();
```

If the attribute name is not delineated, then read the attribute name until either an equals sign or a tag ending greater-than sign is encountered.

```
while (!Character.isWhitespace(source.peek())
  && source.peek() != '='
  && source.peek() != '>' && (source.peek() != -1))
```

```
{
  buffer.append((char) source.read());
}
return buffer.toString();
```

If the attribute name is quoted, simply call **parseString**.

```
} else
{
  return (parseString());
}
```

Finally, return the result, the attribute name.

## Parse Special Characters with parseSpecialCharacter

Certain characters must be encoded when included in HTML documents. Characters such as greater than are encoded as **&gt;**. Additionally you can encode ASCII codes. For example ASCII character 34 could be encoded as **&#34;**.

The **parseSpecialCharacter** function handles these character encodings. This function begins by reading the first character and seeing if it is an ampersand (&). If the first character is an ampersand then a **StringBuilder** object is setup to hold the rest of the character encoding.

```
char ch = (char) source.read();
if (ch == '&')
{
StringBuilder buffer = new StringBuilder();
```

Next, a loop is started that will read the rest of the character encoding up to the semicolon that ends all character encoding.

```
do
{
  ch = (char) source.read();
  if (ch != '&' && ch != ';')
  {
    buffer.append(ch);
  }
```

If a beginning tag less-than character is found, then the character encoding is invalid, so we just return an ampersand. This is the best we can do with regards to decoding the character. The **do/while** loop will continue until a semicolon is found, or we reach the end of the file.

```
  if (ch == '<')
    return '&';
} while (ch != ';' && (ch != -1));
```

Now we have the entire character encoding loaded into the variable named **buffer**. The first thing to check is to see if the first character is a pound sign (#). If the first character is a pound sign, then this is an ASCII encoding. We should parse the number immediately following the pound sign and return that as the encoded character.

```
String b = buffer.toString().trim().toLowerCase();
if (b.charAt(0) == '#')
{
  try
  {
    return (char) (Integer.parseInt(b.substring(1)));
  } catch (NumberFormatException e)
  {
  return '&';
  }
```

If the number is invalid, and a **NumberFormatException** is thrown, then we return an ampersand (&). Again, since this is an error, returning an ampersand is the best we can do with regards to decoding the character.

If it is not an ASCII encoding, then we look up the character in the **charMap**, which was setup earlier. This will give us the ASCII code for the character. For example, the string "quot" is mapped to ASCII 34, which is the ASCII code for a quote.

```
} else
{
  if (charMap.containsKey(b))
  return charMap.get(b);
else
  return '&';
}
} else
return ch;
```

Finally, we return the character, if the very first if-statement failed. This is because there was no character-encoded character.

### Reading Characters

The HTML parse class contains a function, named **read** that is called to read the next character from an HTML file. The function will return zero if an HTML tag is encountered. Additionally it will decode any special HTML characters.

The function begins by looking for a less-than sign. The less-than sign signals the beginning of an HTML tag. If a less-than sign is found, then the **parseTag** method is called, and a zero is returned. Calling the **getTag** function can access the tag, which was parsed by the **parseTag** method.

```
if (source.peek() == '<')
{
  parseTag();
  return 0;
```

If an ampersand is found, then a special character will follow. Calling **parseSpecialCharacter** will handle the special HTML character.

```
} else if (source.peek() == '&')
{
return parseSpecialCharacter();
```

Finally, if it is a regular HTML character, simply return that character.

```
} else
{
  return (source.read());
}
```

## Encapsulating HTML Tags

When you call the **getTag** function of the HTML parse class, you are given an **HTMLTag** object. This object completely encapsulates the HTML tag that was just parsed. The **HTMLTag** class is shown in Listing 6.3.

### Listing 6.3: HTML Tags (HTMLTag.java)

```java
package com.heatonresearch.httprecipes.html;

import java.util.*;

public class HTMLTag
{
  /*
   * The attributes
   */
  private Map<String, String> attributes = new HashMap<String,
String>();

  /**
   * The tag name.
   */
  private String name = "";

  /*
   * Is this both a beginning and ending tag.
   */
  private boolean ending;
```

```java
public void clear()
{
  this.attributes.clear();
  this.name = "";
  this.ending = false;
}

/**
 * Get the value of the specified attribute.
 *
 * @param name
 *          The name of an attribute.
 * @return The value of the specified attribute.
 */
public String getAttributeValue(String name)
{
  return this.attributes.get(name.toLowerCase());
}

/**
 * Get the tag name.
 */
public String getName()
{
  return this.name;
}

/**
 * @return the ending
 */
public boolean isEnding()
{
  return this.ending;
}

/**
 * Set a HTML attribute.
 *
 * @param name
 *          The name of the attribute.
 * @param value
 *          The value of the attribute.
 */
public void setAttribute(String name, String value)
{
```

```
    this.attributes.put(name.toLowerCase(), value);
}


/**
 * @param ending
 *            The ending to set.
 */
public void setEnding(boolean ending)
{
  this.ending = ending;
}


/**
 * Set the tag name.
 */
public void setName(String s)
{
  this.name = s;
}


/**
 * Convert this tag back into string form, with the
 * beginning < and ending >.
 *
 * @param id
 *            A zero based index that specifies the
 *            attribute to retrieve.
 * @return The Attribute object that was found.
 */
@Override
public String toString()
{
  StringBuilder buffer = new StringBuilder("<");
  buffer.append(this.name);

  Set<String> set = this.attributes.keySet();
  for (String key : set)
  {
    String value = this.attributes.get(key);
    buffer.append(' ');

    if (value == null)
    {
      buffer.append("\"");
      buffer.append(key);
      buffer.append("\"");
```

```
    } else
    {
      buffer.append(key);
      buffer.append("=\"");
      buffer.append(value);
      buffer.append("\"");
    }

  }

  if (this.ending)
  {
    buffer.append('/');
  }
  buffer.append(">");
  return buffer.toString();
  }
}
```

The HTML tag class contains two properties, which are used to hold the HTML tag.

- attributes
- name

The **attributes** variable contains a Map, which holds all of the name value pairs that make up the HTML attributes. The **name** attribute contains a **String** that holds the name of the HTML tag.

Most of the code in Listing 6.3 is contained in the **toString** function. The **toString** function is responsible for converting this **HTMLTag** object back into a textual HTML tag.

The first thing that the **toString** function does is to create a **StringBuilder** to hold the textual tag, as it is created. The **StringBuilder** object begins with a less-than character and then the tag name.

```
StringBuilder buffer = new StringBuilder("<");
buffer.append(name);
```

Next, a loop is entered to display each of the attributes. The attribute's value is read into a **String** object, named **value**. A leading space is placed in front of each attribute.

```
Set<String> set = attributes.keySet();
for (String key : set)
{
  String value = attributes.get(key);
  buffer.append(' ');
```

If a value is not present, then just display the **key**, which is the name of the attribute. The key will be enclosed in quotes.

```
if (value == null)
{
  buffer.append("\"");
  buffer.append(key);
  buffer.append("\"");
```

If a value is present, then display the **key** followed by an equals sign, followed by the value. The value will be enclosed in quotes.

```
} else
{
  buffer.append(key);
  buffer.append("=\"");
  buffer.append(value);
  buffer.append("\"");
}
```

Once all of the attributes have been displayed, a trailing greater-than is appended to the **StringBuilder** object, to end the tag.

```
buffer.append(">");
return buffer.toString();
```

Once the loop completes, the **StringBuilder** object is converted to a **String**, by calling its **toString** method. This **String** is returned.

## Recipes

This chapter includes seven recipes. These recipes demonstrate how to extract data from a variety of different HTML page types. Specifically, you will see how to extract data from each of the following:

- Extract data from a choice list
- Extract data from a HTML list
- Extract data from a table
- Extract data from hyperlinks
- Extract images from an HTML page
- Extract data from HTML sub-pages
- Extract data form HTML partial-pages

All of the recipes in this chapter will make use of the HTML parsing classes that were described in the first part of this chapter. We will begin with the first recipe, which shows you how to extract data from a choice list.

### Recipe #6.1: Extracting Data from a Choice List

Many websites contains choice lists. These choice lists, which are usually part of a form, allow you to pick one option from a scrolling list of many different options. This recipe will extract data from the choice list, at the following URL.

**http://www.httprecipes.com/1/6/form.php**

You can see this list in Figure 6.1.

**Figure 6.1: An HTML Choice List**

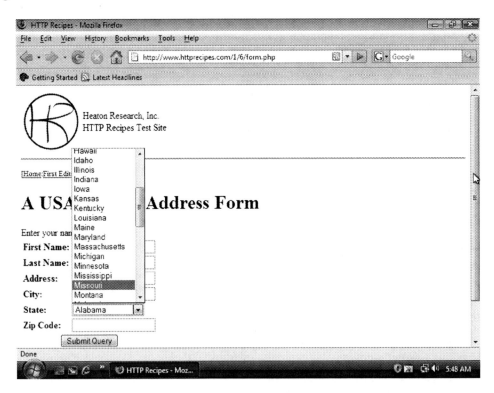

As you can see there is a listing of all fifty US states. This recipe will show how to extract these states, and their abbreviations. The recipe is shown in Listing 6.4.

**Listing 6.4: Parse a Choice List (ParseChoiceList.java)**

```
package com.heatonresearch.httprecipes.ch6.recipe1;

import java.io.*;
import java.net.*;
import com.heatonresearch.httprecipes.html.*;
```

```java
public class ParseChoiceList
{

  /**
   * Called for each option item that is found.
   * @param name The name of the option item.
   * @param value The value of the option item.
   */
  private void processOption(String name, String value)
  {
    StringBuilder result = new StringBuilder();
    result.append('\"');
    result.append(name);
    result.append("\",\"");
    result.append(value);
    result.append('\"');
    System.out.println(result.toString());
  }

  /**
   * Advance to the specified HTML tag.
   * @param parse The HTML parse object to use.
   * @param tag The HTML tag.
   * @param count How many tags like this to find.
   * @return True if found, false otherwise.
   * @throws IOException If an exception occurs while reading.
   */
  private boolean advance(ParseHTML parse, String tag, int count)
      throws IOException
  {
    int ch;
    while ((ch = parse.read()) != -1)
    {
      if (ch == 0)
      {
        if (parse.getTag().getName().equalsIgnoreCase(tag))
        {
          count--;
          if (count <= 0)
            return true;
        }
      }
    }
    return false;
  }
```

```
/**
 * Process the specified URL and extract the option list there.
 * @param url The URL to process.
 * @param optionList Which option list to process, zero
 * for first.
 * @throws IOException Any exceptions that might have
 * occurred while reading.
 */
public void process(URL url, int optionList) throws IOException
{
  String value = "";
  InputStream is = url.openStream();
  ParseHTML parse = new ParseHTML(is);
  StringBuilder buffer = new StringBuilder();

  advance(parse, "select", optionList);

  int ch;
  while ((ch = parse.read()) != -1)
  {
    if (ch == 0)
    {
      HTMLTag tag = parse.getTag();
      if (tag.getName().equalsIgnoreCase("option"))
      {
        value = tag.getAttributeValue("value");
        buffer.setLength(0);
      } else if (tag.getName().equalsIgnoreCase("/option"))
      {
        processOption(buffer.toString(), value);
      } else if (tag.getName().equalsIgnoreCase("/choice"))
      {
        break;
      }
    } else
    {
      buffer.append((char) ch);
    }
  }
}
```

```
/**
 * The main method, create a new instance of the object and call
 * process.
 * @param args not used.
 */
public static void main(String args[])
{
  try
  {
    URL u = new URL("http://www.httprecipes.com/1/6/form.php");
    ParseChoiceList parse = new ParseChoiceList();
    parse.process(u, 1);
  } catch (Exception e)
  {
    e.printStackTrace();
  }
}
}
```

If you examine the HTML source code that makes up the states choice list you will see the following:

```
<select name="state">
<option value="AL">Alabama</option>
<option value="AK">Alaska</option>
<option value="AZ">Arizona</option>
<option value="AR">Arkansas</option>
<option value="CA">California</option>
<option value="CO">Colorado</option>
<option value="CT">Connecticut</option>
<option value="DE">Delaware</option>
...
<option value="WV">West Virginia</option>
<option value="WI">Wisconsin</option>
<option value="WY">Wyoming</option>
</select>
```

In the next section you will see how to parse these **<option>** tags into a comma delineated list of states and abbreviations.

### Parsing the Choice List

We are going to extract the state abbreviation, as well as the state name. The **process** method is used to process the list. This method begins by defining several variables that will be needed to parse the choice list. An **InputStream** is opened to the URL that is being parsed, and a new **ParseHTML** object is constructed.

```
String value = "";
InputStream is = url.openStream();
ParseHTML parse = new ParseHTML(is);
StringBuilder buffer = new StringBuilder();
```

There may be more than one choice list on the page that we are parsing. Each choice list will be surrounded by a beginning **<select>** tag, and an ending **</select>** tag. If there is more than one **<select>** list, then we must advance to the correct one. This is what the **advance** function does.

The **advance** function takes three parameters. The first is the parse object that is being used to parse the HTML. This object will be advanced to the correct location. The second parameter is the name of the tag that we are advancing to. In this case we are advancing to a "select" tag. Finally, the third parameter tells the **advance** function which instance of the second parameter to look for. Zero specifies the first instance; one specifies the second instance, and so on.

```
advance(parse, "select", optionList);
```

Once we have advanced to the correct location it is time to begin parsing for **<option>** tags. We begin with a **while** loop that begins reading data from the **parse** object. As soon as the **read** function returns a zero, we know that we have found an HTML tag.

```
int ch;
while ((ch = parse.read()) != -1)
{
  if (ch == 0)
  {
    HTMLTag tag = parse.getTag();
```

First, we check to see if it is an opening **<option>** tag. If it is, then we read the **value** attribute. This attribute will hold the abbreviation for that state.

```
if (tag.getName().equalsIgnoreCase("option"))
{
  value = tag.getAttributeValue("value");
  buffer.setLength(0);
```

Next we check to see if the tag encountered is an ending **</option>** tag. If it is, then we have found one state. The **processOption** method is called to display that state as part of the comma separated list, which is the output from this recipe.

```
} else if (tag.getName().equalsIgnoreCase("/option"))
```

```
{
  processOption(buffer.toString(), value);
```

If an ending **</choice>** tag is found, then the list has ended, and we are done.

```
} else if (tag.getName().equalsIgnoreCase("/choice"))
{
  break;
}
```

If it was a character that we found, and not a tag, then append it to the **buffer** variable. The **buffer** will hold the state names that are between the **<option>** and **</option>** tags.

```
}else
{
  buffer.append((char) ch);
  }
}
```

Once the loop completes, you will have all fifty states extracted.

## Implementing the Advance Function

As previously mentioned, the **advance** function advances through several instances of a tag, looking for the correct one. To do this the **advance** function enters a **while** loop that will continue until the end of file is reached.

```
int ch;
while ((ch = parse.read()) != -1)
{
```

For each HTML tag encountered, see if the tag name matches the tag we are looking for.

```
if (ch == 0)
{
  if (parse.getTag().getName().equalsIgnoreCase(tag))
  {
```

If the tag name matches, then decrease the **count** and return if the **count** has reached zero. If the count has reached zero, then we have advanced to the correct location and are done.

```
  count--;
  if (count <= 0)
    return true;
}
```

If we fail to find the tag, then return **false**.

```
return false;
```

Several other recipes in this chapter use the **advance** function.

### Recipe #6.2: Extracting Data from an HTML List

Many websites contains lists of data. This recipe will extract data from the HTML list at the following URL:

**http://www.httprecipes.com/1/6/list.php**

You can see this choice list in Figure 6.2.

**Figure 6.2: An HTML List**

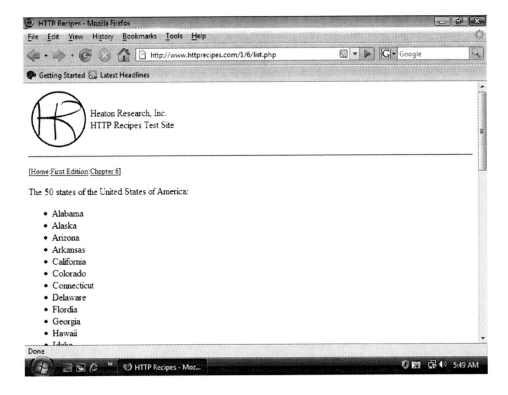

As you can see there is a listing of all fifty US states. This recipe will show how to extract these states. The recipe is shown in Listing 6.5.

## Listing 6.5: Parse an HTML List (ParseList.java)

```java
package com.heatonresearch.httprecipes.ch6.recipe2;

import java.io.*;
import java.net.*;
import com.heatonresearch.httprecipes.html.*;

public class ParseList
{

  /**
   * Advance to the specified HTML tag.
   * @param parse The HTML parse object to use.
   * @param tag The HTML tag.
   * @param count How many tags like this to find.
   * @return True if found, false otherwise.
   * @throws IOException If an exception occurs while reading.
   */
  private boolean advance(ParseHTML parse, String tag, int count)
      throws IOException
  {
    int ch;
    while ((ch = parse.read()) != -1)
    {
      if (ch == 0)
      {
        if (parse.getTag().getName().equalsIgnoreCase(tag))
        {
          count--;
          if (count <= 0)
            return true;
        }
      }
    }
    return false;
  }

  /*
   * Handle each list item, as it is found.
   */
  private void processItem(String item)
  {
    System.out.println(item);
  }
```

```java
/**
 * Called to extract a list from the specified URL.
 * @param url The URL to extract the list from.
 * @param listType What type of list, specify its beginning
 * tag (i.e. <UL>).
 * @param optionList Which list to search, zero for first.
 * @throws IOException Thrown if an IO exception occurs.
 */
public void process(URL url, String listType, int optionList)
    throws IOException
{
  String listTypeEnd = listType + "/";
  InputStream is = url.openStream();
  ParseHTML parse = new ParseHTML(is);
  StringBuilder buffer = new StringBuilder();
  boolean capture = false;

  advance(parse, listType, optionList);

  int ch;
  while ((ch = parse.read()) != -1)
  {
    if (ch == 0)
    {
      HTMLTag tag = parse.getTag();
      if (tag.getName().equalsIgnoreCase("li"))
      {
        if (buffer.length() > 0)
          processItem(buffer.toString());
        buffer.setLength(0);
        capture = true;
      } else if (tag.getName().equalsIgnoreCase("/li"))
      {
        System.out.println(buffer.toString());
        processItem(buffer.toString());
        buffer.setLength(0);
        capture = false;
      } else if (tag.getName().equalsIgnoreCase(listTypeEnd))
      {
        break;
      }
    } else
    {
      if (capture)
        buffer.append((char) ch);
    }
}
```

```
    }
  }

  /**
   * The main method, create a new instance of the object and call
   * process.
   * @param args not used.
   */
  public static void main(String args[])
  {
    try
    {
      URL u = new URL("http://www.httprecipes.com/1/6/list.php");
      ParseList parse = new ParseList();
      parse.process(u, "ul", 1);
    } catch (Exception e)
    {
      e.printStackTrace();
    }
  }
}
```

The **process** method of the **ParseList** class extracts the data from the list. This method begins by creating several variables that will be needed to parse the list. The type of list must be passed in, because there are several list types in HTML, such as **<ul>**, **<ol>**, etc. Because of this, the variable **listTypeEnd** is created to contain the ending tag. For example, an **<ol>** list would end with a **</ol>** tag.

The **capture** variable keeps track of if we are capturing the "non-tag" text or not. This variable will be enabled when we reach a **<li>** tag, which means we need to start capturing the text of the current item.

```
String listTypeEnd = listType + "/";
InputStream is = url.openStream();
ParseHTML parse = new ParseHTML(is);
StringBuilder buffer = new StringBuilder();
boolean capture = false;
```

The **advance** method will take us to the correct list in the HTML page. The advance method is discussed in Recipe 6.1.

```
advance(parse, listType, optionList);
```

Next we begin reading the HTML tags. We continue until the end of the file is reached.

```
int ch;
while ((ch = parse.read()) != -1)
{
  if (ch == 0)
```

```
{
HTMLTag tag = parse.getTag();
```

If we find an **<li>** tag, then we clear the **buffer** and begin capturing. If there was data already in the **buffer**, then we record that item, as it will be one of the fifty states.

```
if (tag.getName().equalsIgnoreCase("li"))
{
  if (buffer.length() > 0)
    processItem(buffer.toString());
  buffer.setLength(0);
  capture = true;
```

If we find an ending **</li>** tag then we clear the **buffer** and prepare for the next tag. Many times the ending **</li>** tag is not used, and as a result this recipe does not require the ending **</li>** tag to be present. To support not having an ending **</li>** tag we first check to see if there is already a tag in the buffer, when we reach the next **<li>** tag.

```
} else if (tag.getName().equalsIgnoreCase("/li"))
{
  System.out.println(buffer.toString());
  processItem(buffer.toString());
  buffer.setLength(0);
  capture = false;
```

If we find the ending tag type, then we are done.

```
} else if (tag.getName().equalsIgnoreCase(listTypeEnd))
{
  break;
}
```

If we found a regular character, and not an HTML tag, then add it to the buffer, if we are currently capturing characters.

```
} else
{
  if (capture)
    buffer.append((char) ch);
}
```

When the loop completes we will have parsed all fifty states from the HTML list.

### Recipe #6.3: Extracting Data from a Table

Many websites contains tables. These tables allow the website to arrange data by rows and columns. This recipe will extract data from the table, at the following URL:

`http://www.httprecipes.com/1/6/table.php`

You can see this table list in Figure 6.3.

## Figure 6.3: An HTML Table

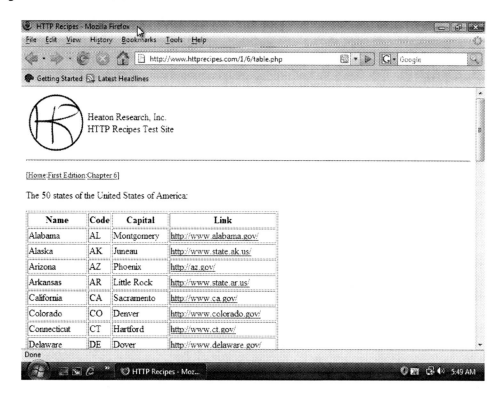

As you can see there is a table of all fifty US states, along with capital cities and official link. This recipe will show how to extract these states, and their this data. The recipe is shown in Listing 6.6.

## Listing 6.6: Parse a Table (ParseTable.java)

```
package com.heatonresearch.httprecipes.ch6.recipe3;

import java.io.*;
import java.net.*;
import java.util.*;
import com.heatonresearch.httprecipes.html.*;

public class ParseTable
{

  /** Advance to the specified HTML tag.
   * @param parse The HTML parse object to use.
```

```java
 * @param tag The HTML tag.
 * @param count How many tags like this to find.
 * @return True if found, false otherwise.
 * @throws IOException If an exception occurs while reading.
 */
private boolean advance(ParseHTML parse, String tag, int count)
    throws IOException
{
  int ch;
  while ((ch = parse.read()) != -1)
  {
    if (ch == 0)
    {
      if (parse.getTag().getName().equalsIgnoreCase(tag))
      {
        count--;
        if (count <= 0)
          return true;
      }
    }
  }
  return false;
}


/**
 * This method is called once for each table row located, it
 * contains a list of all columns in that row.  The method
 * provided
 * simply prints the columns to the console.
 * @param list Columns that were found on this row.
 */
private void processTableRow(List<String> list)
{
  StringBuilder result = new StringBuilder();
  for (String item : list)
  {
    if (result.length() > 0)
      result.append(",");
    result.append('\"');
    result.append(item);
    result.append('\"');

  }
  System.out.println(result.toString());
}
```

```java
/**
 * Called to parse a table.  The table number at the
 * specified URL
 * will be parsed.
 * @param url The URL of the HTML page that contains the table.
 * @param tableNum The table number to parse, zero for
 * the first.
 * @throws IOException Thrown if an error occurs while reading.
 */
public void process(URL url, int tableNum) throws IOException
{
  InputStream is = url.openStream();
  ParseHTML parse = new ParseHTML(is);
  StringBuilder buffer = new StringBuilder();
  List<String> list = new ArrayList<String>();
  boolean capture = false;

  advance(parse, "table", tableNum);

  int ch;
  while ((ch = parse.read()) != -1)
  {
    if (ch == 0)
    {
      HTMLTag tag = parse.getTag();
      if (tag.getName().equalsIgnoreCase("tr"))
      {
        list.clear();
        capture = false;
        buffer.setLength(0);
      } else if (tag.getName().equalsIgnoreCase("/tr"))
      {
        if (list.size() > 0)
        {
          processTableRow(list);
          list.clear();
        }
      } else if (tag.getName().equalsIgnoreCase("td"))
      {
        if (buffer.length() > 0)
          list.add(buffer.toString());
        buffer.setLength(0);
        capture = true;
      } else if (tag.getName().equalsIgnoreCase("/td"))
      {
        list.add(buffer.toString());
```

```
          buffer.setLength(0);
          capture = false;
        } else if (tag.getName().equalsIgnoreCase("/table"))
        {
          break;
        }
      } else
      {
        if (capture)
          buffer.append((char) ch);
      }
    }
  }

  /**
   * The main method, create a new instance of the object and call
   * process.
   * @param args not used.
   */
  public static void main(String args[])
  {
    try
    {
      URL u = new URL("http://www.httprecipes.com/1/6/table.php");
      ParseTable parse = new ParseTable();
      parse.process(u, 2);
    } catch (Exception e)
    {
      e.printStackTrace();
    }
  }
}
```

An HTML table is contained between the tags **<table>** and **</table>**. The table is made up of a series of rows, which are contained between the **<tr>** and **</tr>** tags. Each table row contains several columns, each of which is contained between the **<td>** and **</td>** tags. Additionally, some tables have header columns which are contained between **<th>** and **</th>** tags.

The HTML for the states table is shown below.

```
<table border="1">
<tr>
<th>Name</th>
<th>Code</th>
<th>Capital</th>
<th>Link</th>
```

```
</tr>
<tr>
<td>Alabama</td>
<td>AL</td>
<td>Montgomery</td>
<td>
<a href="http://www.alabama.gov/">http://www.alabama.gov/
</a></td>
</tr>
<tr>
<td>Alaska</td>
<td>AK</td>
<td>Juneau</td>
<td>
<a href="http://www.state.ak.us/">http://www.state.ak.us/
</a></td>
</tr>
...
<tr>
<td>Wyoming</td>
<td>WY</td>
<td>Cheyenne</td>
<td><a href="http://wyoming.gov/">http://wyoming.gov/</a></td>
</tr>
</table>
```

The data that we will parse is located between the **<td>** and **</td>** tags. However, the other tags tell us which row the data belongs to.

## Parsing the Table

The table is parsed by the **process** method of the **ParseTable** class. This method begins by opening an **InputStream** to the URL that contains the table. A **ParseHTML** object is created to parse this **InputStream**. A variable named **buffer** is created to hold the data for each table cell. A variable named **list** is created to hold each column of data for a row. A variable named **capture** is used to keep track of if we are capturing HTML text into the buffer variable or not. Capturing will occur when we are between **<td>** and **</td>** tags.

```
InputStream is = url.openStream();
ParseHTML parse = new ParseHTML(is);
StringBuilder buffer = new StringBuilder();
List<String> list = new ArrayList<String>();
boolean capture = false;
```

The **advance** method will take us to the correct table in the HTML page. The advance method is discussed in Recipe 6.1.

```
advance(parse, "table", tableNum);
```

Next we begin reading the HTML tags. We continue until the end of the file is reached.

```
int ch;
while ((ch = parse.read()) != -1)
{
  if (ch == 0)
  {
    HTMLTag tag = parse.getTag();
```

When a **\<tr\>** tag is located a new table row has begun. This means that we must clear out the last table row.

```
if (tag.getName().equalsIgnoreCase("tr"))
{
  list.clear();
  capture = false;
  buffer.setLength(0);
```

When a **\</tr\>** tag is located a table row has ended. If any columns have been recorded, then call **processTableRow** to process the row that has just ended.

```
} else if (tag.getName().equalsIgnoreCase("/tr"))
{
  if (list.size() > 0)
  {
    processTableRow(list);
    list.clear();
  }
```

When a **\<td\>** tag is located a table column is about to begin. If there was any data already being captured for a column then record it to the list. Set the variable named **capture** to **true** so that the text following the **\<td\>** tag will be captured.

```
} else if (tag.getName().equalsIgnoreCase("td"))
{
  if (buffer.length() > 0)
    list.add(buffer.toString());
  buffer.setLength(0);
  capture = true;
```

When a **\</td\>** tag is located, a column has just ended. This column should be recorded to the variable **list** and capturing should stop.

```
} else if (tag.getName().equalsIgnoreCase("/td"))
{
  list.add(buffer.toString());
  buffer.setLength(0);
capture = false;
```

When a **</table>** tag is located the table has ended. Parsing is now done.

```
} else if (tag.getName().equalsIgnoreCase("/table"))
{
  break;
}
```

If we found a regular character, and not an HTML tag, then add it to the **buffer**, if we are currently capturing characters.

```
} else
{
  if (capture)
    buffer.append((char) ch);
}
```

The loop will continue until all cells of the table have been processed.

### Parsing a Table Row

For each row of data that is recorded the **processRow** method is called. This method simply prints out the data in a comma-delineated format. The first thing that the **processRow** method does is to create a **StringBuilder** and begin iterating over the columns sent to it in the **list** variable.

```
StringBuilder result = new StringBuilder();
for (String item : list)
{
```

For each column recorded add it to the **StringBuilder**. Make sure each column is enclosed in quotes.

```
if (result.length() > 0)
  result.append(",");
result.append('\"');
result.append(item);
result.append('\"');
}
```

Finally, display the complete row.

```
System.out.println(result.toString());
```

This method is called for all rows in the table.

### Recipe #6.4: Extracting Data from Hyperlinks

Hyperlinks are very common on web sites. Hyperlinks are what hold the web together. This recipe will extract the hyperlinks from the following URL:

http://www.httprecipes.com/1/6/link.php

You can see this hyperlink list in Figure 6.4.

### Figure 6.4: Hyperlinks

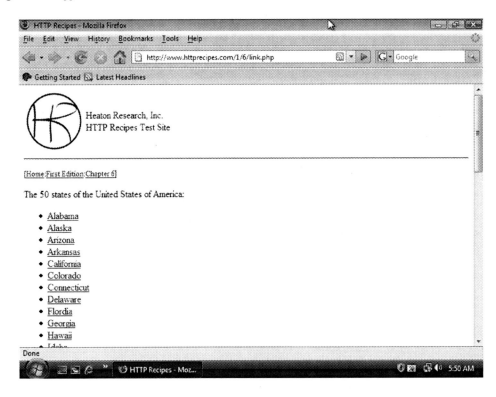

As you can see there is a listing of all fifty US states. This recipe will show how to extract these states, and their links. The recipe is shown in Listing 6.7.

### Listing 6.7: Parse Hyperlinks (ExtractLinks.java)

```
package com.heatonresearch.httprecipes.ch6.recipe4;

import java.io.*;
import java.net.*;
import com.heatonresearch.httprecipes.html.*;


public class ExtractLinks
{

  /**
```

```java
 * Process an individual option tag.  Store the state name
 * and code to a list.
 * @param name The name of the option.
 * @param value The value of the option.
 */
private void processOption(String name, String value)
{
  StringBuilder result = new StringBuilder();
  result.append('\"');
  result.append(name);
  result.append("\",\"");
  result.append(value);
  result.append('\"');
  System.out.println(result.toString());
}

/**
 * Process the specified URL and parse an option list.
 * @param url The URL to process.
 * @param optionList Which option list to process, zero for
 * the first one.
 * @throws IOException Thrown if the page cannot be read.
 */
public void process(URL url, int optionList) throws IOException
{
  String value = "";
  InputStream is = url.openStream();
  ParseHTML parse = new ParseHTML(is);
  StringBuilder buffer = new StringBuilder();

  int ch;
  while ((ch = parse.read()) != -1)
  {
    if (ch == 0)
    {
      HTMLTag tag = parse.getTag();
      if (tag.getName().equalsIgnoreCase("a"))
      {
        value = tag.getAttributeValue("href");
        URL u = new URL(url, value.toString());
        value = u.toString();
        buffer.setLength(0);
      } else if (tag.getName().equalsIgnoreCase("/a"))
      {
        processOption(buffer.toString(), value);
      }
```

```
      } else
      {
        buffer.append((char) ch);
      }
    }
  }

  /**
   * The main method, create a new instance of the object and call
   * process.
   * @param args not used.
   */
  public static void main(String args[])
  {
    try
    {
      URL u = new URL("http://www.httprecipes.com/1/6/link.php");
      ExtractLinks parse = new ExtractLinks();
      parse.process(u, 1);
    } catch (Exception e)
    {
      e.printStackTrace();
    }
  }
}
```

The **process** method of **ExtractLinks** is called to process the hyperlinks. The method begins by creating a few variables that are needed to process the links. This method begins by opening an **InputStream** to the URL that contains the table. A **ParseHTML** object is created to parse this **InputStream**. A variable named **buffer** is created to hold the data for each link.

```
String value = "";
InputStream is = url.openStream();
ParseHTML parse = new ParseHTML(is);
StringBuilder buffer = new StringBuilder();
```

The method loops across every tag and text character in the HTML file.

```
int ch;
while ((ch = parse.read()) != -1)
{
```

When an HTML tag is found it is checked to see if it is an <a> tag. If the tag is an anchor then the **href** attribute is saved to the **value** variable. Additionally, the **buffer** variable is cleared.

```
if (ch == 0)
{
```

```
HTMLTag tag = parse.getTag();
if (tag.getName().equalsIgnoreCase("a"))
{
  value = tag.getAttributeValue("href");
  URL u = new URL(url, value.toString());
  value = u.toString();
  buffer.setLength(0);
```

When the **</a>** tag is found, the tag's text and **href** value are both displayed.

```
} else if (tag.getName().equalsIgnoreCase("/a"))
{
  processOption(buffer.toString(), value);
}
```

If we found a regular character, and not an HTML tag, then add it to the **buffer**.

```
} else
{
  buffer.append((char) ch);
}
```

This loop continues until all links in the file have been processed.

### Recipe #6.5: Extracting Images from HTML

Images are very common on web sites. We have already seen how an image can be downloaded as a binary file. We can also create a bot that examines the **<img>** tags on a site and then downloads the images that it finds. This recipe will extract all of the images from the following URL.

**http://www.httprecipes.com/1/6/image.php**

You can see this image list in Figure 6.5.

**Figure 6.5: HTML Images**

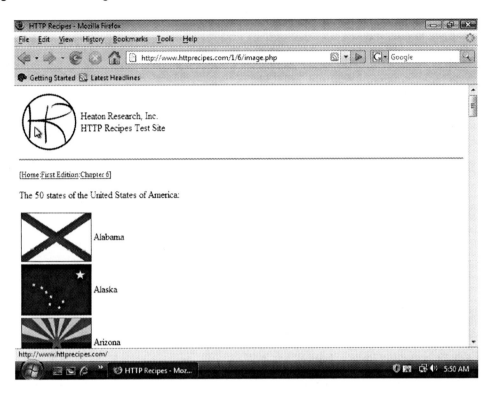

As you can see there are images of the flags of all fifty US states. This recipe will show how to extract these images. The recipe is shown in Listing 6.8.

**Listing 6.8: Extracting Images from HTML (ExtractImages.java)**

```java
package com.heatonresearch.httprecipes.ch6.recipe5;

import java.io.*;
import java.net.*;

import com.heatonresearch.httprecipes.html.*;

public class ExtractImages
{
  /*
   * The size buffer to use for downloading.
   */
  public static int BUFFER_SIZE = 8192;
```

```java
/**
 * Download a binary file from the Internet.
 *
 * @param page The web URL to download.
 * @param filename The local file to save to.
 */
public void downloadBinaryPage(URL url, File file) throws
IOException
{
  byte buffer[] = new byte[BUFFER_SIZE];
  OutputStream os = new FileOutputStream(file);

  InputStream is = url.openStream();
  int size = 0;

  do
  {
    size = is.read(buffer);
    if (size != -1)
      os.write(buffer, 0, size);
  } while (size != -1);

  os.close();
  is.close();
}

/**
 * Extract just the filename from a URL.
 * @param u The URL to extract from.
 * @return The filename.
 */
private String extractFile(URL u)
{
  String str = u.getFile();

  // strip off path information
  int i = str.lastIndexOf('/');
  if (i != -1)
    str = str.substring(i + 1);
  return str;
}

/**
 * Process the specified URL and download the images.
 * @param url The URL to process.
 * @param saveTo A directory to save the images to.
```

```java
     * @throws IOException Thrown if any error occurs.
     */
    public void process(URL url, File saveTo) throws IOException
    {
      InputStream is = url.openStream();
      ParseHTML parse = new ParseHTML(is);

      int ch;
      while ((ch = parse.read()) != -1)
      {
        if (ch == 0)
        {
          HTMLTag tag = parse.getTag();
          if (tag.getName().equalsIgnoreCase("img"))
          {
            String src = tag.getAttributeValue("src");
            URL u = new URL(url, src);
            String filename = extractFile(u);
            File saveFile = new File(saveTo, filename);
            this.downloadBinaryPage(u, saveFile);
          }
        }
      }
    }


    /**
     * The main method, create a new instance of the object and call
     * process.
     * @param args Not used.
     */
    public static void main(String args[])
    {
      try
      {
        URL u = new URL("http://www.httprecipes.com/1/6/image.php");
        ExtractImages parse = new ExtractImages();
        parse.process(u, new File("."));
      } catch (Exception e)
      {
        e.printStackTrace();
      }
    }
}
```

HTML images are stored in the **<img>** tag. This tag contains an attribute, named **src**, that contains the URL for the image to be displayed. A typical HTML image tag looks like this:

```
<img src="/images/logo.gif" width="320" height="200"
alt="Company Logo">
```

The only attribute that this recipe will be concerned with is the **src** attribute. The other tags are option and may, or may not, be present.

## Extracting Images

The method loops across every tag and text character in the HMTL file.

```
InputStream is = url.openStream();
ParseHTML parse = new ParseHTML(is);
```

When an HTML tag is found it is checked to see if it is an <img> tag. If the tag is an image then the **src** attribute is analyzed to determine the path to the image.

```
int ch;
while ((ch = parse.read()) != -1)
{
  if (ch == 0)
  {
    HTMLTag tag = parse.getTag();
    if (tag.getName().equalsIgnoreCase("img"))
    {
String src = tag.getAttributeValue("src");
```

To download the image we need the fully qualified URL. For example, the **<img>** tag's **src** attribute may contain the value **/images/logo.gif**, what we need is **http://www.heatonresearch.com/images/logo.gif**. To obtain this URL we use the **URL** class as follows:

```
URL u = new URL(url, src);
```

Next we extract the filename from the URL and append the filename to a local path to save the file to. The **downloadBinaryPage** method will download the image. This method was covered in Chapter 3.

```
String filename = extractFile(u);
File saveFile = new File(saveTo, filename);
this.downloadBinaryPage(u, saveFile);
```

This method looks across all images on the page.

### Extracting a Filename

The **extractFile** function is used to get the filename portion of a URL. Consider the following URL:

**http://www.heatonresearch.com/images/logo.gif**

The filename portion is **logo.gif**. To extract this part of the URL, the path of the URL is first converted to a string.

```
String str = u.getFile();
```

This string is then searched for the last slash (/) character. Everything to the right of the slash is treated as the filename.

```
// strip off path information
int i = str.lastIndexOf('/');
if (i != -1)
  str = str.substring(i + 1);
return str;
```

This method is used to strip the filename from each image, so that the image can be saved locally to this filename.

### Recipe #6.6: Extracting from Sub-Pages

So far all of the data that we extracted has been on a single HTML page. Often you will want to aggregate data spread across many pages. The last two recipes in this chapter show you how to do this. This recipe shows you how to download data from a list of linked pages. The list is contained here:

**http://www.httprecipes.com/1/6/subpage.php**

You can see this list in Figure 6.6.

**Figure 6.6: A List of Subpages**

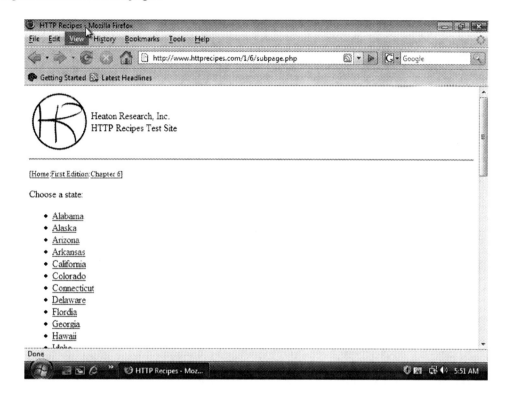

Each state on the list is hyperlinked to a sub-page. For example, the Missouri item links to the following URL:

`http://www.httprecipes.com/1/6/subpage2.php?state=MO`

You can see this sub-page in Figure 6.7.

**Figure 6.7: The Missouri Sub-Page**

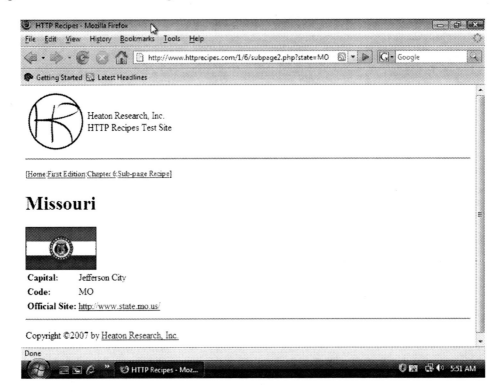

The actual data that we would like to gather is located on the sub-page. However, to find each sub-page we must process the list on the main page. This recipe shows how to extract data from all of the sub-pages. The recipe is shown in Listing 6.9.

**Listing 6.9: Parse HTML Sub-Pages (ExtractSubPage.java)**

```java
package com.heatonresearch.httprecipes.ch6.recipe6;

import java.io.*;
import java.net.*;

import com.heatonresearch.httprecipes.html.*;

public class ExtractSubPage
{
  /*
   * The size buffer to use for downloading.
   */
  public static int BUFFER_SIZE = 8192;
```

```
/**
 * Process each sub page. The sub pages are where the data
 * actually is.
 * @param u The URL of the sub page.
 * @throws IOException Thrown if an error occurs while
 * processing.
 */
private void processSubPage(URL u) throws IOException
{
  String str = downloadPage(u, 5000);
  String code = extractNoCase(str,
    "Code:<b></td><td>", "</td>", 0);
  if (code != null)
  {
    String capital = extractNoCase(str,
      "Capital:<b></td><td>", "</td>", 0);
    String name = extractNoCase(str, "<h1>", "</h1>", 0);
    String flag = extractNoCase(str, "<img src=\"", "\"
      border=\"1\">", 2);
    String site = extractNoCase(str,
      "Official Site:<b></td><td><a href=\"",
      "\"", 0);

    URL flagURL = new URL(u, flag);

    StringBuilder buffer = new StringBuilder();
    buffer.append("\"");
    buffer.append(code);
    buffer.append("\",\"");
    buffer.append(name);
    buffer.append("\",\"");
    buffer.append(capital);
    buffer.append("\",\"");
    buffer.append(flagURL.toString());
    buffer.append("\",\"");
    buffer.append(site);
    buffer.append("\"");
    System.out.println(buffer.toString());
  }
}


/**
 * This method downloads the specified URL into a Java
 * String. This is a very simple method, that you can
 * reused anytime you need to quickly grab all data from
 * a specific URL.
```

```
     *
     * @param url The URL to download.
     * @param timeout The number of milliseconds to wait for
     * connection
     * @return The contents of the URL that was downloaded.
     * @throws IOException Thrown if any sort of error occurs.
     */
public String downloadPage(URL url, int timeout)
  throws IOException
{
  StringBuilder result = new StringBuilder();
  byte buffer[] = new byte[BUFFER_SIZE];

  URLConnection http = url.openConnection();
  http.setConnectTimeout(100);
  InputStream s = http.getInputStream();
  int size = 0;

  do
  {
    size = s.read(buffer);
    if (size != -1)
      result.append(new String(buffer, 0, size));
  } while (size != -1);

  return result.toString();
}

/**
 * This method is very useful for grabbing information from a
 * HTML page.
 *
 * @param url The URL to download.
 * @param token1 The text, or tag, that comes before the
 * desired text
 * @param token2 The text, or tag, that comes after the
 * desired text
 * @param count Which occurrence of token1 to use, 1 for
 * the first
 * @return The contents of the URL that was downloaded.
 * @throws IOException Thrown if any sort of error occurs.
 */
public String extractNoCase(String str, String token1,
  String token2, int count)
{
  int location1, location2;
```

```
  // convert everything to lower case
  String searchStr = str.toLowerCase();
  token1 = token1.toLowerCase();
  token2 = token2.toLowerCase();

  // now search
  location1 = location2 = 0;
  do
  {
    location1 = searchStr.indexOf(token1, location1 + 1);

    if (location1 == -1)
      return null;

    count--;
  } while (count > 0);

  location1 += token1.length();

  // return the result from the original string that has mixed
  // case
  location2 = str.indexOf(token2, location1 + 1);
  if (location2 == -1)
    return null;

  return str.substring(location1, location2);
}


/**
 * Process the specified URL and extract data from all of
 * the sub pages
 * that this page links to.
 * @param url The URL to process.
 * @throws IOException Thrown if an error occurs while
 * reading the URL.
 */
public void process(URL url) throws IOException
{
  String value = "";
  InputStream is = url.openStream();
  ParseHTML parse = new ParseHTML(is);

  int ch;
  while ((ch = parse.read()) != -1)
```

```
      {
        if (ch == 0)
        {
          HTMLTag tag = parse.getTag();
          if (tag.getName().equalsIgnoreCase("a"))
          {
            value = tag.getAttributeValue("href");
            URL u = new URL(url, value.toString());
            value = u.toString();
            processSubPage(u);
          }
        }
      }
    }

  /**
   * The main method, create a new instance of the object and call
   * process.
   * @param args not used.
   */
  public static void main(String args[])
  {
    try
    {
      URL u = new URL(
        "http://www.httprecipes.com/1/6/subpage.php");
      ExtractSubPage parse = new ExtractSubPage();
      parse.process(u);
    } catch (Exception e)
    {
      e.printStackTrace();
    }
  }
}
```

There are two tasks performed by this recipe. First, a list of the sub-pages must be obtained from the main page. Secondly, each sub-page must be loaded, and its data extracted.

### Obtaining the List of Sub-Pages

The **process** method of the **ExtractSubPage** class obtains a list of all sub-pages and passes each sub-page to the **processSubPage** method. This method begins by opening an **InputStream** to the URL that contains the list of hyperlinks. A **ParseHTML** object is created to parse this **InputStream**.

```
String value = "";
InputStream is = url.openStream();
```

```
ParseHTML parse = new ParseHTML(is);
```

The method loops across every tag and text character in the HTML file.

```
int ch;
while ((ch = parse.read()) != -1)
{
  if (ch == 0)
  {
    HTMLTag tag = parse.getTag();
    if (tag.getName().equalsIgnoreCase("a"))
    {
```

When an **<a>** tag is located, its **href** attribute is examined.

```
value = tag.getAttributeValue("href");
```

A new **URL** object is created from the parent URL and the **href** value. This provides the fully qualified URL for the sub-page.

```
URL u = new URL(url, value.toString());
```

The **processSubPage** method is then called for each sub-page.

```
value = u.toString();
processSubPage(u);
```

This method will loop through all sub-pages and call **processSubPage** for each.

## Extracting from the Sub-Pages

Extracting data from the sub-pages is not very different than any of the other data extraction examples. The **extractSubPage** method begins by downloading the HTML page. Next, the method attempts to locate the postal code.

```
String str = downloadPage(u, 5000);
String code = extractNoCase(str, "Code:<b></td><td>", "</td>", 0);
```

If no postal code is located, then we know that there is no US state information on this page. There are several extra links on the parent page, that do not point to state sub-pages. This allows us to quickly discard such pages.

The state's postal code is located by searching for the key text **Code:<b></td><td>**, which occurs just before the postal code in the HTML file. You will also notice that we use a new function, named **extractNoCase**. The **extractNoCase** function is very similar to the **extract** method introduced in Chapter 3. However, **extractNoCase** does not require that the beginning and ending text strings match the case exactly on the HTML page.

```
if (code != null)
{
```

Next we extract the state's capital, name, flag and official site.

```
String capital = extractNoCase(str,
  "Capital:<b></td><td>", "</td>", 0);
String name = extractNoCase(str, "<h1>", "</h1>", 0);
String flag = extractNoCase(str,
  "<img src=\"", "\" border=\"1\">", 2);
String site = extractNoCase(str,
  "Official Site:<b></td><td><a href=\"", "\"", 0);
```

The flag is a URL, so we use the **URL** class to obtain a fully qualified URL to the state flag.

```
URL flagURL = new URL(u, flag);
```

Next store the state's information to a **StringBuilder** as a comma delineated line.

```
StringBuilder buffer = new StringBuilder();
buffer.append("\"");
buffer.append(code);
buffer.append("\",\"");
buffer.append(name);
buffer.append("\",\"");
buffer.append(capital);
buffer.append("\",\"");
buffer.append(flagURL.toString());
buffer.append("\",\"");
buffer.append(site);
buffer.append("\"");
System.out.println(buffer.toString());
```

This method will be called for every sub-page on the system.

### Recipe #6.7: Extracting from Partial-Pages

Many web sites make use of partial pages. A partial page is when you are presented with a list of data. However, you do not see all of your data at once. You are also given options to move forward and backward through a large list of data. Search engine results are a perfect example of this. You can see such a page here:

**http://www.httprecipes.com/1/6/partial.php**

You can see this list in Figure 6.8.

**Figure 6.8: A Partial HTML Page**

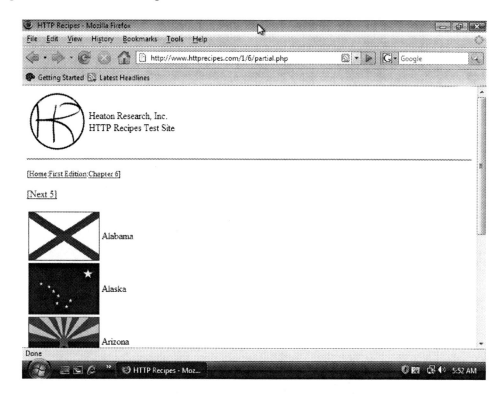

As you can see the images for the states are only shown five at a time. This recipe will process all of the "next page" links until all pages have been downloaded. The recipe is shown in Listing 6.10.

**Listing 6.10: Parse HTML Partial-Pages (ExtractPartial.java)**

```
package com.heatonresearch.httprecipes.ch6.recipe7;

import java.io.*;
import java.net.*;

import com.heatonresearch.httprecipes.html.*;

public class ExtractPartial
{
  /*
   * The size buffer to use for downloading.
   */
  public static int BUFFER_SIZE = 8192;

  /**
```

```
   * This method downloads the specified URL into a Java
   * String. This is a very simple method, that you can
   * reused anytime you need to quickly grab all data from
   * a specific URL.
   *
   * @param url The URL to download.
   * @param timeout The number of milliseconds to wait for
   * connection
   * @return The contents of the URL that was downloaded.
   * @throws IOException Thrown if any sort of error occurs.
   */
public String downloadPage(URL url, int timeout)
   throws IOException
{
   StringBuilder result = new StringBuilder();
   byte buffer[] = new byte[BUFFER_SIZE];

   URLConnection http = url.openConnection();
   http.setConnectTimeout(100);
   InputStream s = http.getInputStream();
   int size = 0;

   do
   {
     size = s.read(buffer);
     if (size != -1)
       result.append(new String(buffer, 0, size));
   } while (size != -1);

   return result.toString();
}


/**
 * Called to process each individual item found.
 * @param official Site The official site for this state.
 * @param flag The flag for this state.
 */
private void processItem(URL officialSite, URL flag)
{
   StringBuilder result = new StringBuilder();
   result.append("\"");
   result.append(officialSite.toString());
   result.append("\",\"");
   result.append(flag.toString());
   result.append("\"");
```

```java
    System.out.println(result.toString());
}


/**
 * This method is very useful for grabbing information from a
 * HTML page.
 *
 * @param url The URL to download.
 * @param token1 The text, or tag, that comes before the
 * desired text.
 * @param token2 The text, or tag, that comes after the
 * desired text.
 * @param count Which occurrence of token1 to use, 1 for
 * the first.
 * @return The contents of the URL that was downloaded.
 * @throws IOException Thrown if any sort of error occurs.
 */
public String extractNoCase(String str, String token1,
  String token2, int count)
{
  int location1, location2;

  // convert everything to lower case
  String searchStr = str.toLowerCase();
  token1 = token1.toLowerCase();
  token2 = token2.toLowerCase();

  // now search
  location1 = location2 = 0;
  do
  {
    location1 = searchStr.indexOf(token1, location1 + 1);

    if (location1 == -1)
      return null;

    count--;
  } while (count > 0);

  location1 += token1.length();

  // return the result from the original string that has mixed
  // case
  location2 = str.indexOf(token2, location1 + 1);
  if (location2 == -1)
    return null;
```

```java
    return str.substring(location1, location2);
}

/**
 * Called to process each partial page.
 * @param url The URL of the partial page.
 * @return Returns the next partial page, or null if no more.
 * @throws IOException Thrown if an exception occurs while
 * reading.
 */
public URL process(URL url) throws IOException
{
  URL result = null;
  StringBuilder buffer = new StringBuilder();
  String value = "";
  String src = "";

  InputStream is = url.openStream();
  ParseHTML parse = new ParseHTML(is);
  boolean first = true;

  int ch;
  while ((ch = parse.read()) != -1)
  {
    if (ch == 0)
    {
      HTMLTag tag = parse.getTag();
      if (tag.getName().equalsIgnoreCase("a"))
      {
        buffer.setLength(0);
        value = tag.getAttributeValue("href");
        URL u = new URL(url, value.toString());
        value = u.toString();
        src = null;
      } else if (tag.getName().equalsIgnoreCase("img"))
      {
        src = tag.getAttributeValue("src");
      } else if (tag.getName().equalsIgnoreCase("/a"))
      {
        if (buffer.toString().equalsIgnoreCase("[Next 5]"))
        {
          result = new URL(url, value);
        } else if (src != null)
        {
          if (!first)
```

```
          {
            URL urlOfficial = new URL(url, value);
            URL urlFlag = new URL(url, src);
            processItem(urlOfficial, urlFlag);
          } else
            first = false;
        }
      }
    } else
    {
      buffer.append((char) ch);
    }
  }

  return result;
}

/**
 * Called to download the state information from several
 * partial pages.
 * Each page displays only 5 of the 50 states, so it is
 * necessary to link
 * each partial page together.  THis method calls "process"
 * which will process
 * each of the partial pages, until there is no more data.
 * @throws IOException Thrown if an exception occurs
 * while reading.
 */
public void process() throws IOException
{
  URL url = new URL(
    "http://www.httprecipes.com/1/6/partial.php");
  do
  {
    url = process(url);
  } while (url != null);

}

/**
 * The main method, create a new instance of the object and call
 * process.
 * @param args not used.
 */
public static void main(String args[])
{
```

```
    try
    {
      ExtractPartial parse = new ExtractPartial();
      parse.process();
    } catch (Exception e)
    {
      e.printStackTrace();
    }
  }
}
```

This recipe works by downloading the first page, then following the "next page" links until the end is reached.

### Processing the First Page

The **process** method of the **ExtractPartial** class is used to access the first page, and download subsequent pages. It is important to note that there are two **process** methods in the **ExtractPartial**. The **process** method used to start downloading is the **process** method that accepts no parameters. It begins by obtaining a URL to the first page.

```
URL url = new URL("http://www.httprecipes.com/1/6/partial.php");
do
{
  url = process(url);
} while (url != null);
```

The URL is passed to the process method that accepts a URL. This process method returns the URL to the next page. This process continues until all pages have been downloaded.

### Processing Individual Pages

The overloaded process method that accepts a **URL** is called for each partial-page that is found. The method begins by creating some variables that will be needed to process the page. The **result** variable holds the next partial-page, or **null** if there is no next page. The **buffer** variable holds non-tag text encountered. The **value** variable holds the **href** attribute for **<a>** tags found. The **src** variable holds the **src** attribute for **<img>** tags encountered.

```
URL result = null;
StringBuilder buffer = new StringBuilder();
String value = "";
String src = "";
```

This method begins by opening an **InputStream** to the URL that contains the table. A **ParseHTML** object is created to parse this **InputStream**. The method then loops over all of the text and tags in the HTML file.

```
InputStream is = url.openStream();
ParseHTML parse = new ParseHTML(is);
boolean first = true;

int ch;
while ((ch = parse.read()) != -1)
{
  if (ch == 0)
  {
    HTMLTag tag = parse.getTag();
    if (tag.getName().equalsIgnoreCase("a"))
    {
```

When an **<a>** tag is encountered, the URL of the image is recorded.

```
buffer.setLength(0);
value = tag.getAttributeValue("href");
URL u = new URL(url, value.toString());
value = u.toString();
src = null;
```

If an **<img>** tag is encountered, the **src** attribute is recorded.

```
} else if (tag.getName().equalsIgnoreCase("img"))
{
  src = tag.getAttributeValue("src");
```

When an ending **</a>** tag is found we need to check the text of the link. If the text of the link was "[Next 5]" then we've found our link to the next page.

```
} else if (tag.getName().equalsIgnoreCase("/a"))
{
  if (buffer.toString().equalsIgnoreCase("[Next 5]"))
  {
```

If the link to the next page has been found, record it so we can return it when this method is done.

```
result = new URL(url, value);
} else if (src != null)
{
```

If this is not the first link on the page, display the link and flag URL found. We do not process the first link on the page because it is not related to a state. It is the link to the homepage.

```
if (!first)
{
  URL urlOfficial = new URL(url, value);
  URL urlFlag = new URL(url, src);
  processItem(urlOfficial, urlFlag);
} else
  first = false;
```

If a tag was not found add the text to the **buffer**.

```
} else
{
  buffer.append((char) ch);
}
```

Finally, return the next page, if it will found.

```
return result;
```

This function will continue returning the next page until it has reached the end of all 50 states.

## Summary

This chapter showed you how to extract data from HTML. Most of the data that a bot would like to access will be in HTML form. Previous chapters showed how to extract data from simple HTML constructs, this chapter expanded on that considerably.

The chapter began by showing you how to create an HTML parser. This HTML parser is fairly short in length, but it can handle any HTML file, even if not properly formatted. The HTML parser built into Java can run into issues with improperly formatted HTML. Unfortunately, there is a fair amount of improperly formatted HTML on the web.

HTML pages can come in a variety of formats. This chapter included seven recipes to show you how to extract data from many of these formats. You were shown how to extract hyperlinks, images, forms, and from multiple pages.

So far the recipes in this book have mostly just downloaded data from a web server. There has not been much interactivity with the web server. In the next chapter you will see how a bot can send form data to a web server. This allows the bot to interact with the web server just like a human using a form.

## CHAPTER 7: RESPONDING TO FORMS

- Understanding Forms
- Responding to a Form with HTTP GET
- Responding to a Form with HTTP POST
- Sending Files with HTTP Upload

Most web sites make use of forms. Forms allow web sites to gather information from a user. Because forms are very important to websites, it is also very important that an HTTP programmer knows how to use Java to interact with forms.

This chapter will show you how to work with the forms you will encounter on web sites. You will see how to work with basic forms that include text, buttons and other controls. You will also be shown how to use multipart forms, which allow the user to upload files to the web server.

I will begin with a review of how forms are constructed.

## Understanding HTML Forms

HTML forms are contained in HTML documents. The HTML form occurs between the beginning `<form>` and ending `</form>` elements. Inside of the form, various `<input>` and other elements allow an assortment of controls to be used with the form.

To see a form in action, load the following URL in a browser. This form demonstrates most of the controls that can be added to a form.

`http://www.httprecipes.com/1/7/input.php`

This form contains a variety of controls and shows what HTML forms are capable of. You can see this form in Figure 7.1.

**Figure 7.1: A HTML form**

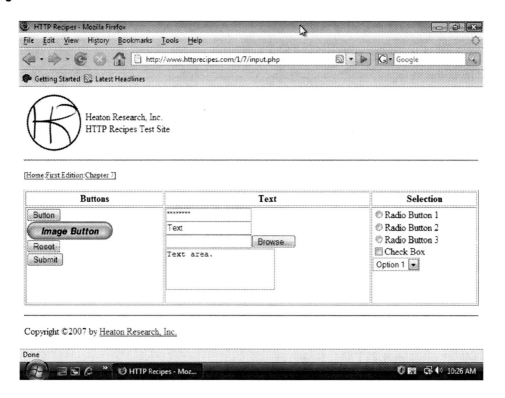

To write a Java program that can respond to a form, you must learn to examine forms in HTML. In this section, we will examine each of the HTML tags that make up a form. If you are already familiar with form HTML code, you can safely skip to the next section.

### Form Tag

The actual **<form>** tag contains two very useful pieces of information. First, the **<form>** tag tells you if the form request should be an HTTP **GET** or an HTTP **POST** request. Each of these two request types are handled differently. Second, the **<form>** tag tells you which URL the HTTP request should be sent to. Consider the following **<form>** tag:

```
<form method="get" action="/process.php">
```

The **method** attribute of this tag tells us that this will be an HTTP **GET** request. The **action** attribute of this tag tells us that the request will go to **/process.php**. A **POST** **<form>** element looks very similar:

```
<form method="post" action="/process.php">
```

The main difference between the two, is that the second tag specifies that this request uses the HTTP **POST**, and not the HTTP **GET**.

Some **\<form\>** elements will not contain an **action** attribute. If this is the case, then the request will be sent back to the same page that contains the form. For example, the following **\<form\>** tag would specify to post back to the page that contains the form.

```
<form method="post">
```

This is a very common practice. Often, the page that contains the **\<form\>** is also capable of processing the data that returns from the form.

### \<input\> Tags

Most form elements are expressed as **\<input\>** tags. The input tag contains a **type** property that tells what type of **\<input\>** tag this is. Table 7.1 summarizes the different **\<input\>** tag types.

**Table 7.1: Common \<input\> Tag Types**

| Tag Type | Purpose |
| --- | --- |
| button | Buttons are used to perform JavaScript actions. |
| checkbox | Checkboxes allow the form to capture true/false data. |
| file | The file type allows files to be uploaded with a multipart form. |
| hidden | Hidden controls hold a value, but cannot be seen or interacted with. |
| image | Images are like buttons, except their appearance is governed by the image. |
| password | Password fields work just like text fields, except you cannot see what is typed. |
| radio | Radio buttons allow a multi-choice input. |
| reset | The reset button sends no data to the web server. It allows you to reset all of the form's controls back to their default values. |
| submit | The submit button submits the form's data to the web server. |
| text | Text fields allow the user to enter single-line text information. |

In the next few sections, each of the controls that can be placed on a form will be explored.

### Form Buttons

There are several types of form buttons that web servers can make use of. The HTML necessary to create each of these button types is shown here.

```
<input type="button" name="button" value="Button">
<input type="image" name="image" value="Image"
src="/images/button.png">
<input type="reset" name="reset" value="Reset">
<input type="submit" name="submit" value="Submit">
```

The most commonly used are the **image** button and the **submit** button. The **image** button allows you to create a button that looks like any image that you choose. The regular **submit** button looks like an ordinary button. Both of these button types will submit the form.

The **reset** button type does not send any data back to the web server. Rather, the **reset** button simply resets all of the form data back to their default values. Reset buttons are not seen on web forms nearly as often as they used to be.

The **button type** attribute is used with JavaScript. JavaScript can be difficult to create a bot for. JavaScript will be covered in Chapter 9, "Handling Javascript".

The **name** attribute of the buttons specifies the name of the button. The name is not displayed to the user. However, the **name** attribute is very important, because it gives the web server a name to identify the button.

The **value** attribute specifies the text of the button that is displayed to the user. Additionally, the **value** attribute is returned, along with the name to allow the web server to further identify the button. For example, consider the following buttons:

```
<input type="submit" name="action" value="Button1">
<input type="submit" name="action" value="Button2">
```

If the user were to click "Button 1", the following data would be returned to the web server:

```
action=Button1
```

This is how data is always returned to the web server, as name-value pairs. This allows you to have more than one button named the same thing. For example, the above two buttons are both named **action**. If the user were to click **Button2**, the following would be returned to the web server.

```
action=Button2
```

This is called a name-value pair. All data returned from HTML forms will be returned as name-value pairs.

## Text Controls

There are several types of form text controls that web servers can make use of. The HTML necessary to create each of these control types is shown here.

```
<input type="password" name="password" value="Password">
<input type="text" name="text" value="Text">
<input type="file" name="file" value="File">
<textarea rows="3" cols="20" name="textarea">Text area.</textarea>
<input type="hidden" name="hidden" value="Hidden">
```

The **text** control displays a rectangular field for the user to enter text into. The **password** control works the same way; however, the user is not allowed to see what is entered. The **hidden** control is simply a name-value pair that is sent directly to the web server. The user cannot see or change a **hidden** control.

The **file** control allows a file to be uploaded. The **file** control works considerably different than any of the other control types, as it requires the form to be posted in a multi-part format. HTTP file uploads will be discussed later in this chapter.

Text controls are also sent to the server as a name-value pair. For example, consider the following text control.

```
<input type="text" name="userid">
```

If you were to enter the user id of "jeff", the following would be sent to the web server.

```
userid=jeff
```

Even the **password** control is transmitted this way. Passwords from web sites are transmitted in a clear-text format. Of course, the best way to secure the password is to use HTTPS so that everything is encrypted.

## Selection Controls

There are several types of form selection lists that web servers can make use of. The HTML necessary to create each of these control types is shown here:

```
<input type="radio" name="radio" value="1">Radio Button 1<br>
<input type="radio" name="radio" value="2">Radio Button 2<br>
<input type="radio" name="radio" value="3">Radio Button 3<br>
```

The above controls are **radio** buttons. Only one **radio** button can be selected at a time. Radio buttons are good for a multi-choice type of question and work just like every other control type, in that they return a name-value pair. For example, if the second **radio** control from the above list was selected, the following name-value pair would be returned to the server:

```
radio=radio2
```

The **checkbox** control works the same way, except that any number of check boxes can be selected.

```
<input type="checkbox" name="checkbox" value="Check Box">Check
Box<br>
```

A **choice** control works just like a radio button, except it takes less space on the page. The user selects from a drop-list of values.

```
<select name="choice">
<option value="1">Option 1</option>
<option value="2">Option 2</option>
<option value="3">Option 3</option>
</select>
```

The drop-list returns data as a name-value pair, just like any other control. For example, if you choose "Option 2" from the above list, the following name-value pair would be returned:

```
choice=2
```

As you can see, to a bot, all controls are handled the same. The controls may look different to the user, but for a bot, they are all just name-value pairs.

# POST or GET

In the previous section we mentioned two different ways of responding to a form: the HTTP **POST** and HTTP **GET**. Both of these two methods are commonly used by web servers and will be utilized by your programs. As an HTTP programmer you will not pick whether to use **POST** or **GET**; rather, you must use whichever protocol your target web server is using. The next two sections will discuss HTTP **POST** and HTTP **GET**.

## Using HTTP GET

HTTP **GET** is the easiest way to respond to a form. It works very similar to HTTP **POST**, in that a series of name-value pairs is transmitted; however, you are limited by the amount of data you can transmit. Most browsers allow the URL like to be only so long. The length varies with the browser; however, most browsers maximum URL length is around 2,000 characters. Also, because all form data is visible on the browser's URL line, it is very easy for the user to tamper with the data sent.

There is no way to tell if a form is **GET** or **POST** just by examining it on the screen. To make this determination, you must examine the HTML source code. A form that makes use of HTTP **GET**, will have a **<form>** tag similar to the following:

```
<form action="somepage.php" method="GET">
```

As you recall from the last section, the data from an HTTP form is nothing more than a series of name-value pairs. Consider a form that has two text fields, one named **first** and the other named **last**. If the user entered "Jeff" for the first field and "Heaton" for the second field, the two name-value pairs would be:

```
first=Jeff
last=Heaton
```

However, when two fields are transmitted, using either **GET** or **POST**, the name-value pairs are concatenated together and separated by an ampersand (&). The two fields above would be encoded as:

```
first=Jeff&last=Heaton
```

In the case of an HTTP **GET**, the name-value pairs are simply concatenated onto the URL. The **<form>** tag above is set to send its data to a page named **somepage.php**. Thus, to send the fields first and last to **test.php**, the following URL would be used:

```
http://www.httprecipes.com/1/test.php?first=Jeff&last=Heaton
```

As you can see, the parameters are concatenated directly onto the end of the URL. A question mark (?) separates the parameters from the rest of the URL.

To see this in action, visit the following URL:

**http://www.httprecipes.com/1/7/get.php**

When you enter a state and click "Search" you will see Figure 7.2.

## Figure 7.2: Using a HTTP GET based Form

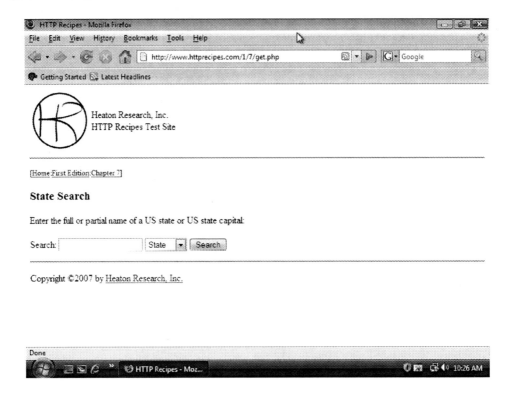

If you examine the browser URL line in Figure 7.2, you will see that the form name-value pairs have been concatenated to the URL.

## Using HTTP POST

HTTP **POST** is slightly more complex than HTTP **GET**. It works very similar to HTTP **GET**, in that a series of name-value pairs is transmitted; however, you are not limited by the amount of data you can transmit. A form that makes use of HTTP **POST** will have a **<form>** tag similar to the following:

```
<form action="somepage.php" method="POST">
```

When data is transmitted using HTTP **POST**, the data is sent as part of the request packet, but it is not visible from the URL. To see how HTTP **POST** data is sent, consider the following URL:

**http://www.httprecipes.com/1/7/post.php**

When you enter a search string and click "Send", the following packet is sent to the web server:

```
POST /1/7/post.php HTTP/1.
Accept: image/gif, image/x-xbitmap, image/jpeg, image/pjpeg, ap-
plication/x-shockwave-flash, */*
Referer: http://www.httprecipes.com/1/7/post.php
Accept-Language: en-us
Content-Type: application/x-www-form-urlencoded
Accept-Encoding: gzip, deflate
User-Agent: Mozilla/4.0 (compatible; MSIE 6.0; Windows NT 5.1;
SV1; .NET CLR 1.1.4322; .NET CLR 2.0.50727)
Host: www.httprecipes.com
Content-Length: 36
Connection: Keep-Alive
Cache-Control: no-cache

search=Missouri&type=s&action=Search
```

As you can see from the above data, the form data is transmitted right after the HTTP headers. Later in this chapter you will be shown how you can quickly generate this data for posts of your own.

## Multipart POST

In addition to the regular post discussed in the last section, there is also a multipart post. Most forms you will encounter are not multipart posts. The only time you will encounter a multipart post is when the form allows you to upload a file. You can easily tell a multipart post by the format of the **<form>** tag:

```
<form enctype="multipart/form-data" action="uploader.php"
method="POST">
```

You can easily identify a multipart form by the **enctype** attribute of the **<form>** element. If the **enctype** is multipart/form-data, then you are dealing with a multipart form.

A multipart **POST** has a much different format than a regular post. In addition to the regular form elements, a multipart post allows files to be sent. You can see an example of a multipart form at the following URL:

**http://www.httprecipes.com/1/7/upload.php**

You can also see the form in Figure 7.3.

### Figure 7.3: A Multipart Form

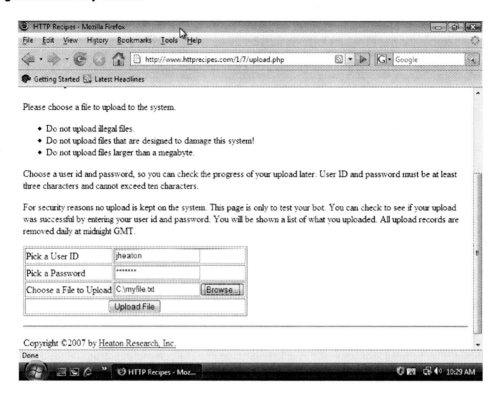

You can easily find the field that allows you to upload a file. The "Browse" button next to the file upload field allows you to navigate through your file system and locate a file to upload.

If you upload using the above form, the following request will be sent to the server:

```
POST /1/7/uploader.php HTTP/1.1
Accept: image/gif, image/x-xbitmap, image/jpeg, image/pjpeg, ap-
plication/x-shockwave-flash, */*
Referer: http://www.httprecipes.com/1/7/upload.php
Accept-Language: en-us
Content-Type: multipart/form-data; boundary=--------------------
-----7d63cf13501b4
Accept-Encoding: gzip, deflate
User-Agent: Mozilla/4.0 (compatible; MSIE 6.0; Windows NT 5.1;
SV1; .NET CLR 1.1.4322; .NET CLR 2.0.50727)
Host: www.httprecipes.com
Content-Length: 571
Connection: Keep-Alive
Cache-Control: no-cache
```

```
---------------------------7d63cf13501b4
Content-Disposition: form-data; name="uid"

jeff
---------------------------7d63cf13501b4
Content-Disposition: form-data; name="pwd"

1234
---------------------------7d63cf13501b4
Content-Disposition: form-data; name="MAX_FILE_SIZE"

1000000
---------------------------7d63cf13501b4
Content-Disposition: form-data; name="uploadedfile"; filename="C:\
Documents and Settings\jeff\Desktop\myfile.txt"
Content-Type: text/plain

This is the contents of myfile.txt.
---------------------------7d63cf13501b4--
```

One of the first things you should notice is the boundary. The boundary is specified in the **Content-Type** header. For this example, the boundary is as follows:

```
---------------------------7d63cf13501b4
```

The boundary is used to separate each of the parts. There is one part for each control on the HTML form. The first two fields, named **uid** and **pwd** contain the user's id and password. These two fields have the values of "jeff" and "1234" respectively. The next field is a hidden field, named **MAX_FILE_SIZE**, which specified the maximum file size that this form will accept. In this case, it is a megabyte.

The final field, named **uploadedfile**, contains the file that we are uploading. The raw binary image of the file is inserted here. For this example, I uploaded a very simple file that contains the text, "This is the contents of myfile.txt". You can see this string in the above form request.

As you can see there are a number of important considerations when responding to a form. In the next section, we will examine a class that can be used to quickly build both multipart and regular responses.

## Processing Forms

All of the recipes in this chapter make use of a simple class named **FormUtility**. This class allows you to quickly create form responses for both regular and multipart form responses. The **FormUtility** class is shown in Listing 7.1.

### Listing 7.1: Form Utility (FormUtility.java)

```java
package com.heatonresearch.httprecipes.html;

import java.io.*;
import java.net.*;
import java.util.*;

public class FormUtility
{
  /*
   * The charset to use for URL encoding. Per URL coding
   * spec, this value should always be UTF-8.
   */
  private final static String encode = "UTF-8";

  /*
   * A Java random number generator.
   */
  private static Random random = new Random();

  /**
   * Generate a boundary for a multipart form.
   *
   * @return The boundary.
   */
  public static String getBoundary()
  {
    return "---------------------------" + randomString() +
      randomString()
        + randomString();
  }

  /**
   * Parse a URL query string. Return a map of all of the
   * name value pairs.
   *
   * @param form
   *           The query string to parse.
   * @return A map of name-value pairs.
   */
  public static Map<String, String> parse(String form)
  {
    Map<String, String> result = new HashMap<String, String>();
    StringTokenizer tok = new StringTokenizer(form, "&");
    while (tok.hasMoreTokens())
    {
```

```java
    String str = tok.nextToken();
    StringTokenizer tok2 = new StringTokenizer(str, "=");
    if (!tok2.hasMoreTokens())
    {
      continue;
    }
    String left = tok2.nextToken();
    if (!tok2.hasMoreTokens())
    {
      left = encode(left);
      result.put(left, null);
      continue;
    }
    String right = tok2.nextToken();
    right = encode(right);
    result.put(left, right);
  }
  return result;
}

/**
 * Encode the specified string. This encodes all special
 * characters.
 *
 * @param str
 *           The string to encode.
 * @return The encoded string.
 */
private static String encode(String str)
{
  try
  {
    return URLEncoder.encode(str, encode);
  } catch (UnsupportedEncodingException e)
  {
    return str;
  }
}

/**
 * Generate a random string, of a specified length. This
 * is used to generate the multipart boundary.
 *
 * @return A random string.
 */
protected static String randomString()
```

```java
{
  return Long.toString(random.nextLong(), 36);
}

/*
 * The boundary used for a multipart post. This field is
 * null if this is not a multipart form and has a value if
 * this is a multipart form.
 */
private String boundary;

/*
 * The stream to output the encoded form to.
 */
private OutputStream os;

/*
 * Keep track of if we're on the first form element.
 */
private boolean first;

/**
 * Prepare to access either a regular, or multipart, form.
 *
 * @param os
 *            The stream to output to.
 * @param boundary
 *            The boundary to be used, or null if this is
 *            not a multipart form.
 */
public FormUtility(OutputStream os, String boundary)
{
  this.os = os;
  this.boundary = boundary;
}

/**
 * Add a file to a multipart form.
 *
 * @param name
 *            The field name.
 * @param file
 *            The file to attach.
 * @throws IOException
 *            If any error occurs while writing.
 */
```

```java
public void add(String name, File file) throws IOException
{
  if (this.boundary != null)
  {
    boundary();
    writeName(name);
    write("; filename=\"");
    write(file.getName());
    write("\"");
    newline();
    write("Content-Type: ");
    String type =
      URLConnection.guessContentTypeFromName(file.getName());
    if (type == null)
    {
      type = "application/octet-stream";
    }
    writeln(type);
    newline();

    byte[] buf = new byte[8192];
    int nread;

    InputStream in = new FileInputStream(file);
    while ((nread = in.read(buf, 0, buf.length)) >= 0)
    {
      this.os.write(buf, 0, nread);
    }

    newline();
  }
}

/**
 * Add a regular text field to either a regular or
 * multipart form.
 *
 * @param name
 *          The name of the field.
 * @param value
 *          The value of the field.
 * @throws IOException
 *          If any error occurs while writing.
 */
public void add(String name, String value) throws IOException
{
```

```
      if (this.boundary != null)
      {
        boundary();
        writeName(name);
        newline();
        newline();
        writeln(value);
      } else
      {
        if (!this.first)
        {
          write("&");
        }
        write(encode(name));
        write("=");
        write(encode(value));
      }
      this.first = false;
  }

  /**
   * Complete the building of the form.
   *
   * @throws IOException
   *              If any error occurs while writing.
   */
  public void complete() throws IOException
  {
    if (this.boundary != null)
    {
      boundary();
      writeln("--");
      this.os.flush();
    }
  }

  /**
   * Generate a multipart form boundary.
   *
   * @throws IOException
   *              If any error occurs while writing.
   */
  private void boundary() throws IOException
  {
    write("--");
    write(this.boundary);
```

```
}

/**
 * Create a new line by displaying a carriage return and
 * linefeed.
 *
 * @throws IOException
 *             If any error occurs while writing.
 */
private void newline() throws IOException
{
  write("\r\n");
}

/**
 * Write the specified string, without a carriage return
 * and line feed.
 *
 * @param str
 *           The String to write.
 * @throws IOException
 *             If any error occurs while writing.
 */
private void write(String str) throws IOException
{
  this.os.write(str.getBytes());
}

/**
 * Write the name element for a multipart post.
 *
 * @param name
 *           The name of the field.
 * @throws IOException
 *             If any error occurs while writing.
 */
private void writeName(String name) throws IOException
{
  newline();
  write("Content-Disposition: form-data; name=\"");
  write(name);
  write("\"");
}

/**
 * Write a string, with a carriage return and linefeed.
```

```
 *
 * @param str
 *           The string to write.
 * @throws IOException
 *             If any error occurs while writing.
 */
protected void writeln(String str) throws IOException
{
  write(str);
  newline();
}

}
```

The next few sections will demonstrate how the **FormUtility** class was constructed. If you are only interested in using the **FormUtility** class, and not with how it works internally, you can safely skip to the recipes.

There are three main features of the **FormUtility** class.

- Add a name-value pair
- Add a file
- Parse a query string

The next three sections will show how each of these features are implemented.

### Add a Name-Value Pair

Adding a name-value pair is a very common operation performed for a form. Every form control results in a name-value pair. Adding a name-value pair is accomplished by calling the **add** method.

The format for a name-value pair is very different when posting using a multipart form compared to a regular form. Therefore, the first thing that the **add** method does, is to determine if this is a multipart response. If the boundary variable is not **null**, then this is a multipart request.

```
if (boundary != null)
{
```

Next, the boundary and name are written.

```
boundary();
writeName(name);
newline();
newline();
writeln(value);
```

If the boundary variable was **null**, meaning this is not a multipart response, then we must check to see if this is the first name-value pair. If it is not the first name-value pair, then an ampersand should be appended.

```
} else
{
if (!first)
  write("&");
```

Next, we encode both the name and value. The name and value are written, separated by an equal sign.

```
  write(encode(name));
  write("=");
  write(encode(value));
}
```

Now that we have completed the first name-value pair, we can set the **first** variable to false.

```
first = false;
```

The name-value pair has now been completed. The **add** method can be called again to add another name-value pair.

### Add a File

Name-value pairs are not the only data that you may respond to a form with. If this is a multipart response, then you can also respond with files. There is an overloaded version of the **add** method that accepts a "File" object.

First, the **add** method makes sure that this is a multipart response. If this is a multipart response, then the boundary variable will not be **null**. If you call the file version of **add** on a non-multipart response, the method call will be ignored.

```
if (boundary != null)
{
```

First, a boundary line is written. Next, the field name is written followed by the filename. To see exactly what this line looks like when written out, refer to the section, earlier in this chapter, about the multipart **POST**.

```
boundary();
writeName(name);
write("; filename=\"");
write(file.getName());
write("\"");
newline();
```

After the name line has been written, the **Content-Type** should be written. The Java function **guessContentTypeFromName** is used to attempt to determine the content type. This function works by looking at the extension and mapping well-known extensions to their proper MIME type. If a MIME type cannot be found, then the MIME type of **application/octet-stream** is used. This type indicates that the file is simply a stream of binary data.

```
write("Content-Type: ");
String type = URLConnection.guessContentTypeFromName(file.get-
Name());
if (type == null)
  type = "application/octet-stream";
writeln(type);
newline();
```

Once the content type has been written, it is time to write the file. The file is transferred byte-by-byte. No data transformation takes place.

First, several variables are set up to transfer the file. A buffer is then created to hold blocks of data. The variable **nread** tracks the amount of data being read.

```
byte[] buf = new byte[8192];
int nread;
```

Once the buffer is established, the file is opened and copied to the output stream.

```
InputStream in = new FileInputStream(file);
while ((nread = in.read(buf, 0, buf.length)) >= 0)
{
  os.write(buf, 0, nread);
}
```

Once the file has been written, add a blank line.

```
  newline();
}
```

These two overloaded versions of the **add** method allow you to add both files and regular fields.

### Parse a Query String

The previous two methods we examined allow you to create a form response. The **parse** method does the opposite. The parse function allows you to parse a name-value pair string and extract values. A common use of this, is when your bot must examine a URL returned by the web server, and extract variables from that URL.

To use this method, we must pass the **parse** function a string containing the name-value pairs, and it will return them parsed as a **Map** object.

This function begins by creating a **Map** object to hold the results. Next, the incoming data is fed to a **StringTokenizer** to parse on ampersands (&).

```
Map<String,String> result = new HashMap<String,String>();
StringTokenizer tok = new StringTokenizer(form,"&");
```

As the **StringTokenizer** parses the ampersands the program loops through all of the tokens. Each token is split into the name and value by parsing on the equal sign that separates the name from the value.

```
while(tok.hasMoreTokens())
{
String str = tok.nextToken();
StringTokenizer tok2 = new StringTokenizer(str,"=");
if(!tok2.hasMoreTokens())
continue;
```

To begin this process, first the **name** is parsed, using a second **StringTokenizer**.

```
String left = tok2.nextToken();
if(!tok2.hasMoreTokens())
{
  left = encode(left);
  result.put(left,null);
  continue;
}
```

Once the name has been parsed, the value is parsed.

```
  String right = tok2.nextToken();
  right = encode(right);
  result.put(left, right);
}
```

Finally, once complete, the **result** map is returned.

```
return result;
```

Using this map, your applications can quickly lookup values.

## Recipes

This chapter includes three recipes. These recipes demonstrate how to process a variety of different HTML forms. Specifically, you will see how to process each of the following form operations:

- Send an HTTP **GET** form response
- Send an HTTP **POST** form response
- Send a file with a multipart form

All of the recipes in this chapter will make use of the form processing class that was described in the first part of this chapter. We will begin with the first recipe, which shows you how to process an HTTP **GET**.

## Recipe #7.1: Using HTTP GET Forms

The first recipe shows how to access a web site and search. The form allows the user to search the US states and capitals. You can see this page at the following URL:

**http://www.httprecipes.com/1/7/get.php**

This page displays a simple form that allows the user to enter a search string and choose if they are searching states or capitals. You can see this recipe in Listing 7.2.

### Listing 7.2: Using HTTP GET (FormGet.java)

```java
package com.heatonresearch.httprecipes.ch7.recipe1;

import java.io.*;
import java.net.*;
import com.heatonresearch.httprecipes.html.*;

public class FormGET
{

  /**
   * Advance to the specified HTML tag.
   * @param parse The HTML parse object to use.
   * @param tag The HTML tag.
   * @param count How many tags like this to find.
   * @return True if found, false otherwise.
   * @throws IOException If an exception occurs while reading.
   */
  private boolean advance(ParseHTML parse, String tag, int count)
      throws IOException
  {
    int ch;
    while ((ch = parse.read()) != -1)
    {
      if (ch == 0)
      {
        if (parse.getTag().getName().equalsIgnoreCase(tag))
        {
          count--;
          if (count <= 0)
            return true;
        }
```

```
    }
  }
  return false;
}

/**
 * Handle each list item, as it is found.
 * @param item The item to be processed.
 */
private void processItem(String item)
{
  System.out.println(item.trim());
}

/**
 * Access the website and perform a search for either
 * states or capitals.
 * @param search A search string.
 * @param type What to search for(s=state, c=capital)
 * @throws IOException Thrown if an IO exception occurs.
 */
public void process(String search, String type)
  throws IOException
{
  String listType = "ul";
  String listTypeEnd = "/ul";
  StringBuilder buffer = new StringBuilder();
  boolean capture = false;

  // build the URL
  ByteArrayOutputStream bos = new ByteArrayOutputStream();
  FormUtility form = new FormUtility(bos, null);
  form.add("search", search);
  form.add("type", type);
  form.add("action", "Search");
  form.complete();

  String surl = "http://www.httprecipes.com/1/7/get.php?" +
    bos.toString();
  URL url = new URL(surl);
  InputStream is = url.openStream();
  ParseHTML parse = new ParseHTML(is);

  // parse from the URL

  advance(parse, listType, 0);
```

```java
    int ch;
    while ((ch = parse.read()) != -1)
    {
      if (ch == 0)
      {
        HTMLTag tag = parse.getTag();
        if (tag.getName().equalsIgnoreCase("li"))
        {
          if (buffer.length() > 0)
            processItem(buffer.toString());
          buffer.setLength(0);
          capture = true;
        } else if (tag.getName().equalsIgnoreCase("/li"))
        {
          processItem(buffer.toString());
          buffer.setLength(0);
          capture = false;
        } else if (tag.getName().equalsIgnoreCase(listTypeEnd))
        {
          processItem(buffer.toString());
          break;
        }
      } else
      {
        if (capture)
          buffer.append((char) ch);
      }
    }
  }

  /**
   * The main method, create a new instance of the object and call
   * process.
   * @param args not used.
   */
  public static void main(String args[])
  {
    try
    {
      FormGET parse = new FormGET();
      parse.process("Mi", "s");
    } catch (Exception e)
    {
      e.printStackTrace();
    }
```

```
    }
}
```

The **process** method of this recipe performs most of the actual work of submitting the form and processing the response. Two parameters are passed to the process method: the first is the search string to use and the second indicates whether we will be doing a state search or a capital search.

The **process** method begins by setting up several variables that will be needed. The states or capitals returned from the search will be in an HTML list. So the starting and ending tags, which in this case are **<ul>** and **</ul>** are stored in the variables **listType** and **listTypeEnd**. Additionally, a **StringBuilder**, named **buffer** is created to hold the HTML text as it is encountered. The **boolean** capture variable indicates if text is currently being captured to the **StringBuilder**.

```
String listType = "ul";
String listTypeEnd = "/ul";
StringBuilder buffer = new StringBuilder();
boolean capture = false;
```

The **FormUtility** class is designed to output to an **OutputStream**. For an HTTP **POST** response, this would be fine. However, since this is an HTTP **GET** request the form data must be encoded into the URL. To do this, we create a **ByteArrayOutputStream**. This stream will allow the **FormUtility** to output the form data to an **OutputStream**, and once it's done we can obtain the formatted name-value pairs.

The three calls to the add method below, set up the different required name-value pairs for the form.

```
// Build the URL.
ByteArrayOutputStream bos = new ByteArrayOutputStream();
FormUtility form = new FormUtility(bos, null);
form.add("search", search);
form.add("type", type);
form.add("action", "Search");
form.complete();
```

Next, the URL must be constructed. The URL is constructed by concatenating the output from the **ByteArrayOutputStream** to the base URL. The URL can then be opened and downloaded. A **ParseHTML** object is then created to parse the HTML.

```
String surl = "http://www.httprecipes.com/1/7/get.php?" + bos.to-
String();
URL url = new URL(surl);
InputStream is = url.openStream();
ParseHTML parse = new ParseHTML(is);
```

With the **ParseHTML** object set up, we can advance to the beginning of the HTML list. The **advance** method was covered in Chapter 6, "Extracting Data".

```
// Parse from the URL.

advance(parse, listType, 0);
```

Now, the HTML will be parsed. Begin looping through, reading each character. When an HTML tag is located, examine it to determine what it is.

```
int ch;
while ((ch = parse.read()) != -1)
{
  if (ch == 0)
  {
    HTMLTag tag = parse.getTag();
```

If the tag is an **<li>** tag, then we have found one of the result items. If there was already data in the buffer, then process it as a valid state or capital.

```
if (tag.getName().equalsIgnoreCase("li"))
{
  if (buffer.length() > 0)
  processItem(buffer.toString());
buffer.setLength(0);
capture = true;
```

Many web sites do not include ending **</li>** items. However, if they are present, then stop capturing text. Process any text already captured as a valid state or capital.

```
} else if (tag.getName().equalsIgnoreCase("/li"))
{
processItem(buffer.toString());
buffer.setLength(0);
capture = false;
```

If the end of the list has been found, then stop processing states and capitals.

```
} else if (tag.getName().equalsIgnoreCase(listTypeEnd))
{
processItem(buffer.toString());
break;
}
```

If the character found was a regular character, and not a tag, then append it to the **StringBuilder**.

```
} else
{
  if (capture)
    buffer.append((char) ch);
}
```

This recipe shows how to access data through an HTTP **GET**. Many web sites make use of HTTP **GET**. In fact, most search engines use HTTP **GET** from their main page.

### Recipe #7.2: Using HTTP POST Forms

The second recipe shows how to access an HTTP **POST** form. The form allows the user to search the US states and capitals, in the same way as Recipe 7.1. You can see this page at the following URL:

**http://www.httprecipes.com/1/7/post.php**

This page displays a simple form that allows the user to enter a search string and select if it is searching states or capitals. You can see this recipe in Listing 7.3.

### Listing 7.3: Using HTTP POST (FormPost.java)

```java
package com.heatonresearch.httprecipes.ch7.recipe2;

import java.io.*;
import java.net.*;

import com.heatonresearch.httprecipes.html.*;

public class FormPOST
{

  /** Advance to the specified HTML tag.
   * @param parse The HTML parse object to use.
   * @param tag The HTML tag.
   * @param count How many tags like this to find.
   * @return True if found, false otherwise.
   * @throws IOException If an exception occurs while reading.
   */
  private boolean advance(ParseHTML parse, String tag, int count)
      throws IOException
  {
    int ch;
    while ((ch = parse.read()) != -1)
    {
      if (ch == 0)
      {
        if (parse.getTag().getName().equalsIgnoreCase(tag))
        {
          count--;
          if (count <= 0)
            return true;
        }
      }
    }
    return false;
```

```java
  }

  /*
   * Handle each list item, as it is found.
   */
  private void processItem(String item)
  {
    System.out.println(item.trim());
  }

  /**
   * Access the website and perform a search for either
   * states or capitals.
   * @param search A search string.
   * @param type What to search for(s=state, c=capital)
   * @throws IOException Thrown if an IO exception occurs.
   */
  public void process(String search, String type)
    throws IOException
  {
    String listType = "ul";
    String listTypeEnd = "/ul";
    StringBuilder buffer = new StringBuilder();
    boolean capture = false;

    // build the URL and POST
    URL url = new URL("http://www.httprecipes.com/1/7/post.php");
    URLConnection http = url.openConnection();
    http.setDoOutput(true);
    OutputStream os = http.getOutputStream();

    FormUtility form = new FormUtility(os, null);
    form.add("search", search);
    form.add("type", type);
    form.add("action", "Search");
    form.complete();

    // read the results
    InputStream is = http.getInputStream();
    ParseHTML parse = new ParseHTML(is);

    // parse from the URL

    advance(parse, listType, 0);

    int ch;
```

```java
    while ((ch = parse.read()) != -1)
    {
      if (ch == 0)
      {
        HTMLTag tag = parse.getTag();
        if (tag.getName().equalsIgnoreCase("li"))
        {
          if (buffer.length() > 0)
            processItem(buffer.toString());
          buffer.setLength(0);
          capture = true;
        } else if (tag.getName().equalsIgnoreCase("/li"))
        {
          processItem(buffer.toString());
          buffer.setLength(0);
          capture = false;
        } else if (tag.getName().equalsIgnoreCase(listTypeEnd))
        {
          processItem(buffer.toString());
          break;
        }
      } else
      {
        if (capture)
          buffer.append((char) ch);
      }
    }
  }

  /**
   * The main method, create a new instance of the object and call
   * process.
   * @param args not used.
   */
  public static void main(String args[])
  {
    try
    {
      FormPOST parse = new FormPOST();
      parse.process("Mi", "s");
    } catch (Exception e)
    {
      e.printStackTrace();
    }
  }
}
```

This recipe is very similar to Recipe 7.1. The only difference is that this recipe uses HTTP **POST** and the previous recipe uses HTTP **GET**. Only the changes necessary to change to HTTP **POST** will be covered here. For information on how this recipe parses the results, refer to Recipe 7.1.

The **process** method for the recipe begins by building a URL object for the target page.

```
// Build the URL and POST.
URL url = new URL("http://www.httprecipes.com/1/7/post.php");
```

Next, a **URLConnection** is opened. The **setDoOutput** method call specifies that this will be an HTTP **POST**. An **OutputStream** is then opened.

```
URLConnection http = url.openConnection();
http.setDoOutput(true);
OutputStream os = http.getOutputStream();
```

The **OutputStream** object is passed to the **FormUtility** constructor. The form data will be output to that stream.

```
FormUtility form = new FormUtility(os, null);
form.add("search", search);
form.add("type", type);
form.add("action", "Search");
form.complete();
```

Once all of the data has been sent for the form, a call to the **complete** method finishes the transaction. Next, the resulting HTML will be parsed. Parsing the resulting HTML is handled exactly as in Recipe 7.1.

### Recipe #7.3: Using Multipart Forms to Upload

The third recipe shows how to upload a file to a form, using HTTP upload. The form allows the user to upload a file to the HTTP recipes website. You can see this page at the following URL:

**http://www.httprecipes.com/1/7/uploadmenu.php**

From this page you have two options:

- Upload a file
- Check the status of a previous upload

You should begin by uploading a file. When you upload a file, you should supply a user id and password. This will allow you to check the status of the upload later using the second option. For security reasons, the files that you upload are immediately deleted. However, their size and type are recorded under your user name and password. This allows you to check to see that your upload was successful.

This recipe must be provided with a user id, password and the file you want to upload. The following command is an example of how to launch the recipe.

```
FormUpload userid password c:\myfile.txt
```

The above command simply shows the abstract format to call this recipe, with the appropriate parameters. For exact information on how to run this recipe refer to Appendix B, C, or D, depending on the operating system you are using. Once you have uploaded your file, you should check to see the status of the file upload. You can do this by selecting the "Check the status of a previous upload" option on the previously mentioned URL. After you enter your user ID and password you will see a page similar to Figure 7.4.

### Figure 7.4: A Successful Upload

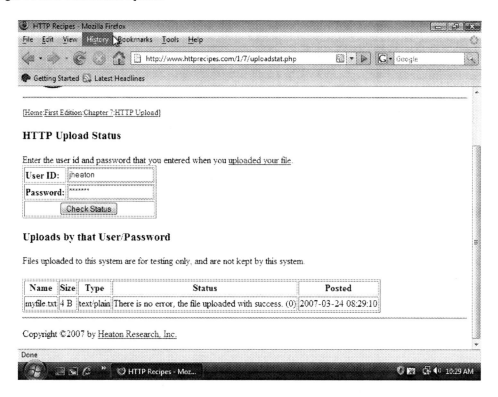

We will now examine how to implement this recipe. You can see this recipe in Listing 7.4.

### Listing 7.4: Using Multipart Forms to Upload (FormUpload.java)

```
package com.heatonresearch.httprecipes.ch7.recipe3;

import java.io.*;
import java.net.*;
```

```
import com.heatonresearch.httprecipes.html.FormUtility;

public class FormUpload
{

  /**
   * Upload a file.
   * @param uid The user id for the form.
   * @param pwd The password for the form.
   * @param file The file to upload.
   * @throws IOException Thrown if any I/O error occurs.
   */
  public void upload(String uid, String pwd, File file)
throws IOException
  {
    // get the boundary used for the multipart upload
    String boundary = FormUtility.getBoundary();
    URLConnection http =
      (new URL("http://www.httprecipes.com/1/7/uploader.php"))
        .openConnection();
    http.setDoOutput(true);
    // specify that we will use a multipart form
    http.setRequestProperty(
      "Content-Type", "multipart/form-data; boundary="
        + boundary);
    OutputStream os = http.getOutputStream();
    // construct a form
    FormUtility form = new FormUtility(os, boundary);
    form.add("uid", uid);
    form.add("pwd", pwd);
    form.add("uploadedfile", file);
    form.complete();
    // perform the upload
    InputStream is = http.getInputStream();
    is.close();
  }

  /**
   * The main method attempts to obtain the user id, password
   * and local filename for the upload.
   * @param args The user id, password and local filename.
   */
  public static void main(String args[])
  {
    try
    {
```

```
      String uid = "";
      String pwd = "";
      String filename = "";

      if (args.length < 3)
      {
        System.out.println("Usage:");
        System.out.println(
"java FormUpload [User ID] [Password] [File to upload]");
      } else
      {
        uid = args[0];
        pwd = args[1];
        filename = args[2];

        FormUpload upload = new FormUpload();
        upload.upload(uid, pwd, new File(filename));
      }
    } catch (IOException e)
    {
      e.printStackTrace();
    }
  }
}
```

Most of the work done by this recipe is done inside of the **FormUtility** class. If you would like to review how any of the methods and functions used in this recipe work, review the section "Multipart Post", from earlier in this chapter.

This recipe starts out by creating a boundary. The boundary is just a random string of characters that is used to separate the different parts of the multipart response.

```
// Get the boundary used for the multipart upload.
String boundary = FormUtility.getBoundary();
```

A connection is opened to the URL that will receive the multipart response.

```
URLConnection http = (new URL("http://www.httprecipes.com/1/7/up-
loader.php"))
.openConnection();
```

Because this is going to be an HTTP **POST** we set the "do output" option to true. We also construct the **Content-Type** header to specify that this will be a multipart response. The boundary is specified inside of the **Content-Type** header.

```
http.setDoOutput(true);
// Specify that we will use a multipart form.
http.setRequestProperty("Content-Type", "multipart/form-data;
boundary="
```

```
+ boundary);
```

An **OutputStream** object is obtained and we construct a new **FormUtility** object. Notice that a boundary is specified on the constructor to the **FormUtility** object. This tells the **FormUtility** object that this is going to be a multipart response. Additionally, the user id and password are added to the form. The names "uid" and "pwd" are the names of the **<input>** tags that the user would normally enter their user id and password into.

```
OutputStream os = http.getOutputStream();
// Construct a form.
FormUtility form = new FormUtility(os, boundary);
form.add("uid", uid);
form.add("pwd", pwd);
```

Next, the actual file is added to the form. This version of the **add** method of the **FormUtility** class takes care of all that is necessary to transmit the file. Finally, the **complete** method is called to complete building the form.

```
form.add("uploadedfile", file);
form.complete();
```

Next, the **InputStream** is obtained and the request is transmitted. The **InputStream** object is immediately closed; we do not care about the response from the upload page.

```
// Perform the upload.
InputStream is = http.getInputStream();
is.close();
```

This recipe can be adapted to any case where you need to upload a file. The **FormUtility** class, used by this recipe, is a short utility class that was introduced earlier in this chapter.

## Summary

Forms are a very common part of many web sites. Most bot programs will have to deal with forms. Forms can be transmitted to the web server in three ways: HTTP **GET**, HTTP **POST** and multipart **POST**.

A form can be sent back to the web server using the HTTP **GET** method. HTTP **GET** places all of the name-value pairs from the form's data onto the URL. When a web site uses HTTP **GET** for a form, the user can see all of their input on the URL line of the browser.

A form can also be sent back to the web server using the HTTP **POST** method. HTTP **POST** sends the data as part of the HTTP packet, and it is not visible to the user. Because the data does not all need to fit onto a URL, much larger amounts of data can be sent with HTTP **POST**.

Finally, a form can also be sent as a multipart **POST**. A multipart **POST** is very useful when you need to send a file back to the web server. Multipart forms are used by many websites when a file is to be uploaded. Though this is by far the least used of the form response types, you will need to make use of it if your bot needs to upload a file.

So far, all of the bots presented have been stateless; that is, the bot can simply jump to the page and retrieve the data. Very often a web server will require you to create a session before you can access any data. Creating a session is usually as easy as logging onto the system. Chapter 8 will show you how to login to websites and handle sessions.

# CHAPTER 8: HANDLING SESSIONS AND COOKIES

- Understanding Sessions
- Using URL Variables to Maintain Sessions
- Using Cookies to Maintain Sessions

State management is a very important concept for many web sites. If a website is to allow a user to log into the system, and present pages customized to that user, state management must be used. State management allows the web server to remember things from one page request to the next.

Consider the example of a user logging onto a system. Once the user has logged onto the system, the system must remember who is logged on. This is called state. Rather than just sending web pages blindly, the web server now knows who the pages are going to. This allows the web server to customize these pages for each user, or perhaps block access to the pages depending on the user.

To access a site, such as this, programmatically requires extra consideration. The program must first login to the website and establish state. To support such a site, a program must be designed to implement state in the way that the target web site expects. There are several ways that web sites implement state; however, most sites fall into one of two categories:

- State through URL Variables
- State through Cookies

Both methods are very common. This chapter will cover both methods and provide a recipe for each.

## URL Variables for State

A very simple way to maintain state is to use the URL line. By placing a variable on the URL that always holds the current state, you can identify who is logged on. It is considered a bad idea to just place the user name on the URL line. So you will not likely see a URL like the following:

```
http://www.httprecipes.com/1/test.php?user=joe
```

This would be terribly insecure. A user would simply have to change the URL line and they could instantly become any user they liked. Usually a session number will be used instead. Consider the following URL:

`http://www.httprecipes.com/1/8/cookieless.php`

This URL presents a login page, as seen in Figure 8.1.

**Figure 8.1: A Login Page**

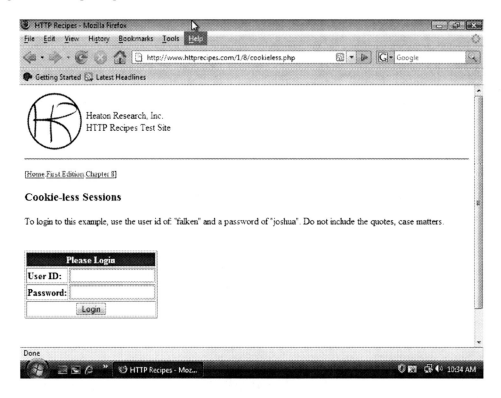

To login to the system, enter the user id of "falken" and the password of "joshua". You will then be taken to a search page. This search page is only available from inside of the web site. You must login to access this page. However, notice the URL. It is now much longer, and will be something similar to:

`http://www.httprecipes.com/1/8/menunc.php?session=9pwoditnygyyvot9`
`7k2jexx8oakelnvz`

This URL specifies a session. A session is usually nothing more than a row in the web server's database that links a session string, as seen above, to a user. The only way to imitate another user, is to try and pick the session number for another user that is currently logged into the system. This will usually not work either, because the web server usually also stores the IP address associated with a session. As a result, if another user tries to hijack a session, the IP addresses will be different, and the attack will be thwarted.

There is nothing special about the session id that you see above. There are no hidden meanings behind the stream of letters and numbers that you see. The session id was randomly created to serve as a unique identifier.

A session is assigned after a successful user login. The session will remain with the user until he logs off the system. If the user does not log off the system, their session will usually expire in some preset time. Having their session expire is no real problem to the user, they are simply asked to re-login to the system.

You have likely already seen session timeouts while using the web. Consider when you log into a web server to check your mail, and then leave the window open overnight. When you try to use the window again in the morning, you will likely be told that you session has "timed out". This is because too much time elapsed, and the web server deleted your session.

When a website uses sessions through the URL, the session variable must be passed to every page on the website. You will always see the session id at the top of the page. If you remove the session part of the URL, or modify it slightly, the site will immediately take you back to the login page. Without a valid session id, you cannot use the site.

One limitation of using the URL to maintain state, is that the session id must be placed on every link generated by the site. Because of this, if even one page removes the session id, the session will be lost. Additionally, if the user temporarily closes the browser, and returns to the site, the state is also lost. If the user types in the session id as part of the URL when they attempt to re-access the site, the state would not be lost; however, this is not likely to be the case.

## Cookies for State

A session id on the URL line is not the only way to maintain state. Cookies can also be used to maintain state. Cookies are different from using the URL to maintain state, in that cookies are invisible to the user. Cookies are stored as part of the request and response headers. Cookies are nothing more than name value pairs. Cookies exist within a specified domain and no two cookies in the same domain can have the same name.

To see cookies in action visit the following URL:

`http://www.httprecipes.com/1/8/cookie.php`

When you access this page you will see a form that allows you to login. To use this form, you should login with the user ID of "falken" and the password of "joshua". Once you are logged in, a cookie will be established with your browser. You will not be able to see this cookie. The cookie is contained inside of the headers of both the request and the response. To see how the cookie is created, we must examine the response that the server sends back when you login to the site. You can see this response here:

```
HTTP/1.1 302 Found
Date: Thu, 31 Aug 2006 23:39:07 GMT
Server: Apache/2.0.40 (Red Hat Linux)
Accept-Ranges: bytes
X-Powered-By: PHP/4.3.2
Set-Cookie: hri-cookie=42252vvf5x4d5d69xq1ub653ltnh9xo7
Location: menuc.php
Content-Length: 0
Connection: close
Content-Type: text/html
```

Notice the cookie? When the server wants to create a cookie, the server returns the **Set-Cookie** header. This specifies that the cookie named **hri-cookie** has the value **42252vvf5x4d5d69xq1ub653ltnh9xo7**.

This tells the browser to always include this cookie in future requests. For example, if you were to perform a search while logged in, your HTTP POST request would look like this:

```
POST /1/8/menuc.php HTTP/1.1
Accept: image/gif, image/x-xbitmap, image/jpeg, image/pjpeg, ap-
plication/x-shockwave-flash, */*
Referer: http://www.httprecipes.com/1/8/menuc.php
Accept-Language: en-us
Content-Type: application/x-www-form-urlencoded
Accept-Encoding: gzip, deflate
User-Agent: Mozilla/4.0 (compatible; MSIE 6.0; Windows NT 5.1;
SV1; .NET CLR 1.1.4322; .NET CLR 2.0.50727)
Host: www.httprecipes.com
Content-Length: 32
Connection: Keep-Alive
Cache-Control: no-cache
Cookie: hri-cookie=42252vvf5x4d5d69xq1ub653ltnh9xo7

search=Miss&type=s&action=Search
```

As you can see, the browser is now sending the cookie back as a request header. When the server requests a cookie, the **Set-Cookie** header is used; when the browser sends this cookie back, the **Cookie** header is used.

## Processing Cookies

The recipes in this chapter will make use of a simple class named **CookieUtility** to process cookies. Any recipe in this book that makes use of cookies will also use this class. In this section, you will see how the **CookieUtility** class was constructed. The **CookieUtility** class is shown in Listing 8.1.

**Listing 8.1: Cookie Utility (CookieUtility.java)**

```java
package com.heatonresearch.httprecipes.html;

import java.net.*;
import java.util.*;

public class CookieUtility
{
  /*
   * Map that holds all of the cookie values.
   */
  private Map<String, String> map = new HashMap<String, String>();

  /**
   * Allows access to the name/value pair list of cookies.
   *
   * @return the map
   */
  public Map<String, String> getMap()
  {
    return this.map;
  }

  /**
   * Load any cookies from the specified URLConnection
   * object. Cookies will be located by their Set-Cookie
   * headers. Any cookies that are found can be moved to a
   * new URLConnection class by calling saveCookies.
   *
   * @param http
   *            The URLConnection object to load the cookies
   *            from.
   */
  public void loadCookies(URLConnection http)
  {
    String str;
    int n = 1;

    do
    {
      str = http.getHeaderFieldKey(n);
      if ((str != null) && str.equalsIgnoreCase("Set-Cookie"))
      {
        str = http.getHeaderField(n);
```

```
          StringTokenizer tok = new StringTokenizer(str, "=");
          String name = tok.nextToken();
          String value = tok.nextToken();
          this.map.put(name, value);
        }
      n++;
    } while (str != null);
  }


  /**
   * Once you have loaded cookies with loadCookies, you can
   * call saveCookies to copy these cookies to a new HTTP
   * request. This allows you to easily support cookies.
   *
   * @param http
   *            The URLConnection object to add cookies to.
   */
  public void saveCookies(URLConnection http)
  {
    StringBuilder str = new StringBuilder();

    Set<String> set = this.map.keySet();
    for (String key : set)
    {
      String value = this.map.get(key);
      if (str.length() > 0)
      {
        str.append("; ");
      }

      str.append(key + "=" + value);
    }

    http.setRequestProperty("Cookie", str.toString());
  }
}
```

The **CookieUtility** class is essentially a collection. It loads cookies from HTTP server responses and then attaches them to outbound browser requests.

### Reading Cookies from the Server

To support cookies from your bot, you should call the **loadCookies** method of the **CookieUtility** class. The **loadCookies** method will scan the **URLConnection** object and extract the cookies from any **Set-Cookie** headers found. The **loadCookies** method begins by declaring a few needed variables.

The **str** variable will hold the header names as they are read in. The variable **n** will keep count of which header we are currently processing.

```
String str;
int n = 1;
```

The **do/while** loop will look until a **null** header is found. A **null** header indicates that there are no more headers to read. Each header is read and checked to see if it is a **Set-Cookie** header.

```
do
{
  str = http.getHeaderFieldKey(n);
  if( (str!=null) && str.equalsIgnoreCase("Set-Cookie"))
  {
```

If it is a **Set-Cookie** header, then the cookie is parsed and saved in cookie map. The cookie map is a Java **Map** collection that maps cookie names to their values.

```
  str = http.getHeaderField(n);
  StringTokenizer tok = new StringTokenizer(str,"=");
  String name = tok.nextToken();
  String value = tok.nextToken();
  map.put(name, value);
}
```

Next, the **loadCookies** method moves on to the next header.

```
  n++;
} while(str!=null);
```

This process continues until all headers have been processed.

### Sending Cookies from the Browser

Once the cookies have been loaded by the **loadCookies** method, they must be attached to future server requests. This is the job of the **saveCookies** method. The cookie name-value pairs for a given site will be concatenated together. The **saveCookies** method begins by declaring a **StringBuilder** that will hold the Cookie header until it is completely constructed.

```
StringBuilder str = new StringBuilder();
```

Next, we iterate over all of the cookie names. As the "for each" loop passes over each cookie in the collection the **key** variable will hold each cookie's name.

```
Set<String> set = map.keySet();
for(String key:set)
{
```

The value of that cookie is then looked up. If this is not the first name-value pair written to the **StringBuilder**, then append a semicolon (;) to the **StringBuilder** before the next name-value pair is added. A semicolon is used to separate individual cookies.

```
String value = map.get(key);
if( str.length()>0 )
{
  str.append("; ");
}
```

Next, the cookie name-value pair is appended to the **StringBuilder**.

```
  str.append(key+"="+value);
}
```

Finally, the Cookie header is added to the **URLConnection** object, which is named **http**.

```
http.setRequestProperty("Cookie", str.toString());
```

By using the **loadCookies** and **saveCookies** methods, you can easily add cookie support to your bots.

## Recipes

This chapter includes two recipes. These recipes demonstrate how to process a variety of different HTML forms. Specifically, you will see how to process each of the following form types:

- Cookieless Session
- Cookie Based Session

We will begin with the first recipe, which shows how to process a session without the use of cookies.

### Recipe #8.1: A Cookieless Session

This recipe shows how to manage a session using only the URL. No cookies are used to maintain state. This recipe shows how to login to a simple system and perform a basic search. This recipe will access the following URL:

**http://www.httprecipes.com/1/8/cookieless.php**

This recipe must go through several steps to get the data requested. First, it must login to the system and obtain a session. Next, it must submit the search. Finally, it must parse the results of the search. These steps are summarized in Table 8.1.

**Table 8.1: Extracting from Cookieless Session**

| Step | Function |
|------|----------|
| Step 1. | Post login information to http://www.httprecipes.com/1/8/cookieless.php |
| Step 2: | Extract session id from http://www.httprecipes.com/1/8/menunc. php?session=[Session id] |
| Step 3. | Be redirected to Post search to http://www.httprecipes.com/1/8/menunc. php?session=[Session id] |
| Step 4. | Parse search results |

This recipe is shown in Listing 8.2.

**Listing 8.2: Cookieless Session (Cookieless.java)**

```java
package com.heatonresearch.httprecipes.ch8.recipe1;

import java.io.*;
import java.net.*;
import java.util.*;

import com.heatonresearch.httprecipes.html.*;

public class Cookieless
{
  /**
   * This method is called to log into the system and return
   * a session id.  Once you have the session ID you can call
   * the search function to perform searches.
   * @param uid The user id to use for login.
   * @param pwd The password to use for login.
   * @return The session id if login was successful, null if
   * it was not.
   * @throws IOException If an exception occurs while reading.
   */
  private String login(String uid, String pwd) throws IOException
  {
    URL url =
      new URL("http://www.httprecipes.com/1/8/cookieless.php");
    URLConnection http = url.openConnection();
    http.setDoOutput(true);
    OutputStream os = http.getOutputStream();
    FormUtility form = new FormUtility(os, null);
    form.add("uid", uid);
    form.add("pwd", pwd);
    form.add("action", "Login");
```

```java
      form.complete();
      http.getInputStream();
      String query = http.getURL().getQuery();
      if (query != null)
      {
        Map<String, String> map = FormUtility.parse(query);
        return map.get("session");
      } else
        return null;
  }


  /** Advance to the specified HTML tag.
   * @param parse The HTML parse object to use.
   * @param tag The HTML tag.
   * @param count How many tags like this to find.
   * @return True if found, false otherwise.
   * @throws IOException If an exception occurs while reading.
   */
  private boolean advance(ParseHTML parse, String tag, int count)
        throws IOException
  {
    int ch;
    while ((ch = parse.read()) != -1)
    {
      if (ch == 0)
      {
        if (parse.getTag().getName().equalsIgnoreCase(tag))
        {
          count--;
          if (count <= 0)
            return true;
        }
      }
    }
    return false;
  }


  /**
   * Use the session to search for the specified state or
   * capital.  The search
   * method can be called multiple times per login.
   * @param session The session to use.
   * @param search The search string to use.
   * @param type What to search for(s=state,c=capital).
   * @return A list of states or capitals.
   * @throws IOException Thrown if a communication failure occurs
```

```java
 */
public List<String> search(String session, String search,
   String type)
      throws IOException
{
   String listType = "ul";
   String listTypeEnd = "/ul";
   StringBuilder buffer = new StringBuilder();
   boolean capture = false;
   List<String> result = new ArrayList<String>();

   // build the URL
   ByteArrayOutputStream bos = new ByteArrayOutputStream();
   FormUtility form = new FormUtility(bos, null);
   form.add("search", search);
   form.add("type", type);
   form.add("action", "Search");
   form.complete();


   URL url = new URL(
      "http://www.httprecipes.com/1/8/menunc.php?session="
         + session);
   URLConnection http = url.openConnection();
   http.setDoOutput(true);
   OutputStream os = http.getOutputStream();
   // perform the post

   os.write(bos.toByteArray());

   // read the results
   InputStream is = http.getInputStream();
   ParseHTML parse = new ParseHTML(is);

   // parse from the URL

   advance(parse, listType, 0);

   int ch;
   while ((ch = parse.read()) != -1)
   {
      if (ch == 0)
      {
         HTMLTag tag = parse.getTag();
         if (tag.getName().equalsIgnoreCase("li"))
```

```
      {
        if (buffer.length() > 0)
          result.add(buffer.toString());
        buffer.setLength(0);
        capture = true;
      } else if (tag.getName().equalsIgnoreCase("/li"))
      {
        result.add(buffer.toString());
        buffer.setLength(0);
        capture = false;
      } else if (tag.getName().equalsIgnoreCase(listTypeEnd))
      {
        result.add(buffer.toString());
        break;
      }
    } else
    {
      if (capture)
        buffer.append((char) ch);
    }
  }

  return result;
}

/**
 * Called to login to the site and download a list of
 * states or capitals.
 * @param uid The user id to use for login.
 * @param pwd The password to use for login.
 * @param search The search string to use.
 * @param type What to search for(s=state,c=capital).
 * @throws IOException Thrown if a communication failure occurs
 */
public void process(String uid, String pwd,
  String search, String type)
    throws IOException
{
  String session = login(uid, pwd);
  if (session != null)
  {
    List<String> list = search(session, search, type);
    for (String item : list)
    {
      System.out.println(item);
    }
```

```
    } else
    {
      System.out.println("Error logging in.");
    }
  }

  /*
   * Simple main method to create an instance of the object and
   * call the process method.
   */
  public static void main(String args[])
  {
    try
    {
      Cookieless cookieless = new Cookieless();
      cookieless.process("falken", "joshua", "Mi", "s");
    } catch (Exception e)
    {
      e.printStackTrace();
    }
  }
}
```

There are three primary methods that are used in this recipe. The first, named **process**, manages the bot's progress and calls the other two methods. The second, named **login**, logs the user into the system. The third, called **search**, is called by the process method to perform the search.

### The Process Method

The **process** method is called by the **main** method. The **process** method is passed four parameters. The parameter **uid** specifies the user id, **pwd** specifies the password, **search** specifies what to search for and **type** specifies the type of search. Two search types are supported: a search type of "s" for states or "c" for capitols.

The **process** method begins by calling the **login** method. If the **login** method was successful, then a session id is returned. This session id will be necessary to perform the search, because the web site requires that you be logged in to perform the search.

```
String session = login(uid, pwd);
if (session != null)
{
```

If a session id was returned, then the **search** function is called. The **search** function returns a list of states that matched the search.

```
List<String> list = search(session, search, type);
for (String item : list)
```

```
{
  System.out.println(item);
}
```

If **null** was returned as the session id, then the login failed. The user id or password were likely incorrect.

```
} else
{
  System.out.println("Error logging in.");
}
```

The **process** method makes use of both the **login** function and the **search** function. The next two sections will describe how these functions work.

### Logging In

The login method is responsible for logging the user into the system and returning a session id. This method begins by posting the user id and password to the web site. To do this, a URL object is constructed to post to the login form. Since this will be a post, **setDoOutput** must be called.

```
URL url =
  new URL("http://www.httprecipes.com/1/8/cookieless.php");
URLConnection http = url.openConnection();
http.setDoOutput(true);
```

Next, an **OutputStream** is obtained to post the data to. This **OutputStream** is passed to the constructor of the **FormUtility** class. Then the user id, password and login button are all added to the form. Since submit buttons can also send data to the form, it is important to designate that the Login button is used here.

```
OutputStream os = http.getOutputStream();
FormUtility form = new FormUtility(os, null);
form.add("uid", uid);
form.add("pwd", pwd);
form.add("action", "Login");
form.complete();
```

The **InputStream** is not needed because we do not need to read any data from the form. We will get the session id from whatever page the login form redirects us to.

```
http.getInputStream();
String query = http.getURL().getQuery();
```

If there is no query string on the URL, then the login failed, and we should return **null**. Otherwise, we call the **parse** method of the **FormUtility** class to extract the **session** attribute from the URL. The **session** attribute contains the session id.

```
if (query != null)
```

```
{
  Map<String, String> map = FormUtility.parse(query);
  return map.get("session");
} else
  return null;
```

Once the session id has been obtained, the **search** function can be called.

### Performing the Search

The **search** method submits the search form and reads the results from that search. The session id must be attached to the URL that is posted to.

The **search** method begins by setting up several variables that will be needed. The states or capitals returned from the search will be in an HTML list. So the starting and ending tags, which in this case are **<ul>** and **</ul>**, are stored in the variables **listType** and **listTypeEnd**. Additionally, a **StringBuilder**, named **buffer** is created to hold the HTML text as it is encountered. The **boolean** capture variable indicates if text is currently being captured to the **StringBuilder**.

```
String listType = "ul";
String listTypeEnd = "/ul";
StringBuilder buffer = new StringBuilder();
boolean capture = false;
List<String> result = new ArrayList<String>();
```

The **FormUtility** class is designed to output to an **OutputStream**. For an HTTP POST response, this will be fine. The three calls to the add method below setup the different required name-value pairs for the form.

```
// Build the URL.
ByteArrayOutputStream bos = new ByteArrayOutputStream();
FormUtility form = new FormUtility(bos, null);
form.add("search", search);
form.add("type", type);
form.add("action", "Search");
form.complete();
```

A **URL** object is created for the form's location plus the session ID. The rest of this procedure is very similar to the list parsing example from recipes 7.1 and 7.2 in Chapter 7.

```
URL url = new URL(
  "http://www.httprecipes.com/1/8/menunc.php?session="
  + session);
URLConnection http = url.openConnection();
http.setDoOutput(true);
OutputStream os = http.getOutputStream();
```

The output from the **FormUtility** object is posted to the form. A **ParseHTML** object is setup to parse the search results.

```
// Perform the post.
os.write(bos.toByteArray());

// Read the results.
InputStream is = http.getInputStream();
ParseHTML parse = new ParseHTML(is);
```

Now the HTML will be parsed. Begin looping through, reading each character. When an HTML tag is located, examine that HTML tag to see what it is.

```
advance(parse, listType, 0);

int ch;
while ((ch = parse.read()) != -1)
{
  if (ch == 0)
  {
    HTMLTag tag = parse.getTag();
```

If the tag is an **<li>** tag, then we have found one of the result items. If there was already data in the buffer, then process it as a valid state or capital.

```
if (tag.getName().equalsIgnoreCase("li"))
{
  if (buffer.length() > 0)
    result.add(buffer.toString());
  buffer.setLength(0);
  capture = true;
```

Many web sites do not include ending **</li>** items; however, if they are present, then stop capturing text. Process any already captured text as a valid state or capitol.

```
} else if (tag.getName().equalsIgnoreCase("/li"))
{
  result.add(buffer.toString());
  buffer.setLength(0);
  capture = false;
```

If we have reached the end of the list, then there is no more data to parse.

```
} else if (tag.getName().equalsIgnoreCase(listTypeEnd))
{
  result.add(buffer.toString());
  break;
}
```

```
} else
{
```

If we are between an **<li>** and **</li>** tag, then we should be capturing text - since this is a list item, and our data is contained in the list items.

```
    if (capture)
    buffer.append((char) ch);
  }
}
```

```
return result;
```

Finally, the list of states is returned.

### Recipe #8.2: A Cookie Based Session

This recipe shows how to manage a session using cookies. Cookies are used to maintain state. This recipe shows how to login to a simple system and perform a basic search, which is the same as Recipe 8.1, except cookies are used. This recipe will access the following URL:

**http://www.httprecipes.com/1/8/cookie.php**

This recipe must go through several steps to get the data requested. First, it must login to the system and obtain a session. Next, it must submit the search. Finally, it must parse the results of the search. These steps are summarized in Table 8.2.

### Table 8.2: Extracting from Cookie Based Session

| Step | Function |
|------|----------|
| Step 1. | Post login information to http://www.httprecipes.com/1/8/cookieless.php |
| Step 2: | Extract session id from the headers returned, look for the Set-Cookie header. |
| Step 3. | Be redirected to Post search to http://www.httprecipes.com/1/8/menu.php use the cookie |
| Step 4. | Parse search results |

This recipe is shown in Listing 8.3.

### Listing 8.3: Cookie-Based Session (Cookie.java)

```
package com.heatonresearch.httprecipes.ch8.recipe2;

import java.io.*;
import java.net.*;
```

```java
import java.util.*;

import com.heatonresearch.httprecipes.html.*;

public class Cookie
{
  /*
   * Holds the cookies used to keep the session.
   */
  private CookieUtility cookies = new CookieUtility();

  /**
   * This method is called to log into the system and establish
   * the cookie.  Once the cookie is established, you can call
   * the search function to perform searches.
   * @param uid The user id to use for login.
   * @param pwd The password to use for login.
   * @return True if the login was successful.
   * @throws IOException If an exception occurs while reading.
   */
  private boolean login(String uid, String pwd) throws IOException
  {
    URL url = new URL(
      "http://www.httprecipes.com/1/8/cookie.php");
    HttpURLConnection http =
      (HttpURLConnection) url.openConnection();
    http.setInstanceFollowRedirects(false);
    http.setDoOutput(true);
    OutputStream os = http.getOutputStream();
    FormUtility form = new FormUtility(os, null);
    form.add("uid", uid);
    form.add("pwd", pwd);
    form.add("action", "Login");
    form.complete();
    http.getInputStream();

    cookies.loadCookies(http);
    return (cookies.getMap().containsKey("hri-cookie"));
  }

  /** Advance to the specified HTML tag.
   * @param parse The HTML parse object to use.
   * @param tag The HTML tag.
   * @param count How many tags like this to find.
   * @return True if found, false otherwise.
   * @throws IOException If an exception occurs while reading.
```

```java
  */
private boolean advance(ParseHTML parse, String tag, int count)
    throws IOException
{
  int ch;
  while ((ch = parse.read()) != -1)
  {
    if (ch == 0)
    {
      if (parse.getTag().getName().equalsIgnoreCase(tag))
      {
        count--;
        if (count <= 0)
          return true;
      }
    }
  }
  return false;
}


/**
 * Use the cookie to search for the specified state
 * or capital.  The search method can be called multiple
 * times per login.
 * @param search The search string to use.
 * @param type What to search for(s=state,c=capital).
 * @return A list of states or capitals.
 * @throws IOException Thrown if a communication failure occurs
 */
public List<String> search(String search, String type)
  throws IOException
{
  String listType = "ul";
  String listTypeEnd = "/ul";
  StringBuilder buffer = new StringBuilder();
  boolean capture = false;
  List<String> result = new ArrayList<String>();

  // build the URL
  ByteArrayOutputStream bos = new ByteArrayOutputStream();
  FormUtility form = new FormUtility(bos, null);
  form.add("search", search);
  form.add("type", type);
  form.add("action", "Search");
  form.complete();
```

```java
URL url = new URL("http://www.httprecipes.com/1/8/menuc.php");
URLConnection http = url.openConnection();
http.setDoOutput(true);
cookies.saveCookies(http);
OutputStream os = http.getOutputStream();
// perform the post

os.write(bos.toByteArray());

// read the results
InputStream is = http.getInputStream();
ParseHTML parse = new ParseHTML(is);

// parse from the URL

advance(parse, listType, 0);

int ch;
while ((ch = parse.read()) != -1)
{
  if (ch == 0)
  {
    HTMLTag tag = parse.getTag();
    if (tag.getName().equalsIgnoreCase("li"))
    {
      if (buffer.length() > 0)
        result.add(buffer.toString());
      buffer.setLength(0);
      capture = true;
    } else if (tag.getName().equalsIgnoreCase("/li"))
    {
      result.add(buffer.toString());
      buffer.setLength(0);
      capture = false;
    } else if (tag.getName().equalsIgnoreCase(listTypeEnd))
    {
      result.add(buffer.toString());
      break;
    }
  } else
  {
    if (capture)
      buffer.append((char) ch);
  }
}
```

```java
    return result;
  }

  /**
   * Called to login to the site and download a list of
   * states or capitals.
   * @param uid The user id to use for login.
   * @param pwd The password to use for login.
   * @param search The search string to use.
   * @param type What to search for(s=state,c=capital).
   * @throws IOException Thrown if a communication failure occurs
   */
  public void process(String uid, String pwd,
    String search, String type)
  throws IOException
  {
    if (login(uid, pwd))
    {
      List<String> list = search(search, type);
      for (String item : list)
      {
        System.out.println(item);
      }
    } else
    {
      System.out.println("Error logging in.");
    }
  }

  /*
   * Simple main method to create an instance of the object and
   * call the process method.
   */
  public static void main(String args[])
  {
    try
    {
      Cookie cookie = new Cookie();
      cookie.process("falken", "joshua", "Mi", "s");
    } catch (Exception e)
    {
      e.printStackTrace();
    }
  }
}
```

The **login** function for Recipe 8.2 is very similar to Recipe 8.1; however, cookies are used to maintain state. This recipe makes use of the **CookieUtility** class to process the cookies.

The **login** method begins by creating a URL object that will be used to perform the POST.

```
URL url = new URL("http://www.httprecipes.com/1/8/cookie.php");
HttpURLConnection http = (HttpURLConnection) url.openConnection();
```

It is very important that we do not follow redirects automatically. Java is not aware of cookies, and as a result, if Java automatically redirects, the cookie will be lost. Additionally, since this is a POST we must call **setDoOutput** with **true**.

```
http.setInstanceFollowRedirects(false);
http.setDoOutput(true);
```

Next, the form must be posted. The user id and password are sent, along with the "Log-in" button.

```
OutputStream os = http.getOutputStream();
FormUtility form = new FormUtility(os, null);
form.add("uid", uid);
form.add("pwd", pwd);
form.add("action", "Login");
form.complete();
```

The **InputStream** is not needed because we do not need to read any data from the form. We will get the session id from the cookie attached to the response.

```
http.getInputStream();
cookies.loadCookies(http);
return (cookies.getMap().containsKey("hri-cookie"));
```

The session id is stored in a cookie named **hri-cookie**. This cookie will automatically be applied when the search is performed. This is accomplished by the following line of code, from the search method:

```
cookies.saveCookies(http);
```

The above method call adds the cookie headers to the HTTP request.

## Summary

Sessions are a very important concept in HTTP programming. You cannot access data from many websites until you have logged on. Logging onto a website establishes a session. To work with such web sites, your bot must support sessions. There are two ways that web sites commonly support sessions: in the URL variables and in cookies.

Both methods work by causing the web browser to keep returning a session id to the web server. This session id is a unique number that identifies this one user from the others. The session id is usually stored in the database and maps the logged in user's session to the identity of the user.

The first method that web sites commonly use to support sessions is the URL line. You can easily attach a session id to a web site's URL line. This session id must be passed to any page that the user will enter on the website.

The other common method to support sessions is to place the session id into a cookie. By setting a cookie, the web server can easily identify who has sent the request. The web browser will automatically set the cookie for future requests to the server. If the web server requires cookies, your bot must send these cookies.

So far, all of the recipes we have examined in this book have not used any client side scripting. In the next two chapters, you will be introduced to ways that your bot can handle client side scripting. Chapter 9 will show how to handle embedded Javascript on a web site. Chapter 10 will show how to use AJAX, which is a specialized Javascript method that combines XML and other technologies.

# CHAPTER 9: USING JAVASCRIPT

- JavaScript and Bots
- Processing Automatic Choice Lists
- Supporting JavaScript Includes
- Processing JavaScript Forms

Many web sites make use of JavaScript. JavaScript is a language that allows you to embed Java-like instructions into a web site. This allows the user's web browsing experience to be much more interactive. However, JavaScript also makes creating a bot, for a JavaScript enabled web site, much more complex.

When a bot encounters JavaScript, the bot will not automatically execute the JavaScript, as a regular browser would do. Rather, you, the bot programmer, must examine the JavaScript first and understand which HTTP requests your bot must send to emulate the browser. This chapter will show you some techniques for how to handle JavaScript.

## Understanding JavaScript

Though JavaScript is similar to Java, there are many important differences. It is a common misunderstanding that Java and JavaScript are the same thing. This is not at all the case. The following are some of the important differences between Java and JavaScript:

- Java uses types, such as **int**
- JavaScript is typeless, everything is an object
- Java and JavaScript use different syntax for functions
- Java was developed by Sun Microsystems
- JavaScript was developed by NetScape, based on Java

It is important that you understand these differences, if you are to create bots that access sites that make use of JavaScript.

JavaScript occurs between a beginning **&lt;script&gt;** and ending **&lt;/script&gt;** tags. For example, the following code fragment defines a JavaScript function.

```
<script type="text/javascript">
function formValidate(form){

if( form.interest.value.length==0 )
     alert("You must enter an interest rate.");
else if( form.principle.value.length==0 )
     alert("You must enter a principle.");
else if( form.term.value.length==0 )
```

```
        alert("You must enter a term.");
else
        form.submit();
}

</script>
```

As you can see, the format for JavaScript is slightly different than Java. For example, the function declaration starts with the keyword **function**. Additionally, none of the variables have a type declaration.

You will find this **<script>** declaration mixed in with regular HTML on web sites. Some older browsers can not properly process JavaScript. These older browsers will simply display the JavaScript code to the end user. To prevent this from happening, HTML comments were often inserted around the JavaScript code.

Though every major browser supports JavaScript, you will still often see JavaScript code enclosed in HTML comments. For example, the above function could also be expressed as follows, using HTML comments:

```
<script type="text/javascript">
<!--
function formValidate(form){

if( form.interest.value.length==0 )
        alert("You must enter an interest rate.");
else if( form.principle.value.length==0 )
        alert("You must enter a principle.");
else if( form.term.value.length==0 )
        alert("You must enter a term.");
else
        form.submit();
}

//-->
</script>
```

In addition to directly inserting JavaScript code into HTML, JavaScript also supports an "include". Using a JavaScript include statement allows JavaScript, from an external file, to be included in the HTML document. This allows you to group commonly used functions into an "include file" that can be accessed from many different HTML documents. The following line of code demonstrates a JavaScript include:

```
<script type="text/javascript" src="include.js"></script>
```

Include files normally end with a **.js** file extension.

## Common JavaScript Techniques

JavaScript can be used to add a wide array of features to a web site; however, there are certain features that are very common. Some of the most common JavaScript enabled features used by web sites include:

- Automatic Choice Lists
- JavaScript Includes
- JavaScript Forms
- Asynchronous JavaScript and XML (AJAX)

Of course, there are many additional JavaScript features and techniques beyond these. However, learning to handle these common techniques will enable you to understand and implement bots to handle other techniques as well.

From a bot's perspective, JavaScript does very little. A bot does not need to actually execute the JavaScript to work properly. The web browsing experience is still just a series of HTTP request sand response packets. You must understand how the JavaScript influences the HTTP request packets, or simply use a packet sniffer to examine them. As long as your bot sends the same HTTP request packets as a browser does, your bot will function correctly.

We will now examine each of the common JavaScript techniques.

### Working with Automatic Choice Lists

Choice lists are very common on web sites. A choice list is a drop-down list that allows the user to select from several options. Choice lists are often part of HTML forms. In addition, you may have also seen automatic choice lists. Automatic choice lists are usually not part of an HTML form, and will navigate when the user selects an item, or with the use of an HTML button next to them.

Automatic choice lists are usually used for site navigation. When you select one of the options on the automatic choice list, you will be instantly taken to a new page on the web site. To see an example of an automatic choice list, visit the following URL:

`http://www.httprecipes.com/1/9/article.php`

You can also view the automatic choice list in Figure 9.1.

**Figure 9.1: An Automatic Choice List**

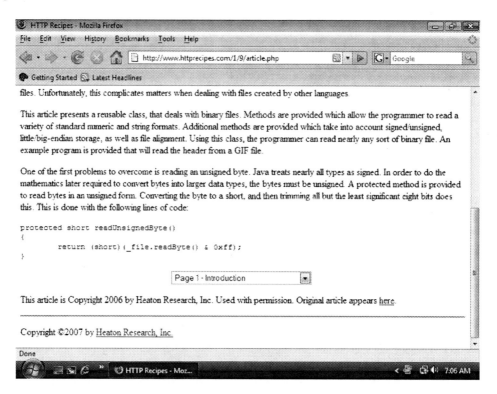

If you examine the HTML for this choice list, you will see that it is implemented with a regular **`<select>`** tag. However, the **`<select>`** tag does not directly operate with a form. You can see this in the HTML code here:

```
<center><select onchange="menuLink(this)">
<option SELECTED VALUE="/1/9/article.php?id=1">
Page 1 - Introduction</option>
<option VALUE="/1/9/article.php?id=2">
Page 2 - Using the BinaryFile Class</option>
<option VALUE="/1/9/article.php?id=3">
Page 3 - String Datatypes</option>
<option VALUE="/1/9/article.php?id=4">
Page 4 - Numeric Datatypes</option>
<option VALUE="/1/9/article.php?id=5">
Page 5 - Alignment</option>
<option VALUE="/1/9/article.php?id=6">
Page 6 - Reading a GIF Header</option>
<option VALUE="/1/9/article.php?id=7">
```

```
Page 7 - Summary</option>
</select></center>
```

As you can see from the above code, the **<select>** tag contains an **onchange** attribute. This attribute tells the browser to execute the **menuLink** function when the value of the choice list changes. Each of the **<option>** tags contains a link to the page that the user is requesting.

Using this information, the **menuLink** function can navigate to the correct page. The **menuLink** function is contained inside of a beginning **<script>** and ending **</script>** tag. You can see this code here:

```
<script type="text/javascript">
function isValidUrl( url )
{
  return !(typeof(url)=="undefined" || url==null ||
  url=="" || url.toLowerCase()=="none" ||
  url.toLowerCase()=="null" || url=="-1");
}

function openPopup( url, width, height, name, left, top )
{
if (isValidUrl(url))
  window.open(url, ((name&&name!="")?name:"popup"),
      ((width&&width!="")?"width="+width+",":"")+
      ((height&&height!="")?"height="+height+",":"")+
      "status=no,toolbar=no,menubar=no,location=no," +
      "scrollbars=yes,resizable=yes"
      +((left&&left!="")?",left="+left:"")+((top&&top!="")?
      ",top="+top:""));
}

function menuLink( menu )
{
  var link   = menu.options[menu.selectedIndex];
  var url    = link.value;
  var target       = link.target;
  if (link.popup == "true")
  {
    openPopup(url, link.popupwidth, link.popupheight, target);
  }
  else if (isValidUrl(url))
  {
    if (url.indexOf("javascript:") != -1)
    {
      eval(url.substr(url.indexOf(":")+1));
      } else if (target && target != "")
```

```
    {
    if (target == "_top")
      window.top.location.href = url;
    else if (target.substr(0,1) != "_")
      window.parent.frames[target].location.href = url;
    else window.location.href = url;
    }
    else
    {
      window.location.href = url;
    }
  }
  menu.selectedIndex = 0;
}
</script>
```

Describing how this JavaScript functions, is beyond the scope of the book. Entire books have been written on JavaScript programming. However, you can see near the bottom, that the code moves the browser to the link specified in the **<option>** tag by the following line of code:

```
window.location.href = url;
```

The **window.location.href** property allows JavaScript to move the browser to a new page. This is often the line of code that a bot programmer is most interested in. Recipe 9.1 shows how to parse the JavaScript and access all pages in this article.

### Working with JavaScript Includes

Not all JavaScript is necessarily located on the page that is making use of it. "JavaScript includes" allow an HTML form to import JavaScript from an external file. This allows commonly used JavaScript code to be placed into files, making them easily accessible across many HTML documents.

To see an example of "JavaScript includes", examine the following URL:

**http://www.httprecipes.com/1/9/includes.php**

You can also view this page in Figure 9.2.

**Figure 9.2: JavaScript Includes**

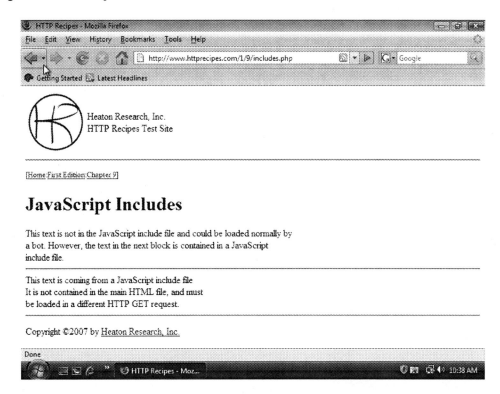

If you examine the HTML at the above URL, you will notice that not all of the text is on that page. If you look at Figure 9.2, you will notice that the text "This text is coming from a JavaScript include file" is present. However, if you examine the HTML from the above URL you will not see this text. You can see the HTML from the page here:

```
<!DOCTYPE HTML PUBLIC "-//W3C//DTD HTML 4.01 Transitional//EN">

<HTML>
<HEAD>
      <TITLE>HTTP Recipes</TITLE>
      <meta http-equiv="Content-Type"
      content="text/html; charset=UTF-8">
      <meta http-equiv="Cache-Control" content="no-cache">
</HEAD>

<BODY>

<table border="0"><tr><td>
<a href="http://www.httprecipes.com/">
<img src="/images/logo.gif" alt="Heaton Research Logo"
border="0"></a>
```

```
</td><td valign="top">Heaton Research, Inc.<br>
HTTP Recipes Test Site
</td></tr>
</table>
<hr><p><small>[<a href="/">Home</a>:<a href="/1/">
First Edition</a>:<a href="/1/9/">Chaper 9</a>]</small></p>

<h1>JavaScript Includes</h1>
This text is not in the JavaScript include file and could be load-
ed normally by<br>

a bot. However, the text in the next block is contained in a
JavaScript<br>
include file.<br>
<hr>
<script type="text/javascript" src="include.js"></script>
<hr>
<p>Copyright 2006 by
<a href="http://www.heatonresearch.com/">Heaton Research, Inc.
</a></p>
</BODY>
</HTML>
```

The JavaScript include statement includes another file, named **include.js**. You can see this include statement here:

```
<script type="text/javascript" src="include.js"></script>
```

This will cause the file **include.js** to be included as part of the HTML file. However, the **include.js** file is assumed to be JavaScript, so no **<script>** tags are necessary inside **include.js**. The **include.js** source is shown below:

```
document.write('This text is coming from a JavaScript include
file<br>');
document.write('It is not contained in the main HTML file, and
must<br>');
document.write('be loaded in a different HTTP GET request.<br>');
```

As a separate request, the web browser will load the **include.js** file. It is a regular web document, which can be found at the following address:

**http://www.httprecipes.com/1/9/include.js**

To process JavaScript includes with a bot, you must examine what they contain and how you will obtain what you need from them. Like the other JavaScript techniques, it is a matter of providing the correct HTTP requests to the server and processing the responses. Recipe 9.2 shows how to process this URL.

## Working with JavaScript Forms

Perhaps one of the most common uses for JavaScript is to validate forms. JavaScript allows you to perform basic validation checks on data before that data is sent to the web server. The following URL has an example of a JavaScript enabled form:

`http://www.httprecipes.com/1/9/form.php`

This form can also be seen in Figure 9.3.

**Figure 9.3: A JavaScript Enabled Form**

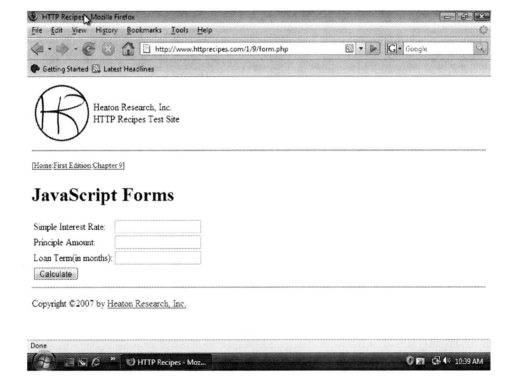

This form allows the user to enter information about a loan. Once the user clicks the "Calculate" button, a loan amortization schedule will be calculated. You can see this amortization schedule in Figure 9.4.

**Figure 9.4: Amortization Data**

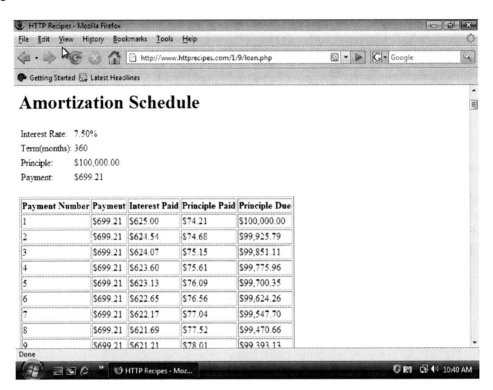

To see how this form is implemented, we will examine its HTML. You can see the form **<input>** tag for the "Calculate" button here:

```
<input type="button" name="action" value="Calculate" onclick="form
Validate(this.form);">
```

As you can see from the above code, the "Calculate" button calls the **formValidate** function when it is clicked. The **formValidate** function is shown here:

```
<script type="text/javascript">
<!--
function formValidate(form){


if( form.interest.value.length==0 )
     alert("You must enter an interest rate.");
else if( form.principle.value.length==0 )
     alert("You must enter a principle.");
else if( form.term.value.length==0 )
     alert("You must enter a term.");
else
```

```
      form.submit();
}
//-->
</script>
```

This is a very simple form checker. This form checker validates that the user has entered a value for each of the three fields. If all fields have been entered, then the form is submitted.

Processing JavaScript forms is usually fairly easy for a bot. A JavaScript validation form often works just like a regular form. Your bot can usually ignore the validations and just post the form as a normal form would be posted. Recipe 9.3 shows how to write a bot for this page.

### Working with AJAX

AJAX is a relatively new technique used by many web sites. It uses JavaScript and XML to exchange data with the web server. AJAX stands for "Asynchronous JavaScript and XML". This allows the web site to interact with a user without moving to a new page. Many AJAX web sites more closely resemble traditional GUI applications than web sites.

AJAX is heavily dependent on JavaScript. Special considerations must be made for web sites that make use of AJAX. Chapter 10 will show you how to create bots for AJAX sites.

### Other JavaScript Techniques

This chapter discusses some of the most common JavaScript techniques. However, this is only the beginning. Web sites make use of JavaScript in many different ways. JavaScript sites are much more complex for bots than non-JavaScript sites. There is no one single method to create a bot for all JavaScript sites.

Creating bots for JavaScript sites means that you, the bot programmer, must understand how these JavaScript sites work and generate the correct HTTP requests and process the responses. It is important to remember that generating the correct HTTP requests is really all there is to creating a bot.

After all, the web server is not aware of JavaScript. JavaScript simply helps the browser to generate HTTP requests. Your bot can generate these same requests, if you understand how the site is using JavaScript. Also, there are many good books and online tutorials for learning JavaScript.

## Implementing JavaScript

It is possible to allow your bot to understand JavaScript; although, this almost always is not necessary. As mentioned in the previous section, it us usually best to custom program the bot after you understand how the JavaScript is being used by the site. If you would like to build JavaScript processing into your bot, it can be done; however, it will be a somewhat large undertaking. Because it is so rarely necessary to do this, direct JavaScript processing is beyond the scope of the book. However, I will point you in the right direction.

The Rhino project, which is provided by Mozilla, allows you to add JavaScript support to Java programs. As described at Rhino's website, "Rhino is an open-source implementation of JavaScript written entirely in Java. It is typically embedded into Java applications to provide scripting to end users." Rhino can be obtained from the following URL:

`http://www.mozilla.org/rhino/`

Using Rhino, you can create bots that are capable of executing the JavaScript that they encounter.

## Recipes

This chapter includes three recipes. These recipes demonstrate how to construct bots that navigate and extract data from JavaScript enabled web pages. Specifically, you will see how to process these JavaScript techniques:

- Automatic Choice Lists
- JavaScript Includes
- JavaScript Forms

These recipes will show you how a bot can be adapted to several very common JavaScript techniques. The first recipe demonstrates automatic choice lists.

### Recipe #9.1: Automatic Choice Lists

Automatic choice lists are a common use of JavaScript. They are usually used as a navigational aid. You are allowed to select an option from a choice list. Once you select an item, you will be instantly taken to the web page that corresponds to the option you chose.

This recipe will show how to extract data from a site that makes use of automatic choice lists. This site presents a multi-page article that allows you to select which page to view using an automatic choice list. This recipe will extract data from the following URL:

`http://www.httprecipes.com/1/9/article.php`

This recipe is shown in Listing 9.1.

## Listing 9.1: Automatic Choice Lists (DownloadAtricle.java)

```java
package com.heatonresearch.httprecipes.ch9.recipe1;

import java.io.*;
import java.net.*;

import com.heatonresearch.httprecipes.html.*;

public class DownloadArticle
{
  /**
   * The size of the download buffer.
   */
  public static int BUFFER_SIZE = 8192;

  /**
   * This method downloads the specified URL into a Java
   * String. This is a very simple method, that you can
   * reused anytime you need to quickly grab all data from
   * a specific URL.
   *
   * @param url The URL to download.
   * @return The contents of the URL that was downloaded.
   * @throws IOException Thrown if any sort of error occurs.
   */
  public String downloadPage(URL url) throws IOException
  {
    StringBuilder result = new StringBuilder();
    byte buffer[] = new byte[BUFFER_SIZE];

    InputStream s = url.openStream();
    int size = 0;

    do
    {
      size = s.read(buffer);
      if (size != -1)
        result.append(new String(buffer, 0, size));
    } while (size != -1);

    return result.toString();
  }

  /**
   * This method is very useful for grabbing information from a
   * HTML page.
```

```
 *
 * @param url The URL to download.
 * @param token1 The text, or tag, that comes before the
 * desired text
 * @param token2 The text, or tag, that comes after the
 * desired text
 * @param count Which occurrence of token1 to use, 1 for
 * the first
 * @return The contents of the URL that was downloaded.
 * @throws IOException Thrown if any sort of error occurs.
 */
public String extractNoCase(String str, String token1,
  String token2, int count)
{
  int location1, location2;

  // convert everything to lower case
  String searchStr = str.toLowerCase();
  token1 = token1.toLowerCase();
  token2 = token2.toLowerCase();

  // now search
  location1 = location2 = 0;
  do
  {
    location1 = searchStr.indexOf(token1, location1 + 1);

    if (location1 == -1)
      return null;

    count--;
  } while (count > 0);

  // return the result from the original string that has mixed
  // case
  location2 = str.indexOf(token2, location1 + 1);
  if (location2 == -1)
    return null;

  return str.substring(location1 + token1.length(), location2);
}
```

```
/**
 * This method is called to download article text from each
 * article page.
 * @param url The URL to download from.
 * @return The article text from the specified page.
 * @throws IOException Thrown if a communication error occurs.
 */
private String downloadArticlePage(URL url) throws IOException
{
  final String token = "<center>";
  String contents = downloadPage(url);
  String result = extractNoCase(contents,token,token,0);
  return token+result;
}


/**
 * This method looks for each of the <option> tags that contain
 * a link to each of the pages.  For each page found the
 * downloadArticlePage method is called.
 */
public void process()
    throws IOException
{
  URL url =
    new URL("http://www.httprecipes.com/1/9/article.php");
  InputStream is = url.openStream();
  ParseHTML parse = new ParseHTML(is);

  int ch;
  while ((ch = parse.read()) != -1)
  {
    if (ch == 0)
    {
      HTMLTag tag = parse.getTag();
      if (tag.getName().equalsIgnoreCase("option"))
      {
        String str = tag.getAttributeValue("value");
        URL u = new URL(url,str);
        System.out.println(downloadArticlePage(u));
      }
    }
  }
}
```

```
/**
 * The main method, create a new instance of the object and call
 * process.
 * @param args not used.
 */
public static void main(String args[])
{
  try
  {
    DownloadArticle parse = new DownloadArticle();
    parse.process();
  } catch (Exception e)
  {
    e.printStackTrace();
  }
}
}
```

This recipe is structured around two functions. The first function, named **process**, reads the automatic choice list and extracts URLs from it. These URLs will be the URLs for all of the pages in the article. Next, the **process** method calls the **downloadArticlePage** method for each URL extracted.

The next two sections will describe these two functions. First, we will examine the **process** function.

### Reading the Choice List

The **process** function reads the **<option>** tags that will be passed to the Java-Script. This will give us a complete list of where all seven pages are stored. You can see the option tags that we will be parsing here:

```
<option SELECTED VALUE="/1/9/article.php?id=1">
Page 1 - Introduction</option>
<option VALUE="/1/9/article.php?id=2">
Page 2 - Using the BinaryFile Class</option>
<option VALUE="/1/9/article.php?id=3">
Page 3 - String Datatypes</option>
<option VALUE="/1/9/article.php?id=4">
Page 4 - Numeric Datatypes</option>
<option VALUE="/1/9/article.php?id=5">
Page 5 - Alignment</option>
<option VALUE="/1/9/article.php?id=6">
Page 6 - Reading a GIF Header</option>
<option VALUE="/1/9/article.php?id=7">
Page 7 - Summary</option>
```

The **VALUE** attribute of each of the above option tags defines the URL that we will access to find that page.

This function begins by opening the URL to the first page.

```
URL url = new URL("http://www.httprecipes.com/1/9/article.php");
InputStream is = url.openStream();
```

A **ParseHTML** object will be used to parse the HTML. The **ParseHTML** class was discussed in Chapter 6, "Extracting Data".

```
ParseHTML parse = new ParseHTML(is);

int ch;
while ((ch = parse.read()) != -1)
{
```

As the data is read from the HTML page, each tag is processed. If the tag found is an **<option>** tag, then we will look for a URL.

```
  if (ch == 0)
  {
    HTMLTag tag = parse.getTag();
    if (tag.getName().equalsIgnoreCase("option"))
    {
```

If an **<option>** tag is found, then construct a URL object for it and call the **downloadArticlePage** function.

```
      String str = tag.getAttributeValue("value");
      URL u = new URL(url,str);
      System.out.println(downloadArticlePage(u));
    }
  }
}
```

The **downloadArticlePage** function returns a string for every page downloaded. This string is then displayed.

## Reading Each Article Page

Reading the data from each of the article pages is fairly straightforward. First, let's examine the HTML page that contains each page of the article. You can see this HTML here:

```
<center>
<h1>Programming Binary Files in Java</h1>
<h3>Introduction</h3></center>
<p>Java contains an extensive array of classes for file access.
A series of readers, writers and filters make up
```

```
... article continues here ...
```

```
</p>
<center><select onchange="menuLink(this)">
```

To extract the article text, we must find the HTML tags that completely enclose the article. The article begins with a **<center>** tag. The article also ends with a **<center>** tag (not a **</center>** tag). This is because the ending **<center>** tag is actually used to center the automatic choice list; and the automatic choice list occurs at the end of the article text.

If you are extracting data from other web sites, you will need to find the bounding tags for that article. It may even be a series of tags, for example **</p></center>** could be the ending tag for a page. It all depends on the data you are reading.

To do this, the **extractNoCase** function is used.

```
final String token = "<center>";

String contents = downloadPage(url);
String result = extractNoCase(contents,token,token,0);
return token+result;
```

Once the page has been read, the article text is returned.

### Recipe #9.2: JavaScript Includes

"JavaScript includes" are another common use of JavaScript. They allow an HTML document to include JavaScript from another HTML document. This recipe will demonstrate how to read an HTML document that uses "JavaScript includes". This recipe will output a "compound document" that will replace the JavaScript include statements with the text that is contained in these included JavaScript documents.

This recipe will read the HTML text located at the following URL:

**http://www.httprecipes.com/1/9/includes.php**

This recipe is shown in Listing 9.2.

### Listing 9.2: JavaScript Includes (Includes.java)

```
package com.heatonresearch.httprecipes.ch9.recipe2;

import java.io.*;
import java.net.*;

import com.heatonresearch.httprecipes.html.*;
```

```
public class Includes
{
  /**
   * The size of the download buffer.
   */
  public static int BUFFER_SIZE = 8192;

  /**
   * This method is very useful for grabbing information from a
   * HTML page.
   *
   * @param url The URL to download.
   * @param token1 The text, or tag, that comes before the
   * desired text.
   * @param token2 The text, or tag, that comes after the
   * desired text.
   * @param count Which occurrence of token1 to use, 1 for
   * the first.
   * @return The contents of the URL that was downloaded.
   * @throws IOException Thrown if any sort of error occurs.
   */
  public String extractNoCase(String str, String token1,
    String token2, int count)
  {
    int location1, location2;

    // convert everything to lower case
    String searchStr = str.toLowerCase();
    token1 = token1.toLowerCase();
    token2 = token2.toLowerCase();

    // now search
    location1 = location2 = 0;
    do
    {
      location1 = searchStr.indexOf(token1, location1 + 1);

      if (location1 == -1)
        return null;

      count--;
    } while (count > 0);

    // return the result from the original string that has mixed
```

```java
    // case
    location2 = str.indexOf(token2, location1 + 1);
    if (location2 == -1)
      return null;

    return str.substring(location1 + token1.length(), location2);
  }


  /**
   * This method downloads the specified URL into a Java
   * String. This is a very simple method, that you can
   * reused anytime you need to quickly grab all data from
   * a specific URL.
   *
   * @param url The URL to download.
   * @return The contents of the URL that was downloaded.
   * @throws IOException Thrown if any sort of error occurs.
   */
  public String downloadPage(URL url) throws IOException
  {
    StringBuilder result = new StringBuilder();
    byte buffer[] = new byte[BUFFER_SIZE];

    InputStream s = url.openStream();
    int size = 0;

    do
    {
      size = s.read(buffer);
      if (size != -1)
        result.append(new String(buffer, 0, size));
    } while (size != -1);

    return result.toString();
  }


  /**
   * Called to download the text from a page.  If any JavaScript
   * include is found, the text from that page is read too.
   */
  public void process()
      throws IOException
  {
    URL url = new URL(
      "http://www.httprecipes.com/1/9/includes.php");
    InputStream is = url.openStream();
```

```java
    ParseHTML parse = new ParseHTML(is);
    StringBuilder buffer = new StringBuilder();

    int ch;
    while ((ch = parse.read()) != -1)
    {
      if (ch == 0)
      {
        HTMLTag tag = parse.getTag();
        if (tag.getName().equalsIgnoreCase("script")
          && tag.getAttributeValue("src")!=null)
        {
          String src = tag.getAttributeValue("src");
          URL u = new URL(url,src);
          String include = downloadPage(u);
          buffer.append("<script>");
          buffer.append(include);
          buffer.append("</script>");
        }
        else
        {
          buffer.append(tag.toString());
        }
      }
      else
      {
        buffer.append((char)ch);
      }
    }

    System.out.println(buffer.toString());
}

/**
 * The main method, create a new instance of the object and call
 * process.
 * @param args not used.
 */
public static void main(String args[])
{
  try
  {
    Includes parse = new Includes();
    parse.process();
  } catch (Exception e)
  {
```

```
            e.printStackTrace();
        }
    }
}
```

This recipe begins by opening a connection to the URL it will download from.

```
URL url = new URL("http://www.httprecipes.com/1/9/includes.php");
InputStream is = url.openStream();
```

A **ParseHTML** object will be used to parse the HTML. The **ParseHTML** class was discussed in Chapter 6.

```
ParseHTML parse = new ParseHTML(is);
StringBuilder buffer = new StringBuilder();
```

As the data is read from the HTML page, each tag is processed. If the tag found is a **<script>** tag, then we will look to see if it is a JavaScript include. Additionally, a **StringBuilder** is setup to hold the compound document.

```
int ch;
while ((ch = parse.read()) != -1)
{
    if (ch == 0)
    {
```

If this tag is a **<script>** tag, and it has a **src** attribute, then the tag will be processed as a JavaScript include.

```
HTMLTag tag = parse.getTag();
if (tag.getName().equalsIgnoreCase("script") &&
tag.getAttributeValue("src")!=null)
{
```

The included page is loaded and appended to the main document. Included JavaScript pages do not have a beginning **<script>** and ending **</script>** tags of their own, so these tags are added.

```
    String src = tag.getAttributeValue("src");
    URL u = new URL(url,src);
    String include = downloadPage(u);
    buffer.append("<script>");
    buffer.append(include);
    buffer.append("</script>");
}
else
{
```

If this is a regular HTML tag, then append it to the **StringBuilder**.

```
    buffer.append(tag.toString());
```

```
     }
}
```

If this is a regular HTML text character, then append it to the **StringBuilder**.

```
else
{
  buffer.append((char)ch);
}
```

```
System.out.println(buffer.toString());
```

Finally, once the entire document has been read, it is displayed.

### Recipe #9.3: JavaScript Forms

Another very common use for JavaScript is to validate forms. Usually these forms can be treated as normal forms. However, sometimes these forms will make use of an **<input   type="button">** tag to submit, rather than the usual **<input   type="submit">**. If an **<input>** tag makes use of the **button** type, rather than **submit**, then JavaScript must be used to submit the form. This recipe will show how to process such a form. You can see the form that this recipe will process at the following URL:

**http://www.httprecipes.com/1/9/form.php**

This recipe is shown in Listing 9.3:

### Listing 9.3: JavaScript Forms (JavaScriptForms.java)

```
package com.heatonresearch.httprecipes.ch9.recipe3;

import java.io.*;
import java.net.*;
import java.util.*;
import com.heatonresearch.httprecipes.html.*;

public class JavaScriptForms
{

  /** Advance to the specified HTML tag.
   * @param parse The HTML parse object to use.
   * @param tag The HTML tag.
   * @param count How many tags like this to find.
   * @return True if found, false otherwise.
   * @throws IOException If an exception occurs while reading.
   */
  private boolean advance(ParseHTML parse, String tag, int count)
```

```java
      throws IOException
  {
    int ch;
    while ((ch = parse.read()) != -1)
    {
      if (ch == 0)
      {
        if (parse.getTag().getName().equalsIgnoreCase(tag))
        {
          count--;
          if (count <= 0)
            return true;
        }
      }
    }
    return false;
  }


  /**
   * This method is called once for each table row located, it
   * contains a list of all columns in that row.  The method
   * provided simply prints the columns to the console.
   * @param list Columns that were found on this row.
   */
  private void processTableRow(List<String> list)
  {
    StringBuilder result = new StringBuilder();
    for (String item : list)
    {
      if (result.length() > 0)
        result.append(",");
      result.append('\"');
      result.append(item);
      result.append('\"');

    }
    System.out.println(result.toString());
  }
```

```
/**
 * This method will download an amortization table for the
 * specified parameters.
 * @param interest The interest rate for the loan.
 * @param term The term(in months) of the loan.
 * @param principle The principle amount of the loan.
 * @throws IOException Thrown if a communication error occurs.
 */
public void process(double interest,int term,int principle)
throws IOException
{


  URL url = new URL("http://www.httprecipes.com/1/9/loan.php");
  URLConnection http = url.openConnection();
  http.setDoOutput(true);
  OutputStream os = http.getOutputStream();
  FormUtility form = new FormUtility(os,null);
  form.add("interest", ""+interest);
  form.add("term", ""+term);
  form.add("principle", ""+principle);
  form.complete();
  InputStream is = http.getInputStream();
  ParseHTML parse = new ParseHTML(is);
  StringBuilder buffer = new StringBuilder();
  List<String> list = new ArrayList<String>();
  boolean capture = false;

  advance(parse,"table",3);

  int ch;
  while ((ch = parse.read()) != -1)
  {
    if (ch == 0)
    {
      HTMLTag tag = parse.getTag();
      if (tag.getName().equalsIgnoreCase("tr"))
      {
        list.clear();
        capture = false;
        buffer.setLength(0);
      } else if (tag.getName().equalsIgnoreCase("/tr"))
      {
        if (list.size() > 0)
        {
          processTableRow(list);
          list.clear();
```

```
        }
      } else if (tag.getName().equalsIgnoreCase("td"))
      {
        if (buffer.length() > 0)
          list.add(buffer.toString());
        buffer.setLength(0);
        capture = true;
      } else if (tag.getName().equalsIgnoreCase("/td"))
      {
        list.add(buffer.toString());
        buffer.setLength(0);
        capture = false;
      } else if (tag.getName().equalsIgnoreCase("/table"))
      {
        break;
      }
    } else
    {
      if (capture)
        buffer.append((char) ch);
    }
  }
}

/**
 * The main method, create a new instance of the object and call
 * process.
 * @param args not used.
 */
public static void main(String args[])
{
  try
  {
    JavaScriptForms parse = new JavaScriptForms();
    parse.process(7.5,12,10000);
  } catch (Exception e)
  {
    e.printStackTrace();
  }
}
}
```

This recipe submits data to a JavaScript enabled form. This form collects information about a loan and displays the loan's amortization table. Figure 9.4 from earlier in this chapter, shows the amortization schedule.

To produce an amortization schedule, the user must enter the principle loan amount, the interest rate, and the term. These values will all be transmitted to the form by the bot, and the resulting amortization table will be parsed.

This recipe begins by opening a connection to the **loan.php** page. This is the page that the form will **POST** to.

```
URL url = new URL("http://www.httprecipes.com/1/9/loan.php");
URLConnection http = url.openConnection();
http.setDoOutput(true);
```

First, a **FormUtility** object is constructed to construct our response to the form. Chapter 7. "Responding to Forms" explains how to use the **FormUtility** class.

```
OutputStream os = http.getOutputStream();
FormUtility form = new FormUtility(os,null);
```

The three form variables; interest, term and principle, are added to the form.

```
form.add("interest", ""+interest);
form.add("term", ""+term);
form.add("principle", ""+principle);
form.complete();
```

The form is now posted. Next, we parse the results that are returned.

```
InputStream is = http.getInputStream();
ParseHTML parse = new ParseHTML(is);
StringBuilder buffer = new StringBuilder();
List<String> list = new ArrayList<String>();
boolean capture = false;
```

The data that we are looking for is in the third table. We begin parsing the HTML; looking for the tags that make up the table that holds the amortization schedule. Table parsing was covered in greater detail in Chapter 6, "Extracting Data".

```
advance(parse,"table",3);

int ch;
while ((ch = parse.read()) != -1)
{
  if (ch == 0)
  {
```

If the tag is an opening table row tag, **<tr>**, then we clear the list to begin capturing a table row.

```
HTMLTag tag = parse.getTag();
if (tag.getName().equalsIgnoreCase("tr"))
{
  list.clear();
```

```
capture = false;
buffer.setLength(0);
```

If the tag is an ending table row tag, **</tr>**, then we can display the row we just extracted. This display is handled by the **processTableRow** method.

```
} else if (tag.getName().equalsIgnoreCase("/tr"))
{
if (list.size() > 0)
{
  processTableRow(list);
  list.clear();
}
```

If the tag is an opening table column tag, **<td>**, begin capturing the data contained in that column.

```
} else if (tag.getName().equalsIgnoreCase("td"))
{
if (buffer.length() > 0)
  list.add(buffer.toString());
buffer.setLength(0);
capture = true;
```

If the tag is an ending table column tag, **</td>**, then we have captured one complete column. Add that column to the row's list and stop capturing text.

```
} else if (tag.getName().equalsIgnoreCase("/td"))
{
  list.add(buffer.toString());
  buffer.setLength(0);
  capture = false;
```

Finally, if we reach an ending table tag, **</table>**, then we are done.

```
} else if (tag.getName().equalsIgnoreCase("/table"))
{
  break;
}
} else
{
```

When characters are encountered while we are capturing, we should append them to the **buffer**.

```
if (capture)
  buffer.append((char) ch);
```

Once the loop ends, the entire amortization table will be parsed.

## Summary

This chapter showed how to handle JavaScript enabled web sites when writing a bot. The web server does not handle JavaScript; it is a web browser only technology. As a result, your bot does not need to be directly concerned with JavaScript. Rather, you the bot programmer must understand the JavaScript code and ensure that the bot sends the same HTTP requests that a browser running the JavaScript would.

There are several common JavaScript techniques. One of the most common is using JavaScript to validate data entered into a form. JavaScript is also often used to provide automatic choice lists, as well as JavaScript includes. This chapter showed recipes that demonstrate how to handle each of these situations.

Additionally, you can also include a JavaScript interpreter in your programs. Although, the Rhino JavaScript engine allows your Java applications to execute JavaScript, a bot program rarely needs this functionality.

The next chapter will examine one of the most popular ways to use JavaScript. AJAX is a technology that combines JavaScript and asynchronous HTTP messages to provide very rich and interactive experiences for the user. In addition, there are special considerations that will be discussed regarding AJAX processing.

# CHAPTER 10: WORKING WITH AJAX SITES

- Understanding AJAX
- Understanding the Components of AJAX
- Parsing XML
- Generating XML

AJAX (Asynchronous JavaScript and XML ) is a web development technology that has become very popular. AJAX web sites look much more like traditional GUI applications, than they do regular web sites. When you access a regular web site, you move from one web page to another, as you use the web site. AJAX applications usually use a single page, and update only what needs to be updated.

In an attempt to respond quicker to the user and behave more like traditional applications, AJAX web applications attempt to limit movement from one web page to another. Your browser's URL line stays the same, and only the part of the page that actually changed is updated. There are many commercial websites that make use of AJAX, such as:

- Google
- Digg
- Yahoo Mail
- Writely

There are still HTTP requests and responses being transmitted between the web browser and web server; however, the HTTP responses do not move the user to a new page. Rather, JavaScript interprets these HTTP responses on the web browser. This allows for much more real-time interaction with the user.

AJAX is an acronym for Asynchronous JavaScript and XML. As implied by the name, AJAX employs a number of existing web technologies. Because AJAX is based on existing web technologies, AJAX works on nearly every web browser. Table 10.1 summarizes the technologies used by AJAX.

**Table 10.1: AJAX Components**

| Technology | AJAX Use |
|---|---|
| HTML/XHTML and CSS | CSS allows AJAX applications to format their display. By using CSS, the HTML documents can be kept relatively simple, which makes them easier to be modified by the DOM. |
| DOM | The Document Object Model allows JavaScript to modify the data currently displayed on the web browser. The DOM also allows JavaScript to parse XML. |
| XMLHttpRequest Object | The XMLHttpRequest object allows you to exchange data asynchronously with the web server through HTTP requests and responses. Some AJAX applications use an embedded <iframe> to accomplish this as well. |
| XML | XML, or some other textual format, is the format usually used for AJAX applications to communicate with the web server. |

AJAX web sites can actually be easier to navigate with a bot than regular web sites. AJAX web sites tend to be designed so that their JavaScript can request information from the server in short simple XML packets. This can be ideal for a bot. Programming a bot is just a matter of understanding what format these small requests are in.

# Understanding AJAX

To understand this format, you must understand how AJAX works. There are entire books dedicated to AJAX. This chapter will just present a brief introduction to AJAX. The focus is on how to access AJAX with a bot, not how to actually program AJAX.

Another option, beyond understanding how AJAX works, is simply to use a network analyzer. If you use a network analyzer, you can watch the web browser communicate to the web server. You will see the AJAX requests and responses. From this information, you can then build a bot to send these same requests. Using a network analyzer to analyze AJAX will be discussed later in this chapter.

In the next few sections, this chapter will present a brief overview of how AJAX works.

## Using HTML/XHTML and CSS

AJAX web sites will use the Document Object Model (DOM) to modify their HTML programmatically. Rather than calling on the web server to completely redraw the entire HTML page, AJAX applications will request data from the server and then modify the page the user is already looking at. Because if this, it is best to keep the HTML as simple as possible. Cascading Style Sheets (CSS) is a great way to do this.

Consider using traditional HTML to display the message, "This is a note", in a red font and bold type. The following HTML would have to be used:

```
<font color="red"><p><b>This is a note</b></p></font>
```

There is quite a bit of "overhead" HTML here that has nothing to do with the text that is being displayed. Each place that you want to use this style of text you would need to include the additional "overhead" HTML that specifies the formatting properties for the text.

With CSS, you can define styles. Styles are either included in a separate style file, or defined between a beginning **\<style\>** and ending **\</style\>** tag. Using CSS to format the text above, you would simply include the following style:

```
.note {
color: red;
font-weight: bold;
}
```

Now, anytime you want to apply this style, you simply use a class attribute, such as:

```
<p class="note">This is a note</p>
```

This is very advantageous for bots. The above HTML example is far easier to parse than the preceding traditional HTML example.

XHTML is often used in place of HTML in AJAX applications. XHTML looks almost identical to HTML with the main difference being that XHTML must follow XML formatting rules. For example, the following example is fine under HTML, but is unacceptable in XHTML:

```
Line 1<br>
Line 2<br>
<ul>
<li>Option 1
<li>Option 2
<li>Option 3
</ul>
```

There are several missing end tags. The above document, recreated as XHTML would look like this:

```
Line 1<br/>
Line 2<br/>
<ul>
<li>Option 1</li>
<li>Option 2</li>
<li>Option 3</li>
</ul>
```

The advantage is that this method makes it much easier for a parser, such as the DOM, to understand the document.

## Understanding Document Object Model

The Document Object Model (DOM) is a series of JavaScript objects that allows a Java-Script application to access and modify both XML and HTML information. There are two primary functions that most AJAX web sites use the DOM for. They are summarized here:

- Parsing XML received from the web server
- Making dynamic changes to the web page displayed on the browser

When the web server sends an HTML document to the web browser, the web browser has a copy of the document, separate from the web server. This separate copy, which the web browser stores in memory, is the copy of the web page that the user is looking at. Using the DOM, it is possible for a JavaScript program to make changes to the copy of the web page the user is viewing. This allows the browser to update individual parts of the document, but does not change the document on the web server.

This is how AJAX gets by with not having to update the entire page. AJAX applications use the DOM to update parts of the page in response to packets sent to the AJAX application from the web server. It is also important to note that when AJAX updates the HTML of a page, only the local browser copy is changed. The actual HTML on the web server is never changed.

It is very easy to view a web page as it is seen from the DOM. For example, consider the web page stored at the following URL:

`http://www.httprecipes.com/1/10/example1.html`

This page stores a simple table and some text. You can see this web page in Figure 10.1.

**Figure 10.1: A Simple HTML Page**

The FireFox web browser includes a special tool named "DOM Inspector" that allows you to see your document as the DOM sees it. The DOM inspector can be found under the tools menu in Firefox. Some versions of FireFox require you to do a "custom" install and choose "developer tools" to access the "DOM Inspector". Selecting the "DOM Inspector" will show you how this page is viewed by the DOM. Figure 10.2 shows what this page looks like in the "DOM Inspector".

**Figure 10.2: A Simple Page in the DOM Inspector**

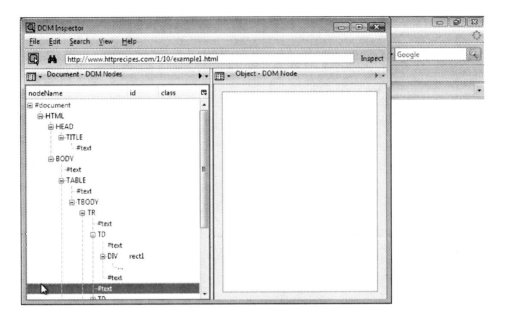

The DOM provides a programmatic way to access the contents of the web site. For example, the following JavaScript code would change the text "One", from Figure 10.1 to "Hello World".

```
document.getElementById('rect1').innerHTML='Hello World';
```

As you can see from the above code, the value of the tag, named **rect1** can be changed on the fly. Here it is being changed to the words "Hello World".

This is the heart of AJAX programming. You modify the page that is currently being displayed. This limits the number of times the web browser has to go back to the web server for a complete page.

## Communicating using the XMLHttpRequest Object

The **XMLHttpRequest** object allows JavaScript to communicate directly with the web server. This communication occurs through the HTTP protocol. However, the data exchanged with the **XMLHttpRequest** objects goes to the JavaScript program and does not redisplay the entire page. The AJAX browser application can then interpret the HTTP response as needed and update itself using the DOM.

Despite the fact that the **XMLHttpRequest** object has the XML acronym as part of its name, it does not require that you use XML. You can use the **XMLHttpRequest** object to exchange text information just as well as XML. However, if you are using XML, the **XMLHttpRequest** object will conveniently package the incoming XML with the DOM.

The **XMLHttpRequest** object is not the only method that can be used to exchange information with the web server. Another common technique is to use an **<iframe>**. The **<iframe>** tag allows you to embed one web page inside of another.

The **<iframe>** tag has a URL that defines what HTML it is to display. This URL property can be modified with JavaScript. If the URL is modified, the **<iframe>** will load the data contained at the new URL. Some sites simply hide the **<iframe>** and change its URL to the page that they would like to retrieve a message from. The browser will then fill the **<iframe>** element with the data received from the URL. The JavaScript can then harvest the data. Because the **<iframe>** element is hidden, the user will not see any of this.

### Interpreting XML

XML is an ideal protocol to exchange information between the web server and the AJAX program running on the web browser. Because the DOM can easily parse XML, JavaScript is very well equipped to handle XML messages.

To see what XML messages might be sent, consider an AJAX web application that maintains an employee database. One such function that an AJAX application would need to implement would be an employee search. Consider an employee search function where the user enters the first and last name of an employee and the system attempts to locate that employee's record.

For such a system, the AJAX application running on the web browser would construct and send an XML message similar to the following:

```
<request type="employeeSearch">
  <searchFor>
    <first>John</first>
    <last>Smith</last>
  </searchFor>
</request>
```

When the server sends back the requested employee, it will be as an XML message. The following message could be sent back:

```
<response type="employeeSearch">
  <employee>
    <first>John</first>
    <last>John</last>
    <phone>636-555-1212</phone>
    <address>102 Main Street</address>
```

```
      <city>St. Louis</city>
      <state>MO</state>
      <zip>63017</zip>
   </employee>
</response>
```

The AJAX web browser application will take the above XML information and use the DOM to parse it. The data extracted from the message will be displayed on the current web page. The data will be displayed using the DOM.

Again, it is not necessary to use XML with an AJAX application. Some AJAX applications will transmit HTML or raw text messages. XML is particularly convenient because JavaScript can use the DOM to parse it.

### What AJAX Means to Bots

Supporting AJAX from a bot is very similar to supporting JavaScript from a bot. Just as with JavaScript, the user's web browsing experience boils down to a series of HTTP requests. The web server is not aware that AJAX is being used. The web server is simply accepting HTTP requests and issuing HTTP responses. How these responses are interpreted is up to the web browser.

To create a bot that supports an AJAX site, you must provide the same HTTP requests as the AJAX web application. Your bot will then examine the responses and extract the needed information from these responses.

There are two ways to do this. If you know JavaScript and how to use AJAX, you can examine the target AJAX site and learn to construct the same requests as the AJAX application. However, a much easier approach is to use a network analyzer to examine the AJAX web site as you use it. The network analyzer will show you the format of the HTTP requests and responses. This approach also allows you to not need an in-depth knowledge of AJAX.

## Recipes

One of the quickest ways to determine how to create a bot for an AJAX site is to use a network analyzer. The network analyzer will allow you to examine the HTTP requests and responses that are sent between the web browser and the web server.

The first recipe for this chapter will show how to use a network analyzer to construct the bot. This chapter will demonstrate two different recipes:

- Extract data from a non-XML based AJAX site
- Extract data from an XML based AJAX site

We will begin with a non-XML based AJAX site.

### Recipe #10.1: A Non-XML Based AJAX Site

Some AJAX sites do not use XML to transfer messages between the web browser and web server. One common format is HTML. It is often very convenient for an AJAX application to simply transmit new HTML that must be displayed to part of the web browser. To see an example of this visit the following URL:

`http://www.httprecipes.com/1/10/ajaxnonxml.php`

This page contains two AJAX features. First, as you type the name of a US state, a drop list is shown to help you narrow in on what state you would like to view. You can see this in Figure 10.3. If you do not see the drop list, as you type the state name, make sure you have JavaScript enabled.

### Figure 10.3: An AJAX Drop-List

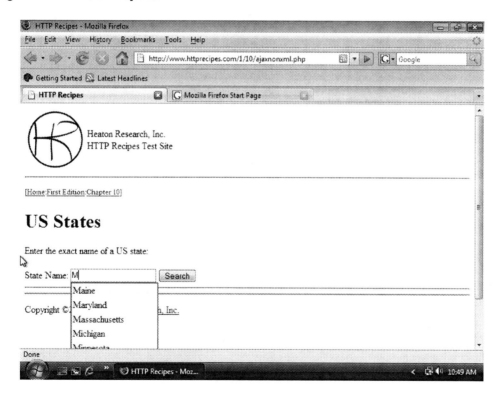

Once you select a state and click the "Search" button, you will see the second AJAX feature of this web site. Information about the state you choose is displayed. However, only the information about the state you choose was transmitted to the web browser. You will notice that you are still at the same URL. You can see a state displayed in Figure 10.4.

**Figure 10.4: Viewing Missouri**

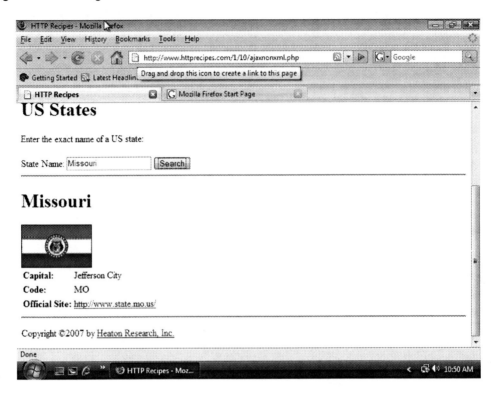

In the next section we will analyze the traffic that occurs to support these AJAX requests.

## Analyzing the HTTP Traffic

To display this drop list, as well as information about the selected state, HTML is downloaded from the web server as needed. To see this happening, use the WireShark network analyzer. This was covered in Chapter 2, "Using Network Analyzers". You can view WireShark following the AJAX traffic in Figure 10.5.

**Figure 10.5: WireShark Examining AJAX**

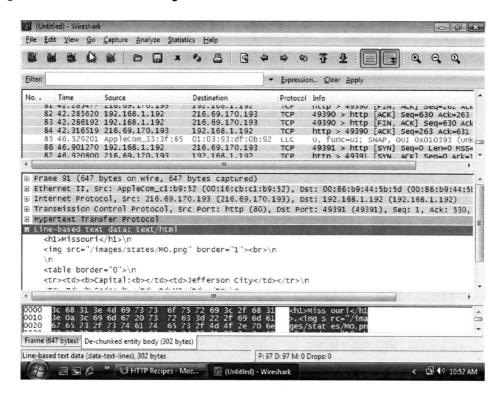

Only the very top request shown in Figure 10.5 is actually used display a complete HTTP page. All of the other requests are to handle receiving the state's name, and displaying the drop-down.

As you type in the state's name, the web browser repeatedly requests a list of states that match what you have typed so far. This data is obtained from the following URL:

**http://www.httprecipes.com/1/10/states.php**

As the state name is typed, the JavaScript on the page sends requests to the above URL to obtain a list of states that match what has been typed so far. For example, if the user had typed "Mi", the following message would be returned.

```
<ul>
<li>Michigan
<li>Minnesota
<li>Mississippi
<li>Missouri
</ul>
```

This list will be displayed in the drop down list.

Once you actually select a state, the following request is sent:

**http://www.httprecipes.com/1/10/statehtml.php?state=MO**

The above URL requests state information for Missouri, which has the postal code of "MO". The following HTML would be returned:

```
<h1>Missouri</h1>
<img src="/images/states/MO.png" border="1"><br>

<table border="0">
<tr><td><b>Capital:<b></td><td>Jefferson City</td></tr>
<tr><td><b>Code:<b></td><td>MO</td></tr>
<tr><td><b>Official Site:<b></td><td><a href="http://www.state.
mo.us/">http://www.state.mo.us/</a></td></tr>
</table>
```

Of course, this is not a complete HTML page. There is no **\<html\>** or **\<body\>** tags. This HTML will be displayed under the input area, once the user selects the desired state.

### Writing a Bot for the Non-XML AJAX Site

We will now construct a bot that can download the state information. When you want to write a bot for an AJAX site, your job is to send the same requests as the web browser. The bot we are creating will send the same request as the web server when the state information was requested. You can see this recipe in Listing 10.1.

### Listing 10.1: Non-XML AJAX Bot (AjaxNonXML.java)

```java
package com.heatonresearch.httprecipes.ch10.recipe1;

import java.io.*;
import java.net.*;

public class AjaxNonXML
{
  // the size of a buffer
  public static int BUFFER_SIZE = 8192;

  /**
   * This method downloads the specified URL into a Java
   * String. This is a very simple method, that you can
   * reused anytime you need to quickly grab all data from
   * a specific URL.
   *
```

```
 * @param url The URL to download.
 * @param timeout The number of milliseconds to wait for
 * connection.
 * @return The contents of the URL that was downloaded.
 * @throws IOException Thrown if any sort of error occurs.
 */
public String downloadPage(URL url, int timeout)
  throws IOException
{
  StringBuilder result = new StringBuilder();
  byte buffer[] = new byte[BUFFER_SIZE];

  URLConnection http = url.openConnection();
  http.setConnectTimeout(100);
  InputStream s = http.getInputStream();
  int size = 0;

  do
  {
    size = s.read(buffer);
    if (size != -1)
      result.append(new String(buffer, 0, size));
  } while (size != -1);

  return result.toString();
}


/**
 * This method will extract data found between two tokens,
 * which are usually tags.  This method does not care about
 * the case of the tokens.
 *
 * @param url The URL to download.
 * @param token1 The text, or tag, that comes before the
 * desired text.
 * @param token2 The text, or tag, that comes after the
 * desired text.
 * @param count Which occurrence of token1 to use, 1 for
 * the first.
 * @return The contents of the URL that was downloaded.
 * @throws IOException Thrown if any sort of error occurs.
 */
public String extractNoCase(String str, String token1,
  String token2, int count)
{
  int location1, location2;
```

```java
    // convert everything to lower case
    String searchStr = str.toLowerCase();
    token1 = token1.toLowerCase();
    token2 = token2.toLowerCase();

    // now search
    location1 = location2 = 0;
    do
    {
      if( location1>0 )
        location1++;

      location1 = searchStr.indexOf(token1, location1 );

      if (location1 == -1)
        return null;

      count--;
    } while (count > 0);

    // return the result from the original string that has mixed
    // case
    location2 = str.indexOf(token2, location1
    + token1.length() + 1);
    if (location2 == -1)
      return null;

    return str.substring(location1 + token1.length(), location2);
  }

  /**
   * This method will download data from the specified state.
   * This data will come in as a partial HTML document,
   * the necessary data will be extracted from there.
   * @param state The state you want to download (i.e. Missouri).
   * @throws IOException Thrown if a communication error occurs.
   */
  public void process(String state) throws IOException
  {
    URL url = new URL(
"http://www.httprecipes.com/1/10/statehtml.php?state="+state);
    String buffer = downloadPage(url,10000);
    String name = this.extractNoCase(buffer,"<h1>", "</h1>", 0);
    String capital = this.extractNoCase(buffer,
"Capital:<b></td><td>", "</td>", 0);
```

```
    String code = this.extractNoCase(buffer,
      "Code:<b></td><td>", "</td>", 0);
    String site = this.extractNoCase(buffer,
      "Official Site:<b></td><td><a href=\"", "\"", 0);

    System.out.println("State name:" + name);
    System.out.println("State capital:"+ capital);
    System.out.println("Code:"+code);
    System.out.println("Site:"+site);
  }


  /**
   * Typical Java main method, create an object, and then
   * start the object passing arguments. If insufficient
   * arguments are provided, then display startup
   * instructions.
   *
   * @param args Program arguments.
   */
  public static void main(String args[])
  {
    try
    {
      if (args.length != 1)
      {
        System.out.println(
          "Usage:\njava AjaxNonXML [state, i.e. Missouri]");
      } else
      {
        AjaxNonXML d = new AjaxNonXML();
        d.process(args[0]);
      }
    } catch (Exception e)
    {
      e.printStackTrace();
    }
  }
}
```

Most of the work for this recipe is done inside of the **process** method. The **process** method begins by downloading the contents of the URL.

```
URL url = new URL("http://www.httprecipes.com/1/10/statehtml.
php?state="+state);
String buffer = downloadPage(url,10000);
```

Next, the state name, capital, code and site are all extracted from the HTML download-ed.

```
String name = this.extractNoCase(buffer,"<h1>", "</h1>", 0);
String capital = this.extractNoCase(buffer,
  "Capital:<b></td><td>", "</td>", 0);
String code = this.extractNoCase(buffer,"Code:<b></td><td>",
  "</td>", 0);
String site = this.extractNoCase(buffer,
  "Official Site:<b></td><td><a href=\"", "\"", 0);
```

Once the data has been extracted, it is displayed.

```
System.out.println("State name:" + name);
System.out.println("State capital:"+ capital);
System.out.println("Code:"+code);
System.out.println("Site:"+site);
```

This recipe can be adapted to web sites that transfer HTML data with AJAX.

### Recipe #10.2: A XML Based AJAX Site

Many AJAX sites use XML to transfer messages between the web browser and web server. This recipe will demonstrate how to write a bot for an AJAX web site that makes use of XML. To see a web site that makes use of AJAX XML communication, examine the following URL:

**http://www.httprecipes.com/1/10/ajaxxml.php**

This page allows you to search for a list of states. For example, if you enter the string "Miss" you will see the states "Mississippi" and "Missouri". You can see this in Figure 10.6.

**Figure 10.6: Searching for States**

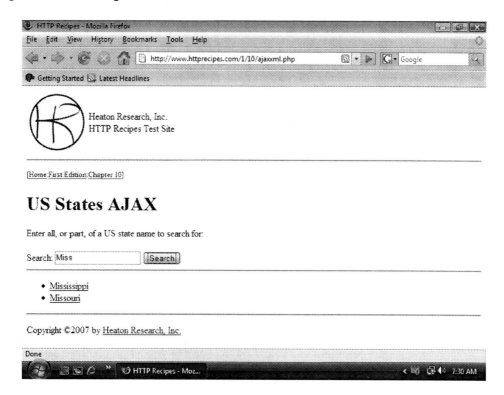

You can open any of the states returned for more information. Clicking on Missouri will produce Figure 10.7.

**Figure 10.7: Displaying a State**

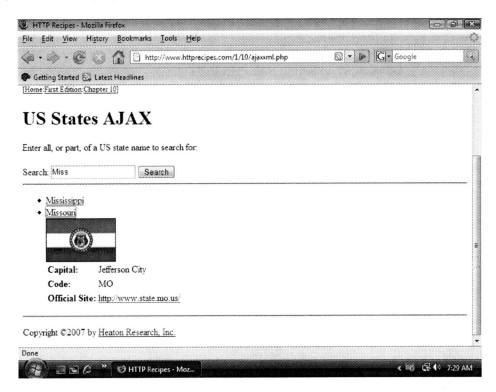

You can click on as many states as are returned from the search. The HTML will be build dynamically to add the additional information for the states.

We will now examine the XML messages that the web browser exchanges with the web server to preset this information.

## XML AJAX Messages

There are two different XML request/response pairs that are sent. The first request/response pair performs the search. If you enter the string "Miss" and select search, the following XML message will be sent to the web server:

```
<request type="search">
  <search>Miss</search>
</request>
```

There is no specified XML format for AJAX websites. You will have to analyze the messages sent by an AJAX site to see what its structure is. This can be done with a tool such as WireShark. WireShark was covered in Chapter 2, "Using Network Analyzers".

When the above search request is sent to the web server, it will respond with the following response:

```
<result>
  <state>
    <code>MS</code>
    <name>Mississippi</name>
  </state>
  <state>
    <code>MO</code>
    <name>Missouri</name>
  </state>
</result>
```

Once you have decided on a state that you would like displayed and click it, the following request will be sent:

```
<request type="state">
<code>MO</code>
</request>
```

The above request asks for information about the state of Missouri. The web server will respond as follows:

```
<result>
    <state id="25">
    <code>MO</code>
    <name>Missouri</name>
    <capital>Jefferson City</capital>
    <url>http://www.state.mo.us/</url>
  </state>
</result>
```

The above response is used by the JavaScript to display information about Missouri.

### Writing a Bot for the XML AJAX Site

We will now create a bot that can download and process the XML data from the AJAX web site. This recipe is shown in Listing 10.2.

#### Listing 10.2: XML AJAX Bot (AjaxXML.java)

```
package com.heatonresearch.httprecipes.ch10.recipe2;

import java.io.*;
import java.net.*;
import java.util.*;
import javax.xml.parsers.*;
import org.w3c.dom.*;
import org.xml.sax.SAXException;
```

```java
public class AjaxXML
{
  // the size of a buffer
  public static int BUFFER_SIZE = 8192;


  /**
   * Obtains a XML node.  Specify a name such as "state.name"
   * to nest several layers of nodes.
   * @param e The parent node.
   * @param name The child node to search for. Specify levels
   * with .'s.
   * @return Returns the node found.
   */
  private Node getXMLNode(Node e,String name)
  {
    StringTokenizer tok = new StringTokenizer(name,".");
    Node node = e;
    while( tok.hasMoreTokens() )
    {
      String currentName = tok.nextToken();

      NodeList list = node.getChildNodes();
      int len = list.getLength();
      for(int i=0;i<len;i++)
      {
        Node n = list.item(i);
        if( n.getNodeName().equals(currentName) )
        {
          node = n;
          break;
        }
      }
    }
    return node;
  }

  /**
   * Obtain the specified XML attribute from the specified node.
   * @param e The XML node to obtain an attribute from.
   * @param name The name of the attribute.
   * @return Returns the value of the attribute.
   */
  private String getXMLAttribute(Node e,String name)
  {
```

```java
    NamedNodeMap map = e.getAttributes();
    Attr attr = (Attr)map.getNamedItem(name);
    return attr.getNodeValue();
  }

  /**
   * Get the text for the specified XML node.
   * @param e The parent node.
   * @param name The child node to search for. Specify levels
   * with .'s.
   * @return The text for the specified XML node.
   */
  private String getXMLText(Element e, String name)
  {
    Node node = getXMLNode(e,name);
    NodeList nl = node.getChildNodes();
    for(int i=0;i<nl.getLength();i++)
    {
      Node n = nl.item(i);
      if( n.getNodeType() == Node.TEXT_NODE )
        return n.getNodeValue();

    }
    return null;
  }

  /**
   * Download the information for the specified state.  This
   * bot uses
   * a AJAX web site to obtain the XML message.
   * @param state The state code to look for(i.e. MO).
   * @throws IOException Thrown if there is a communication error.
   * @throws SAXException Thrown if there is an error parsing XML.
   * @throws ParserConfigurationException Thrown if there
   * is an error obtaining the parser.
   */
  public void process(String state)
throws IOException, SAXException, ParserConfigurationException
  {
    URL url = new URL(
      "http://www.httprecipes.com/1/10/request.php");

    String request =
      "<request type=\"state\"><code>"+state
      +"</code></request>";
```

```
    URLConnection http = url.openConnection();
    http.setDoOutput(true);
    OutputStream os = http.getOutputStream();
    os.write(request.getBytes());
    InputStream is = http.getInputStream();

    DocumentBuilderFactory factory =
      DocumentBuilderFactory.newInstance();
    Document d = factory.newDocumentBuilder().parse(is);

    Element e = d.getDocumentElement();
    Node stateNode = getXMLNode(e,"state");
    String id = getXMLAttribute(stateNode,"id");
    System.out.println( "State Name:"
      + getXMLText(e,"state.name") );
    System.out.println( "Code:" + getXMLText(e,"state.code") );
    System.out.println( "Capital:"
      + getXMLText(e,"state.capital") );
    System.out.println( "URL:" + getXMLText(e,"state.url") );
    System.out.println( "ID:" + id);
  }


  /**
   * Typical Java main method, create an object, and then
   * start the object passing arguments. If insufficient
   * arguments are provided, then display startup
   * instructions.
   *
   * @param args Program arguments.
   */
  public static void main(String args[])
  {
    try
    {
      if (args.length != 1)
      {
        System.out.println(
          "Usage:\njava AjaxXML [state code, i.e. MO]");
      } else
      {
        AjaxXML d = new AjaxXML();
        d.process(args[0]);
      }
    } catch (Exception e)
    {
```

```
        e.printStackTrace();
      }
    }
  }
}
```

The **process** method is called to download a state's information. The **process** method is passed a variable, named state, that contains the code for the state that is to be downloaded.

The **process** method begins by constructing a URL to which the XML request will be posted.

```
URL url = new URL("http://www.httprecipes.com/1/10/request.php");
```

Next, the XML request is constructed.

```
String request = "<request type=\"state\"><code>"+state
+"</code></request>";
```

A connection is opened, and the request is posted to the web server.

```
URLConnection http = url.openConnection();
http.setDoOutput(true);
OutputStream os = http.getOutputStream();
os.write(request.getBytes());
InputStream is = http.getInputStream();
```

The response will be in XML format, as discussed earlier. Java contains many classes to support the parsing of XML. To do this, we must first create a **DocumentBuilderFactory**. Once a **DocumentBuilderFactory** is constructed, we can pass it the **InputStream** from the HTTP connection. The XML from the **InputStream** will be parsed and loaded into a **Document** object. The **Document** implements the Document Object Model (DOM) for Java. As already discussed, the DOM allows Java to parse XML and HTML.

```
DocumentBuilderFactory factory = DocumentBuilderFactory.newIn-
stance();
Document d = factory.newDocumentBuilder().parse(is);
```

The root element is obtained from the DOM.

```
Element e = d.getDocumentElement();
```

The **getXMLNode** function is called to obtain the **state** node from the XML. The implementation of the **getXMLNode** function will be explained later in this chapter. The **getXMLAttribute** function is also called to read the **id** attribute from the **state** node.

```
Node stateNode = getXMLNode(e,"state");
String id = getXMLAttribute(stateNode,"id");
```

Each of the attributes are read from the **state** node.

```
System.out.println( "State Name:" +
getXMLNode(e,"state.name").getTextContent() );
System.out.println( "Code:" +
getXMLNode(e,"state.code").getTextContent() );
System.out.println( "Capital:" +
getXMLNode(e,"state.capital").getTextContent() );
System.out.println( "URL:" +
getXMLNode(e,"state.url").getTextContent() );
System.out.println( "ID:" + id);
```

In the above example, we made use of **getXMLNode** and **getXMLAttribute** functions. These are not built in Java functions. They are functions I created to make working with the DOM easier. They will be discussed in the next two sections.

### Implementing getXMLNode

The **getXMLNode** function is a simple function that allows you to quickly take apart XML and get to the data you need. To understand how it works, consider the following XML:

```
<firstLevel>
  <secondLevel>
    <thirdLevel>
    </thirdLevel>
  </secondLevel>
</firstLevel>
```

If you wanted to access the **<thirdLevel>** node, using only the DOM, you would have to iterate through each level.

Using the **getXMLNode** function makes this much easier. To return the **<thirdLevel>** node, you would use the following code:

```
Node node = getXMLNode(documentRoot,"firstLevel.secondLevel.third-
Level");
```

The **getXMLNode** method is fairly short. It begins by creating a **StringTokenizer** object to break the name up by periods. For example, the name "firstLevel.secondLevel.third-Level" would be broken in to three names.

```
StringTokenizer tok = new StringTokenizer(name,".");
Node node = e;
while( tok.hasMoreTokens() )
{
```

As each component of the name is parsed, we attempt to find it at the current level.

```
String currentName = tok.nextToken();
```

```
NodeList list = node.getChildNodes();
int len = list.getLength();
for(int i=0;i<len;i++)
{
```

Once the current name segment is found, we move it to the **node** variable and **break** out of the search loop. The function will now return if there are no more search elements, or continue searching if there are.

```
Node n = list.item(i);
if( n.getNodeName().equals(currentName) )
{
  node = n;
  break;
}
```

Finally, the **node** that was found is returned.

```
return node;
```

Once you have read a node you will likely either want to get its content text, or obtain an attribute from that node. To access the content text, you simply call the **getTextContent** function of the node, as follows:

```
System.out.println("Value is: " + node.getTextContent() );
```

Obtaining an attribute from a node is discussed in the next section.

### Implementing getXMLAttribute

Some XML tags have attributes. The **getXMLAttribute** method can be called to quickly retrieve the attribute from an XML tag. Consider the following XML tag:

```
<state id="25">
```

This XML tag has one property named **id** that has a value of **25**. To access this value, the **getXMLAttribute** function is used. This function begins by obtaining a map of all attributes. Calling **getNamedItem** looks up the attribute, then the node value is returned.

```
NamedNodeMap map = e.getAttributes();
Attr attr = (Attr)map.getNamedItem(name);
return attr.getNodeValue();
```

This obtains the attribute value.

## Summary

This chapter showed you how to create bots that access sites that make use of AJAX. AJAX stands for Asynchronous JavaScript with XML. AJAX web sites usually make use of HTML/XML, CSS, and the **XMLHttpRequestObject**. However, some of these components can be exchanged for other components. For example, some web sites make use of **<iframe>** tags instead of the **XMLHttpRequestObject**. Additionally, not all AJAX websites make use of XML.

This chapter presented two recipes that showed how to communicate with the different types of AJAX web sites. You were shown how to process data from an AJAX web site that exchanges information using XML. You were also shown how to access data from an AJAX web site that did not use XML.

The biggest challenge in creating a bot for an AJAX web site is figuring out the communication protocol between the web server and the web browser. You must understand what HTTP requests and responses are flowing between the web server and the web browser. This will allow your bot to send the same requests and process the same responses as a web browser would. The challenges are similar to working with JavaScript, as was covered in the last chapter. This demonstrates that AJAX sites are just an advanced application of JavaScript.

Some web sites are designed to allow you to transfer XML requests with them. Such services are called web services. Exchanging XML with a web service is very similar to communicating with an AJAX web site. Building bots to work with web services will be covered in the next chapter.

# CHAPTER 11: HANDLING WEB SERVICES

- Understanding Web Services
- Notable Public Web Services
- Using the Google Search API
- Creating Hybrid Bots
- Using the AXIS Framework

A bot is a program that accesses HTML and AJAX web sites that were designed for human visitors. This is often complex for the bot because the HTML is formatted for a human to read. This is not the case with a web service. A web service is a web site that was designed from the start to be accessed by other computers.

Web Services are an important aspect of HTTP programming. Web Services communicate using HTTP. The data exchanged between a Web Service server and client is usually in XML (Extensible Markup Language). This makes it very easy for a Java program to interpret.

A program that accesses a web service is not typically called a bot. However, some bots make use of Web Services to help them find other HTML sites to process. Such a bot is called a hybrid bot. Hybrid bots will be discussed later in this chapter. Additionally, this chapter will present one recipe that implements a hybrid bot.

## Notable Public Web Services

Many different companies offer web services. Many major web sites offer some sort of web service. If the web site you wish to work with offers a web service, this is the preferred means of communicating with that site. Table 11.1 lists some of the most commonly used Web Services.

**Table 11.1: Large Websites Offering Web Services**

| Web Site | Web Services Offered |
|---|---|
| Alexa | Alexa web services allow access to their web site directory and web site thumbnails. |
| Amazon | Amazon allows access to their product database through their web services. This allows web sites to create a complete Amazon based online store, complete with a shopping cart. |
| Blogger | Blogger web services allow blog entries to be posted. |
| Digg | Digg web services allow you to digg a web link, as well as other access to the Digg API. |
| EBay | EBay web services allow you to place and modify auction listings. |
| Flickr | Flickr web services allow access to their image database. |
| Google | Google web services allow access to their search database, and other services. |
| MSN | MSN web services allow access to their search database. |
| Paypal | Paypal web services allow you to process payments. |
| United States Postal Service | The USPS web services allow you to calculate shipping rates. |
| Yahoo | Yahoo web services allow access to their search database. |

For more information on any of these web services you should consult their web site. Most web sites that make web services available have documentation on how to implement their service using Java.

## Using the Google API

Google offers a wide variety of web services. One of the most useful to bot programmers, is the Google Search API. Information about the Google Search API can be found at the following address:

```
http://www.google.com/apis/index.html
```

The Google Search API allows access to Google search information. You can perform any of the following using the Google search API:

- Spell check
- Search for a term
- View Googles cache for a site
- Find sites that link to a URL
- And more

In the next two sections, you will be shown how to make use of the Google Search API. First, you will have to register with Google. Secondly, you will have to obtain Google's JAR file that allows your Java application to access Google.

### Registering for the Google API

When you request information from the Google API, you must send a key along with your request. This key allows Google to track where requests are coming from. Before you can use the Google Search API, you must register to obtain one of these keys. Once you register with Google, your key will be mailed to you. To register with Google, visit the "Google Developer Network."

```
http://code.google.com/
```

The Google key is just a long stream of seemingly random characters. For example, the Google key might look something like the following:

```
jWKfuw78WHdiwe8dfHs
```

This is not an actual Google key, and as a result would not work properly with the Google Search API. To use any of the Google examples in this chapter, you will have to obtain a Google API key of your own.

### Using the Google API

The Google API provides a JAR file for you to use with your Java applications. You should download this JAR file and include it with the **classpath** of any Java application that you wish to use the Google API with.

For precise instructions on how to include the Google API with your Java project, refer to the documentation that was included with the Google JAR file you downloaded. It will contain up to date information on how to include the most current JAR file with your application.

Once you have added the Google JAR file to your application, you are ready to make use of it. The Google JAR file provides several new classes for your applications to use. To access these classes, you must import them with the following **import** command:

```
import com.google.soap.search.*;
```

Now that you have included the Google package, you can make use of the Google classes. Some of the more common Google classes that you will make use of are:

- GoogleSearch
- GoogleSearchResult
- GoogleSearchResultElement

The recipes shown later in this chapter will demonstrate how to make use of these classes.

## Hybrid Bots

A hybrid bot makes use of both web services and conventional HTML based web access. The Google web services API is very useful for creating hybrid bots. The Google search API allows you to quickly locate pages for your bot to visit.

Consider if you wanted to create a bot that downloaded information about "George Washington". It would take a very long time to construct a bot that would visit every site on the web looking for information about "George Washington".

Thanks to the Google search API, you do not need to construct such a bot. You can submit a search request to the Google API, and you will be given a list of all web pages that contain the name "George Washington". Your bot can then access these sites using the methods previously discussed in this book. Recipe 11.3 demonstrates a hybrid bot.

## Understanding SOAP

When you make use of the Google API, your computer is sending requests to Google and receiving responses back. You might be wondering what format these requests and responses are in. Most web services make use of the HTTP protocol called Simple Object Access Protocol (SOAP) to send and receive requests and responses.

SOAP is a standard format for representing web service requests and responses. SOAP is XML based and can be processed using the Document Object Model (DOM) or any of a large number of framework libraries designed to make it easy to access SOAP. Later in this chapter you will be shown how to use AXIS, which is a SOAP access framework provided by Apache. For now, we will examine SOAP directly, and see what messages are sent and received by it.

You can see a simple SOAP server at the following URL:

`http://www.httprecipes.com/1/11/`

This SOAP server translates English to "Pig Latin". Pig Latin is a simple language game based on English. English can be quickly translated to Pig Latin by following a set of rules. For more information on Pig Latin visit the following URL:

**http://en.wikipedia.org/wiki/Pig latin**

It is not important to understand Pig Latin for this example. It is simply used to create a simple web service.

## Using WSDL Information

Most web services make use of a single HTTP page that describes the types of requests that a SOAP server can handle. This page is in a special XML format called the Web Service Definition Language (WSDL). The Pig Latin web server supports such a page. To see the WSDL from the Pig Latin SOAP server, visit the following URL:

**http://www.httprecipes.com/1/11/soap/?wsdl**

You can see the output from the above URL in Listing 11.1:

### Listing 11.1: Pig Latin Server's WSDL

```
<?xml version="1.0" encoding="ISO-8859-1"?>
<definitions
xmlns:SOAP-ENV="http://schemas.xmlsoap.org/soap/envelope/"
xmlns:xsd="http://www.w3.org/2001/XMLSchema"
xmlns:xsi="http://www.w3.org/2001/XMLSchema-instance"
xmlns:SOAP-ENC="http://schemas.xmlsoap.org/soap/encoding/"
xmlns:tns="http://www.httprecipes.com/1/11/soap/"
xmlns:soap="http://schemas.xmlsoap.org/wsdl/soap/"
xmlns:wsdl="http://schemas.xmlsoap.org/wsdl/"
xmlns="http://schemas.xmlsoap.org/wsdl/"
targetNamespace="http://www.httprecipes.com/1/11/soap/">

<types>
<xsd:schema
targetNamespace="http://www.httprecipes.com/1/11/soap/">
<xsd:import
namespace="http://schemas.xmlsoap.org/soap/encoding/" />
<xsd:import namespace="http://schemas.xmlsoap.org/wsdl/" />
</xsd:schema>
</types>

<message name="translateRequest">
<part name="inputString" type="xsd:string" />
</message>
```

```
<message name="translateResponse">
<part name="return" type="xsd:string" />
</message>

<portType name="PigLatinTranslatorPortType">
<operation name="translate">
<input message="tns:translateRequest"/>
<output message="tns:translateResponse"/>
</operation>
</portType>

<binding name="PigLatinTranslatorBinding"
type="tns:PigLatinTranslatorPortType">
<soap:binding style="rpc"
transport="http://schemas.xmlsoap.org/soap/http"/>
<operation name="translate">
<soap:operation
soapAction=
"http://www.httprecipes.com/1/11/soap/index.php/translate"
style="rpc"/>
<input>
<soap:body use="encoded"
namespace="http://www.httprecipes.com/1/11/soap/"
encodingStyle="http://schemas.xmlsoap.org/soap/encoding/"/>
</input>
<output>
<soap:body use="encoded"
namespace="http://www.httprecipes.com/1/11/soap/"
encodingStyle="http://schemas.xmlsoap.org/soap/encoding/"/>
</output>
</operation>
</binding>
<service name="PigLatinTranslator">
<port name="PigLatinTranslatorPort"
binding="tns:PigLatinTranslatorBinding">
<soap:address
location="http://www.httprecipes.com/1/11/soap/index.php"/>
</port>
</service>
</definitions>
```

It is not important to understand the exact format of WSDL unless you are going to implement a SOAP framework. Later in this chapter you will see how to use the AXIS framework to generate Java class files from the above WSDL.

In the next two sections, you will see how to use the Pig Latin server to translate "Hello World" into Pig Latin. You will be shown both the request and response for this operation. Finally, you will be shown how to use AXIS to generate Java classes that perform all of these operations for you.

## SOAP Requests

SOAP requests and responses work very similar to Java method calls. For the Pig Latin server, think of it as calling a very simple function, such as this:

```
public String translate(String str);
```

The **translate** function accepts a string, which is the text to be translated, then returns a translated string. To accomplish this, an XML request is built according to the SOAP specification that contains the name of the function to call, as well as the text to translate. Listing 11.2 shows how to call the translate function with the text "Hello World".

### Listing 11.2: Pig Latin SOAP Request

```
<?xml version="1.0" encoding="UTF-8" standalone="no"?>
<SOAP-ENV:Envelope
xmlns:SOAP-ENV="http://schemas.xmlsoap.org/soap/envelope/"
xmlns:xsd="http://www.w3.org/2001/XMLSchema"
xmlns:xsi="http://www.w3.org/2001/XMLSchema-instance"
xmlns:tns="http://www.httprecipes.com/1/11/soap/"
xmlns:soap="http://schemas.xmlsoap.org/wsdl/soap/"
xmlns:wsdl="http://schemas.xmlsoap.org/wsdl/"
xmlns:SOAP-ENC="http://schemas.xmlsoap.org/soap/encoding/">
<SOAP-ENV:Body>
<mns:translate
xmlns:mns="http://www.httprecipes.com/1/11/soap/"
SOAP-ENV:encodingStyle=
"http://schemas.xmlsoap.org/soap/encoding/">
<inputString xsi:type="xsd:string">Hello World</inputString>
</mns:translate>
</SOAP-ENV:Body>
</SOAP-ENV:Envelope>
```

There is considerable overhead XML that tells the SOAP server what kind of request this is; however, you can still see the function name (translate) and the text passed to the function (Hello World).

## SOAP Responses

Once the SOAP server receives the request, the text is translated and returned. The text is returned as a SOAP formatted response. The response is seen in Listing 11.3.

### Listing 11.3: Pig Latin Server's SOAP Response

```
<?xml version="1.0" encoding="ISO-8859-1"?>
<SOAP-ENV:Envelope
SOAP-ENV:encodingStyle=
"http://schemas.xmlsoap.org/soap/encoding/"
xmlns:SOAP-ENV="http://schemas.xmlsoap.org/soap/envelope/"
xmlns:xsd="http://www.w3.org/2001/XMLSchema"
xmlns:xsi="http://www.w3.org/2001/XMLSchema-instance"
xmlns:SOAP-ENC="http://schemas.xmlsoap.org/soap/encoding/">
<SOAP-ENV:Body>
<ns1:translateResponse xmlns:ns1=
"http://www.httprecipes.com/1/11/soap/">
<return xsi:type="xsd:string">ellohay orldway</return>
</ns1:translateResponse></SOAP-ENV:Body>
</SOAP-ENV:Envelope>
```

As you can see, the translated text is returned.

It can be complex to build and parse SOAP requests and responses. Because of this, programmers often use a framework to help. In the next section, you will learn about the Apache AXIS framework.

### Using AXIS

If you need to access a SOAP based web service from Java, one of the easiest ways is to use the AXIS framework. The Apache Foundation offers the AXIS framework. This framework allows you to quickly construct Java objects that allow you to access a web service. You can download the AXIS framework from the following URL:

**http://ws.apache.org/axis/**

Downloading and installing AXIS will provide you with a directory named **c:\axis-1_4\** or similar, depending on the current version. The first step is to run the **wsdl2java** utility. This utility accepts the URL of a WSDL file, and generates Java classes needed to access the web service.

The **wsdl2java** utility is written in Java; and it must be run, along with its required JAR files. The following Java command would run the **wsdl2java** utility and process the Pig Latin server.

```
java -cp lib\axis.jar;lib\commons-discovery-0.2.jar;lib\commons-
logging-1.0.4.jar;
lib\jaxrpc.jar;lib\log4j-1.2.8;lib\saaj.jar;lib\wsdl4j-1.5.1.jar
org.apache.axis.wsdl.WSDL2Java http://www.httprecipes.com/1/11/
soap/?wsdl
```

Of course, you would issue this command all as one single line. For more information on using **wsdl2java,** refer to the AXIS documentation.

The **wsdl2java** utility can be used on any web service that supports WSDL and SOAP. Recipe 11.2 will use the classes generated by **wsdl2java** for the Pig Latin server.

# Recipes

This chapter includes three recipes. These recipes demonstrate how to construct bots to work with web services or a combination of web services and regular HTTP programming. Specifically, you will see how to perform the following techniques:

- Using Google
- Access a SOAP Server
- Constructing a Hybrid Bot

These recipes cover a combination of web service and hybrid bot programming.

### Recipe #11.1: Scanning for Links

One of the key components determining how high a search engine will place a particular site, is the number of other sites linked to that site. Because of this, it can be beneficial to scan for which sites are linked to a particular site.

This recipe will display all inbound links to a particular site, based on the Google Search API. This recipe also displays how many links each of those sites have as well. Consider Figure 11.1.

**Figure 11.1: Links Between Sites**

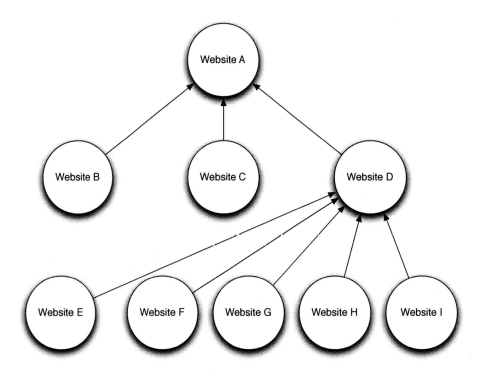

Our website is site A. You can see that we have three inbound links, from sites B, C, and D. Site B and C have no links of their own, so they are not valued terribly high by a search engine. Site D, on the other hand, has five links of its own. As a result, site D is far more valuable of a link to Site A than both Site B and Site C.

This is why this recipe returns how many links each inbound link has. The inbound link with the higher number, and therefore more links, is more valuable.

A very useful technique is to run this recipe for a competitor's web site. You will quickly see which links are most valuable to your competitor. You can then see about getting links from those sites to your site as well.

Listing 11.4 shows this recipe.

**Listing 11.4: Scanning for Links (ScanLinks.java)**

```
package com.heatonresearch.httprecipes.ch11.recipe1;

import com.google.soap.search.*;
import java.util.*;
```

```java
public class ScanLinks
{
  /*
   * The key that Google provides anyone who uses their API.
   */
  static String key;

  /*
   * The search object to use.
   */
  static GoogleSearch search;

  /**
   * This method queries Google for the specified search, all
   * URL's found by Google are returned.
   *
   * @param query What to search for.
   * @return The URL's that google returned for the search.
   */
  public static Collection<GoogleSearchResultElement>
getResults(String query)
  {
    Collection<GoogleSearchResultElement> result =
      new ArrayList<GoogleSearchResultElement>();
    int resultCount = 0;
    int top = 0;

    do
    {
      search.setQueryString(query);
      search.setStartResult(top);
      GoogleSearchResult r = null;
      try
      {
        r = search.doSearch();
      } catch (GoogleSearchFault e)
      {
        e.printStackTrace();
      }

      if (r != null)
      {
        Object list[] = r.getResultElements();
        resultCount = list.length;
        for (int i = 0; i < resultCount; i++)
```

```
        {
          GoogleSearchResultElement element =
           (GoogleSearchResultElement) list[i];
          result.add(element);
        }
      }
      top = top + 10;
      System.out.println(top);
    } while (resultCount >= 10);

    return result;
  }

  /**
   * For the given URL check how many links the URL has.
   *
   * @param url The URL to check.
   * @return The number of links that URL has.
   */
  public static int getLinkCount(String url)
  {
    int result = 0;
    search.setQueryString("link:" + url);
    GoogleSearchResult r = null;
    try
    {
      r = search.doSearch();
    } catch (GoogleSearchFault e)
    {
      e.printStackTrace();
    }

    result = r.getEstimatedTotalResultsCount();
    return result;

  }

  /**
   * The main method processes the command line arguments and
   * then calls getResults to build up the list.
   *
   * @param args Holds the Google key and the site to search.
   */
  public static void main(String args[])
  {
    if (args.length < 2)
```

```
  {
    System.out.println("ScanLinks [Google Key] [Site to Scan]");
  } else
  {

    key = args[0];
    search = new GoogleSearch();
    search.setKey(key);

    Collection<GoogleSearchResultElement> c =
      getResults("\"" + args[1] + "\"");

    for( GoogleSearchResultElement element:c)
    {
      StringBuilder str = new StringBuilder();
      str.append(getLinkCount(element.getURL()));
      str.append(":");
      str.append(element.getTitle() );
      str.append(" (");
      str.append(element.getURL());
      str.append(")");
      System.out.println(str.toString());


    }
   }
  }
}
```

This recipe should be run with two parameters. The first parameter is the your Google key, which was obtained from Google. The second parameter is the URL of the site you wish to scan. For example, to scan the HTTP Recipes site you would use the following command:

```
ScanLinks [Google Key] [URL to Scan]
```

The above command simply shows where the abstract format to call this recipe, with the appropriate parameters. For exact information on how to run this recipe refer to Appendix B, C, or D, depending on the operating system you are using. The main method begins by obtaining the key and passing it onto the **GoogleSearch** object.

```
key = args[0];
search = new GoogleSearch();
search.setKey(key);
```

Next, the URL to be scanned is passed to the **getResults** function. This function will be discussed in the next section.

```
Collection<GoogleSearchResultElement> c =
getResults("\"" + args[1] + "\"");
```

The **getResults** function returns a Collection of **GoogleSearchResultElement** objects. These objects are displayed.

```
for( GoogleSearchResultElement element:c)
{
```

Each element is displayed. For each element, the **getLinkCount** function is called to display the number of links found.

```
  StringBuilder str = new StringBuilder();
  str.append(getLinkCount(element.getURL()));
  str.append(":");
  str.append(element.getTitle() );
  str.append("(");
  str.append(element.getURL());
  str.append(")");
  System.out.println(str.toString());
}
```

Each of the elements will be displayed.

### Searching Google

In the last section, we saw that the **getResults** function returns a list of pages from the Google search engine. In this section, we will see how the **getResults** function works. It begins by creating a collection of **GoogleSearchResultElement** objects.

```
Collection<GoogleSearchResultElement> result =
new ArrayList<GoogleSearchResultElement>();
int resultCount = 0;
int top = 0;
```

Next, the **getResults** function begins a loop and obtains the search results. Google returns the search results ten items at a time.

```
do
{
  search.setQueryString(query);
  search.setStartResult(top);
  GoogleSearchResult r = null;
```

The search is performed.

```
try
{
  r = search.doSearch();
} catch (GoogleSearchFault e)
{
  e.printStackTrace();
```

```
}
```

For each search, a **GoogleSearchResult** object is returned. This object is accessed to obtain the **GoogleSearchResultElement** objects, which contain the actual URL's found by the Google search.

```
if (r != null)
{
  Object list[] = r.getResultElements();
  resultCount = list.length;
```

Next, look through and obtain all of the **GoogleSearchResultElement** objects.

```
for (int i = 0; i < resultCount; i++)
{
  GoogleSearchResultElement element =
   (GoogleSearchResultElement) list[i];
  result.add(element);
}
```

If fewer than ten items were returned in the search, then we have reached the end of the search.

```
  top = top + 10;
  System.out.println(top);
} while (resultCount >= 10);
```

```
return result;
```

When the **getResults** function completes, we will have a list of all pages that contain a reference to the target web site.

### Getting a Link Count

It is also very easy to get a link count from Google. Simply perform a search on the target URL, with the prefix "link:", as seen here:

```
int result = 0;
search.setQueryString("link:" + url);
GoogleSearchResult r = null;
```

Next, the search is performed.

```
try
{
  r = search.doSearch();
} catch (GoogleSearchFault e)
{
  e.printStackTrace();
```

```
}
```

Now, rather than looping through all the results, as was done in the last section, we simply call **getEstimatedTotalResultsCount** to see how many links were found.

```
result = r.getEstimatedTotalResultsCount();
return result;
```

The number of results found is returned.

### Recipe #11.2: Using AXIS to Access a SOAP Server

In the previous recipe, we accessed the Google Search API. The Google web service provides Java classes for us to access Google. However, not all web services provide such classes. When a web service does not provide such classes, you should use Apache AXIS to generate such classes for you.

This recipe demonstrates how to use Apache AXIS to access a web server. You can view this recipe in Listing 11.5 below:

### Listing 11.5: Using AXIS to Access a SOAP Server (PigLatin.java)

```java
package com.heatonresearch.httprecipes.ch11.recipe2;

import java.rmi.RemoteException;
import javax.xml.rpc.ServiceException;
import com.httprecipes.www._1._11.soap.*;

public class PigLatin
{
  /***
   * The main method.
   * @param args Not used.
   * @throws RemoteException Thrown if there is an error
   * connecting the remote system.
   */
  public static void main(String args[]) throws RemoteException
  {

    try
    {
      PigLatinTranslatorLocator locator =
        new PigLatinTranslatorLocator();
      PigLatinTranslatorBindingStub trans =
        (PigLatinTranslatorBindingStub)
        locator.getPigLatinTranslatorPort();
      System.out.println( trans.translate("Hello world!") );
```

```
    } catch (ServiceException e)
    {
      e.printStackTrace();
    }

  }
}
```

This recipe uses several classes that were generated by the **wsdl2java** utility, which was discussed earlier in this chapter. These classes were generated from the web service located at the following URL:

**http://www.httprecipes.com/1/11/soap/**

The URL where the web service resides forms part of the package name created by AXIS. The following **import** statement accesses the classes used to access the above web service.

```
import com.httprecipes.www._1._11.soap.*;
```

As you can see, the above package name is based on the URL.

Once the classes have been imported, it is very easy to make use of the web service. First, create a locator object. This is used to locate the web service.

```
PigLatinTranslatorLocator locator = new PigLatinTranslatorLoca-
tor();
```

Next, a binding is created between the locator and a local class to access the web service.

```
PigLatinTranslatorBindingStub trans = (PigLatinTranslatorBindingS-
tub) locator.getPigLatinTranslatorPort();
```

Now that the web service has been bound, you can call any method on the web service by using the bound object, which in this case is named **trans**.

```
System.out.println( trans.translate("Hello world!") );
```

As you can see, the AXIS framework makes it very easy to use web services.

### Recipe #11.3: A Google Hybrid Bot

It is also possible to create a hybrid bot. A hybrid bot uses both traditional HTML parsing, as discussed in the preceding chapters, as well as web services. The Google Search API is a great choice for hybrid bots. You can use the Google Search API to locate web pages that match your criteria, and then use a traditional HTML bot to scan these sites for what you are looking for.

This recipe will create a bot that will scan sites that contain information about a famous person that you will choose. The bot will attempt to obtain the person's birth year. The bot works by calling on Google to find web sites that contain the person's name. The bot then scans the HTML of each of these pages looking for the person's birth year.

This recipe is shown in Listing 11.6.

### Listing 11.6: A Google Hybrid Bot (WhenBorn.java)

```java
package com.heatonresearch.httprecipes.ch11.recipe3;

import com.google.soap.search.*;
import com.heatonresearch.httprecipes.html.ParseHTML;

import java.io.IOException;
import java.io.InputStream;
import java.net.URL;
import java.net.URLConnection;
import java.util.*;

public class WhenBorn
{
  /*
   * The key that Google provides anyone who uses their API.
   */
  static String key;

  /*
   * The search object to use.
   */
  static GoogleSearch search;

  /*
   * This map stores a mapping between a year, and how
   * many times that year has come up as a potential birth year.
   */
  private Map<Integer, Integer> results =
    new HashMap<Integer, Integer>();


  /**
   * Perform a Google search and return the results. Only return
   * 100 results.
   * @param query What to search for.
   * @return The results of the Google search.
   */
  public Collection<GoogleSearchResultElement>
```

```java
  getResults(String query)
{
  Collection<GoogleSearchResultElement> result =
    new ArrayList<GoogleSearchResultElement>();
  int resultCount = 0;
  int top = 0;

  do
  {
    search.setQueryString("\"" + query + "\"");
    search.setStartResult(top);
    GoogleSearchResult r = null;
    try
    {
      r = search.doSearch();
    } catch (GoogleSearchFault e)
    {
      e.printStackTrace();
    }

    if (r != null)
    {
      Object list[] = r.getResultElements();
      resultCount = list.length;
      for (int i = 0; i < resultCount; i++)
      {
        GoogleSearchResultElement element =
          (GoogleSearchResultElement) list[i];
        result.add(element);
      }
    }
    top = top + 10;
  } while ((resultCount >= 10) && (result.size() < 100));

  return result;
}


/**
 * Examine a sentence and see if it contains the word born
 * and a number.
 *
 * @param sentence The sentence to search.
 * @return The number that was found.
 */
private int extractBirth(String sentence)
```

```
{
  boolean foundBorn = false;
  int result = -1;

  StringTokenizer tok = new StringTokenizer(sentence);
  while (tok.hasMoreTokens())
  {
    String word = tok.nextToken();

    try
    {
      result = Integer.parseInt(word);
    } catch (NumberFormatException e)
    {
      if (word.equalsIgnoreCase("born"))
        foundBorn = true;
    }
  }

  if (!foundBorn)
    result = -1;

  return result;
}

/**
 * Increase the specified year's count in the map.
 * @param year The year to increase.
 */
private void increaseYear(int year)
{
  Integer count = results.get(year);
  if (count == null)
    count = new Integer(1);
  else
    count = new Integer(count.intValue() + 1);
  results.put(year, count);
}

/**
 * Check the specified URL for a birth year.  This will occur
 * if one sentence is found that has the word born, and a
 * numeric value less than 3000.
 *
 * @param url The URL to check.
 * @throws IOException Thrown if a communication error occurs.
 */
```

```java
public void checkURL(URL url) throws IOException
{
  int ch;
  StringBuilder sentence = new StringBuilder();

  URLConnection http = url.openConnection();
  http.setConnectTimeout(1000);
  http.setReadTimeout(1000);
  InputStream is = http.getInputStream();
  ParseHTML html = new ParseHTML(is);
  do
  {
    ch = html.read();
    if ((ch != -1) && (ch != 0))
    {
      if (ch == '.')
      {
        String str = sentence.toString();
        int year = extractBirth(str);
        if ((year > 1) && (year < 3000))
        {
          System.out.println("URL supports year: " + year);
          increaseYear(year);
        }
        sentence.setLength(0);
      } else
        sentence.append((char) ch);
    }
  } while (ch != -1);

}



/**
 * Get birth year that occurred the largest number of times.
 *
 * @return The birth year that occurred the largest
 * number of times.
 */
public int getResult()
{
  int result = -1;
  int maxCount = 0;

  Set<Integer> set = results.keySet();
  for (int year : set)
```

```
  {
    int count = results.get(year);
    if (count > maxCount)
    {
      result = year;
      maxCount = count;
    }
  }

  return result;
}



/**
 * This method is called to determine the birth year for a
 * person.  It obtains 100 web pages that Google returns
 * for that person.  Each of these pages is then searched
 * for the birth year of that person.
 * Which ever year is selected the largest number of times
 * is selected as the birth year.
 *
 * @param name The name of the person you are seeing the
 * birth year for.
 * @throws IOException Thrown if a communication error occurs.
 */
public void process(String name) throws IOException
{
  search = new GoogleSearch();
  search.setKey(key);

  System.out.println("Getting search results form Google.");
  Collection<GoogleSearchResultElement> c = getResults(name);
  int i = 0;

  System.out.println("Scanning URL's from Google.");
  for (GoogleSearchResultElement element : c)
  {
    try
    {
      i++;
      URL u = new URL(element.getURL());
      System.out.println("Scanning URL: " + i + "/"
        + c.size() + ":" + u);
      checkURL(u);
    } catch (IOException e)
    {
```

```
      }
    }

    int resultYear = getResult();
    if (resultYear == -1)
    {
      System.out.println("Could not determine when "
        + name + " was born.");
    } else
    {
      System.out.println(name + " was born in " + resultYear);
    }
  }

  /**
   * The main method processes the command line arguments and
   * then calls process method to determine the birth year.
   *
   * @param args Holds the Google key and the site to search.
   */
  public static void main(String args[])
  {
    if (args.length < 2)
    {
      System.out.println(
        "Usage:\njava WhenBorn [Google Key] [Famous Person]");
    } else
    {
      try
      {
        key = args[0];
        WhenBorn when = new WhenBorn();
        when.process(args[1]);
      } catch (Exception e)
      {
        e.printStackTrace();
      }
    }
  }

}
```

This program completes three phases to obtain the information needed. First, the famous person is presented to Google to get a list of web sites that contain this person's name. Secondly, each of the search results is scanned for a birth year. These birth years are accumulated in a list. Finally, the program determines which birth year was the most prevalent. This birth year is then assumed to be the birth year of the famous person.

This recipe begins by submitting the name of the famous person to Google. The results are read by calling the **getResults** function.

```
search = new GoogleSearch();
search.setKey(key);

System.out.println("Getting search results form Google.");
Collection<GoogleSearchResultElement> c = getResults(name);
int i = 0;
```

Next, each of the URLs returned from Google are checked. Because some of the URLs returned from Google may no longer be valid, a **try/catch** block is used inside of the loop to catch errors. This is not really an issue to the program. Such URLs are simply skipped and the loop continues to the next iteration.

Each URL that is found is passed to the **checkURL** method. This method will be covered in a later section.

```
System.out.println("Scanning URL's from Google.");
for (GoogleSearchResultElement element : c)
{
  try
  {
    i++;
    URL u = new URL(element.getURL());
    System.out.println("Scanning URL: " + i + "/" + c.size()
      + ":" + u);
    checkURL(u);
  }


  catch (IOException e)
  {
  }
}
```

Once all of the URLs have been processed, the **getResult** function is called to determine which birth year is the famous person's actual birth year.

```
int resultYear = getResult();
if (resultYear == -1)
{
```

```
System.out.println("Could not determine when "
  + name + " was born.");
} else
{
  System.out.println(name + " was born in " + resultYear);
}
```

In some cases, the program may not be able to determine the person's birth year. If this occurs, the user is informed.

### Searching Google

The first step is to submit the search to Google and get the results back.

```
Collection<GoogleSearchResultElement> result = new ArrayList<Googl
eSearchResultElement>();
int resultCount = 0;
int top = 0;
```

The search is submitted.

```
do
{
  search.setQueryString("\"" + query + "\"");
  search.setStartResult(top);
  GoogleSearchResult r = null;
try
{
  r = search.doSearch();
} catch (GoogleSearchFault e)
{
  e.printStackTrace();
}
```

If search results were found, add them to the list and continue. Google returns **GoogleSearchResultElement** objects for each of the URLs found.

```
if (r != null)
{
  Object list[] = r.getResultElements();
  resultCount = list.length;

  for (int i = 0; i < resultCount; i++)
  {
    GoogleSearchResultElement element =
      (GoogleSearchResultElement)    list[i];
    result.add(element);
  }
}
```

```
top = top + 10;
```

Only look at up to 100 pages.

```
} while ((resultCount >= 10) && (result.size() < 100));
```

```
return result;
```

Finally, the complete list is returned.

### Checking a Search Result

Each URL that was located by Google must be processed. These URLs will be downloaded and parsed into sentences. If a sentence contains both the word "born" and a number that looks like a year, that number is assumed to be a birth year. Numbers that are between 1 and 3000 are considered as possible years. People born before 1 AD are out of the scope for the program.

The **checkURL** method begins by creating a **StringBuilder** that will hold each sentence as it is parsed.

```
int ch;
StringBuilder sentence = new StringBuilder();
```

A connection is opened to the URL and a **ParseHTML** object is constructed to parse the HTML found at this site. We are not really interested in the HTML. The main purpose of the parser is to strip the HTML tags away from the text. We are only interested in the text. The **ParseHTML** class was explained in Chapter 6.

```
URLConnection http = url.openConnection();
http.setConnectTimeout(1000);
http.setReadTimeout(1000);
InputStream is = http.getInputStream();
ParseHTML html = new ParseHTML(is);
```

Next, we loop across all of the characters in the HTML file. A value of zero is returned if an HTML tag is encountered. Any HTML tags are ignored.

```
do
{
  ch = html.read();
  if ((ch != -1) && (ch != 0))
  {
    if (ch == '.')
    {
```

Once we have accumulated a complete sentence, which ends in a period, we check the sentence for the birth year. This is not the most accurate way to break up sentences, but it works well enough for this recipe. If a few sentences run on, or are cut short, it really does not impact the final output of the program. This program is all about finding many birth years and then using a sort of "majority rules" approach to determining the correct one. If a few are lost in the noise, it does not hurt.

If a valid birth year is found, it is recorded and the program continues.

```
String str = sentence.toString();
int year = extractBirth(str);
  if ((year > 1) && (year < 3000))
  {
    System.out.println("URL supports year: " + year);
    increaseYear(year);
  }
  sentence.setLength(0);
  } else
  sentence.append((char) ch);
}
} while (ch != -1);
```

This process is continued until the end of the HTML document is reached.

### Extracting a Birth Year

Each "sentence" that is found must be scanned for a birth year. To do this, the sentence is broken up into "words", which are defined as groups of characters separated by spaces.

```
boolean foundBorn = false;
int result = -1;

StringTokenizer tok = new StringTokenizer(sentence);
while (tok.hasMoreTokens())
{
```

Each word must first be checked to see if it is a number. If it is a number, that number is recorded and the program sentence parsing continues. If more than one number is found in a sentence, only the last number is used.

```
String word = tok.nextToken();

try
{
  result = Integer.parseInt(word);
} catch (NumberFormatException e)
{
```

If the word "born" is found, a boolean is set to record that it was found.

```
if (word.equalsIgnoreCase("born"))
  foundBorn = true;

if (!foundBorn)
  result = -1;

return result;
```

If a number and the word "born" were both found, then the number is returned. We have found a potential birth year. If only one, or neither, are found a negative one is returned.

### Finding the Correct Birth Year

Once the program finishes scanning the URLs identified with a famous person, we are left with a list of potential birth years. The program also tracks how many times each of those potential birth years were located. The **getResult** function is now called to determine which year had the largest number of "votes".

The function begins by creating two variables. The **result** variable holds the year with the largest count. The second variable, named **maxCount**, holds the number of votes held by the current value of the **result** variable.

```
int result = -1;
int maxCount = 0;
```

Next, a **Set** is created that contains each birth year. Each birth year is checked and at the end, the birth year with the largest count is held in the **result** variable.

```
Set<Integer> set = results.keySet();
for (int year : set)
{
  int count = results.get(year);
  if (count > maxCount)
  {
    result = year;
    maxCount = count;
  }
}

return result;
```

If no birth years were found, then the result variable stays at negative one. This will indicate to the calling method that no birth year was found.

## Summary

HTML was designed primarily for humans to access web sites. If a web site is designed for computers to access it, usually XML and web services are used. This chapter shows how to access a variety of web services.

Many web services make use of Simple Object Access Protocol (SOAP). SOAP is an XML based protocol that specifies how a web service server and client should communicate. Most SOAP web services include a Web Service Definition Language (WSDL) file that provides information to the program on how to access the web service.

Apache AXIS can be used to quickly create a set of classes to access any SOAP based web service. AXIS includes a simple utility named **wsdl2java** that can quickly create Java class files for any web service that provides a WSDL file.

The Google Search API is a very commonly used web service. It is based on SOAP; however, Google provides a set of classes you can download and use. The Google Search API allows you to easily construct and submit search requests to the Google search engine.

You can also construct Hybrid bots. A hybrid bot makes use of both web services and traditional HTML parsing. The Google search API is commonly used to construct hybrid bots. You can submit a search term to Google, then use a traditional HTML bot to scan all of the results returned from Google.

Three recipes were presented in this chapter. The first showed how to use the Google Search API to display information about all of the sites linking to a particular site. The second recipe showed how to use the AXIS framework to utilize a web service. The third recipe showed how to create a hybrid bot that used both the Google Search API, as well as a traditional HTML bot.

The next chapter will discuss Real-time Site Syndication (RSS). RSS is an XML format that allows you to keep up with new content on web sites.

# CHAPTER 12: WORKING WITH RSS FEEDS

- Understanding RSS
- Differences Between RSS 1.0 and RSS 2.0
- Parsing RSS
- Find the RSS Link Tag

RSS feeds provide a means for web sites to communicate links to their newest content. Users who are interested in particular web sites can instruct their browsers, and other software, to follow the RSS feeds from that site. When new content is posted to the feed, the user will know about it.

RSS is communicated using the HTTP protocol and the "file format" used for RSS is XML based. Because of these two features, it is easy to add RSS support to a bot. RSS data can be valuable to bots that monitor web sites. In this chapter, you will be shown how to access RSS with Java.

RSS is an acronym which can stand for several different things. These different meanings are summarized here:

- Really Simple Syndication (RSS 2.0)
- Rich Site Summary (RSS 0.91, RSS 1.0)
- RDF Site Summary (RSS 0.9 and 1.0)

To the end user, all versions of RSS operate similarly. In the next section, we will see how users typically use RSS.

## Using RSS with a Web Browser

Most modern web browsers include support for RSS. An RSS feed is usually implemented as a sort of dynamic bookmark in most web browsers. Firefox alerts you to the presence of RSS with a simple icon displayed on the URL line. If you access the following URL, you will see an RSS icon in Firefox.

```
http://www.httprecipes.com/
```

Figure 12.1 shows this icon.

**Figure 12.1: An RSS Enabled Site**

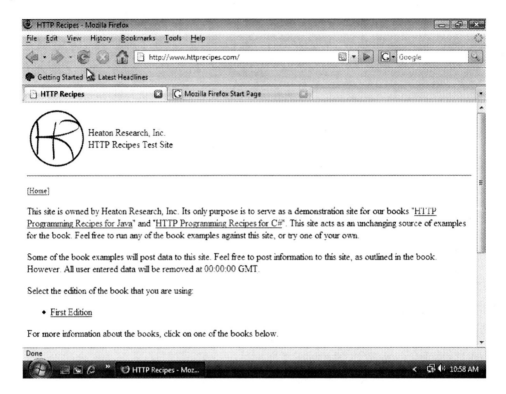

Can you see the RSS icon in Figure 12.1? It looks like several small waves on an orange background. It is located to the far right of the URL input area.

Clicking this icon will allow you to add the RSS Feed to your browser. Figure 12.2 shows a user accessing the HTTP Recipes RSS feed.

**Figure 12.2: The HTTP Recipes Feed**

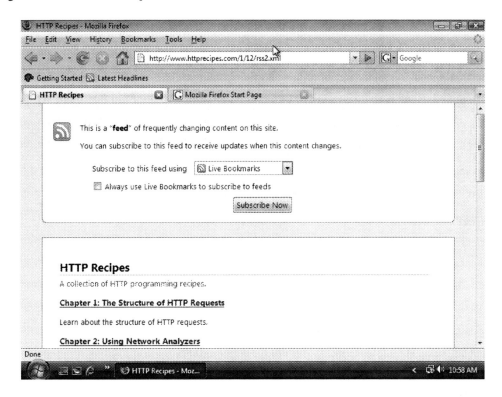

This allows the user to easily keep up with new pages posted to a web site of interest.

# RSS Format

RSS follows a specific format. In the next two sections, this book will cover the two most common RSS formats:

- RSS 1.0
- RSS 2.0

A sample containing the same data will be shown for each format. In this way, you can easily see the differences between the two formats.

### Understanding RSS 1.0

RSS 1.0 allows a web site to publish a list of links to that site's newest content. An RSS 1.0 feed is always accessed directly from a URL. To see a sample RSS 1.0 feed from the HTTP recipes site, access the following URL:

```
http://www.httprecipes.com/1/12/rss1.xml
```

The contents of this URL are shown in Listing 12.1.

### Listing 12.1: A RSS 1.0 File

```xml
<?xml version="1.0"?>

<rdf:RDF
xmlns:rdf="http://www.w3.org/1999/02/22-rdf-syntax-ns#"
xmlns="http://purl.org/rss/1.0/">

<channel rdf:about="http://www.httprecipes.com/1/12/rss1.xml">
<title>HTTP Recipes</title>
<link>http://www.httprecipes.com/</link>
<description>
A collection of HTTP programming recipes.
</description>

</channel>

<item rdf:about="http://www.httprecipes.com/1/1/">
<title>Chapter 1: The Structure of HTTP Requests</title>
<link>http://www.httprecipes.com/1/1/</link>
<description>
Learn about the structure of HTTP requests.
</description>
</item>

<item rdf:about="http://www.httprecipes.com/1/2/">
<title>Chapter 2: Using Network Analyzers</title>
<link>http://www.httprecipes.com/1/2/</link>
<description>
Learn to use Network Analyzers to make bot programming
easier.
</description>
</item>
<item rdf:about="http://www.httprecipes.com/1/3/">

<title>Chapter 3: Simple Requests</title>
<link>http://www.httprecipes.com/1/3/</link>
<description>
Learn to construct simple HTTP requests in Java.
</description>
</item>


... Chapters 4-13 continue here ...
```

```
<item rdf:about="http://www.httprecipes.com/1/14/">
<title>Chapter 14: Well Behaved Spiders and Bots</title>
<link>http://www.httprecipes.com/1/14/</link>
<description>
Learn to create bots that are well behaved.
</description>

</item>

</rdf:RDF>
```

The file begins with some header information about the feed. The **<title>** tag speci-fies the title of the RSS feed. The **<link>** tag specifies the location of the site producing the RSS feed. The **<description>** tag gives a description of the feed.

There are also several **<item>** tags. These are the individual items, or articles, that the feed provides information about. Inside of the **<item>** tag, you will find several other tags that define this item. The **<title>** tag gives the name of this item. The **<link>** tag gives a link to this item, which is a URL. The **<description>** tag provides a description of this item.

### Understanding RSS 2.0

RSS 2.0, like RSS 1.0, allows a web site to publish a list of links to that site's newest con-tent. Also like RSS 1.0, an RSS 2.0 feed is always accessed directly from a URL. The main difference is in the placement of the elements. To see a sample RSS 2.0 feed from the HTTP recipes site, access the following URL:

**http://www.httprecipes.com/1/12/rss2.xml**

The contents of this URL are shown in Listing 12.2.

### Listing 12.2: An RSS 2.0 File

```
<?xml version="1.0"?>
<rss version="2.0">
<channel>
<title>HTTP Recipes</title>
<link>http://www.httprecipes.com/</link>
<description>A collection of HTTP programming recipes.
</description>
<language>en-us</language>
<pubDate>Sun, 8 Oct 2006 04:00:00 GMT</pubDate>

<docs>http://blogs.law.harvard.edu/tech/rss</docs>
```

```
<item>
<title>Chapter 1: The Structure of HTTP Requests</title>
<pubDate>Sun, 8 Oct 2006 04:00:00 GMT</pubDate>
<link>http://www.httprecipes.com/1/1/</link>
<description>

Learn about the structure of HTTP requests.
</description>
</item>
<item>
<title>Chapter 2: Using Network Analyzers</title>
<pubDate>Sun, 8 Oct 2006 04:00:00 GMT</pubDate>
<link>http://www.httprecipes.com/1/2/</link>
<description>

Learn to use Network Analyzers to make bot programming
easier.
</description>
</item>
<item>
<title>Chapter 3: Simple Requests</title>
<pubDate>Sun, 8 Oct 2006 04:00:00 GMT</pubDate>
<link>http://www.httprecipes.com/1/3/</link>
<description>

Learn to construct simple HTTP requests in Java.
</description>
</item>


... Chapters 4-13 continue here ...


<item>
<title>Chapter 14: Well Behaved Spiders and Bots</title>
<pubDate>Sun, 8 Oct 2006 04:00:00 GMT</pubDate>
<link>http://www.httprecipes.com/1/14/</link>
<description>

Learn to create bots that are well behaved.
</description>
</item>

</channel>
</rss>
```

Did you notice the difference? The biggest difference between the RSS 2.0 and RSS 1.0 formats that we need to contend with, is the placement of the **\<item\>** elements. RSS 2.0 places the **\<item\>** elements inside of the **\<channel\>** element. RSS 1.0 places the **\<item\>** elements at the same level as the **\<channel\>** element.

Additionally, RSS 1.0 **\<item\>** elements do not contain a **\<pubDate\>** element. However, RSS 2.0 does include a **\<pubDate\>** element. The **\<pubDate\>** element contains the date that the article or channel was last updated. RSS stores dates in the following format:

```
Sun, 8 Oct 2006 04:00:00 GMT
```

To work with RSS in Java, this date will need to be converted to a Java **Date** object.

# Parsing RSS Files

In this section, we will develop a package of classes that can parse RSS data. This package will be used by the RSS recipes presented in this chapter. There will be only two classes in this relatively simple package. These classes are:

- RSS
- RSSItem

The **RSS** class is the main entry point for this package. Using the RSS class, you can parse RSS data. The **RSSItem** class holds individual RSS items, or articles, found when parsing the RSS feed. In the next two sections, we will examine each of these classes.

This RSS parser is designed to work with either RSS 1.0 or RSS 2.0 feeds. The program automatically adapts to each type of feed.

### The RSS Class

The **RSS** class is the main class of the RSS parsing package and the class that you will instruct to parse **RSS**. Additionally, the **RSS** class is used to navigate the RSS data that was retrieved. The **RSS** class is shown below in Listing 12.3.

### Listing 12.3: The RSS Class (RSS.java)

```
package com.heatonresearch.httprecipes.rss;

import java.io.*;
import java.net.*;
import java.text.*;
import java.util.*;

import javax.xml.parsers.*;

import org.w3c.dom.*;
```

```java
import org.xml.sax.*;

public class RSS
{
  /*
   * All of the attributes for this RSS document.
   */
  private Map<String, String> attributes = new HashMap<String,
String>();

  /*
   * All RSS items, or stories, found.
   */
  private List<RSSItem> items = new ArrayList<RSSItem>();

  /**
   * Simple utility function that converts a RSS formatted date
   * into a Java date.
   * @param datestr The RSS formatted date.
   * @return A Java java.util.date
   */
  public static Date parseDate(String datestr)
  {
    try
    {
      DateFormat formatter =
        new SimpleDateFormat("E, dd MMM yyyy HH:mm:ss Z");
      Date date = (Date) formatter.parse(datestr);
      return date;
    } catch (Exception e)
    {
      return null;
    }
  }

  /**
   * Load the specified RSS item, or story.
   * @param item A XML node that contains a RSS item.
   */
  private void loadItem(Node item)
  {
    RSSItem rssItem = new RSSItem();
    rssItem.load(item);
    items.add(rssItem);
  }
```

```java
/**
 * Load the channle node.
 * @param channel A node that contains a channel.
 */
private void loadChannel(Node channel)
{
  NodeList nl = channel.getChildNodes();
  for (int i = 0; i < nl.getLength(); i++)
  {
    Node node = nl.item(i);
    String nodename = node.getNodeName();
    if (nodename.equalsIgnoreCase("item"))
    {
      loadItem(node);
    } else
    {
      if (node.getNodeType() != Node.TEXT_NODE)
        attributes.put(nodename, RSS.getXMLText(node));
    }
  }
}

/**
 * Load all RSS data from the specified URL.
 * @param url URL that contains XML data.
 * @throws IOException Thrown if an IO error occurs.
 * @throws SAXException Thrown if there is an error while
 * parsing XML.
 * @throws ParserConfigurationException Thrown if there
 * is an XML
 * parse config error.
 */
public void load(URL url) throws IOException, SAXException,
    ParserConfigurationException
{
  URLConnection http = url.openConnection();
  InputStream is = http.getInputStream();

  DocumentBuilderFactory factory =
    DocumentBuilderFactory.newInstance();
  Document d = factory.newDocumentBuilder().parse(is);

  Element e = d.getDocumentElement();
  NodeList nl = e.getChildNodes();
  for (int i = 0; i < nl.getLength(); i++)
  {
```

```java
      Node node = nl.item(i);
      String nodename = node.getNodeName();

      // RSS 2.0
      if (nodename.equalsIgnoreCase("channel"))
      {
        loadChannel(node);
      }
      // RSS 1.0
      else if (nodename.equalsIgnoreCase("item"))
      {
        loadItem(node);
      }
    }

  }

  /**
   * Simple utility method that obtains the text of an XML
   * node.
   * @param n The XML node.
   * @return The text of the specified XML node.
   */
  public static String getXMLText(Node n)
  {
    NodeList list = n.getChildNodes();
    for (int i = 0; i < list.getLength(); i++)
    {
      Node n2 = list.item(i);
      if (n2.getNodeType() == Node.TEXT_NODE)
        return n2.getNodeValue();
    }
    return null;
  }

  /**
   * Get the list of attributes.
   * @return the attributes
   */
  public Map<String, String> getAttributes()
  {
    return attributes;
  }

  /**
   * Convert the object to a String.
```

```
 * @return The object as a String.
 */
public String toString()
{
  StringBuilder str = new StringBuilder();
  Set<String> set = attributes.keySet();
  for (String item : set)
  {
    str.append(item);
    str.append('=');
    str.append(attributes.get(item));
    str.append('\n');
  }
  str.append("Items:\n");
  for (RSSItem item : items)
  {
    str.append(item.toString());
    str.append('\n');
  }
  return str.toString();
}

}
```

It is very easy to use the **RSS** class. Simply call the **load** method, and pass an **InputStream** that contains RSS data. Once you have loaded the RSS data, you can call the **getAttributes** function of the RSS class to access any attributes of the **<channel>** element. Additionally, you can call the **getItems** function to gain access to the **RSSItems** that were parsed.

This chapter includes two recipes that demonstrate exactly how to use the **RSS** class to parse RSS data. In the next several sections, you will see how the RSS parsing class was constructed.

### Loading the RSS File

Calling the **load** method of the **RSS** class will load RSS data at the specified URL. The first thing that the **load** method does, is to open a connection and obtain an **InputStream** to the URL that contains the RSS data.

```
URLConnection http = url.openConnection();
InputStream is = http.getInputStream();
```

Next, the DOM is setup to parse the XML data from the **InputStream**.

```
DocumentBuilderFactory factory =
  DocumentBuilderFactory.newInstance();
Document d = factory.newDocumentBuilder().parse(is);
```

Then iterate over all of the top-level document elements of the RSS data.

```
Element e = d.getDocumentElement();
NodeList nl = e.getChildNodes();
for (int i = 0; i < nl.getLength(); i++)
{
  Node node = nl.item(i);
  String nodename = node.getNodeName();
```

Once we find the **\<channel\>** element, the **loadChannel** method is called to load the channel data.

```
// RSS 2.0
if (nodename.equalsIgnoreCase("channel"))
{
  loadChannel(node);
}
```

If this is an RSS 1.0 feed, then there will be **\<item\>** elements at the top level. If any item tags are encountered, then we call **loadItem** to process them.

```
// RSS 1.0
else if (nodename.equalsIgnoreCase("item"))
{
  loadItem(node);
}
```

This process continues until all top level elements have been processed.

### Loading the Channel

The **loadChannel** method is called to load a **\<channel\>** element. This method begins by looping across all of the child elements of the **\<channel\>** element.

```
NodeList nl = channel.getChildNodes();
for (int i = 0; i < nl.getLength(); i++)
{
```

Once a child node is located, examine the name of that node.

```
Node node = nl.item(i);
String nodename = node.getNodeName();
```

If this is an **\<item\>** element, then call **loadItem** to load that item.

```
if (nodename.equalsIgnoreCase("item"))
{
  loadItem(node);
}
```

Otherwise, add the item to the **attributes** collection.

```
else
{
  if(node.getNodeType()!=Node.TEXT_NODE)
    attributes.put(nodename, RSS.getXMLText(node));
}
}
```

The **attributes** collection stores all of the attributes that were loaded with the **<channel>** element.

## Parse an RSS Format Date

The RSS standard specifies a very specific format for dates. The **parseDate** method of the RSS class converts these dates to Java **Date** objects. As previously mentioned, the following is the format that RSS expects a date to be in.

```
Sun, 8 Oct 2006 04:00:00 GMT
```

To parse the date, the **SimpleDateFormat** class of Java is used. The **SimpleDateFormat** object is constructed to accept a date that matches the above format. Once the date is parsed, it is returned.

```
try
{
DateFormat formatter =
  new SimpleDateFormat("E, dd MMM yyyy HH:mm:ss Z");
Date date = (Date) formatter.parse(datestr);
return date;
```

If an error occurs while parsing the date, then a value of **null** is returned for the date.

```
} catch (Exception e)
{
  return null;
}
```

This method is made **static** so that it can be called directly from the **RSSItem** class.

## The RSSItem Class

The **RSSItem** class is the class that holds individual RSS items, or articles. The **RSSItem** class also holds all of the attributes that were parsed from each of the **<item>** elements in the RSS feed. You may view the **RSSItem** class below in Listing 12.4.

### Listing 12.4: The RSSItem Class (RSSItem.java)

```
package com.heatonresearch.httprecipes.rss;
```

```java
import java.util.*;

import org.w3c.dom.*;

public class RSSItem
{

  /*
   * The title of this item.
   */
  private String title;

  /*
   * The hyperlink to this item.
   */
  private String link;

  /*
   * The description of this item.
   */
  private String description;

  /*
   * The date this item was published.
   */
  private Date date;

  /**
   * Get the publication date.
   * @return The publication date.
   */
  public Date getDate()
  {
    return date;
  }

  /**
   * Set the publication date.
   * @param date The new publication date.
   */
  public void setDate(Date date)
  {
    this.date = date;
  }
```

```java
/**
 * Get the description.
 * @return The description.
 */
public String getDescription()
{
  return description;
}

/**
 * Get the description.
 * @param description The new description.
 */
public void setDescription(String description)
{
  this.description = description;
}

/**
 * Get the hyperlink.
 * @return The hyperlink.
 */
public String getLink()
{
  return link;
}

/**
 * Set the hyperlink.
 * @param link The new hyperlink.
 */
public void setLink(String link)
{
  this.link = link;
}


/**
 * Get the item title.
 * @return The item title.
 */
public String getTitle()
{
  return title;
}
```

```java
/**
 * Set the item title.
 * @param title The new item title.
 */
public void setTitle(String title)
{
  this.title = title;
}


/**
 * Load an item from the specified node.
 * @param node The Node to load the item from.
 */
public void load(Node node)
{
  NodeList nl = node.getChildNodes();
  tor (int i = 0; i < nl.getLength(); i++)
  {
    Node n = nl.item(i);
    String name = n.getNodeName();

    if (name.equalsIgnoreCase("title"))
      title = RSS.getXMLText(n);
    else if (name.equalsIgnoreCase("link"))
      link = RSS.getXMLText(n);
    else if (name.equalsIgnoreCase("description"))
      description = RSS.getXMLText(n);
    else if (name.equalsIgnoreCase("pubDate"))
    {
      String str = RSS.getXMLText(n);
      if (str != null)
        date = RSS.parseDate(str);
    }

  }
}

/**
 * Convert the object to a String.
 * @return The object as a String.
 */
public String toString()
{
  StringBuilder builder = new StringBuilder();
  builder.append('[');
  builder.append("title=\"");
```

```
      builder.append(title);
      builder.append("\",link=\"");
      builder.append(link);
      builder.append("\",date=\"");
      builder.append(date);
      builder.append("\"]");
      return builder.toString();
   }
}
```

The **RSSItem** class holds all of the attributes that are parsed from individual **<item>** elements. These attributes, which can be accessed using getters, are listed here:

- Title
- Description
- Link
- Date

The **RSSItem** class includes a method, named **load**, which loads the item from an **<item>** element. This method begins by looping through all of the child elements of the **<item>** element.

```
NodeList nl = node.getChildNodes();
for (int i = 0; i < nl.getLength(); i++)
{
Node n = nl.item(i);
String name = n.getNodeName();
```

Each of the elements are checked to see if it is a **<title>**, **<description>**, **<link>** or **<date>** element. If the element is one of these, then the value of that element is copied into the correct property.

```
if (name.equalsIgnoreCase("title"))
  title = RSS.getXMLText(n);
else if (name.equalsIgnoreCase("link"))
  link = RSS.getXMLText(n);
else if (name.equalsIgnoreCase("description"))
  description = RSS.getXMLText(n);
else if (name.equalsIgnoreCase("pubDate"))
{
```

If the element is a date, then the date is parsed.

```
  String str = RSS.getXMLText(n);
  if (str != null)
    date = RSS.parseDate(str);
  }
}
```

This continues until all child elements of the **<item>** element have been processed.

## Recipes

This chapter includes two recipes. These recipes demonstrate how to parse RSS feeds. Specifically, you will see how to perform the following techniques:

- Parse an RSS Feed
- Find an RSS Feed from a Link Tag

These recipes will show you how a bot can be adapted to work with RSS feeds. The first recipe demonstrates how to display an RSS feed.

### Recipe #12.1: Display an RSS Feed

This recipe demonstrates how to open an RSS feed and parse it. The recipe will work with either an RSS 1.0 or RSS 2.0 feed. It relies on the RSS parser, which was constructed earlier in this chapter. This recipe is shown in Listing 12.5.

### Listing 12.5: Display an RSS Feed (LoadRSS.java)

```java
package com.heatonresearch.httprecipes.ch12.recipe1;

import java.io.*;
import java.net.*;
import javax.xml.parsers.*;
import org.xml.sax.*;
import com.heatonresearch.httprecipes.rss.*;

public class LoadRSS
{

  /**
   * Display an RSS feed.
   * @param url The URL of the RSS feed.
   * @throws IOException Thrown if an IO exception occurs.
   * @throws SAXException Thrown if an XML parse exception occurs.
   * @throws ParserConfigurationException Thrown if there is
   * an error setting up the parser.
   */
  public void process(URL url) throws IOException, SAXException,
      ParserConfigurationException
  {
    RSS rss = new RSS();
    rss.load(url);
    System.out.println(rss.toString());
  }

  /**
   * The main method processes the command line arguments and
```

```
 * then calls process to display the feed.
 *
 * @param args Holds the RSS feed to download.
 */
public static void main(String args[])
{
  try
  {
    URL url;

    if (args.length != 0)
      url = new URL(args[0]);
    else
      url = new URL("http://www.httprecipes.com/1/12/rss1.xml");

    LoadRSS load = new LoadRSS();
    load.process(url);
  } catch (Exception e)
  {
    e.printStackTrace();
  }
}
}
```

This recipe is very simple. It begins by creating a new **RSS** object. The **RSS** class was constructed earlier in this chapter.

```
RSS rss = new RSS();
```

Next, the load method is called to load a RSS feed.

```
rss.load(url);
```

Finally, the RSS feed is displayed by calling the RSS object's **toString** function.

```
System.out.println(rss.toString());
```

If you need to access the RSS items directly, you can easily use the **getItems** function to obtain a list of **RSSItem** objects.

### Recipe #12.2: Find an RSS Feed

Many web sites contain a special **<link>** tag that shows you where the RSS feed for that site resides. By parsing for this **<link>** tag, you can easily obtain the RSS feed for a web site. The HTTP Recipes site contains such a tag. If you examine the source at the following URL, you will see this tag.

**http://www.httprecipes.com/**

The above URL contains the following **<link>** tag:

```
<link rel="alternate"
type="application/rss+xml"
href="http://www.httprecipes.com/1/12/rss2.xml">
```

The **href** attribute of this tag tells us that we can find the RSS feed for the HTTP Recipes site at the following URL:

**http://www.httprecipes.com/1/12/rss2.xml**

This recipe will show how to access the HTTP Recipes site, find the **<link>** tag for the RSS Feed, and then download the RSS feed. This recipe is shown in Listing 12.6.

### Listing 12.6: Find an RSS Feed (FindRSS.java)

```java
package com.heatonresearch.httprecipes.ch12.recipe2;

import java.io.*;
import java.net.*;

import javax.xml.parsers.*;

import org.xml.sax.*;

import com.heatonresearch.httprecipes.html.*;
import com.heatonresearch.httprecipes.rss.*;

public class FindRSS
{
  /**
   * Display an RSS feed.
   * @param url The URL of the RSS feed.
   * @throws IOException Thrown if an IO exception occurs.
   * @throws SAXException Thrown if an XML parse exception occurs.
   * @throws ParserConfigurationException Thrown if there is
   * an error setting
   * up the parser.
   */
  public void processRSS(URL url) throws IOException,
  SAXException, ParserConfigurationException
  {
    RSS rss = new RSS();
    rss.load(url);
    System.out.println(rss.toString());
  }
```

```java
/**
 * This method looks for a link tag at the specified URL.  If
 * a link tag is found that specifies an RSS feed, then
 * that feed is displayed.
 * @param url The URL of the web site.
 * @throws IOException Thrown if an IO exception occurs.
 * @throws SAXException Thrown if an XML parse exception occurs.
 * @throws ParserConfigurationException Thrown if there is
 * an error setting
 * up the parser.
 */
public void process(URL url)
  throws IOException, SAXException,
  ParserConfigurationException
{
  String href = null;
  InputStream is = url.openStream();
  ParseHTML parse = new ParseHTML(is);
  int ch;
  do
  {
    ch = parse.read();
    if (ch == 0)
    {
      HTMLTag tag = parse.getTag();
      if (tag.getName().equalsIgnoreCase("link"))
      {
        String type = tag.getAttributeValue("type");
        if (type != null && type.indexOf("rss") != -1)
        {
          href = tag.getAttributeValue("href");
        }
      }
    }
  } while (ch != -1);

  if (href == null)
  {
    System.out.println("No RSS link found.");
  } else
    processRSS(new URL(href));

}
```

```
/**
 * The main method processes the command line arguments and
 * then calls process to display the feed.
 *
 * @param args Holds the RSS feed to download.
 */
public static void main(String args[])
{
  try
  {
    URL url;

    if (args.length != 0)
      url = new URL(args[0]);
    else
      url = new URL("http://www.httprecipes.com/");

    FindRSS load = new FindRSS();
    load.process(url);
  } catch (Exception e)
  {
    e.printStackTrace();
  }


}

}
```

This recipe begins by opening a connection to the web site which we will scan for an RSS URL. A **ParseHTML** object is setup to parse the HTML. The **ParseHTML** class was discussed in Chapter 6.

```
String href = null;
InputStream is = url.openStream();
ParseHTML parse = new ParseHTML(is);
int ch;
```

The program will look through all of the tags in the document, ignoring the text between HTML tags. Because this program is only looking for a **<link>** tag, the actual text does not matter.

```
do
{
ch = parse.read();
  if (ch == 0)
  {
    HTMLTag tag = parse.getTag();
```

Once a **<link>** tag is found, we check to see if the **type** attribute specifies RSS. If this **<link>** tag contains the type tag, then we store the **<link>** tag's **href** attribute into a variable also named **href**.

```
if (tag.getName().equalsIgnoreCase("link"))
{
  String type = tag.getAttributeValue("type");
  if (type != null && type.indexOf("rss") != -1)
  {
    href = tag.getAttributeValue("href");
  }
}
}
}
```

This process continues until the end of the HTML document is reached.

```
} while (ch != -1);
```

If no RSS tag was found, then we inform the user.

```
if (href == null)
{
  System.out.println("No RSS link found.");
} else
processRSS(new URL(href));
```

Once the link is found, call the **processRSS** method to display the RSS feed. The **processRSS** method works the same as the process method from Recipe 12.1.

## Summary

This chapter showed how to create Java applications that can work with RSS. RSS is a very simple way of keeping up with new content on web sites. Using RSS, your bot can quickly query a web site and find out what new documents are available.

There are two major versions of RSS: RSS 1.0 and RSS 2.0. Though these two formats are very similar, there are some important differences. This chapter showed how to construct an RSS parser class that is capable of parsing either type of RSS feed.

RSS feeds return a list of new articles on the web site, as well as hyperlinks to the original article. Because of this, bots can easily use RSS to get a listing of URLs on a web site that contain new content. Some web sites also include a **<link>** tag that specifies the location of the site's RSS feed. By looking for this tag, your bot can automatically locate the RSS feed for most web sites.

This chapter includes two recipes. The first recipe simply displays the contents of an RSS feed from a web site. The second recipe scans a web site, looking for an RSS **<link>** tag. Once the site's RSS feed is located, it is displayed.

The next chapter will show how to construct a spider. A spider is a program that crawls a web site. Spiders can be used to download the contents of web site, or scan a site for specific information.

# CHAPTER 13: USING A SPIDER

- Understanding when to Use a Spider
- Introducing the Heaton Research Spider
- Using Thread Pools
- Using Memory to Track URLs
- Using SQL to Track URLs
- Spidering Many Web Sites

A spider is a special type of bot that is designed to crawl the World Wide Web, just like a biological spider crawls its web. While bots are usually designed to work with one specific site, spiders are usually designed to work with a vast number of web sites.

A spider always starts on one single page. This page is scanned for links. All links to other pages, are stored in a list. The spider will then visit the next URL on the list and scan for links again. This process continues endlessly as the spider finds new pages.

Usually, some restriction is placed on the spider to limit what pages it will visit. If no restrictions were placed on the spider, the spider would theoretically visit every page on the entire Internet.

Most of the recipes in this book have been fairly self-contained, usually requiring only a class or two to function. This presents the reader with an efficient solution, with minimum overhead. This strategy does not work so well with a spider. To create a truly effective spider, there are many considerations, such as:

- Thread pooling and synchronization
- Storing a very large URL list
- HTML parsing
- Working with an SQL database
- Reporting results

These considerations do not lend themselves to a concise example. This book will show you how to use the "Heaton Research Spider". The Heaton Research Spider is an ever-evolving open source spider produced by the publisher of this book. The Heaton Research Spider is also available in C#, as well as Java, and can be obtained from the following URL:

`http://www.heatonresearch.com/projects/spider/`

This book uses v1.0 of the Heaton Research Spider which is included with the companion download of this book. New releases will likely be available after the publication of this book. Adapting to later versions of the spider should be relatively easy as backwards compatibility is a very important design consideration for the spider.

The Heaton Research Spider is not an immense project. The spider seeks to be as capable as possible, without including a great deal of overhead. This chapter will show you how to use the spider.

## Using the Heaton Research Spider

In this section you will learn to use the Heaton Research Spider. The Heaton Research Spider can be configured to perform a wide variety of tasks. There are three primary steps when using the Heaton Research Spider:

- Configure the spider
- Provide a class for the spider to report its findings
- Start the spider

### Configuring the Spider

You will now be shown how to configure the Heaton Research Spider. The Heaton Research Spider is easily configured one of two ways:

- Programmatically (or Directly)
- With a Configuration File

Each of these methods will be discussed in the next two sections.

### Configuring the Spider Directly

To configure the Heaton Research Spider you should use the **SpiderOptions** class. The **SpiderOptions** class contains several properties, implemented as public members. We chose to use public members to allow the class to be quickly loaded from a file using Java reflection. These properties are shown in Table 13.1.

**Table 13.1: Spider Configuration Options**

| Configuration Option | Purpose |
|---|---|
| timeout | How long to wait for a connection/read (in milliseconds). |
| maxDepth | How deep to search for links (1 for homepage only, -1 infinite depth). |
| userAgent | What user agent to report, blank to report the Java user agent. |
| corePoolSize | Core thread pool size, the minimum number of threads to use. |
| maximumPoolSize | Maximum thread pool size. |
| keepAliveTime | How long to keep an idle thread alive (seconds). |
| dbURL | The JDBC URL of a database to use. |
| dbClass | The full class name of a JDBC driver to use. |
| workloadManager | The full class name of a workload manager to use. |
| startup | What to do on startup. Specify "clear" to clear the workload or "resume" to resume processing. |
| filter | The full class path of a filter class. More than one filter can be specified. |

The timeout value allows you to define the amount of time, in milliseconds that you will wait for a page to load.

The **userAgent** property allows you to specify the **User-Agent** header that the spider will report when accessing web sites. It is usually a good idea to create a specific user agent for your spider so that it can be identified. If you set this value to **null**, then the default Java user agent will be used.

The **corePoolSize**, **maximumPoolSize**, and **keepAliveTime** properties allow you to define how the thread pool works. The thread pool is a pool of threads that waits to handle tasks assigned to it by the spider. Using a thread pool makes a spider very efficient. This is because a spider is often waiting for a web server to respond. If a spider can be waiting on multiple pages at the same time, the over all performance is greatly increased. The **maximumPoolSize** property states the maximum number of threads in the pool. If a single thread has no work to do after the number of seconds specified by the **keepAliveTime** property, then the thread will be killed. No threads will be killed once the thread pool has reached the size specified by the **corePoolSize** property.

The **dbURL** and **dbClass** properties allow you to define a JDBC database. For more information on how to set these values, refer to the next chapter.

The **workloadManager** property allows you to specify what sort of a workload manager will handle the URL list. To specify an in-memory workload manager, use the following option:

```
com.heatonresearch.httprecipes.spider.workload.memory.MemoryWork-
loadManager
```

To specify an SQL based workload manager, use the following option:

```
com.heatonresearch.httprecipes.spider.workload.sql.SQLWorkloadMa-
nager
```

If you are going to use an SQL workload manager, you must also specify the **dbURL** and **dbClass**. Additionally, you must also create a database that has the required tables. This is covered in the next chapter. There are no options that need to be specified for a memory workload.

A memory workload is more simple to setup than an SQL workload. However, a memory workload can hold a limited number of sites and the memory workload manager is capable of spidering only a single host. If you would like to spider multiple hosts, or very large hosts, you must use an SQL workload manager.

There are two values you can specify for the **startup** property. First, if you specify the value of **clear**, the entire workload will be erased, and the spider will start over. Secondly, if you specify the value of **resume**, the spider will resume where it left off from the last run.

The **filter** property allows you to specify one or more filters to use. You should always make sure you use at least the **RobotsFilter**. This filter ensures that your bot is compliant with the "Bot Exclusion Standard". The Bot Exclusion Standard will be covered in Chapter 16, "Well Behaved Bots".

The following code shows how you might initialize a **SpiderOptions** object:

```
SpiderOptions options = new SpiderOptions();

spiderOptions.timeout(60000);
spiderOptions.maxDepth(-1);
spiderOptions.userAgent(null);
spiderOptions.corePoolSize(100);
spiderOptions.maximumPoolSize(100);
spiderOptions.keepAliveTime(60);
spiderOptions.dbURL(
"jdbc:mysql://127.0.0.1/spider?user="+
"testuser&password=testpassword");
spiderOptions.dbClass("com.mysql.jdbc.Driver");
spiderOptions.workloadManager(
"com.heatonresearch.httprecipes.spider."+
```

```
"workload.sql.SQLWorkloadManager");
spiderOptions.startup("clear");
spiderOptions.filters.add(
"com.heatonresearch.httprecipes.spider.filter.RobotsFilter");
```

You can also configure the spider using a configuration file. This is discussed in the next section.

## Configuring with a Configuration File

It is often more convenient to use a configuration file than directly setting the values of the **SpiderOptions**. To use a configuration file, create a text file that contains a single line for each configuration option. Each configuration option is a name-value pair. A colon(:) separates the name and value. The name corresponds to the property name in the **SpiderOptions** class. See Table 13.1 for a complete list of configuration options. Also, a sample configuration file is shown in Listing 13.1.

### Listing 13.1: A Configuration file for the Spider (spider.conf)

```
timeout:      60000
maxDepth:     -1
userAgent:
corePoolSize:       100
maximumPoolSize:  100
keepAliveTime:    60
dbURL:            jdbc:mysql://192.168.1.10/spider
dbClass:      com.mysql.jdbc.Driver
dbUID:            root
dbPWD:            test
workloadManager:com.heatonresearch.httprecipes.spider.workload.
sql.SQLWorkloadManager
startup:      clear
filter: com.heatonresearch.httprecipes.spider.filter.RobotsFilter
```

Once the configuration file is setup, it is relatively easy to tell the spider to make use of it. Simply call the load method on the **SpiderOptions** object as follows:

```
SimpleReport report = new SimpleReport();
SpiderOptions options = new SpiderOptions();
options.load("c:\\spider.conf");
Spider spider = new Spider(options,report);
```

Once the **SpiderOptions** object has been loaded, it is passed to the spider's constructor. You will also notice that a report variable is passed which the spider uses to report its findings. This will be discussed in the next section.

### Setting up the Database

If you are going to use the **SQLWorkloadManager**, then you must prepare a database to use with the workload manager. The **SQLWorkloadManager** requires two tables to be present in the database. They are listed here:

- spider_host
- spider_workload

There can be additional tables; however, the spider will simply ignore them.

The **spider_host** table keeps a list of hosts that the spider has encountered. The fields contained in the **spider_host** table are summarized in Table 13.2.

**Table 13.2: The spider_host Table**

| Field Name | SQL Type | Purpose |
|---|---|---|
| host_id | int(10) | The primary key for the table. |
| host | varchar(255) | The host name (i.e. www.httprecipes.com) |
| status | varchar(1) | The status of the host. |
| urls_done | int(11) | The number of URLs successfully processed for this host. |
| urls_error | int(11) | The number of URLs that resulted in an error for this host. |

The **spider_workload** table contains a complete list of every URL that the spider has encountered. The fields contained in the **spider_workload** table are summarized in Table 13.3.

**Table 13.3: The Spider_workload Table**

| Field Name | SQL Type | Purpose |
|---|---|---|
| workload_id | int(10) | The primary key for this table. |
| host | int(10) | The host id that this URL corresponds to. |
| url | varchar(2083) | The URL used for this workload element. |
| status | varchar(1) | This status of this workload element. |
| depth | int(10) | The depth of this URL. |
| url_hash | int(11) | A hash code that allows the URL to be quickly looked up. |
| source_id | int(11) | The ID of the URL where this URL was found. |

Both of the tables can be created using a data definition language (DDL) script. The DDL script for MySQL is shown in Listing 13.2.

**Listing 13.2: Example Create Table DDL for MySQL**

```
SET NAMES latin1;
SET FOREIGN_KEY_CHECKS = 0;

CREATE TABLE 'spider_host' (
'host_id' int(10) unsigned NOT NULL auto_increment,
'host' varchar(255) NOT NULL default '',
'status' varchar(1) NOT NULL default '',
'urls_done' int(11) NOT NULL,
'urls_error' int(11) NOT NULL,
PRIMARY KEY ('host_id')
) ENGINE=MyISAM AUTO_INCREMENT=5929 DEFAULT CHARSET=latin1;

CREATE TABLE 'spider_workload' (
'workload_id' int(10) unsigned NOT NULL auto_increment,
'host' int(10) unsigned NOT NULL,
'url' varchar(2083) NOT NULL default '',
'status' varchar(1) NOT NULL default '',
'depth' int(10) unsigned NOT NULL,
'url_hash' int(11) NOT NULL,
'source_id' int(11) NOT NULL,
PRIMARY KEY (`workload_id`),
KEY `status` (`status`),
KEY `url_hash` (`url_hash`),
KEY `host` (`host`)
) ENGINE=MyISAM AUTO_INCREMENT=2 DEFAULT CHARSET=latin1;

SET FOREIGN_KEY_CHECKS = 1;
```

There is a status field contained in both tables. The status field contains a single character that specifies the status of either the host or workload entry. These status codes are summarized in Table 13.4.

**Table 13.4: Spider Status Codes**

| Status Code | Purpose |
|---|---|
| D | Processed successfully. |
| E | Error while processing. |
| P | Currently processing. |
| W | Waiting to be processed. |

For more information on setting up your database, including examples for databases other than MySQL, refer to Appendix F, "Setting Up your Database".

### How the Spider Reports its Findings

The spider uses the **SpiderReportable** interface to report its findings. For each spider you create, you should create a class that implements the **SpiderReportable** interface. The **SpiderReportable** interface is shown in Listing 13.3.

### Listing 13.3: The SpiderReportable Interface (SpiderReportable.java)

```java
package com.heatonresearch.httprecipes.spider;

import java.io.*;
import java.net.*;

public interface SpiderReportable {

  /**
   * The types of link that can be encountered.
   */
  public enum URLType {
    HYPERLINK, IMAGE, SCRIPT, STYLE
  }

  /**
   * This function is called when the spider is ready to
   * process a new host.
   *
   * @param host
   *            The new host that is about to be processed.
   * @return True if this host should be processed, false
   *            otherwise.
   */
  public boolean beginHost(String host);

  /**
   * Called when the spider is starting up. This method
   * provides the SpiderReportable class with the spider
   * object.
   *
   * @param spider
   *            The spider that will be working with this
   *            object.
   */
  public void init(Spider spider);
```

```
/**
 * Called when the spider encounters a URL.
 *
 * @param url
 *           The URL that the spider found.
 * @param source
 *           The page that the URL was found on.
 * @param type
 *           The type of link this URL is.
 * @return True if the spider should scan for links on
 *           this page.
 */
public boolean spiderFoundURL(URL url, URL source,
  URLType type);

/**
 * Called when the spider is about to process a NON-HTML
 * URL.
 *
 * @param url
 *           The URL that the spider found.
 * @param stream
 *           An InputStream to read the page contents from.
 * @throws IOException
 *            Thrown if an IO error occurs while processing
 *            the page.
 */
public void spiderProcessURL(URL url, InputStream stream)
    throws IOException;

/**
 * Called when the spider is ready to process an HTML
 * URL.
 *
 * @param url
 *           The URL that the spider is about to process.
 * @param parse
 *           An object that will allow you you to parse the
 *           HTML on this page.
 * @throws IOException
 *            Thrown if an IO error occurs while processing
 *            the page.
 */
public void spiderProcessURL(URL url, SpiderParseHTML parse)
    throws IOException;
```

```
/**
 * Called when the spider tries to process a URL but gets
 * an error.
 *
 * @param url
 *           The URL that generated an error.
 */
public void spiderURLError(URL url);

}
```

Any class that implements this interface must provide implementations for each of the methods and functions contained in the above listing. These methods and function are summarized in Table 13.5.

**Table 13.5: Functions and Methods of the SpiderReportable Interface**

| Name | Purpose |
|---|---|
| beginHost | Called when the spider begins processing a new host. |
| init | Called to setup the object. The object is provided with a reference to the spider at this point. |
| spiderFoundURL | Called when the spider finds a URL. Return true if links from this URL should be processed. |
| spiderProcessURL (HTML) | Called when the spider encounters an HTML page. A SpiderHTMLParse object is provided to parse the HTML. |
| spiderProcesURL (binary) | Called to download a binary page, such as an image. An InputStream is provided to download the page. |
| spiderURLError | Called when a URL results in an error while loading. |

By providing a class that implements the **SpiderReportable** interface, you are able to process all of the data the spider finds. This is how you really define the sort of a spider you are creating. The recipes section of this chapter will demonstrate several **SpiderReportable** implementations.

### Starting the Spider

Now that you have seen how to configure and setup the spider, you are ready to learn how to actually start the spider. The spider can be started with the following lines of code:

```
URL base = new URL("http://www.httprecipes.com/");
SimpleReport report = new SimpleReport();
SpiderOptions options = new SpiderOptions();
```

```
options.load("spider.conf");
Spider spider = new Spider(options,report);
spider.addURL(base, null, 1);
spider.process();
System.out.println(spider.getStatus());
```

First, a variable named **base** is created that contains the **base** URL with which the spider begins. Next, a **SimpleReport** object is created named **report**. The **SimpleReport** class implements a spider **ReportableInterface**, and is provided by the Heaton Research Spider. However, the **SimpleReport** does nothing more than allow the spider to continue crawling, no data is processed. It is suitable only for testing the spider.

Next, a **SpiderOptions** object, named **options** is created. The **options** object loads configuration data from a file named **spider.conf**. Now that we have both a configuration and report object, we can create a Spider object named **spider**.

Finally, the **base** URL is added to the spider object, and the **process** method is called. The **process** method will not return until the spider is finished. If you wish to cancel the spider processing early, you must call the **cancel** method on the **spider** object.

Of course you could also directly create the **SpiderOptions** object, as discussed earlier in the chapter. To set options directly, simply remove the call to the **load** method and set each of the properties of the **options** object.

# Recipes

This chapter includes four recipes. These recipes demonstrate how to construct spiders that check links, download sites, and which attempt to access a large number of sites. Additionally, a recipe is provided that tracks the progress of a spider. Specifically, you will see how to perform the following techniques:

- Find Site Broken Links
- Download Site Contents
- Access Numerous Internet Sites
- Track Spider Progress

These recipes will also show you how a bot can be adapted to perform several very common spider techniques. The first recipe below demonstrates how to find bad links.

### Recipe #13.1: Broken Links

A broken link is a link on a web site that leads to a non-existent page or image. Broken links make a web site look unprofessional. Spiders are particularly adept at finding broken links on a web site. This recipe shows how to create a spider that will scan a web site for broken links.

To run this spider, simply pass the URL of the website you wish to check as the first argument. For example, to spider the HTTP Recipes site, use the following command:

```
CheckLinks http://www.heatonreserach.com
```

The above command simply shows the abstract format to call this recipe, with the appropriate parameters. For exact information on how to run this recipe refer to Appendix B, C, or D, depending on the operating system you are using. This recipe is made up of two classes. The first, named **CheckLinks**, configures the spider and then begins processing. The next class, named **LinkReport**, receives information from the spider and compiles a list of bad links. We will examine each of classes, starting with **CheckLinks**.

### Creating the Broken Links Spider

The **CheckLinks** class contains the main method for the recipe. Listing 13.4 shows the **CheckLinks** class.

#### Listing 13.4: Find Broken Links (CheckLinks.java)

```java
package com.heatonresearch.httprecipes.ch13.recipe1;

import java.net.*;

import com.heatonresearch.httprecipes.spider.*;
import com.heatonresearch.httprecipes.spider.workload.*;
import com.heatonresearch.httprecipes.spider.workload.memory.*;

public class CheckLinks {

  /**
   * Main method for the application.
   *
   * @param args
   *            Holds the website to check (i.e.
   *            http://www.httprecipes.com/)
   */
  static public void main(String args[]) {

    try {
      if (args.length != 1) {
        System.out.println(
          "Usage: CheckLinks [website to check]");
      } else {
        CheckLinks links = new CheckLinks();
        links.check(new URL(args[0]));
      }

    } catch (Exception e) {
```

```
      e.printStackTrace();
    }
  }

  /**
   * This method is called by main to check a link. After
   * spidering through the site, the final list of bad links
   * is displayed.
   *
   * @param url
   *            The URL to check for bad links.
   * @throws WorkloadException
   * @throws ClassNotFoundException
   * @throws IllegalAccessException
   * @throws InstantiationException
   *
   */
  public void check(URL url) throws InstantiationException,
      IllegalAccessException,
      ClassNotFoundException, WorkloadException {
    SpiderOptions options = new SpiderOptions();
    options.workloadManager =
      MemoryWorkloadManager.class.getCanonicalName();
    LinkReport report = new LinkReport();
    Spider spider = new Spider(options, report);
    spider.addURL(url, null, 1);
    spider.process();
    System.out.println(spider.getStatus());

    if (report.getBad().size() > 0) {
      System.out.println("Bad Links Found:");
      for (String str : report.getBad()) {
        System.out.println(str);
      }
    } else {
      System.out.println("No bad links were found.");
    }

  }

}
```

All of the work performed by this recipe is accomplished inside of the **checkLink**
method. This method begins by creating a **SpiderOptions** object named **options**.
Then a **MemoryWorkloadManager** is specified. A **MemoryWorkloadManager**
will work with relatively large sites; however, if you are going to check an extremely large
site, you may want to use an **SQLWorkloadManager**.

```
SpiderOptions options = new SpiderOptions();
options.workloadManager = MemoryWorkloadManager.class.getCanoni-
calName();
```

Next, a **LinkReport** object is created. The **LinkReport** class will be discussed in the next section. The spider is then created and the URL to check is added to the spider's workload.

```
LinkReport report = new LinkReport();
Spider spider = new Spider(options, report);
spider.addURL(url, null, 1);
```

Calling the **process** method starts the spider. Once the spider is completed, its status is displayed.

```
spider.process();
System.out.println(spider.getStatus());
```

If bad links are found, then they are displayed in a list.

```
if (report.getBad().size() > 0) {
  System.out.println("Bad Links Found:");
  for (String str : report.getBad()) {
    System.out.println(str);
}
```

Finally, if there are no bad links found, the user is informed.

```
} else {
  System.out.println("No bad links were found.");
}
```

The **LinkReport** class processes all of the bad links. The **LinkReport** class will be described in the next section.

### Receiving Data for the Broken Links Spider

The Heaton Research Spider requires that any spider include a class that implements the **SpiderReportable** interface. This object manages the spider and receives all information found by the spider. The broken links spider uses the **LinkReport** class to implement the **SpiderReportable** interface.

Listing 13.5 shows the **LinkReport** class.

### Listing 13.5: Report Broken Links (LinkReport.java)

```
package com.heatonresearch.httprecipes.ch13.recipe1;

import java.io.*;
import java.net.*;
import java.util.*;
```

```java
import java.util.logging.*;

import com.heatonresearch.httprecipes.spider.*;
import com.heatonresearch.httprecipes.spider.workload.*;

public class LinkReport implements SpiderReportable {
  /**
   * For logging.
   */
  private static Logger logger = Logger
      .getLogger("com.heatonresearch.httprecipes.spider.Spider");

  /**
   * The host we are working with.
   */
  private String base;

  /**
   * The bad URL's.
   */
  private List<String> bad = new ArrayList<String>();

  /**
   * The workload manager being used.
   */
  private WorkloadManager workloadManager;

  /**
   * This function is called when the spider is ready to
   * process a new host. This function simply stores the
   * value of the current host.
   *
   * @param host
   *            The new host that is about to be processed.
   * @return True if this host should be processed, false
   *            otherwise.
   */
  public boolean beginHost(String host) {
    if (this.base == null) {
      this.base = host;
      return true;
    } else {
      return false;
    }
  }
}
```

```java
/**
 * @return the bad
 */
public List<String> getBad() {
  return this.bad;
}

/**
 * Called when the spider is starting up. This method
 * provides the SpiderReportable class with the spider
 * object.
 *
 * @param spider
 *           The spider that will be working with this
 *           object.
 */
public void init(Spider spider) {
  this.workloadManager = spider.getWorkloadManager();
}

/**
 * @param bad
 *           the bad to set
 */
public void setBad(List<String> bad) {
  this.bad = bad;
}

public boolean spiderFoundURL(URL url, URL source,
    SpiderReportable.URLType type) {

  if ((this.base != null) &&
      (!this.base.equalsIgnoreCase(url.getHost()))) {
    return false;
  }

  return true;
}
```

```java
/**
 * Called when the spider is about to process a NON-HTML
 * URL.
 *
 * @param url
 *             The URL that the spider found.
 * @param stream
 *             An InputStream to read the page contents from.
 * @throws IOException
 *                Thrown if an IO error occurs while processing
 *                the page.
 */
public void spiderProcessURL(URL url, InputStream stream) {
}

/**
 * Called when the spider is ready to process an HTML
 * URL.
 *
 * @param url
 *             The URL that the spider is about to process.
 * @param parse
 *             An object that will allow you you to parse the
 *             HTML on this page.
 * @throws IOException
 *                Thrown if an IO error occurs while processing
 *                the page.
 */
public void spiderProcessURL(URL url, SpiderParseHTML parse) {
  try {
    parse.readAll();
  } catch (IOException e) {
    logger.log(Level.INFO, "Error reading page:"
      + url.toString());
  }
}

/**
 * Called when the spider tries to process a URL but gets
 * an error.
 *
 * @param url
 *             The URL that generated an error.
 */
public void spiderURLError(URL url) {
  URL source;
```

```
    try {
      source = this.workloadManager.getSource(url);
      StringBuilder str = new StringBuilder();
      str.append("Bad URL:");
      str.append(url.toString());
      str.append(" found at ");
      str.append(source.toString());
      this.bad.add(str.toString());
    } catch (WorkloadException e) {
      e.printStackTrace();
    }
  }

}
```

The **ReportLinks** class implements all of the functions and methods defined by the **SpiderReportable** interface. To review what these methods and functions are for, refer to Table 13.1.

The **foundURL** function is called each time a new URL is found. Because this spider only operates on a single web server, the **foundURL** method ensures that all new URLs are on the same server.

```
if ((this.base != null) &&
  (!this.base.equalsIgnoreCase(url.getHost()))) {
  return false;
}
return true;
```

If the new URL's host varies from the starting host, the **foundURL** function will return **false**, causing the spider to ignore the new URL. The above lines of code can be reused in any spider that is to operate only on a single host.

The **processURL** method, which usually downloads a URL, is fairly simple. Because we are only checking links, we do not need to actually download the page. This can be done by calling the **readAll** method of the **ParseHTML** object.

```
try {
  parse.readAll();
} catch (IOException e) {
  logger.log(Level.INFO, "Error reading page:" + url.toString());
}
```

There is no need to record the **IOException** that was caught, since it would most likely be caused by a timeout on the web server and not by a missing page. Timeouts are caused by a variety of events. One of which, is an overloaded web server. A missing page would throw an exception when it is first opened, not during the transfer of information. Therefore, since a timeout is only a temporary server issue, we do not record that page as a bad link.

The Heaton Research Spider calls the **spiderURLError** method whenever a bad URL is found. This URL is displayed, along with the page it was found on, and added to the **bad** list.

```
URL source;
try {
  source = this.workloadManager.getSource(url);
  StringBuilder str = new StringBuilder();
  str.append("Bad URL:");
  str.append(url.toString());
  str.append(" found at ");
  str.append(source.toString());
  this.bad.add(str.toString());
} catch (WorkloadException e) {
  e.printStackTrace();
}
```

These bad URLs are accumulated in the **LinkReport** class until the spider finished. Then the bad URL list is displayed.

### Recipe #13.2: Downloading HTML and Images

Another common use for spiders, is to create an offline copy of a web site. This recipe will show how to do this. To start this spider, you must provide three arguments. The first argument is the name of spider configuration file. Through the spider configuration file, you can specify to use either an SQL or memory based workload manager. Listing 13.1 shows an example spider configuration file. Next, a local directory must be specified to which you will download the site. Finally, the starting URL must be given.

The following shows how you might start the spider:

```
DownloadSite spider.conf c:\temp\ http://www.example.com
```

The above command simply shows the abstract format to call this recipe, with the appropriate parameters. For exact information on how to run this recipe refer to Appendix B, C, or D, depending on the operating system you are using. Now that you have seen how to use the download spider, we will examine how it was constructed.

## Creating the Download Spider

The **DownloadSite** class contains the main method for the recipe, which is shown in Listing 13.6.

### Listing 13.6: Download a Site (DownloadSite.java)

```java
package com.heatonresearch.httprecipes.ch13.recipe2;

import java.io.*;
import java.net.*;

import com.heatonresearch.httprecipes.spider.*;
import com.heatonresearch.httprecipes.spider.workload.*;

public class DownloadSite {
  /**
   * The main method.
   *
   * @param args
   *            Specifies the path to the config file, the
   *            path to download to, and the starting URL.
   */
  public static void main(String args[]) {
    try {
      if (args.length < 3) {
        System.out
            .println(
        "Usage: DownloadSite [Path to spider.conf] [Path to down-
load to] [URL to download]");
      } else {
        DownloadSite download = new DownloadSite();
        download.download(args[0], new URL(args[2]), args[1]);
      }
    } catch (Exception e) {
      e.printStackTrace();
    }
  }

  /**
   * Download an entire site.
   *
   * @param config
   *            The spider configuration file to use.
   * @param base
   *            The URL to start from.
   * @param local
```

```
 *            The local path to save files to.
 * @throws IOException
 *              Thrown if an I/O error occurs.
 * @throws SpiderException
 *              Thrown if there is an error connecting to the
 *              database.
 * @throws InstantiationException
 *              Thrown if there is an error parsing the
 *              config file.
 * @throws IllegalAccessException
 *              Thrown if the database driver can not be
 *              loaded.
 * @throws ClassNotFoundException
 *              Thrown if the database driver can not be
 *              located.
 * @throws WorkloadException
 *              Thrown if there is an error reading the
 *              config file.
 */
public void download(String config, URL base, String local)
    throws IOException, SpiderException,
    InstantiationException,
    IllegalAccessException, ClassNotFoundException,
    WorkloadException
{
  SpiderReport report = new SpiderReport(local);
  SpiderOptions options = new SpiderOptions();
  options.load(config);
  Spider spider = new Spider(options, report);
  spider.addURL(base, null, 1);
  spider.process();
  System.out.println(spider.getStatus());
}
}
```

The majority of the work done by this recipe is performed inside of the **download** method. The **download** method is very similar to Recipe 13.1, except that the configuration is read from a file. This recipe begins by creating a **SpiderReport** object, named **report**, and a **SpiderOptions** object, named **options**. The configuration is then loaded from a file.

```
SpiderReport report = new SpiderReport(local);
SpiderOptions options = new SpiderOptions();
options.load(config);
```

Next, the spider is constructed, and the starting URL is added.

```
Spider spider = new Spider(options, report);
```

```
spider.addURL(base, null, 1);
```

Once the spider has been created, it can be started by calling the process method. Once the spider is finished, the status is displayed.

```
spider.process();
System.out.println(spider.getStatus());
```

The actual downloading is performed by the SpiderReport class, which is discussed in the next section.

### Receiving Data for the Download Spider

As in the last recipe, this spider is required to have a class that implements the **SpiderReportable** interface. This object manages the spider and receives all information found by the spider. The site Download spider uses the **SpiderReport** class to implement the **SpiderReportable** interface.

Listing 13.7 shows the **SpiderReport** class.

### Listing 13.7: Report Download Information (SpiderReport.java)

```java
package com.heatonresearch.httprecipes.ch13.recipe2;

import java.io.*;
import java.net.*;

import com.heatonresearch.httprecipes.html.*;
import com.heatonresearch.httprecipes.spider.*;

public class SpiderReport implements SpiderReportable {
  /*
   * The base host. Only URL's from this host will be
   * downloaded.
   */
  private String base;

  /*
   * The local path to save downloaded files to.
   */
  private String path;

  /**
   * Construct a SpiderReport object.
   *
   * @param path
   *            The local file path to store the files to.
   */
```

```java
public SpiderReport(String path) {
  this.path = path;
}

/**
 * This function is called when the spider is ready to
 * process a new host. This function simply stores the
 * value of the current host.
 *
 * @param host
 *           The new host that is about to be processed.
 * @return True if this host should be processed, false
 *           otherwise.
 */
public boolean beginHost(String host) {
  if (this.base == null) {
    this.base = host;
    return true;
  } else {
    return false;
  }
}

/**
 * Called when the spider is starting up. This method
 * provides the SpiderReportable class with the spider
 * object. This method is not used in this manager.
 *
 * @param spider
 *           The spider that will be working with this
 *           object.
 */
public void init(Spider spider) {
}

/**
 * Called when the spider encounters a URL. If the URL is
 * on the same host as the base host, then the function
 * will return true, indicating that the URL is to be
 * processed.
 *
 * @param url
 *           The URL that the spider found.
 * @param source
 *           The page that the URL was found on.
 * @param type
```

```
 *            The type of link this URL is.
 * @return True if the spider should scan for links on
 *            this page.
 */
public boolean spiderFoundURL(URL url, URL source,
    SpiderReportable.URLType type) {

  if ((this.base != null)
      && (!this.base.equalsIgnoreCase(url.getHost()))) {
    return false;
  }

  return true;
}

/**
 * Called when the spider is about to process a NON-HTML
 * URL.
 *
 * @param url
 *            The URL that the spider found.
 * @param stream
 *            An InputStream to read the page contents from.
 * @throws IOException
 *            Thrown if an IO error occurs while processing
 *            the page.
 */
public void spiderProcessURL(URL url, InputStream stream)
  throws IOException {
  byte[] buffer = new byte[1024];

  int length;
  String filename =
    URLUtility.convertFilename(this.path, url, true);

  try {
    OutputStream os = new FileOutputStream(filename);
    do {
      length = stream.read(buffer);
      if (length != -1) {
        os.write(buffer, 0, length);
      }
    } while (length != -1);
    os.close();

  } catch (FileNotFoundException e) {
```

```
      e.printStackTrace();
    }
  }


  /**
   * Called when the spider is ready to process an HTML
   * URL. Download the contents of the URL to a local file.
   *
   * @param url
   *          The URL that the spider is about to process.
   * @param parse
   *          An object that will allow you you to parse the
   *          HTML on this page.
   * @throws IOException
   *            Thrown if an IO error occurs while processing
   *            the page.
   */
  public void spiderProcessURL(URL url, SpiderParseHTML parse)
      throws IOException {
    String filename =
      URLUtility.convertFilename(this.path, url, true);
    OutputStream os = new FileOutputStream(filename);
    parse.getStream().setOutputStream(os);
    parse.readAll();
    os.close();

  }


  /**
   * Called when the spider tries to process a URL but gets
   * an error. This method is not used in tries manager.
   *
   * @param url
   *          The URL that generated an error.
   */
  public void spiderURLError(URL url) {
  }

}
```

Much of Recipe 13.2's **SpiderReportable** implementation is similar to Recipe 13.1. However, unlike 13.1, Recipe 13.2 will actually download what it finds. This downloading functionality is implemented in the two overloaded instances of the **spiderProcessURL** methods. The first **spiderProcessURL** method is designed to take an **InputStream**.

```
public void spiderProcessURL(URL url, InputStream stream)
```

This method is called to download images and other binary objects. Anything that is not HTML is downloaded by this method. HTML is handled differently because HTML contains links to other pages. This method begins by creating a buffer to read the binary data.

```
byte[] buffer = new byte[1024];
int length;
```

Next, a filename is created. The filename uses the **convertFilename** function to convert the URL into a file that can be saved to the local computer. The **convertFilename** function also creates the directory structure to hold the specified file.

```
String filename = URLUtility.convertFilename(this.path, url,
true);
```

Next, the data is read in. It is read using the **buffer** variable that was created earlier.

```
try {
  OutputStream os = new FileOutputStream(filename);
do {
  length = stream.read(buffer);
  if (length != -1) {
  os.write(buffer, 0, length);
  }
} while (length != -1);
```

Once the data has been read, the output stream can be closed.

```
os.close();
```

If any exceptions are caught, they are displayed to the user.

```
} catch (FileNotFoundException e) {
  e.printStackTrace();
}
```

This recipe also has to handle HTML data. If a URL has HTML data, then the second form of the **spiderProcessURL** method is used.

```
public void spiderProcessURL(URL url, SpiderParseHTML parse)
```

First, a filename is generated, just as was done for the binary URL. An **OutputStream** is opened to write the file to.

```
String filename =
  URLUtility.convertFilename(this.path, url, true);
OutputStream os = new FileOutputStream(filename);
```

The **OutputStream** is then attached to the **ParseHTML** object, so that any data ready from the HTML stream is also written to the **OutputStream**. This saves the HTML file to the local computer.

```
parse.getStream().setOutputStream(os);
```

Finally, **readAll** is called to read the entire HTML file. The HTML file will be written to the attached **OutputStream**, as it is parsed.

```
parse.readAll();
os.close();
```

Now that the file has been written, the **OutputStream** can be closed.

## Recipe #13.3: Spider the World

Perhaps the most well known of all spiders, are the search engine spiders. These are the spiders used by sites, such as Google, to add new sites to their search engines. Such spiders are not designed to stay on one specific site. In this recipe I will show you how to create a spider that will not restrict itself to one site; rather, this spider will keep following links endlessly. It is important to note, it is very unlikely that this spider will ever finish, since it will have to visit nearly every public URL on the Internet to do so.

To start this spider, you must provide three arguments. The first argument is the name of the spider configuration file. Through the spider configuration file, you can specify to use either an SQL or memory based workload manager. Listing 13.1 shows an example spider configuration file. Next, a local directory must be specified to download the site to. Finally, the starting URL must be specified.

The following shows how you might start the spider.

```
WorldSpider spider.conf c:\temp\ http://www.example.com
```

The above command simply shows the abstract format to call this recipe, with the appropriate parameters. For exact information on how to run this recipe refer to Appendix B, C, or D, depending on the operating system you are using. This spider is designed to access a large number of sites. You should use the **SQLWorkloadManager** class with this spider. Because the **MemoryWorkloadManager** is only designed to work with one single host, it would not be compatible with this spider.

Now that you have seen how to use the world spider we will examine how it was constructed.

## Creating the World Spider

The **WorldSpider** class contains the **main** method for the recipe. Listing 13.8 shows the **WorldSpider** class.

### Listing 13.8: Download the World (WorldSpider.java)

```
package com.heatonresearch.httprecipes.ch13.recipe3;

import java.io.*;
import java.net.*;
```

```
import com.heatonresearch.httprecipes.spider.*;
import com.heatonresearch.httprecipes.spider.workload.*;

public class WorldSpider {


  /**
   * The main method.
   *
   * @param args
   *            Specifies the path to the config file, the
   *            path to download to, and the starting URL.
   */
  public static void main(String args[]) {
    try {
      if (args.length < 3) {
        System.out
            .println(
"Usage: WorldSpider [Path to spider.conf] "
+"[Path to download to] [URL to start]");
      } else {
        WorldSpider download = new WorldSpider();
        download.download(args[0], new URL(args[2]), args[1]);
      }
    } catch (Exception e) {
      e.printStackTrace();
    }
  }


  /**
   * Download an entire site.
   *
   * @param config
   *            The spider configuration file to use.
   * @param base
   *            The URL to start from.
   * @param local
   *            The local path to save files to.
   * @throws IOException
   *             Thrown if an I/O error occurs.
   * @throws SpiderException
   *             Thrown if there is an error connecting to the
   *             database.
   * @throws InstantiationException
   *             Thrown if there is an error parsing the
```

```
    *            config file.
    * @throws IllegalAccessException
    *            Thrown if the database driver can not be
    *            loaded.
    * @throws ClassNotFoundException
    *            Thrown if the database driver can not be
    *            located.
    * @throws WorkloadException
    *            Thrown if there is an error reading the
    *            config file.
    */
  public void download(String config, URL base, String local)
      throws IOException, SpiderException, InstantiationException,
      IllegalAccessException, ClassNotFoundException, WorkloadEx-
ception {
    WorldSpiderReport report = new WorldSpiderReport(local);
    SpiderOptions options = new SpiderOptions();
    options.load(config);
    Spider spider = new Spider(options, report);
    spider.addURL(base, null, 1);
    spider.process();
    System.out.println(spider.getStatus());
  }
}
```

The **download** method for the world spider is essentially the same as Recipe 13.2. The difference is in the **WorldSpiderReport** class, which manages the spider.

### Receiving Data for the World Spider

Just like the last two recipes, this spider must have a class that implements the **SpiderReportable** interface. This object manages the spider and receives all information found by the spider. The site world spider uses the **WorldSpiderReport** class to implement the **SpiderReportable** interface.

Listing 13.9 displays the **SpiderReport** class.

#### Listing 13.9: Report for World Spider (WorldSpiderReport.java)

```
package com.heatonresearch.httprecipes.ch13.recipe3;

import java.io.*;
import java.net.*;

import com.heatonresearch.httprecipes.html.*;
import com.heatonresearch.httprecipes.spider.*;
```

```java
public class WorldSpiderReport implements SpiderReportable {
  /*
   * The base host. Only URL's from this host will be
   * downloaded.
   */
  private String base;

  /*
   * The local path to save downloaded files to.
   */
  private String path;

  /**
   * Construct a SpiderReport object.
   *
   * @param path
   *             The local file path to store the files to.
   */
  public WorldSpiderReport(String path) {
    this.path = path;
  }

  /**
   * This function is called when the spider is ready to
   * process a new host. This function simply stores the
   * value of the current host.
   *
   * @param host
   *             The new host that is about to be processed.
   * @return True if this host should be processed, false
   *             otherwise.
   */
  public boolean beginHost(String host) {
    if (this.base == null) {
      this.base = host;
      return true;
    } else {
      return false;
    }
  }

  /**
   * Called when the spider is starting up. This method
   * provides the SpiderReportable class with the spider
   * object. This method is not used in this manager.
   *
```

```
 * @param spider
 *           The spider that will be working with this
 *           object.
 */
public void init(Spider spider) {
}

/**
 * Called when the spider encounters a URL. This function
 * will always return true. Because this spider will
 * theoretically visit every URL on the Internet, all
 * URL's will be processed.
 *
 * @param url
 *           The URL that the spider found.
 * @param source
 *           The page that the URL was found on.
 * @param type
 *           The type of link this URL is.
 * @return True if the spider should scan for links on
 *           this page.
 */
public boolean spiderFoundURL(URL url, URL source,
    SpiderReportable.URLType type) {
  return true;
}

/**
 * Called when the spider is about to process a NON-HTML
 * URL.
 *
 * @param url
 *           The URL that the spider found.
 * @param stream
 *           An InputStream to read the page contents from.
 * @throws IOException
 *            Thrown if an IO error occurs while processing
 *            the page.
 */
public void spiderProcessURL(URL url, InputStream stream)
  throws IOException {
  byte[] buffer = new byte[1024];

  int length;
  String filename = URLUtility.convertFilename(this.path, url,
true);
```

```java
    try {
      OutputStream os = new FileOutputStream(filename);
      do {
        length = stream.read(buffer);
        if (length != -1) {
          os.write(buffer, 0, length);
        }
      } while (length != -1);
      os.close();

    } catch (FileNotFoundException e) {
      e.printStackTrace();
    }
  }

  /**
   * Called when the spider is ready to process an HTML
   * URL. Download the contents of the URL to a local file.
   *
   * @param url
   *            The URL that the spider is about to process.
   * @param parse
   *            An object that will allow you you to parse the
   *            HTML on this page.
   * @throws IOException
   *             Thrown if an IO error occurs while processing
   *             the page.
   */
  public void spiderProcessURL(URL url, SpiderParseHTML parse)
      throws IOException {
    String filename = URLUtility.convertFilename(this.path, url,
true);
    OutputStream os = new FileOutputStream(filename);
    parse.getStream().setOutputStream(os);
    parse.readAll();
    os.close();

  }
```

```
/**
 * Called when the spider tries to process a URL but gets
 * an error. This method is not used in this manager.
 *
 * @param url
 *           The URL that generated an error.
 */
public void spiderURLError(URL url) {
}

}
```

The unique functionality with the world spider is the way that it handles new URLs when **spiderFoundURL** is called. Unlike the previous spiders, no checks are made to determine if the URL is on the same host. Any URL is a candidate to be visited.

```
public boolean spiderFoundURL(URL url, URL source,
SpiderReportable.URLType type) {
return true;
}
```

As you can see, the **spiderFoundURL** simply returns **true**.

This spider shows how you would setup a spider that would access a large number of web sites. Of course, this spider is only the beginning of a search engine; but it does demonstrate how to configure the Heaton Research Spider to access a large amount of sites.

### Recipe #13.4: Display Spider Statistics

Because the **SQLWorkloadManager** class stores the workload in a database, it is possible for other programs to monitor the progress of the spider. This recipe will show you how to create a simple program that monitors the spider progress using the Heaton Research spider database.

This recipe makes use of a Heaton Research Spider configuration file, just like previous recipes. To start this recipe, specify the name of the configuration file as the first argument. The following code demonstrates how you might start the spider:

```
SpiderStats spider.conf c:\temp\ http://www.example.com
```

The above command simply shows the abstract format to call this recipe, with the appropriate parameters. For exact information on how to run this recipe refer to Appendix B, C, or D, depending on the operating system you are using. Figure 13.1 shows this program monitoring a spider's progress.

**Figure 13.1: Monitoring a Spider**

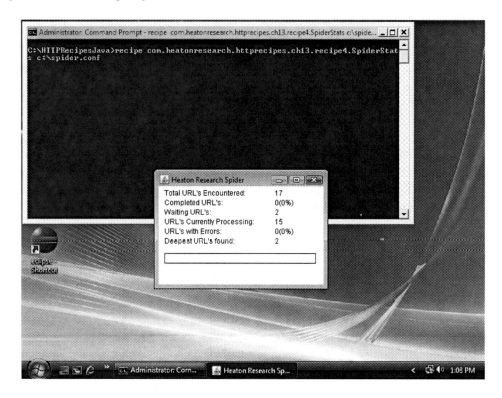

The spider monitor is shown in Listing 13.10.

**Listing 13.10: Display Spider Statistics (SpiderStats.java)**

```java
package com.heatonresearch.httprecipes.ch13.recipe4;

import java.awt.*;
import java.io.*;
import java.sql.*;
import java.text.*;

import javax.swing.*;

import com.heatonresearch.httprecipes.spider.*;

public class SpiderStats extends JFrame implements Runnable {
  /**
   * Serial id.
   */
  private static final long serialVersionUID = 1L;
```

```java
/**
 * Start the program.
 *
 * @param args
 *            The first argument contains a path to a spider
 *            configuration file.
 */
public static void main(String args[]) {
  try {
    if (args.length < 1) {
      System.out.println(
        "Usage: SpiderStats [path to config file]");
    } else {
      JFrame frame = new SpiderStats(args[0]);
      frame.setSize(new Dimension(300, 200));
      frame.setVisible(true);
    }
  } catch (Exception e) {
    e.printStackTrace();
  }
}

/**
 * Contains information about how to connect to the
 * database.
 */
private SpiderOptions options;

/**
 * A JDBC connection.
 */
private Connection connection;

/**
 * Get a count by status.
 */
private final String sqlStatus =
"select status,count(*) from spider_workload group by status;";

/**
 * Get the maximum depth
 */
private final String sqlDepth =
"SELECT MAX(depth) from spider_workload";
```

```
/**
 * Prepared statement for status.
 */
private PreparedStatement stmtStatus;

/**
 * Prepared statement for depth.
 */
private PreparedStatement stmtDepth;

/**
 * How many URL's are waiting.
 */
private int waiting;

/**
 * How many URL's are done.
 */
private int done;

/**
 * How many URL's are being processed.
 */
private int processing;

/**
 * How many URL's resulted in an error.
 */
private int error;

/**
 * What is the maximum depth encountered so far.
 */
private int depth;

/**
 * The background thread.
 */
private Thread thread;

/**
 * Percent done.
 */
private double donePercent;
```

```java
/**
 * Percent error.
 */
private double errorPercent;

/**
 * Construct a SpiderStats object.
 *
 * @param config
 *            A path to a spider configuration file.
 * @throws IOException
 *             Thrown if an I/O error occurs.
 * @throws SpiderException
 *             Thrown if the options can not be loaded.
 */
public SpiderStats(String config)
  throws IOException, SpiderException {
  this.options = new SpiderOptions();
  this.options.load(config);
  this.thread = new Thread(this);
  this.thread.start();
}

/**
 * Display the stats.
 *
 * @param g
 *            The graphics object.
 */
public void displayStats(Graphics g) {
  final String stat1 = "Total URL\'s Encountered:";
  final String stat2 = "Completed URL\'s:";
  final String stat3 = "Waiting URL\'s:";
  final String stat4 = "URL\'s Currently Processing:";
  final String stat5 = "URL\'s with Errors:";
  final String stat6 = "Deepest URL\'s found:";

  FontMetrics fm = g.getFontMetrics();
  int y = fm.getHeight();
  g.setColor(Color.WHITE);
  g.fillRect(0, 0, getWidth(), getHeight());
  g.setColor(Color.BLACK);
  int total = this.processing + this.error
    + this.done + this.waiting;

  NumberFormat numFormat = NumberFormat.getInstance();
```

```
    NumberFormat percentFormat =
      NumberFormat.getPercentInstance();

    if ((this.waiting + this.processing + this.done) == 0) {
      this.donePercent = 0;
    } else {
      this.donePercent = (double) this.done
      / (double) (this.waiting + this.processing + this.done);
    }

    if (total == 0) {
      this.errorPercent = 0;
    } else {
      this.errorPercent = (double) this.error / (double) total;
    }

    g.drawString(stat1, 10, y);
    g.drawString("" + numFormat.format(total), 200, y);
    y += fm.getHeight();

    g.drawString(stat2, 10, y);
    g.drawString("" + numFormat.format(this.done) + "("
        + percentFormat.format(this.donePercent) + ")", 200, y);
    y += fm.getHeight();

    g.drawString(stat3, 10, y);
    g.drawString("" + numFormat.format(this.waiting), 200, y);
    y += fm.getHeight();

    g.drawString(stat4, 10, y);
    g.drawString("" + numFormat.format(this.processing), 200, y);
    y += fm.getHeight();

    g.drawString(stat5, 10, y);
    g.drawString("" + numFormat.format(this.error) + "("
        + percentFormat.format(this.errorPercent) + ")", 200, y);
    y += fm.getHeight();

    g.drawString(stat6, 10, y);
    g.drawString("" + numFormat.format(this.depth), 200, y);
    y += fm.getHeight();

    displayProgressBar(g, y);

  }
```

```java
/**
 * Run the background thread.
 */
public void run() {
  Graphics g = null;
  for (;;) {
    if (this.connection == null) {
      open();
    }

    if (g == null) {
      g = getContentPane().getGraphics();
    }

    if (g != null) {
      getStats();
      displayStats(g);
    }

    try {
      Thread.sleep(10000);
    } catch (InterruptedException e) {
      return;
    }
  }

}

/**
 * Draw a progress bar.
 *
 * @param g
 *          The graphics object.
 * @param y
 *          The y position to draw the progress bar.
 */
private void displayProgressBar(Graphics g, int y) {
  int width = getWidth();
  int progressWidth = width - 20;
  g.setColor(Color.GREEN);
  g.fillRect(10, y, (int)
    (progressWidth * this.donePercent), 16);
  g.setColor(Color.BLACK);
  g.drawRect(10, y, progressWidth, 16);

}
```

```java
/**
 * Load the stats from the database.
 */
private void getStats() {
  try {
    this.waiting = this.processing = this.error = this.done = 0;
    ResultSet rs = this.stmtStatus.executeQuery();
    while (rs.next()) {
      String status = rs.getString(1);
      int count = rs.getInt(2);
      if (status.equalsIgnoreCase("W")) {
        this.waiting = count;
      } else if (status.equalsIgnoreCase("P")) {
        this.processing = count;
      } else if (status.equals("E")) {
        this.error = count;
      } else if (status.equals("D")) {
        this.done = count;
      }
    }
    rs.close();

    this.depth = 0;
    rs = this.stmtDepth.executeQuery();
    if (rs.next()) {
      this.depth = rs.getInt(1);
    }
  } catch (SQLException e) {
    e.printStackTrace();
  }
}

/**
 * Open a connection to the database.
 */
private void open() {
  try {
    setTitle("Heaton Research Spider");
    Class.forName(this.options.dbClass).newInstance();
    this.connection =
      DriverManager.getConnection(
        this.options.dbURL, this.options.dbUID,
          this.options.dbPWD);
    this.stmtStatus = this.connection.prepareStatement(
      this.sqlStatus);
```

```
      this.stmtDepth = this.connection.prepareStatement(
        this.sqlDepth);
    } catch (InstantiationException e) {
      e.printStackTrace();
    } catch (IllegalAccessException e) {
      e.printStackTrace();
    } catch (ClassNotFoundException e) {
      e.printStackTrace();
    } catch (SQLException e) {
      e.printStackTrace();
    }


  }
}
```

This program begins by creating its window and then creating a background thread. The background thread, contained in the **run** method, allows the application to update the statistics on a regular basis. The **run** method begins by entering an endless loop and opening a connection to the database and obtaining a **Graphics** object.

```
Graphics g = null;
for (;;) {
  if (this.connection == null) {
  open();
}

if (g == null) {
  g = getContentPane().getGraphics();
}
```

The database connection is established by calling the **open** method, which will be covered in the next section. If the **Graphics** object, named **g**, was obtained successfully, the **getStats** method is called to obtain the current statistics from the database. Next, the **displayStats** method is called to display the current statistics.

```
if (g != null) {
getStats();
displayStats(g);
}
```

Then the program will wait for 10,000 milliseconds, or 10 seconds, before polling for stats again.

```
try {
  Thread.sleep(10000);
} catch (InterruptedException e) {
  return;
}
}
}
```

This process continues endlessly, as long as the program is allowed to run.

## Opening a Database Connection

Before any SQL commands can be issued to obtain stats, a connection must be opened to the database. This is done by the **open** method. The **open** method will also create several **PreparedStatements** that will execute the two SQL statements that this program uses to obtain its statistics. The **open** method begins by using the information from a **SpiderOptions** object to establish a connection. The **SpiderOptions** object was loaded from a spider configuration file, discussed in previous recipes in this chapter.

```
try {
  setTitle("Heaton Research Spider");
  Class.forName(this.options.dbClass).newInstance();
  this.connection = DriverManager.getConnection(
    this.options.dbURL, this.options.dbUID,
    this.options.dbPWD);
```

Next, two prepared statements are created for the two SQL statements that this program uses to obtain statistics.

```
this.stmtStatus = this.connection.prepareStatement(this.sqlSta-
tus);
this.stmtDepth = this.connection.prepareStatement(this.sqlDepth);
```

Finally, **catch** statements are used to trap any of the errors that can occur while establishing a database connection.

```
} catch (InstantiationException e) {
  e.printStackTrace();
} catch (IllegalAccessException e) {
  e.printStackTrace();
} catch (ClassNotFoundException e) {
  e.printStackTrace();
} catch (SQLException e) {
  e.printStackTrace();
}
```

If any error does occur, a stack trace is printed, and the method ends.

## Obtaining the Statistics

Now that the database connection has been opened, the statistics can be obtained. Calling the **obtainStats** method does this. The **obtainStats** method begins by clearing out all of the totals and executing the **stmtStatus** query. This query obtains a count for each of the status types in the **spider_workload** table.

```
this.waiting = this.processing = this.error = this.done = 0;
ResultSet rs = this.stmtStatus.executeQuery();
```

Next, the results will be examined. The SQL was constructed so that each of the status types will be returned in a separate row, along with a count. As we loop over everything that was returned, we examine the **status** of each row and assign it to the correct total variable.

```
while (rs.next()) {
  String status = rs.getString(1);
  int count = rs.getInt(2);
  if (status.equalsIgnoreCase("W")) {
  this.waiting = count;
  } else if (status.equalsIgnoreCase("P")) {
    this.processing = count;
  } else if (status.equals("E")) {
    this.error = count;
  } else if (status.equals("D")) {
    this.done = count;
  }
}
rs.close();
```

Once this completes, we can close the result set.

Next, we execute the **stmtDepth** query. This simple SQL query obtains the maximum depth that was recorded in the **spider_workload** table.

```
this.depth = 0;
rs = this.stmtDepth.executeQuery();
if (rs.next()) {
  this.depth = rs.getInt(1);
}
rs.close();
```

Once the depth has been obtained, the result set can be closed.

```
} catch (SQLException e) {
  e.printStackTrace();
}
```

If any errors occur, a stack trace is displayed.

### Displaying the Statistics

Now that we have obtained the statistics from the database, we can display them. First, a string is created for each of the statistics that will be displayed.

```
final String stat1 = "Total URL\'s Encountered:";
final String stat2 = "Completed URL\'s:";
final String stat3 = "Waiting URL\'s:";
final String stat4 = "URL\'s Currently Processing:";
```

```
final String stat5 = "URL\'s with Errors:";
final String stat6 = "Deepest URL\'s found:";
```

Next, a **FontMetrics** object is created to properly space all of the text. Drawing a white rectangle clears the display area.

```
FontMetrics fm = g.getFontMetrics();
int y = fm.getHeight();
g.setColor(Color.WHITE);
g.fillRect(0, 0, getWidth(), getHeight());
g.setColor(Color.BLACK);
int total = this.processing + this.error + this.done + this.wait-
ing;
```

Both **NumberFormat** and **PercentFormat** objects are created to format the numbers.

```
NumberFormat numFormat = NumberFormat.getInstance();
NumberFormat percentFormat = NumberFormat.getPercentInstance();
```

If a percent done can be calculated, then calculate it. Otherwise put a zero into percent done.

```
if ((this.waiting + this.processing + this.done) == 0) {
  this.donePercent = 0;
} else {
  this.donePercent = (double) this.done / (double) (this.waiting +
this.processing + this.done);
}
```

If a percent error can be calculated, then calculate it. Otherwise put a zero into percent error.

```
if (total == 0) {
  this.errorPercent = 0;
} else {
  this.errorPercent = (double) this.error / (double) total;
}
```

Display the total number of URLs found and move the **y** variable down by the correct amount.

```
g.drawString(stat1, 10, y);
g.drawString("" + numFormat.format(total), 200, y);
y += fm.getHeight();
```

Display the total number of URLs done and the percent done. Move the **y** variable down by the correct amount.

```
g.drawString(stat2, 10, y);
g.drawString("" + numFormat.format(this.done) + "("
```

```
+ percentFormat.format(this.donePercent) + ")", 200, y);
y += fm.getHeight();
```

Display the total number of URLs waiting to be processed and move the **y** variable down by the correct amount.

```
g.drawString(stat3, 10, y);
g.drawString("" + numFormat.format(this.waiting), 200, y);
y += fm.getHeight();
```

Display the total number of URLs that are currently being processed and move the **y** variable down by the correct amount.

```
g.drawString(stat4, 10, y);
g.drawString("" + numFormat.format(this.processing), 200, y);
y += fm.getHeight();
```

Display the total number of URLs that resulted in an error, and the error percent. Move the **y** variable down by the correct amount.

```
g.drawString(stat5, 10, y);
g.drawString("" + numFormat.format(this.error) + "("
+ percentFormat.format(this.errorPercent) + ")", 200, y);
y += fm.getHeight();
```

Display the deepest URL processed and move the **y** variable down by the correct amount.

```
g.drawString(stat6, 10, y);
g.drawString("" + numFormat.format(this.depth), 200, y);
y += fm.getHeight();
```

Finally, display a progress bar indicating how close we are to being finished.

```
displayProgressBar(g, y);
```

Of course, the progress bar is a very rough approximation. The spider does not know how many URL's it will find ahead of time. So the percent done is simply the ratio of the number of URLs processed against the total number of URLs found.

### Displaying the Progress Bar

The progress bar is a simple green rectangle that is drawn to display the percent done. (The percent done was calculated in the previous section.) First, the total width is calculated.

```
int width = getWidth();
int progressWidth = width - 20;
```

Next, a green bar is drawn that is a percent of the total width.

```
g.setColor(Color.GREEN);
```

```
g.fillRect(10, y, (int) (progressWidth * this.donePercent), 16);
```

Finally, a black border is drawn around the total width of the progress bar. This allows the user to see a white region that represents how much longer it will take to process.

```
g.setColor(Color.BLACK);
g.drawRect(10, y, progressWidth, 16);
```

The bar will be updated until it reaches 100%.

## Summary

A spider is a special kind of bot. A spider scans HTML pages and looks for more pages to visit. A spider would theoretically continue finding URLs forever, or until it has visited every URL on the Internet. However, there are two factors that limit a spider from doing this. First, a spider is often given a maximum depth to visit. If a page is deeper, relative to the home page, than this depth, the spider will not visit it. Secondly, spiders are often instructed to stay within a specified set of hosts. This set is often just one host.

This chapter showed how to use the Heaton Research Spider. The Heaton Research Spider is an open source spider, written in Java and C#, and is available for free from Heaton Research, Inc. To use the Heaton Research Spider you must create two objects.

First, a **SpiderOptions** object must be created to provide the spider with some basic configuration options. The **SpiderOptions** properties can either be set directly, or loaded from a file.

Second, a **WorkloadManager** is also required. For simple spiders, you may choose to use the **MemoryWorkloadManager**. This will store all URLs in the computer's memory. For larger spiders, you should use the **SQLWorkloadManager**. The **SQLWorkloadManager** stores the URL workload in an SQL database.

This chapter provided four recipes. The first recipe showed how to use a spider to check for bad links on a web site. The second recipe showed how to use a spider to download a site. The third recipe showed how to create a spider that accesses a large number of URLs that did not restrict itself to a single host. The fourth recipe showed how to display the statistics from the database, as a spider executes.

Now that you know how to use the Heaton Research Spider, the next chapter will take you through the internals of how the Heaton Research Spider works. If you are content with only using the Heaton Research Spider and do not wish to learn the internals of how to build a spider yet, you may safely skip to Chapter 16 and learn how to create well behaved bots; otherwise, continue through Chapters 14 and 15 and learn the internals of the Heaton Research Spider.

# CHAPTER 14: INSIDE THE HEATON RESEARCH SPIDER

- The Spider Class
- How Workloads are Managed
- Reading Configuration files
- Thread Pools
- The Memory-Based Workload Manager
- Spider HTML Parsing
- Spider Streams

Chapter 13 taught you how to use the Heaton Research Spider. The Heaton Research Spider is an advanced and very extensible spider that can be applied to both small and large spider tasks. This chapter goes beyond showing you how to use the spider; it will show you how the Heaton Research Spider is constructed. Because the Heaton Research Spider is open source, you are free to download the source code and make your own modifications.

The Heaton Research Spider is an on going open source project. Because of this, there may have been enhancements made to the spider after the publication of this book. You can always check the Heaton Research Spider's home page for the latest updates. The latest version of the Heaton Research Spider can always be found at:

`http://www.heatonresearch.com/projects/spider/`

If you are content simply using the Heaton Research Spider and are not currently interested in how it works internally, you can safely skip to Chapter 16, "Well Behaved Bots". However, you may still wish to visit the above URL to obtain the latest version. Additionally, there is a forum at the above URL where you can discuss using and modifying the Heaton Research Spider.

The Heaton Research Spider is made up of several different classes. These classes are shown in Table 14.1 and are summarized in Table 14.1.

**Table 14.1: The Heaton Research Spider Classes**

| Class | Purpose |
|---|---|
| MemoryWorkloadManager | Manage the set of URLs the spider knows about using the computer's memory. |
| OracleHolder | Holds the SQL statements used by the OracleWorkload-Manager. |
| OracleWorkloadManager | Manage the set of URLs the spider knows about using an Oracle Database. |
| RepeatableStatement | Holds an SQL statement that can be repeated. SQL statements are repeated if the connection is broken. |
| RobotsFilter | Filter URLs using the bot exclusion file (robots.txt). |
| SimpleReport | A very simple SpiderReportable implementation. This class does nothing with the data reported by the spider. |
| Spider | The main class for the spider. Through this class you will command the spider. |
| SpiderException | Thrown when the spider encounters an error it can not handle. |
| SpiderFilter | An interface that defines how to create filters for the spider. Filters allow specific URLs to be excluded. |
| SpiderFormatter | A JDK logging formatter to display the spider's log output in a simple way. |
| SpiderInputStream | A special InputStream that also writes everything it reads to an OutputStream. This class allows the spider to both save HTML and parse it, at the same time. |
| SpiderOptions | Holds configuration items for the spider. It also loads the configuration from a file. |
| SpiderParseHTML | A special version of the HTML parser for the spider. This version records any links found as the user program parses the HTML. |
| SpiderReportable | An interface that defines a class that the spider can report its findings to. |
| SpiderWorker | Performs the actual work of the spider. The SpiderWorker class is used to perform work in the thread pool. |
| SQLHolder | All of the SQL statements used by the spider are contained here. |
| SQLWorkloadManager | Manages the set of URLs the spider knows about, using an SQL database. |
| Status | The status of a URL, held in the SQL workload manager. |

| URLStatus | The status of a URL, held in the memory workload manager. |
|---|---|
| WorkloadException | Thrown when the workload manager encounters a problem. |
| WorkloadManager | An interface that defines the spider's workload manager. Workload managers hold all of the URLs that the spider has encountered. |

We will review all but the simplest classes shown in Table 14.1, beginning with the Spider class.

## The Spider Class

As you will recall from Chapter 13, one of the most important classes in the Heaton Research Spider is the **Spider** class. In this section, we will examine the **Spider** class. The **Spider** class is shown in Listing 14.1.

### Listing 14.1: The Spider Class (Spider.java)

```java
package com.heatonresearch.httprecipes.spider;

import java.io.*;
import java.net.*;
import java.util.*;
import java.util.concurrent.*;
import java.util.logging.*;

import com.heatonresearch.httprecipes.spider.filter.*;
import com.heatonresearch.httprecipes.spider.workload.*;

public class Spider
{
  /**
   * The logger.
   */
  private static Logger logger = Logger
      .getLogger("com.heatonresearch.httprecipes.spider.Spider");

  /**
   * The object that the spider reports its findings to.
   */
  private SpiderReportable report;

  /**
   * A flag that indicates if this process should be
   * canceled.
```

```
  */
private boolean cancel = false;

/**
 * The workload manager, the spider can use any of several
 * different workload managers. The workload manager
 * tracks all URL's found.
 */
private WorkloadManager workloadManager;

/**
 * The Java thread executor that will manage the thread
 * pool.
 */
private ThreadPoolExecutor threadPool;

/*
 * The BlockingQueue that will hold tasks for the thread
 * pool.
 */
private BlockingQueue<Runnable> tasks;

/**
 * The options for the spider.
 */
private SpiderOptions options;

/**
 * Filters used to block specific URL's.
 */
private List<SpiderFilter> filters =
  new ArrayList<SpiderFilter>();

/**
 * The time that the spider began.
 */
private Date startTime;

/**
 * The time that the spider ended.
 */
private Date stopTime;

/**
 * Construct a spider object. The options parameter
 * specifies the options for this spider. The report
```

```
 * parameter specifies the class that the spider is to
 * report progress to.
 *
 * @param report
 *           A class that implements the SpiderReportable
 *           interface, that will receive information that
 *           the spider finds.
 * @param timeout
 *           How many miliseconds to wait for data.
 * @throws ClassNotFoundException
 *             Thrown if an error occurs while creating the
 *             workload manager.
 * @throws IllegalAccessException
 *             Thrown if an error occurs while creating the
 *             workload manager.
 * @throws InstantiationException
 *             Thrown if an error occurs while creating the
 *             workload manager.
 * @throws WorkloadException
 *             Exception thrown if there are any issues with
 *             the workload.
 */
public Spider(SpiderOptions options, SpiderReportable report)
    throws InstantiationException, IllegalAccessException,
    ClassNotFoundException, WorkloadException
{
  this.options = options;
  this.report = report;

  this.workloadManager = (WorkloadManager) Class.forName(
      options.workloadManager).newInstance();
  this.workloadManager.init(this);
  report.init(this);

  this.tasks = new SynchronousQueue<Runnable>();
  this.threadPool = new ThreadPoolExecutor(
    options.corePoolSize,
    options.maximumPoolSize,
    options.keepAliveTime,
    TimeUnit.SECONDS,
      this.tasks);
  this.threadPool.setRejectedExecutionHandler(
    new ThreadPoolExecutor.CallerRunsPolicy());

  // add filters
  if (options.filter != null)
```

```
    {
      for (String name : options.filter)
      {
        SpiderFilter filter = (SpiderFilter)
          Class.forName(name).newInstance();
        this.filters.add(filter);
      }
    }

    // perform startup
    if (options.startup.equalsIgnoreCase(
      SpiderOptions.STARTUP_RESUME))
    {
      this.workloadManager.resume();
    } else
    {
      this.workloadManager.clear();
    }
  }

  /**
   * Add a URL for processing. Accepts a SpiderURL.
   *
   * @param url
   * @throws WorkloadException
   *            Exception thrown if there are any issues with
   *            the workload.
   */
  public void addURL(URL url, URL source, int depth)
    throws WorkloadException
  {
    // check the depth
    if ((this.options.maxDepth != -1) &&
        (depth > this.options.maxDepth))
    {
      return;
    }

    // see if it does not pass any of the filters
    for (SpiderFilter filter : this.filters)
    {
      if (filter.isExcluded(url))
      {
        return;
      }
    }
```

```java
  // add the item
  if (this.workloadManager.add(url, source, depth))
  {
    StringBuilder str = new StringBuilder();
    str.append("Adding to workload: ");
    str.append(url);
    str.append(" (depth=");
    str.append(depth);
    str.append(")");
    logger.fine(str.toString());
  }
}

/**
 * Set a flag that will cause the begin method to return
 * before it is done.
 */
public void cancel()
{
  this.cancel = true;
}

/**
 * Get the list of filters for the spider.
 *
 * @return The list of filters for the spider.
 */
public List<SpiderFilter> getFilters()
{
  return this.filters;
}

/**
 * Get the options for this spider.
 *
 * @return The options for this spider.
 */
public SpiderOptions getOptions()
{
  return this.options;
}
```

```java
/**
 * Get the object that the spider reports to.
 *
 * @return The object that spider reports to.
 */
public SpiderReportable getReport()
{
  return this.report;
}


/**
 * Generate basic status information about the spider.
 *
 * @return The status of the spider.
 */
public String getStatus()
{
  StringBuilder result = new StringBuilder();
  result.append("Start time:");
  result.append(this.startTime.toString());
  result.append('\n');
  result.append("Stop time:");
  result.append(this.stopTime.toString());
  result.append('\n');
  result.append("Minutes Elapsed:");
  result.append((this.stopTime.getTime() -
    this.startTime.getTime()) / 60000);
  result.append('\n');

  return result.toString();
}


/**
 * Get the workload manager.
 *
 * @return The workload manager.
 */
public WorkloadManager getWorkloadManager()
{
  return this.workloadManager;
}

/**
 * Called to start the spider.
 *
 * @throws WorkloadException
```

```
*             Exception thrown if there are any issues with
*             the workload.
* @throws InterruptedException
*             Called if any blocking operation is
*             interrupted.
*/
public void process() throws WorkloadException
{
  this.cancel = false;
  this.startTime = new Date();

  // process all hosts
  do
  {
    processHost();
  } while (this.workloadManager.nextHost() != null);

  this.threadPool.shutdown();
  this.stopTime = new Date();
}

public void setReport(SpiderReportable report)
{
  this.report = report;
}

/**
 * Process one individual host.
 *
 * @throws WorkloadException
 *             Exception thrown if there are any issues with
 *             the workload.
 */
private void processHost() throws WorkloadException
{
  URL url = null;

  String host = this.workloadManager.getCurrentHost();

  // first notify the manager
  if (!this.report.beginHost(host))
  {
    return;
  }

  // second, notify any filters of a new host
```

```java
      for (SpiderFilter filter : this.filters)
      {
        try
        {
          filter.newHost(host, this.options.userAgent);
        } catch (IOException e)
        {
          logger.log(Level.INFO,
            "Error while reading robots.txt file:"
              + e.getMessage());
        }
      }

      // now process this host
      do
      {
        url = this.workloadManager.getWork();
        if (url != null)
        {
          SpiderWorker worker = new SpiderWorker(this, url);
          this.threadPool.execute(worker);
        } else
        {
          this.workloadManager.waitForWork(60, TimeUnit.SECONDS);
        }
      } while (((url != null) ||
              (this.threadPool.getActiveCount() > 0))
          && !this.cancel);
    }

}
```

As you can see from the above listing, the spider uses a number of instance variables. The spider uses these to track its current state, as well as to remember configuration information. These instance variables are summarized in Table 14.2.

**Table 14.2: Instance Variables for the Spider Class**

| Instance Variable | Purpose |
|---|---|
| cancel | A flag that indicates if this process should be canceled. |
| filters | Filters used to block specific URLs. |
| logger | The object that the spider reports its findings to. |
| options | The configuration options for the spider. |
| startTime | The time that the spider began. |
| stopTime | The time that the spider ended. |
| tasks | The BlockingQueue that will hold tasks for the thread pool. |
| threadPool | The Java thread executor that will manage the thread pool. |
| workloadManager | The workload manager, the spider can use any of several different workload managers. The workload manager tracks all URL's found. |

There are also a number of methods and functions that perform important tasks for the **Spider** class. These will be discussed in the next few sections.

### The Spider Constructor

The **Spider** class' constructor begins by saving the **SpiderOptions** and **WorkloadManager** objects that was passed to instance variables. This will allow the spider to refer to these important objects later.

```
this.options = options;
this.report = report;
```

Next, a workload manager is instantiated from the class name provided in the **SpiderOptions** class. The **init** method is then called on the workload manager.

```
this.workloadManager = (WorkloadManager) Class.forName(
options.workloadManager).newInstance();
this.workloadManager.init(this);
report.init(this);
```

The thread pool is set up next. This uses the JDK 1.5 **ThreadPoolExecutor** to implement the spider's thread pool. The thread pool is started with the options specified in the **SpiderOptions** object.

Additionally, the thread pool is started with **CallerRunsPolicy**. This policy specifies that once there is no more room to queue new tasks, the thread pool begins running new tasks with the main thread. This allows us to make use of all threads and also throttles the spider when it gets too much work. Since the main thread will be processing work when the queue fills, the main thread will not have a chance to generate more work. Once the queue goes down, the main thread is allowed to continue filling up the queue.

The queue is a **SynchronousQueue**, which is a Java class that holds waiting tasks for the spider. The Java thread pool requires that some sort of **BlockingQueue** be used to hold the workload.

```
this.tasks = new SynchronousQueue<Runnable>();
this.threadPool = new ThreadPoolExecutor(options.corePoolSize,
options.maximumPoolSize, options.keepAliveTime,
TimeUnit.SECONDS,this.tasks);
this.threadPool.setRejectedExecutionHandler(
new ThreadPoolExecutor.CallerRunsPolicy());
```

If any filters were specified, they are loaded at this point.

```
// Add filters.
if (options.filter != null) {
  for (String name : options.filter) {
    SpiderFilter filter = (SpiderFilter)
      Class.forName(name).newInstance();
    this.filters.add(filter);
  }
}
```

Finally, we are ready to perform the startup operation that was specified in the **SpiderOptions** configuration. If the user requests **STARUP_RESUME** then the workload manager is instructed to set up the resume from the last spider run. Otherwise, the workload will be cleared.

```
// Perform startup.
if (options.startup.equalsIgnoreCase(
  SpiderOptions.STARTUP_RESUME)) {
  this.workloadManager.resume();
} else {
  this.workloadManager.clear();
}
```

After the constructor completes, the spider is ready to run. The Heaton Research Spider is designed that you should create a new Spider object for each spider that runs.

## Adding a URL

When you first create a **Spider** object, you are to add one or more URLs to begin processing. If you do not add a URL, then the spider will have no work. These URLs are added through the spider's **addURL** method. Additionally, when the spider finds other URLs, the spider uses its own **addURL** method to add URLs. This is helpful because the spider's **addURL** method performs checks on the URL to make sure it should be added to the workload.

First, the spider checks to see if the URL being added is beyond the specified maximum depth.

```
if ((this.options.maxDepth != -1) &&
    (depth > this.options.maxDepth)) {
  return;
}
```

Next, the spider makes sure that any filters have not excluded the URL.

```
for (SpiderFilter filter : this.filters) {
  if (filter.isExcluded(url)) {
    return;
  }
}
```

Finally, the URL is passed on to the workload manager. If the workload manager returns **true**, then the URL was added. The workload manager also performs additional filtering on URLs. Specifically, if the workload manager determines that the URL has already been found, then the URL is not reprocessed.

```
// Add the item.
if (this.workloadManager.add(url, source, depth)) {
  StringBuilder str = new StringBuilder();
  str.append("Adding to workload: ");
  str.append(url);
  str.append(" (depth=");
  str.append(depth);
  str.append(")");
  logger.fine(str.toString());
}
```

Finally, if the URL was added, then it is logged.

## Processing All Hosts

When the **process** method is called, the spider begins working. The **process** method will not return until the spider has no more work to do. The **process** method begins by clearing the **cancel** flag and recording the starting time for the spider.

```
this.cancel = false;
this.startTime = new Date();
```

The spider then loops until there are no more hosts to process. If at least one URL has been added, there will be at least one host to process. You should always add at least one URL to the spider; otherwise, it has no work to do.

```
do {
  processHost();
} while (this.workloadManager.nextHost() != null);
```

Finally, the spider shuts down the thread pool, and records the stopping time.

```
this.threadPool.shutdown();
this.stopTime = new Date();
```

At this point the spider is complete, and the **process** method returns.

### Processing One Host

The **processHost** method is called for each host the spider needs to process. This method will begin processing URLs on the workload that correspond to the current host. The **processHost** method is called in a loop, by the **process** method, until all hosts have been processed.

The **processHost** method begins by obtaining the current host.

```
URL url = null;

String host = this.workloadManager.getCurrentHost();
```

Next, the spider manager is notified that a new host is beginning.

```
if (!this.report.beginHost(host)) {
  return;
}
```

Next, all filters are notified that we are moving to a new host.

```
for (SpiderFilter filter : this.filters) {
try {
  filter.newHost(host, this.options.userAgent);
} catch (IOException e) {
  logger.log(Level.INFO,
    "Error while reading robots.txt file:"
    + e.getMessage());
  }
}
```

Now that everything has been notified, we begin processing the host. To do this, we attempt to obtain a URL from the workload manager. If no URL was available, then we wait for up to 60 seconds, and then try the process again.

```
do {
  url = this.workloadManager.getWork();
  if (url != null) {
    SpiderWorker worker = new SpiderWorker(this, url);
    this.threadPool.execute(worker);
  } else {
    this.workloadManager.waitForWork(60, TimeUnit.SECONDS);
  }
} while (((url != null) || (this.threadPool.getActiveCount() > 0))
&& !this.cancel);
```

This process continues until there is no more work left for the current host.

## Other Important Classes in the Heaton Research Spider

When you make use of the Heaton Research Spider, you will deal primarily with the **Spider** class. However, there are other important classes in the Heaton Research Spider that you will also make use of. Particularly, the Heaton Research Spider supports several interfaces and is also capable of throwing several exceptions.

### Spider Interfaces

There are two interfaces that the Heaton Research Spider makes use of. These interfaces allow you to define how the spider acts.

The first interface is the **SpiderReportable** interface. To make use of the Heaton Research Spider, you must provide a class that implements the **SpiderReportable** interface. This class is responsible for processing the data that the spider finds.

The second interface is the **WorkloadManager** interface. The **WorkloadManager** class allows the spider to use more than one type of workload manager. There are two workload managers provided with the spider. The **SQLWorkloadManager** stores URLs in an SQL database. The **MemoryWorkloadManager** stores URLs in memory.

### Spider Exceptions

There are two exceptions that can be thrown by the spider. These exceptions will be required to be caught when you are working with the spider. Which exception you must catch is determined by the operation you are performing with the spider.

The first exception is the **SpiderException**. The **Spider** class throws the **SpiderException** when a severe error occurs. This must be a real error that prevents the spider from continuing. Errors that are internal to individual web pages are not thrown as spider errors.

The second exception is the **WorkloadException**. The **WorkloadException** is thrown when there is an error with the workload. That can be an SQL exception, or another communication error when dealing with an SQL based workload manager. Usually classes external to the spider are not exposed to the **WorkloadException**. Rather, these classes will throw the **WorkloadException** as a **SpiderException**.

### Configuring the Spider

The **SpiderOptions** class is used to configure the spider. This class can accept configuration directly from other Java classes when they modify the public properties on the **SpiderOptions** object. The **SpiderOptions** class can also load configuration options from a file. Listing 14.2 shows the **SpiderOptions** class.

### Listing 14.2: Configuring the Spider (SpiderOptions.java)

```
package com.heatonresearch.httprecipes.spider;

import java.io.*;
import java.lang.reflect.*;
import java.util.*;

public class SpiderOptions {
  /**
   * Specifies that when the spider starts up it should
   * clear the workload.
   */
  public static final String STARTUP_CLEAR = "CLEAR";

  /**
   * Specifies that the spider should resume processing its
   * workload.
   */
  public static final String STARTUP_RESUME = "RESUME";

  /**
   * How many milliseconds to wait when downloading pages.
   */
  public int timeout = 60000;
```

```
/**
 * The maximum depth to search pages. -1 specifies no
 * maximum depth.
 */
public int maxDepth = -1;

/**
 * What user agent should be reported to the web site.
 * This allows the web site to determine what browser is
 * being used.
 */
public String userAgent = null;

/**
 * The core thread pool size.
 */
public int corePoolSize = 100;

/**
 * The maximum thread pool size.
 */
public int maximumPoolSize = 100;

/**
 * How long to keep inactive threads alive. Measured in
 * seconds.
 */
public long keepAliveTime = 60;

/**
 * The URL to use for JDBC databases. Used to hold the
 * workload.
 */
public String dbURL;

/**
 * The user id to use for JDBC databases. Used to hold the
 * workload.
 */
public String dbUID;

/**
 * The password to use for JDBC databases. Used to hold
 * the workload.
 */
public String dbPWD;
```

```java
/**
 * The class to use for JDBC connections. Used to hold the
 * workload.
 */
public String dbClass;

/**
 * What class to use as a workload manager.
 */
public String workloadManager;

/**
 * What to do when the spider starts up. This specifies if
 * the workload should be cleared, or resumed.
 */
public String startup = STARTUP_CLEAR;

/*
 * Specifies a class to be used a filter.ß
 */
public List<String> filter = new ArrayList<String>();

/**
 * Load the spider settings from a configuration file.
 *
 * @param inputFile
 *            The name of the configuration file.
 * @throws IOException
 *             Thrown if an I/O error occurs.
 * @throws SpiderException
 *             Thrown if there is an error mapping
 *             configuration items between the file and this
 *             object.
 */
public void load(String inputFile)
  throws IOException, SpiderException {
  FileReader f = new FileReader(new File(inputFile));
  BufferedReader r = new BufferedReader(f);
  String line;
  while ((line = r.readLine()) != null) {
    try {
      parseLine(line);
    } catch (IllegalArgumentException e) {
      throw (new SpiderException(e));
```

```
      } catch (SecurityException e) {
        throw (new SpiderException(e));
      } catch (IllegalAccessException e) {
        throw (new SpiderException(e));
      } catch (NoSuchFieldException e) {
        throw (new SpiderException(e));
      }
    }
  }
  r.close();
  f.close();
}

/**
 * Process each line of a configuration file.
 *
 * @param line
 *          The line of text read from the configuration
 *          file.
 * @throws IllegalArgumentException
 *            Thrown if an invalid argument is specified.
 * @throws SecurityException
 *            Thrown if a security exception occurs.
 * @throws IllegalAccessException
 *            Thrown if a field cannot be accessed.
 * @throws NoSuchFieldException
 *            Thrown if an invalid field is specified.
 */
@SuppressWarnings("unchecked")
private void parseLine(String line)
  throws IllegalArgumentException,
    SecurityException, IllegalAccessException,
    NoSuchFieldException
{
  String name, value;
  int i = line.indexOf(':');
  if (i == -1) {
    return;
  }
  name = line.substring(0, i).trim();
  value = line.substring(i + 1).trim();

  if (value.trim().length() == 0) {
    value = null;
  }

  Field field = this.getClass().getField(name);
```

```
    if (field.getType() == String.class) {
      field.set(this, value);
    } else if (field.getType() == List.class) {
      List<String> list = (List<String>) field.get(this);
      list.add(value);
    } else {
      int x = Integer.parseInt(value);
      field.set(this, x);
    }
  }
}
}
```

The **load** and **loadLine** methods of the **SpiderOptions** class are used to load data from a spider configuration file. The **load** method works by reading a simple configuration file that consists of name value pairs. For each name that is found in the file, the **loadLine** method uses Java reflection to determine how to set the variable in a **SpiderOptions** object. This allows us to quickly add new variables by adding them to the **SpiderOptions** object. No additional parsing code is needed for any new property.

### Reading a Configuration File

The **load** method reads the spider configuration file. For each line encountered by the load method, the **loadLine** method is called. The **load** method begins by opening the file and creating a **BufferedReader**. The **BufferedReader** will allow us to read the file on a line-by-line basis.

```
FileReader f = new FileReader(new File(inputFile));
BufferedReader r = new BufferedReader(f);
```

Next, a single line is read from the file. If the line is **null**, then the program is done reading the file.

```
String line;
while ((line = r.readLine()) != null) {
```

The line that was read is passed on to the **parseLine** method. Any exceptions that can occur are thrown as a **SpiderException**.

```
try {
  parseLine(line);
} catch (IllegalArgumentException e) {
  throw (new SpiderException(e));
} catch (SecurityException e) {
  throw (new SpiderException(e));
} catch (IllegalAccessException e) {
  throw (new SpiderException(e));
} catch (NoSuchFieldException e) {
throw (new SpiderException(e));
```

Finally, the file is closed.

```
r.close();
f.close();
```

The real work of loading the configuration file is done by the **loadLine** method, which is discussed in the next section.

### Reading a Line from the Configuration File

The **loadLine** method begins by checking for a colon (:) character. This character separates a name from a value. If no colon is found, then the line is invalid, so it is simply ignored.

```
String name, value;
int i = line.indexOf(':');
if (i == -1) {
  return;
}
```

The **name** and **value** variables are extracted from each side of the colon.

```
name = line.substring(0, i).trim();
value = line.substring(i + 1).trim();
```

If the value has no length, then it is assumed to be **null**.

```
if (value.trim().length() == 0) {
  value = null;
}
```

Next, reflection is used to look up the **name** variable. The names in the configuration file must match the names of the properties in the **SpiderOptions** class. If the variable can not be found, then an error will be thrown, which is caught by the **load** method.

```
Field field = this.getClass().getField(name);
```

If the variable is of type **String**, then we simply set the variable to the **value** variable that was parsed earlier.

```
if (field.getType() == String.class) {
  field.set(this, value);
}
```

If the variable is a **List**, then the value variable is simply added to the **List**.

```
if (field.getType() == List.class) {
  List<String> list = (List<String>) field.get(this);
  list.add(value);
```

Finally, if the variable is numeric, then the **value** variable is parsed as an integer.

```
} else {
  int x = Integer.parseInt(value);
  field.set(this, x);
}
```

This process is repeated for each line of the configuration file.

### Understanding the Thread Pool

The spider uses a thread pool to perform its tasks. A thread pool programming pattern creates N number of threads to perform tasks. These tasks are organized in a queue. This queue then feeds a workload to the number of threads. As soon as a thread completes its task, it will request the next task from the queue until all tasks have been completed. At this point, the thread can then terminate, or sleep, until there are new tasks available. The number of threads is tuned to increase overall performance.

Thread pools address two different problems. First, they usually provide improved performance when executing large numbers of asynchronous tasks. This is due to reduced overhead of recreating threads. Secondly, a thread pool provides a means of managing the resources consumed (including threads), when executing a collection of tasks.

As of JDK 1.5, Java now provides direct support of thread pools. This is done through the use of the **ThreadPoolExecutor**. In addition to creating a **ThreadPoolExecutor**, you must also create a class that implements the **BlockingQueue**. Using these two objects, you can implement a thread pool.

To use the thread pool, you submit tasks to run. These tasks are objects created from classes that implement the **Runnable** interface. As new tasks are submitted to the thread pool, they are moved to the queue until the thread pool has time to execute them.

The thread pool is particularly valuable to a spider. Even on a single processor computer, using a thread pool will considerably increase the performance of the spider. This is because a spider spends a good deal of time waiting. When a spider submits a request to a web sever the spider immediately begins waiting for the response. It is much faster to wait on several web pages instead of just one.

### Constructing a Worker Class

To use a Java thread pool, you must add objects which implement the **Runnable** interface. These objects are the individual workers that perform the actual work being performed by the thread pool. The Heaton Research Spider uses the **SpiderWorker** class for this purpose. The **SpiderWorker** class is shown in Listing 14.3.

**Listing 14.3: The Worker Class (SpiderWorker.java)**

```java
package com.heatonresearch.httprecipes.spider;

import java.io.*;
import java.net.*;
import java.util.logging.*;

import com.heatonresearch.httprecipes.spider.workload.*;

public class SpiderWorker implements Runnable {
  /**
   * The logger.
   */
  private static Logger logger = Logger.getLogger(
    "com.heatonresearch.httprecipes.spider.SpiderWorker");

  /**
   * The URL being processed.
   */
  private URL url;

  /**
   * The Spider object that this worker belongs to.
   */
  private Spider spider;

  /**
   * Construct a SpiderWorker object.
   *
   * @param spider
   *          The spider this worker will work with.
   * @param url
   *          The URL to be processed.
   */
  public SpiderWorker(Spider spider, URL url) {
    this.spider = spider;
    this.url = url;
  }

  /*
   * This method is called by the thread pool to process one
   * single URL.
   */
  public void run() {
    URLConnection connection = null;
    InputStream is = null;
```

```
try {
  logger.fine("Processing: " + this.url);
  // get the URL's contents
  connection = this.url.openConnection();
  connection.setConnectTimeout(
    this.spider.getOptions().timeout);
  connection.setReadTimeout(this.spider.getOptions().timeout);
  if (this.spider.getOptions().userAgent != null) {
    connection.setRequestProperty("User-Agent",
        this.spider.getOptions().userAgent);
  }

  // read the URL
  is = connection.getInputStream();

  // parse the URL
  if (connection.getContentType().equalsIgnoreCase(
    "text/html")) {
    SpiderParseHTML parse = new SpiderParseHTML(
      connection.getURL(),
       new SpiderInputStream(is, null), this.spider);
    this.spider.getReport().spiderProcessURL(this.url, parse);
  } else {
    this.spider.getReport().spiderProcessURL(this.url, is);
  }

} catch (IOException e) {
  logger.log(Level.INFO,
    "I/O error on URL:" + this.url.toString());
  try {
    this.spider.getWorkloadManager().markError(this.url);
  } catch (WorkloadException e1) {
    logger.log(Level.WARNING,
      "Error marking workload(1).", e);
  }
  this.spider.getReport().spiderURLError(this.url);
  return;
} catch (Throwable e) {
  try {
    this.spider.getWorkloadManager().markError(this.url);
  } catch (WorkloadException e1) {
    logger.log(Level.WARNING,
      "Error marking workload(2).", e);
  }
}
```

```
      logger.log(Level.SEVERE,
        "Caught exception at URL:" + this.url.toString(), e);
      this.spider.getReport().spiderURLError(this.url);
      return;
    } finally {
      if (is != null) {
        try {
          is.close();
        } catch (IOException e) {
        }
      }
    }
  }

  try {
    // mark URL as complete
    this.spider.getWorkloadManager().markProcessed(this.url);
    logger.fine("Complete: " + this.url);
    if (!this.url.equals(connection.getURL())) {
      // save the URL(for redirect's)
      this.spider.getWorkloadManager().add(
        connection.getURL(), this.url,
          this.spider.getWorkloadManager().getDepth(
            connection.getURL())));
      this.spider.getWorkloadManager().markProcessed(
        connection.getURL());
    }
  } catch (WorkloadException e) {
    logger.log(Level.WARNING, "Error marking workload(3).", e);
  }

  }

}
```

As the thread pool processes the **SpiderWorker** objects presented to it, the **run** methods from these **SpiderWorker** classes are executed. The **run** method begins by logging the URL that it is currently processing. Then a connection is opened to that URL.

```
try {
  logger.fine("Processing: " + this.url);
// Get the URL's contents.
connection = this.url.openConnection();
```

Next, the timeout values are set. The same timeout value is used for both connection and read timeouts.

```
connection.setConnectTimeout(this.spider.getOptions().timeout);
connection.setReadTimeout(this.spider.getOptions().timeout);
```

If a **User-Agent** was specified, then the user agent is set.

```
if (this.spider.getOptions().userAgent != null) {
connection.setRequestProperty("User-Agent",
this.spider.getOptions().userAgent);
}
```

The spider is now ready to read the contents of the URL. First, the spider checks to see if the data from the URL is of the MIME type **text/html**. If this is a **text/html** document, then a new **SpiderParseHTML** object is created and the **spiderProcessURL** method is called for the **SpiderReportable** object.

The **SpiderParseHTML** object works exactly the same as the **ParseHTML** class, except that it allows the spider to gather links as the **spiderProcessURL** method parses the HTML. This makes the spider link gathering transparent to the class using the spider.

```
// Read the URL.
is = connection.getInputStream();

// Parse the URL.
if (connection.getContentType().equalsIgnoreCase("text/html")) {
  SpiderParseHTML parse = new SpiderParseHTML(connection.getURL(),
  new SpiderInputStream(is, null), this.spider);
  this.spider.getReport().spiderProcessURL(this.url, parse);
} else {
  this.spider.getReport().spiderProcessURL(this.url, is);
}
```

If an I/O exception occurs while reading the page, then the exception is logged.

```
} catch (IOException e) {
  logger.log(Level.INFO, "I/O error on URL:"
    + this.url.toString());
try {
```

In addition to logging the exception, the page is also marked with "error" in the workload manager.

```
this.spider.getWorkloadManager().markError(this.url);
} catch (WorkloadException e1) {
  logger.log(Level.WARNING, "Error marking workload(1).", e);
}
this.spider.getReport().spiderURLError(this.url);
return;
```

The spider also traps any **Throwable** exceptions that occur. This prevents errors that occur in the **SpiderReportable** class from causing the spider to crash. If an exception occurs, it is logged, and the spider continues.

```
} catch (Throwable e) {
try {
  this.spider.getWorkloadManager().markError(this.url);
} catch (WorkloadException e1) {
  logger.log(Level.WARNING, "Error marking workload(2).", e);
}

logger.log(Level.SEVERE, "Caught exception at URL:" + this.url.
toString(), e);
this.spider.getReport().spiderURLError(this.url);
return;
```

A **finally** block ensures that the **InputStream** is closed.

```
} finally {
  if (is != null) {
try {
  is.close();
} catch (IOException e) {
}
```

If no exceptions have occurred by this point, the URL can be marked as processed in the workload manager.

```
try {
// Mark URL as complete.
this.spider.getWorkloadManager().markProcessed(this.url);
logger.fine("Complete: " + this.url);
if (!this.url.equals(connection.getURL())) {
```

Sometimes the spider will request one URL and get another. This is the case with an HTTP redirect. One requested URL could redirect the browser to another. If this happens, we need to mark the redirect URL as processed as well. The following lines of code do this.

```
this.spider.getWorkloadManager().add(connection.getURL(),
this.url,
this.spider.getWorkloadManager().getDepth(connection.getURL()));
this.spider.getWorkloadManager().markProcessed(connection.ge-
tURL());
}
```

If any errors occur marking the workload, they are logged.

```
} catch (WorkloadException e) {
  logger.log(Level.WARNING, "Error marking workload(3).", e);
}
```

The thread pool will continue processing **SpiderWorker** objects until the spider has no more work to do.

### Spider HTML Parsing

The Heaton Research Spider provides a **SpiderHTMLParse** object to the **spiderProcessURL** method of a **SpiderReportable** object. This object allows the HTML found by the spider to be parsed. However, it also allows the spider to extract links from the HTML. The **SpiderHTMLParse** class is shown in Listing 14.4.

### Listing 14.4: HTML Parsing (SpiderHTMLParse.java)

```java
package com.heatonresearch.httprecipes.spider;

import java.io.*;
import java.net.*;
import java.util.logging.*;

import com.heatonresearch.httprecipes.html.*;
import com.heatonresearch.httprecipes.spider.workload.*;

public class SpiderParseHTML extends ParseHTML {
  /**
   * The logger.
   */
  private static Logger logger = Logger
      .getLogger("com.heatonresearch.httprecipes.spider.Spider-
ParseHTML");

  /**
   * The Spider that this page is being parsed for.
   */
  private Spider spider;

  /**
   * The URL that is being parsed.
   */
  private URL base;

  /**
   * The depth of the page being parsed.
   */
  private int depth;

  /**
   * The InputStream that is being parsed.
   */
  private SpiderInputStream stream;
```

```
/**
 * Construct a SpiderParseHTML object. This object allows
 * you to parse HTML, while the spider collects link
 * information in the background.
 *
 * @param base
 *           The URL that is being parsed, this is used for
 *           relative links.
 * @param is
 *           The InputStream being parsed.
 * @param spider
 *           The Spider that is parsing.
 * @throws WorkloadException
 *            An error occurred with the workload
 *            management.
 */
public SpiderParseHTML(URL base, SpiderInputStream is,
  Spider spider)
    throws WorkloadException {
  super(is);
  this.stream = is;
  this.spider = spider;
  this.base = base;
  this.depth = spider.getWorkloadManager().getDepth(base);
}


/**
 * Get the InputStream being parsed.
 *
 * @return The InputStream being parsed.
 */
public SpiderInputStream getStream() {
  return this.stream;
}


/**
 * Read a single character. This function will process any
 * tags that the spider needs for navigation, then pass
 * the character on to the caller. This allows the spider
 * to transparently gather its links.
 *
 * @return The character read.
 * @throws IOException
 *            I/O error.
 */
@Override
```

```java
public int read() throws IOException {
  int result = super.read();
  if (result == 0) {
    HTMLTag tag = getTag();
    if (tag.getName().equalsIgnoreCase("a")) {
      String href = tag.getAttributeValue("href");
      handleA(href);
    } else if (tag.getName().equalsIgnoreCase("img")) {
      String src = tag.getAttributeValue("src");
      addURL(src, SpiderReportable.URLType.IMAGE);
    } else if (tag.getName().equalsIgnoreCase("style")) {
      String src = tag.getAttributeValue("src");
      addURL(src, SpiderReportable.URLType.STYLE);
    } else if (tag.getName().equalsIgnoreCase("link")) {
      String href = tag.getAttributeValue("href");
      addURL(href, SpiderReportable.URLType.SCRIPT);
    } else if (tag.getName().equalsIgnoreCase("base")) {
      String href = tag.getAttributeValue("href");
      this.base = new URL(this.base, href);
    }

  }
  return result;
}

/**
 * Read all characters on the page. This will discard
 * these characters, but allow the spider to examine the
 * tags and find links.
 *
 * @throws IOException
 *            I/O error.
 */
public void readAll() throws IOException {
  while (read() != -1) {
    ;
  }
}

/**
 * Used internally, to add a URL to the spider's workload.
 *
 * @param u
 *            The URL to add.
 * @param type
 *            What type of link this is.
```

```java
 * @throws IOException
 *             Thrown if an I/O error occurs.
 */
private void addURL(String u, SpiderReportable.URLType type)
    throws IOException {
  if (u == null) {
    return;
  }

  try {
    URL url = URLUtility.constructURL(this.base, u, true);
    url = this.spider.getWorkloadManager().convertURL(
      url.toString());

    if (url.getProtocol().equalsIgnoreCase("http")
        || url.getProtocol().equalsIgnoreCase("https")) {
      if (this.spider.getReport().spiderFoundURL(url,
        this.base, type)) {
        try {
          this.spider.addURL(url, this.base, this.depth + 1);
        } catch (WorkloadException e) {
          throw new IOException(e.getMessage());
        }
      }
    }
  }

  catch (MalformedURLException e) {
    logger.log(Level.INFO, "Malformed URL found:" + u);
  } catch (WorkloadException e) {
    logger.log(Level.INFO, "Invalid URL found:" + u);
  }
}

/**
 * This method is called when an anchor(A) tag is found.
 *
 * @param href
 *             The link found.
 * @throws IOException
 *             I/O error.
 */
private void handleA(String href) throws IOException {

  if (href != null) {
    href = href.trim();
```

```
        }

    if ((href != null) &&
        !URLUtility.containsInvalidURLCharacters(href)) {
        if (!href.toLowerCase().startsWith("javascript:")
            && !href.toLowerCase().startsWith("rstp:")
            && !href.toLowerCase().startsWith("rtsp:")
            && !href.toLowerCase().startsWith("news:")
            && !href.toLowerCase().startsWith("irc:")
            && !href.toLowerCase().startsWith("mailto:")) {
          addURL(href, SpiderReportable.URLType.HYPERLINK);
        }
      }
    }
  }
}
```

There are several methods and functions that make up the **SpiderParseHTML** class. These will be discussed in the next sections.

### Constructing a SpiderParseHTML Object

The constructor for the **SpiderParseHTML** class is relatively simple. It accepts several parameters and uses them to initialize the object. As you can see from the following lines of code, each of the instance variables is initialized in the constructor.

```
super(is);
this.stream = is;
this.spider = spider;
this.base = base;
this.depth = spider.getWorkloadManager().getDepth(base);
```

Once the instance variables are initialized the **SpiderParseHTML** object is ready for use.

### Reading Data from a SpiderParseHTML Object

The **read** function is called to read individual characters as the HTML is parsed. This works the same as a regular **ParseHTML** object. The **ParseHTML** class was covered in Chapter 6, "Extracting Data". The **read** function begins by calling the parent's **read** function.

```
int result = super.read();
if (result == 0) {
```

If the **read** function returns zero, then a tag was found. The tag is checked to see if it matches any of the tag types that contain a link.

```
HTMLTag tag = getTag();
if (tag.getName().equalsIgnoreCase("a")) {
```

```
    String href = tag.getAttributeValue("href");
    handleA(href);
} else if (tag.getName().equalsIgnoreCase("img")) {
    String src = tag.getAttributeValue("src");
    addURL(src, SpiderReportable.URLType.IMAGE);
} else if (tag.getName().equalsIgnoreCase("style")) {
    String src = tag.getAttributeValue("src");
    addURL(src, SpiderReportable.URLType.STYLE);
} else if (tag.getName().equalsIgnoreCase("link")) {
    String href = tag.getAttributeValue("href");
    addURL(href, SpiderReportable.URLType.SCRIPT);
} else if (tag.getName().equalsIgnoreCase("base")) {
    String href = tag.getAttributeValue("href");
    this.base = new URL(this.base, href);
}
}
return result;
```

For most tag types, the **addURL** method will be called. However, the anchor tag is handled differently with a call to the **handleA** method.

### Adding a URL

The **addURL** method is called to add a URL. It begins by rejecting any **null** URLs.

```
if (u == null) {
    return;
}
```

First, the URL is converted to the fully qualified form. For example, if the **href** of "images/me.gif" were found on the   page, then the fully qualified URL would be **http://www.httprecipes.com/1/images/me.gif**.

```
try {
    URL url = URLUtility.constructURL(this.base, u, true);
    url = this.spider.getWorkloadManager().convertURL(url.to-
String());
```

Next, the protocol is checked. If the URL's protocol is anything other than **http** or **https**, the URL is ignored.

```
if (url.getProtocol().equalsIgnoreCase("http")
|| url.getProtocol().equalsIgnoreCase("https")) {
```

The **spiderFoundURL** function is then called to determine if the URL should be added. If the URL should be added, then the spider's **addURL** method is called.

```
if (this.spider.getReport().spiderFoundURL(url, this.base, type))
{
    try {
```

```
      this.spider.addURL(url, this.base, this.depth + 1);
      } catch (WorkloadException e) {
throw new IOException(e.getMessage());
}
```

Some URLs require additional processing. The anchor tag is discussed in the next section.

### Adding an Anchor URL

Anchor tags sometimes have a prefix such as "javascript:". These are not web addresses and cannot be parsed through the **URL** class. The **handleA** method was designed to take care of these prefixes. The **handleA** method begins by trimming the **href** value.

```
if (href != null) {
href = href.trim();
}
```

If the URL has any of the following known prefixes, then it will be ignored. Otherwise, the URL will be added to the spider's workload.

```
if ((href != null) &&
  !URLUtility.containsInvalidURLCharacters(href)) {
  if (!href.toLowerCase().startsWith("javascript:")
    && !href.toLowerCase().startsWith("rstp:")
    && !href.toLowerCase().startsWith("rtsp:")
    && !href.toLowerCase().startsWith("news:")
    && !href.toLowerCase().startsWith("irc:")
    && !href.toLowerCase().startsWith("mailto:")) {
  addURL(href, SpiderReportable.URLType.HYPERLINK);
  }
}
```

This allows non-standard URLs to be ignored without throwing a **MalformedURLException**.

### Spider Input Stream

The spider also includes an **InputStream** derived class named **SpiderInputStream**. This stream works just like a regular **InputStream**, except that it holds an **OutputStream**. This **OutputStream** is sent a copy of everything read by the **SpiderInputStream**. This allows the raw HTML to be written out to a file as it is parsed. The **SpiderInputStream** is shown in Listing 14.5.

**Listing 14.5: Spider Input Stream (SpiderInputStream.java)**

```
package com.heatonresearch.httprecipes.spider;

import java.io.*;
```

```java
public class SpiderInputStream extends InputStream {
  /**
   * The InputStream to read from.
   */
  private InputStream is;

  /**
   * The OutputStream to write to.
   */
  private OutputStream os;

  /**
   * Construct the SpiderInputStream. Whatever is read from
   * the InputStream will also be written to the
   * OutputStream.
   *
   * @param is
   *            The InputStream.
   * @param os
   *            The OutputStream.
   */
  public SpiderInputStream(InputStream is, OutputStream os) {
    this.is = is;
    this.os = os;
  }

  /*
   * Read a single byte from the stream. @throws IOException
   * If an I/O exception occurs. @return The character that
   * was read from the stream.
   */
  @Override
  public int read() throws IOException {
    int ch = this.is.read();
    if (this.os != null) {
      this.os.write(ch);
    }
    return ch;
  }
}
```

```
/**
 * Set the OutputStream.
 *
 * @param os
 *           The OutputStream.
 */
public void setOutputStream(OutputStream os) {
  this.os = os;
}

}
```

The **read** function performs the work done by this class. The **read** function reads from the parent class and writes that value to the **OutputStream**. Then the value is returned to the calling method or function.

## Workload Management

A workload manager is a class that manages the list of URLs for the spider. The workload manager tracks which URLs the spider has yet to visit, as well as which URLs resulted in an error.

As URLs are found by the spider, they are added to the workload. Initially, they are in a waiting state. However, as the URL is processed by the spider, the state will change accordingly. Table 14.3 lists the states that a URL will go through as it is processed.

**Table 14.3: URL States**

| State | Purpose |
|---|---|
| ERROR | The URL has resulted in an error. The URL will not enter a new state after this one. |
| PROCESSED | The URL was processed successfully. The URL will not enter a new state after this one. |
| WAITING | The URL is waiting to be processed. The URL will enter the WORKING state once the spider is ready to process it. |
| WORKING | The spider is currently processing the URL. If processing the URL is successful, the URL will enter the PROCESSED state after this state. If processing the URL results in an error, the URL will enter the ERROR state after this state. |

Figure 14.1 summarizes these states as a state diagram.

**Figure 14.1: URL State Diagram**

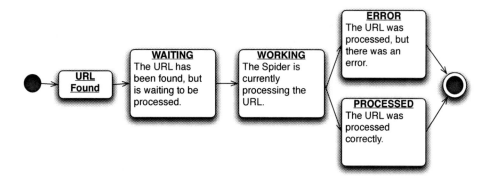

Any class that is to serve as a workload manager must implement the **WorkloadManager** interface. This interface defines the methods and functions necessary to track a list of URLs for the spider. The workload manager class is shown in Listing 14.6.

**Listing 14.6: Workload Manager (WorkloadManager.java)**

```
package com.heatonresearch.httprecipes.spider.workload;

import java.net.*;
import java.util.concurrent.*;

import com.heatonresearch.httprecipes.spider.*;

public interface WorkloadManager {
  /**
   * Add the specified URL to the workload.
   *
   * @param url
   *          The URL to be added.
   * @param source
   *          The page that contains this URL.
   * @param depth
   *          The depth of this URL.
   * @return True if the URL was added, false otherwise.
   * @throws WorkloadException
   */
  public boolean add(URL url, URL source, int depth)
    throws WorkloadException;
```

```java
/**
 * Clear the workload.
 *
 * @throws WorkloadException
 *             An error prevented the workload from being
 *             cleared.
 */
public void clear() throws WorkloadException;

/**
 * Determine if the workload contains the specified URL.
 *
 * @param url
 * @return
 * @throws WorkloadException
 */
public boolean contains(URL url) throws WorkloadException;

/**
 * Convert the specified String to a URL. If the string is
 * too long or has other issues, throw a
 * WorkloadException.
 *
 * @param url
 *          A String to convert into a URL.
 * @return The URL.
 * @throws WorkloadException
 *             Thrown if, The String could not be
 *             converted.
 */
public URL convertURL(String url) throws WorkloadException;

/**
 * Get the current host.
 *
 * @return The current host.
 */
public String getCurrentHost();

/**
 * Get the depth of the specified URL.
 *
 * @param url
 *             The URL to get the depth of.
 * @return The depth of the specified URL.
 * @throws WorkloadException
```

```
*               Thrown if the depth could not be found.
 */
public int getDepth(URL url) throws WorkloadException;


/**
 * Get the source page that contains the specified URL.
 *
 * @param url
 *             The URL to seek the source for.
 * @return The source of the specified URL.
 * @throws WorkloadException
 *               Thrown if the source of the specified URL
 *               could not be found.
 */
public URL getSource(URL url) throws WorkloadException;


/**
 * Get a new URL to work on. Wait if there are no URL's
 * currently available. Return null if done with the
 * current host. The URL being returned will be marked as
 * in progress.
 *
 * @return The next URL to work on,
 * @throws WorkloadException
 *               Thrown if the next URL could not be obtained.
 */
public URL getWork() throws WorkloadException;


/**
 * Setup this workload manager for the specified spider.
 *
 * @param spider
 *             The spider using this workload manager.
 * @throws WorkloadException
 *               Thrown if there is an error setting up the
 *               workload manager.
 */
public void init(Spider spider) throws WorkloadException;


/**
 * Mark the specified URL as error.
 *
 * @param url
 *             The URL that had an error.
 * @throws WorkloadException
 *               Thrown if the specified URL could not be
```

```
   *              marked.
   */
  public void markError(URL url) throws WorkloadException;


  /**
   * Mark the specified URL as successfully processed.
   *
   * @param url
   *              The URL to mark as processed.
   * @throws WorkloadException
   *              Thrown if the specified URL could not be
   *              marked.
   */
  public void markProcessed(URL url) throws WorkloadException;


  /**
   * Move on to process the next host. This should only be
   * called after getWork returns null.
   *
   * @return The name of the next host.
   * @throws WorkloadException
   *              Thrown if the workload manager was unable to
   *              move to the next host.
   */
  public String nextHost() throws WorkloadException;


  /**
   * Setup the workload so that it can be resumed from where
   * the last spider left the workload.
   *
   * @throws WorkloadException
   *              Thrown if we were unable to resume the
   *              processing.
   */
  public void resume() throws WorkloadException;


  /**
   * If there is currently no work available, then wait
   * until a new URL has been added to the workload.
   *
   * @param time
   *              The amount of time to wait.
   * @param length
   *              What time unit is being used.
   */
  public void waitForWork(int time, TimeUnit length);
```

```
/**
 * Return true if there are no more workload units.
 *
 * @return Returns true if there are no more workload
 *          units.
 * @throws WorkloadException
 *              Thrown if there was an error determining if
 *              the workload is empty.
 */
public boolean workloadEmpty() throws WorkloadException;

}
```

As you can see from the above listing, there are quite a few required functions and methods that a class must implement to serve as a workload manager. These methods and functions are summarized in Table 14.4.

**Table 14.4: Methods and Functions in the WorkloadManager Interface**

| Method or Function | Purpose |
|---|---|
| add | Add the specified URL to the workload. Return true if the URL was added, false otherwise. |
| clear | Clear the workload. |
| contains | Returns true if the workload contains the specified URL. |
| convertURL | Convert the specified String to a URL. If the string is too long or has other issues, throw a WorkloadException. Returns the URL with any necessary conversion. |
| getCurrentHost | Returns the current host. |
| getDepth | Returns the depth for the specified URL. |
| getSource | Returns the source for the specified URL. |
| getWork | Returns the next URL that needs to be processed. Also marks this URL as currently being processed. |
| init | Sets up the workload manager. |
| markError | Marks the specified URL as having an error. |
| markProcessed | Marks the specified URL as successfully processed. |
| nextHost | Returns the next host to be processed. |
| resume | Called to set up the workload to resume from a previous attempt. |
| waitForWork | If there is currently no work available, then wait until a new URL has been added to the workload. |
| workloadEmpty | Returns true if the workload is empty. |

By defining a workload management interface, the Heaton Research Spider can be programmed to use a variety of workload managers. Currently, there are only two workload managers defined for the Heaton Research Spider. These workload managers are listed here:

- Memory Workload Management
- SQL Workload Management

Each of these workload managers are discussed in the next few sections.

### Memory Workload Management

The most basic workload management type provided by the spider is the memory-based workload. The memory-based workload is contained in the class **MemoryWorkloadManager**. This class stores the complete list of URLs in memory.

The advantage to the **MemoryWorkloadManager** is that it is very easy to setup. Just create a new instance of the **MemoryWorkloadManager**, and your spider is ready to go. Because everything is stored in memory, there is no database or file system set up.

The main disadvantage to a **MemoryWorkloadManager**, is that it is unable to hold a large number of URLs. Because of this, the **MemoryWorkloadManager** is limited to processing URLs from only a single host. If you would like to process URLs from many different web hosts, you will need to use the **SQLWorkloadManager**.

### SQL Workload Management

The **SQLWorkloadManager** uses an SQL database to hold the list of URLs. This allows the **SQLWorkloadManager** to process a much larger amount of data than the **MemoryWorkloadManager**. Additionally, the **SQLWorkloadManager** can process multiple hosts.

The main disadvantage to the **SQLWorkloadManager**, is that it is complex to setup. For example, you must create a database, with the correct table structure. You must verify that the spider has the correct login information and drivers for the database. None of this is terribly difficult; however, it is more complex than the simple **MemoryWorkloadManager**.

### Other Workload Managers

Some databases require specialized workload managers. One such example is Oracle. A specialized workload manager is provided for Oracle named **OracleWorkloadManager**. Oracle requires slightly different forms for several of the SQL statements used by the workload manager. As a result, it is necessary to create a special workload manager for Oracle. The **OracleWorkloadManager** class is very short. It simply inherits from **WorkloadManagement** and replaces a few of the SQL statements.

Currently, the **OracleWorkloadManager**, the **MemoryWorkloadManager** and the **SQLWorkloadManager** are the only supported workload managers, although others may be supported in the future. One example might be a **FileSystemWorkloadManager**. This workload manager would use a directory on the file system to store the URL list. This would have a similar capacity as the **SQLWorkloadManager**, but would not require a relational database.

## Implementing a Memory Based WorkloadManager

You will now see how the **MemoryWorkloadManager** class is implemented. The memory workload manager stores the list of URLs in several memory-based objects. The **MemoryWorkloadManager** is shown in Listing 14.7.

**Listing 14.7: Memory Workload Manager (MemoryWorkloadManager.java)**

```java
package com.heatonresearch.httprecipes.spider.workload.memory;

import java.net.*;
import java.util.*;
import java.util.concurrent.*;

import com.heatonresearch.httprecipes.spider.*;
import com.heatonresearch.httprecipes.spider.workload.*;

public class MemoryWorkloadManager implements WorkloadManager {
  /**
   * The current workload, a map between URL and URLStatus
   * objects.
   */
  private Map<URL, URLStatus> workload =
    new HashMap<URL, URLStatus>();

  /**
   * The list of those items, which are already in the
   * workload, that are waiting for processing.
   */
  private BlockingQueue<URL> waiting =
    new LinkedBlockingQueue<URL>();

  /**
   * How many URL's are currently being processed.
   */
  private int workingCount = 0;

  /*
   * Because the MemoryWorkloadManager only supports a
   * single host, the currentHost is set to the host of the
   * first URL added.
   */
  private String currentHost;

  /**
   * Add the specified URL to the workload.
   *
   * @param url
   *            The URL to be added.
   * @param source
   *            The page that contains this URL.
```

```
 *  @param depth
 *              The depth of this URL.
 *  @return True if the URL was added, false otherwise.
 *  @throws WorkloadException If any error occurs.
 */
public boolean add(URL url, URL source, int depth) {
  if (!contains(url)) {
    this.waiting.add(url);
    setStatus(url, source, URLStatus.Status.WAITING, depth);
    if (this.currentHost == null) {
      this.currentHost = url.getHost().toLowerCase();
    }
    return true;
  }
  return false;

}


/**
 * Clear the workload.
 *
 * @throws WorkloadException
 *              An error prevented the workload from being
 *              cleared.
 */
public void clear() {
  this.workload.clear();
  this.waiting.clear();
  this.workingCount = 0;
}

/**
 * Determine if the workload contains the specified URL.
 *
 * @param url
 * @return
 * @throws WorkloadException
 */
public boolean contains(URL url) {
  return (this.workload.containsKey(url));
}

/**
 * Convert the specified String to a URL. If the string is
 * too long or has other issues, throw a
 * WorkloadException.
```

```
   *
   * @param url
   *           A String to convert into a URL.
   * @return The URL.
   * @throws WorkloadException
   *              Thrown if, The String could not be
   *              converted.
   */
  public URL convertURL(String url) throws WorkloadException {
    try {
      return new URL(url);
    } catch (MalformedURLException e) {
      throw new WorkloadException(e);
    }
  }


  /**
   * Get the current host.
   *
   * @return The current host.
   */
  public String getCurrentHost() {
    return this.currentHost;
  }


  /**
   * Get the depth of the specified URL.
   *
   * @param url
   *           The URL to get the depth of.
   * @return The depth of the specified URL.
   * @throws WorkloadException
   *              Thrown if the depth could not be found.
   */
  public int getDepth(URL url) {
    URLStatus s = this.workload.get(url);
    assert (s != null);
    if (s != null) {
      return s.getDepth();
    } else {
      return 1;
    }
  }
```

```
/**
 * Get the source page that contains the specified URL.
 *
 * @param url
 *            The URL to seek the source for.
 * @return The source of the specified URL.
 * @throws WorkloadException
 *            Thrown if the source of the specified URL
 *            could not be found.
 */
public URL getSource(URL url) {
  URLStatus s = this.workload.get(url);
  if (s == null) {
    return null;
  } else {
    return s.getSource();
  }
}


/**
 * Get a new URL to work on. Wait if there are no URL's
 * currently available. Return null if done with the
 * current host. The URL being returned will be marked as
 * in progress.
 *
 * @return The next URL to work on,
 * @throws WorkloadException
 *            Thrown if the next URL could not be obtained.
 */
public URL getWork() {
  URL url;
  try {
    url = this.waiting.poll(5, TimeUnit.SECONDS);
    if (url != null) {
      setStatus(url, null, URLStatus.Status.WORKING, -1);
      this.workingCount++;
    }
    return url;
  } catch (InterruptedException e) {
    return null;
  }

}
```

```java
/**
 * Setup this workload manager for the specified spider.
 * This method is not used by the MemoryWorkloadManager.
 *
 * @param spider
 *            The spider using this workload manager.
 * @throws WorkloadException
 *            Thrown if there is an error setting up the
 *            workload manager.
 */
public void init(Spider spider) throws WorkloadException {
}

/**
 * Mark the specified URL as error.
 *
 * @param url
 *            The URL that had an error.
 * @throws WorkloadException
 *            Thrown if the specified URL could not be
 *            marked.
 */
public void markError(URL url) {
  this.workingCount--;
  assert this.workingCount > 0;
  this.waiting.remove(url);
  setStatus(url, null, URLStatus.Status.ERROR, -1);

}

/**
 * Mark the specified URL as successfully processed.
 *
 * @param url
 *            The URL to mark as processed.
 * @throws WorkloadException
 *            Thrown if the specified URL could not be
 *            marked.
 */
public void markProcessed(URL url) {
  this.workingCount--;
  assert this.workingCount > 0;
  this.waiting.remove(url);
  setStatus(url, null, URLStatus.Status.PROCESSED, -1);
}
```

```
/**
 * Move on to process the next host. This should only be
 * called after getWork returns null. Because the
 * MemoryWorkloadManager is single host only, this
 * function simply returns null.
 *
 * @return The name of the next host.
 * @throws WorkloadException
 *             Thrown if the workload manager was unable to
 *             move to the next host.
 */
public String nextHost() {
  return null;
}


/**
 * Setup the workload so that it can be resumed from where
 * the last spider left the workload.
 *
 * @throws WorkloadException
 *             Thrown if we were unable to resume the
 *             processing.
 */
public void resume() throws WorkloadException {
  throw (new WorkloadException(
      "Memory based workload managers can not resume."));
}


/**
 * If there is currently no work available, then wait
 * until a new URL has been added to the workload. Because
 * the MemoryWorkloadManager uses a blocking queue, this
 * method is not needed. It is implemented to support the
 * interface.
 *
 * @param time
 *             The amount of time to wait.
 * @param length
 *             What tiem unit is being used.
 */
public void waitForWork(int time, TimeUnit length) {
}


/**
 * Return true if there are no more workload units.
 *
```

```
 * @return Returns true if there are no more workload
 *          units.
 * @throws WorkloadException
 *              Thrown if there was an error determining if
 *              the workload is empty.
 */
public boolean workloadEmpty() {
  if (!this.waiting.isEmpty()) {
    return false;
  }

  return (this.workingCount < 1);
}

/**
 * Set the source, status and depth for the specified URL.
 *
 * @param url
 *          The URL to set.
 * @param source
 *          The source of this URL.
 * @param status
 *          The status of this URL.
 * @param depth
 *          The depth of this URL.
 */
private void setStatus(URL url, URL source,
  URLStatus.Status status, int depth) {
  URLStatus s = this.workload.get(url);
  if (s == null) {
    s = new URLStatus();
    this.workload.put(url, s);
  }
  s.setStatus(status);

  if (source != null) {
    s.setSource(source);
  }

  if (depth != -1) {
    s.setDepth(depth);
  }
}

}
```

There are several instance variables that are used by the **MemoryWorkloadManager**. These instance variables are summarized in Table 14.5.

**Table 14.5: Instance Variables of the MemoryWorkloadManager**

| Property | Purpose |
|---|---|
| workload | The current workload, a map between URL and URLStatus objects. |
| waiting | The list of those items, which are already in the workload, that are waiting for processing. |
| workingCount | How many URLs are currently being processed. |
| currentHost | Because the MemoryWorkloadManager only supports a single host, the currentHost is set to the host of the first URL added. |

The **MemoryWorkloadManager** class must implement all of the methods and functions in the **WorkloadManager** interface. These functions and methods will be covered in the next few sections.

### Adding URL's

The **addURL** method is called to add a URL to the workload. First, the workload is checked to see if this URL is already part of the workload. If the URL has not previously been added to the workload, then it is processed.

```
if (!contains(url)) {
```

The URL is added to the **waiting** list, and the status for the URL is set to waiting. Additionally, the depth is recorded.

```
this.waiting.add(url);
setStatus(url, source, URLStatus.Status.WAITING, depth);
```

If the **currentHost** variable has not been set, then set it to the host of the URL being added. The **MemoryWorkloadManager** can only process one host. If you would like to process more than one host, you must use the **SQLWorkloadManager**.

```
if (this.currentHost == null) {
  this.currentHost = url.getHost().toLowerCase();
}
  return true;
}
return false;
```

If the URL was not added to the workload, then return **false**, otherwise return **true**.

### Clearing the Workload

Clearing the workload is easy. The **workload** and **waiting** variables are cleared and the **workingCount** is set to zero.

```
this.workload.clear();
this.waiting.clear();
this.workingCount = 0;
```

The **resume** method is not implemented because the memory workload will not persist its data between runs of the program. There will be nothing to resume.

### Getting the Depth of a URL

An important aspect of the workload management is to track the depth of each URL encountered. The depth of the URL was stored when the URL was added to the workload. To determine the URL of a workload, the **URLStatus** is read from the map.

```
URLStatus s = this.workload.get(url);
assert (s != null);
if (s != null) {
  return s.getDepth();
} else {
  return 1;
}
```

An **assert** is used to ensure that the URL is found. If the spider is seeking the depth of a URL that has not been added yet, that is an error.

### Getting the Source of a URL

Along with the depth of a URL, the source of a URL is also tracked. The source of a URL is the page the URL was found on. Finding the source of a URL is very similar to finding the depth of a URL. It is read from the **URLStatus** entry in the map.

```
URLStatus s = this.workload.get(url);
if (s == null) {
  return null;
} else {
  return s.getSource();
}
```

If a URL status is not found for the specified URL, then **null** is returned.

## Getting Work

The **getWork** method is used by the spider to receive individual URLs for the **SpiderWorker** objects to work on. The **getWork** method begins by polling the **waiting** queue. The program will wait up to five seconds for something to be placed in the queue.

```
URL url;
try {
  url = this.waiting.poll(5, TimeUnit.SECONDS);
```

Once a URL is located, the URL's status is set to **WORKING** and the **workingCount** is increased.

```
if (url != null) {
  setStatus(url, null, URLStatus.Status.WORKING, -1);
  this.workingCount++;
}
```

Return any URL that was found.

```
return url;
} catch (InterruptedException e) {
return null;
}
```

If the **poll** was interrupted, then return a **null**. This indicates that no work could be found.

## Marking a URL as Error

If an error occurs while processing a URL, then that URL is marked as **ERROR** and the **workingCount** is decreased. If this value falls below zero, this is an error, and the URL is removed from the waiting queue.

```
this.workingCount--;
assert this.workingCount > 0;
this.waiting.remove(url);
setStatus(url, null, URLStatus.Status.ERROR, -1);
```

Finally, the URL's status is set to **ERROR**.

## Marking a URL as Processed

If a URL has been successfully processed, then that URL is marked as **PROCESSED** and the **workingCount** is decreased. If this value falls below zero, this is an error, and the URL is removed from the waiting queue.

```
this.workingCount--;
assert this.workingCount > 0;
```

```
this.waiting.remove(url);
setStatus(url, null, URLStatus.Status.PROCESSED, -1);
```

Finally, the URL's status is set to **PROCESSED**.

### Setting a URL Status

Both the **markProcessed** and **markError** methods rely on the **setStatus** method to actually set the status for a URL. The **setStatus** accepts a URL, a **status**, a page **source** and a page **depth**. Setting the **status** and **depth** is optional. If you do not wish to affect the **source** then pass **null** for source. If you do not wish to affect **depth**, then pass negative one for **depth**.

The **setStatus** method begins by attempting to access the **URLStatus** object in the map for the specified URL. If no status object is found, then one is created.

```
URLStatus s = this.workload.get(url);
if (s == null) {
  s = new URLStatus();
  this.workload.put(url, s);
}
s.setStatus(status);
```

If a value was specified for **source**, then set the source for the **URLStatus** object.

```
if (source != null) {
  s.setSource(source);
}
```

If a value was specified for **depth**, then set the source for the **URLStatus** object.

```
if (depth != -1) {
  s.setDepth(depth);
}
```

The workload manager uses this method internally any time the status is set.

## Summary

In Chapter 13 you saw how to use the Heaton Research Spider. In this chapter you saw how the Heaton Research Spider was constructed. This chapter is intended for those who want to see the inner workings of the Heaton Research Spider, rather than simply using it.

The spider uses thread pools to work more efficiently. In addition to allowing the spider to execute more effectively on multi-processor systems, the thread pool allows even a single processor system to execute more efficiently. This is because the spider spends a great deal of time waiting. A thread pool allows the spider to be waiting on a large number of URLs at the same time.

The spider also uses workload managers. Any workload manager used by the spider must implement the **WorkloadManager** interface. The workload managers manage the URL list. There are two workload managers provided with the Heaton Research Spider. The **MemoryWorkloadManager** class stores the workload in memory. The **SQLWorkloadManager** class stores the workload in an SQL database.

This chapter introduced internals of the Heaton Research Spider. You also saw how the **MemoryWorkloadManager** was constructed. In the next chapter, you will see how the **SQLWorkloadManager** class was constructed and how the Heaton Research Spider interacts with an SQL based workload manager.

# CHAPTER 15: USING AN SQL WORKLOAD

- Dealing with Broken Connections
- Using PreparedStatements
- Creating Hash Codes for URLs
- Working with Multiple Hosts

The Heaton Research Spider includes an SQL based workload manager. The SQL workload manager allows the Heaton Research Spider to store its lists of URLs to a JDBC SQL database. This allows the spider to manage a very large set of URLs. This chapter will discuss the internals of how the **SQLWorkloadManager** class was implemented.

If you are only interested in using the **SQLWorkloadManager**, you should refer to Chapter 13. Chapter 13 contains a complete description of how to use the Heaton Research Spider. Chapter 14 shows you how the Heaton Research Spider itself was constructed. This chapter focuses exclusively on how the **SQLWorkloadManager** class was constructed.

There are three different classes that make up the SQL workload manager. All three of these classes are in the following package:

```
com.heatonresearch.httprecipes.spider.workload.sql
```

The classes contained in the above package are listed here:

- RepeatableStatement
- SQLWorkloadManager
- Status

The **RepeatableStatement** holds an SQL statement that can be repeated if the connection to the database is broken. The **SQLWorkloadManager** is the main class for the SQL workload manager. The **Status** class is just a simple data holder which is used to hold the status of each URL in the workload. The **RepeatableStatement** and **SQLWorkloadManager** classes will be discussed in the next sections.

## Repeatable Statements

Java provides a class, named **PreparedStatement**, that allows you to compile SQL into objects that can quickly be executed. Because the SQL workload manager only executes a little over a dozen unique SQL statements, it makes sense to package each of these SQL statements as a **PreparedStatement**. This will allow the SQL statements to be executed more quickly. However, it is very important that no two threads use the same **PreparedStatement**. Because of this, it is necessary to create a class that will keep the **PreparedStatement** objects from different threads apart.

Additionally, we need to build in the ability to repeat an SQL statement. The spider is designed to potentially run for days or weeks when using an SQL workload. The connection to the database could be broken in that time period; therefore, we need a way to continue re-executing an SQL statement if it fails. To accomplish both of these design requirements, the **RepeatableStatement** class was developed.

Before I show you how the **RepeatableStatement** class was constructed, we will briefly examine how it is used. The following code uses a **RepeatableStatement** to execute a simple SQL query.

```
String sql = "SELECT * from table_name where name = ?";

RepeatableStatement statement = new RepeatableStatement(sql);
statement.create(manager);
RepeatableStatement.Result result = statement.
executeQuery("Fred");
```

You will notice that the SQL contains a question mark (?). This is a parameter. The parameters you pass on the **execute** or **executeQuery** function calls will be substituted for the question mark. In the above example, the value of "Fred" is passed in for the question mark.

The **RepeatableStatement** class is shown in Listing 15.1.

### Listing 15.1: Repeatable Statements (RepeatableStatement.java)

```
package com.heatonresearch.httprecipes.spider.workload.sql;

import java.sql.*;
import java.util.*;
import java.util.concurrent.*;
import java.util.logging.*;

import com.heatonresearch.httprecipes.spider.workload.*;
```

```java
public class RepeatableStatement
{

  /**
   * Simple internal class that holds the ResultSet from a
   * query.
   *
   * @author jeff
   *
   */
  public class Results
  {

    /**
     * The PreparedStatement that generated these results.
     */
    private PreparedStatement statement;

    /**
     * The ResultSet that was generated.
     */
    private ResultSet resultSet;

    /**
     * Construct a Results object.
     *
     * @param statement
     *           The PreparedStatement for these results.
     * @param resultSet
     *           The ResultSet.
     */
    public Results(PreparedStatement statement,
      ResultSet resultSet)
    {
      this.statement = statement;
      this.resultSet = resultSet;
    }

    /**
     * Close the ResultSet.
     */
    public void close()
    {
      try
      {
        this.resultSet.close();
```

```
    } catch (SQLException e)
    {
      logger.log(Level.SEVERE, "Failed to close ResultSet", e);
    }
    releaseStatement(this.statement);
  }

  /**
   * Get the ResultSet.
   *
   * @return The ResultSet.
   */
  public ResultSet getResultSet()
  {
    return this.resultSet;
  }
}

/**
 * The logger.
 */
private static Logger logger =
  Logger.getLogger(
    "com.heatonresearch.httprecipes.spider."
    +"workload.sql.RepeatableStatement");

/**
 * The SQLWorkloadManager that created this object.
 */
private SQLWorkloadManager manager;

/**
 * The SQL for this statement.
 */
private String sql;

/**
 * A mutex to make sure that only one thread at a time is
 * in the process of getting a PreparedStatement assigned.
 * More than one thread at a time can have a
 * PreparedStatement, however only one can be in the
 * obtainStatement function at a time.
 */
private Semaphore mutex;

/**
```

```
 * The PreparedStatements that are assigned to each
 * thread.
 */
private List<PreparedStatement> statementCache = new ArrayList<P
reparedStatement>();

/**
 * Construct a repeatable statement based on the
 * specified SQL
 * @param sql The SQL to base this statement
 * on.
 */
public RepeatableStatement(String sql)
{
  this.sql = sql;
  this.mutex = new Semaphore(1);
}

/*
 * Close the statement.
 */
public void close()
{
  try
  {
    try
    {
      this.mutex.acquire();
    } catch (InterruptedException e1)
    {
      // TODO Auto-generated catch block
      e1.printStackTrace();
    }

    for (PreparedStatement statement : this.statementCache)
    {
      try
      {
        statement.close();
      } catch (SQLException e)
      {
        logger.log(Level.SEVERE,
          "Failed to close PreparedStatement", e);
      }
    }
  } finally
```

```
      {
        this.mutex.release();
      }
    }

    /**
     * Create the statement, so that it is ready to assign
     * PreparedStatements.
     *
     * @param manager
     *          The manager that created this statement.
     * @throws SQLException
     *          Thrown if an exception occurs.
     */
    public void create(SQLWorkloadManager manager)
      throws SQLException
    {
      close();
      this.manager = manager;
    }

    /**
     * Execute SQL that does not return a result set. If an
     * error occurs, the statement will be retried until it is
     * successful. This handles broken connections.
     *
     * @param parameters
     *          The parameters for this SQL.
     * @throws WorkloadException
     *          Thrown if the SQL cannot be executed, and
     *          retrying the statement has failed.
     */
    public void execute(Object... parameters)
      throws WorkloadException
    {
      PreparedStatement statement = null;

      try
      {
        statement = obtainStatement();

        for (;;)
        {
          try
          {
            for (int i = 0; i < parameters.length; i++)
```

```
        {
          if (parameters[i] == null)
          {
            statement.setNull(i, Types.INTEGER);
          } else
          {
            statement.setObject(i + 1, parameters[i]);
          }
        }
        long time = System.currentTimeMillis();
        statement.execute();
        time = System.currentTimeMillis() - time;

        return;
      } catch (SQLException e)
      {
        logger.log(Level.SEVERE, "SQL Exception", e);
        if (!(e.getCause() instanceof SQLException))
        {
          this.manager.tryOpen();
        } else
        {
          throw (new WorkloadException(e));
        }
      }
    }
  } catch (SQLException e)
  {
    throw (new WorkloadException(e));
  } finally
  {
    if (statement != null)
    {
      releaseStatement(statement);
    }
  }
}

/**
 * Execute an SQL query that returns a result set. If an
 * error occurs, the statement will be retried until it is
 * successful. This handles broken connections.
 *
 * @param parameters
 *          The parameters for this SQL.
 * @return The results of the query.
```

```
 * @throws WorkloadException
 *               Thrown if the SQL cannot be executed, and
 *               retrying the statement has failed.
 */
public Results executeQuery(Object... parameters)
  throws WorkloadException
{

  for (;;)
  {
    try
    {
      PreparedStatement statement = obtainStatement();

      for (int i = 0; i < parameters.length; i++)
      {
        statement.setObject(i + 1, parameters[i]);
      }
      long time = System.currentTimeMillis();
      ResultSet rs = statement.executeQuery();
      time = System.currentTimeMillis() - time;
      // System.out.println( time + ":" + sql);
      return (new Results(statement, rs));
    } catch (SQLException e)
    {
      logger.log(Level.SEVERE, "SQL Exception", e);
      if (!(e.getCause() instanceof SQLException))
      {
        this.manager.tryOpen();
      } else
      {
        throw (new WorkloadException(e));
      }
    }
  }

}

/**
 * Obtain a statement. Each thread should use their own
 * statement, and then call the releaseStatement method
 * when they are done.
 *
 * @return A PreparedStatement object.
 * @throws SQLException
 *               Thrown if the statement could not be
```

```
  *           obtained.
  */
private PreparedStatement obtainStatement() throws SQLException
{
  PreparedStatement result = null;

  try
  {
    this.mutex.acquire();
    if (this.statementCache.size() == 0)
    {
      result =
        this.manager.getConnection().prepareStatement(this.sql);
    } else
    {
      result = this.statementCache.get(0);
      this.statementCache.remove(0);
    }

  } catch (InterruptedException e)
  {
    return null;
  } finally
  {
    this.mutex.release();
  }

  return result;
}

/**
 * This method releases statements after the thread is
 * done with them. These statements are not closed, but
 * rather cached until another thread has need of them.
 *
 * @param stmt
 *           The statement that is to be released.
 */
private void releaseStatement(PreparedStatement stmt)
{
  try
  {
    try
    {
      this.mutex.acquire();
    } catch (InterruptedException e)
```

```
      {
         return;
      }
      this.statementCache.add(stmt);
   } finally
   {
      this.mutex.release();
   }
  }
}
```

As you can see from the above listing, the **RepeatableStatement** class defines several instance variables. These instance variables are defined in Table 15.1.

**Table 15.1: Instance Variables of the RepeatableStatement Class**

| Instance Variable | Purpose |
|---|---|
| manager | The SQLWorkloadManager that created this object. This is used to reopen the database connection, when needed. |
| sql | The SQL for this statement. This is used to recreate the Prepared-Statement when needed. |
| mutex | A mutex to make sure that only one thread at a time is in the process of getting a PreparedStatement assigned. More than one thread at a time can have a PreparedStatement; however, only one can be in the obtainStatement function at a time. |
| statementCache | The PreparedStatements that are assigned to each thread. |

There are also several methods and functions that make up the **RepeatableStatement** class. These methods and functions will be discussed in the next few sections.

### Executing SQL Commands

The **execute** method is used to execute SQL commands that do not return a **ResultSet**. The **execute** method makes use of the variable argument count feature of JDK 1.5. This allows a number of parameters to be included with the SQL command. Parameters were discussed earlier in this chapter.

```
public void execute(Object... parameters) throws WorkloadException
{
   PreparedStatement statement = null;
```

Next, a statement is obtained by calling the **obtainStatement** function. The **obtainStatement** function will be covered later in this chapter.

```
try {
statement = obtainStatement();
```

Now, we enter a loop to execute the statement. This loop will execute until the statement executes successfully.

```
for (;;) {
try {
```

The arguments are copied to the statement.

```
for (int i = 0; i < parameters.length; i++) {
  if (parameters[i] == null) {
    statement.setNull(i, Types.INTEGER);
  } else {
    statement.setObject(i + 1, parameters[i]);
  }
}
```

The current time is taken before and after the SQL is executed. Adding a statement to log this time can be helpful when tuning the SQL statements and queries.

```
long time = System.currentTimeMillis();
statement.execute();
time = System.currentTimeMillis() - time;
return;
```

If a **SQLException** is thrown while trying to execute the SQL statement, then the connection is reopened and the SQL is tried again.

```
} catch (SQLException e) {
logger.log(Level.SEVERE, "SQL Exception", e);
    if (!(e.getCause() instanceof SQLException)) {
      this.manager.tryOpen();
    } else {
      throw (new WorkloadException(e));
    }
  }
}
} catch (SQLException e) {
  throw (new WorkloadException(e));
} finally {
  if (statement != null) {
    releaseStatement(statement);
}
```

Once the SQL statement has been executed, the statement can be released.

The **executeQuery** function works almost identically to the execute method. The only difference is that the **executeQuery** function returns a **ResultSet**.

### Obtaining a PreparedStatement

Other than allowing statements to be repeated, the other major function provided by the **RepeatableStatement** class is the ability to allocate **PreparedStatement** objects to threads. Two threads cannot use the same **PreparedStatement** object at the same time. To keep threads from using the same **PreparedStatement** object, the **obtainStatement** and **releaseStatement** functions are used.

The first thing that the **obtainStatement** function does, is to check to see if it can acquire the **mutex**. This prevents two threads from calling **obtainStatement** at exactly the same time.

```
PreparedStatement result = null;

try {
  this.mutex.acquire();
```

If there are no extra statements already in the cache, then create a new **PreparedStatement**.

```
if (this.statementCache.size() == 0) {
result = this.manager.getConnection().prepareStatement(this.sql);
```

If there is an extra **PreparedStatement** in the cache, then return that **PreparedStatement** and remove it from the cache.

```
  } else {
    result = this.statementCache.get(0);
    this.statementCache.remove(0);
  }
} catch (InterruptedException e) {
return null;
```

Once we are done, we can release the **mutex**.

```
} finally {
  this.mutex.release();
}
```

```
return result;
```

Once you are finished with the **PreparedStatement** that we obtained, call **releaseStatement** to return it to the cache.

### Releasing a PreparedStatement

When a **PreparedStatement** is released by calling **releaseStatment**, the **PreparedStatement** is not actually released. Rather, it is simply returned to the **PreparedStatement** cache. This saves the program the overhead of allocating and releasing large numbers of **PreparedStatement** objects.

The **releaseStatement** method first obtains a **mutex**. This is the same **mutex** used by the **obtainStatement** function. This ensures that no two threads are accessing the **PreparedStatement** cache at the same time.

```
try {
  try {
    this.mutex.acquire();
  } catch (InterruptedException e) {
  return;
}
```

The **PreparedStatement** is added to the cache.

```
this.statementCache.add(stmt);
```

Finally, the **mutex** is released.

```
} finally {
  this.mutex.release();
}
```

Once the **releaseStatement** method is complete, the **PreparedStatement** is back on the cache awaiting the next thread that needs it.

## Implementing an SQL Based Workload Manager

The SQL based workload manager is implemented in the **SQLWorkloadManager** class. In this section, I will show you some of the internals of how this class works. This class makes extensive use of SQL. Teaching extensive SQL is beyond the scope of this book; however, many of the methods and functions of the **SQLWorkloadManager** are simply wrappers for SQL statements. All of the SQL statements used by the spider are relatively simple, if you know SQL basics. This section will focus on explaining how the class works and not what the actual SQL does.

The SQL queries used by this class should work with nearly any SQL database, once the database is set up. For more information about how to set up the database, see Appendix F. The **SQLWorkloadManager** class is shown in Listing 15.2.

### Listing 15.2: SQL Workload Management (SQLWorkloadManager.java)

```
package com.heatonresearch.httprecipes.spider.workload.sql;

import java.net.*;
import java.sql.*;
import java.util.*;
import java.util.concurrent.*;
import java.util.logging.*;

import com.heatonresearch.httprecipes.spider.*;
```

```java
import com.heatonresearch.httprecipes.spider.workload.*;

/**
 * The Heaton Research Spider
 * Copyright 2007 by Heaton Research, Inc.
 *
 * HTTP Programming Recipes for Java ISBN: 0-9773206-6-9
 * http://www.heatonresearch.com/articles/series/16/
 *
 * SQLWorkloadManager: This workload manager stores the URL
 * lists in an SQL database. This workload manager uses two
 * tables, which can be created as follows:
 *
 * CREATE TABLE 'spider_host' (
 * 'host_id' int(10) unsigned NOT NULL auto_increment,
 * 'host' varchar(255) NOT NULL default '',
 * 'status' varchar(1) NOT NULL default '',
 * 'urls_done' int(11) NOT NULL,
 * 'urls_error' int(11) NOT NULL,
 * PRIMARY KEY  ('host_id')
 * )
 *
 * CREATE TABLE 'spider_workload' (
 * 'workload_id' int(10) unsigned NOT NULL auto_increment,
 * 'host' int(10) unsigned NOT NULL,
 * 'url' varchar(2083) NOT NULL default '',
 * 'status' varchar(1) NOT NULL default '',
 * 'depth' int(10) unsigned NOT NULL,
 * 'url_hash' int(11) NOT NULL,
 * 'source_id' int(11) NOT NULL,
 * PRIMARY KEY  ('workload_id'),
 * KEY 'status' ('status'),
 * KEY 'url_hash' ('url_hash'),
 * KEY 'host' ('host')
 * )
 *
 *
 * This class is released under the:
 * GNU Lesser General Public License (LGPL)
 * http://www.gnu.org/copyleft/lesser.html
 *
 * @author Jeff Heaton
 * @version 1.1
 */
public class SQLWorkloadManager implements WorkloadManager
{
```

```
/**
 * The logger.
 */
private static Logger logger = Logger
    .getLogger("com.heatonresearch.httprecipes.spider.workload.
sql.SQLWorkloadManager");

private SQLHolder holder = new SQLHolder();
private RepeatableStatement stmtClear;
private RepeatableStatement stmtClear2;
private RepeatableStatement stmtAdd;
private RepeatableStatement stmtAdd2;
private RepeatableStatement stmtGetWork;
private RepeatableStatement stmtGetWork2;
private RepeatableStatement stmtWorkloadEmpty;
private RepeatableStatement stmtSetWorkloadStatus;
private RepeatableStatement stmtSetWorkloadStatus2;
private RepeatableStatement stmtGetDepth;
private RepeatableStatement stmtGetSource;
private RepeatableStatement stmtResume;
private RepeatableStatement stmtResume2;
private RepeatableStatement stmtGetWorkloadID;
private RepeatableStatement stmtGetHostID;
private RepeatableStatement stmtGetNextHost;
private RepeatableStatement stmtSetHostStatus;
private RepeatableStatement stmtGetHost;

/**
 * The driver for the JDBC connection.
 */
private String driver;

/**
 * The URL for the JDBC connection.
 */
private String url;

/**
 * The UID for the JDBC connection.
 */
private String uid;

/**
 * The PWD for the JDBC connection.
 */
private String pwd;
```

```
/**
 * Only one thread at a time is allowed to add to the
 * workload.
 */
private Semaphore addLock;

/**
 * Is there any work?
 */
private CountDownLatch workLatch;

/**
 * The maximum size a URL can be.
 */
private int maxURLSize;

/**
 * The maximum size that a host can be.
 */
private int maxHostSize;

/**
 * All of the RepeatableStatement objects.
 */
private List<RepeatableStatement> statements =
  new ArrayList<RepeatableStatement>();

/**
 * Used to obtain the next URL.
 */
private RepeatableStatement.Results workResultSet = null;

/**
 * Used to obtain the next host.
 */
private RepeatableStatement.Results hostResultSet = null;

/**
 * A connection to a JDBC database.
 */
private Connection connection;

/**
 * The current host.
 */
```

```java
private String currentHost;

/**
 * The ID of the current host.
 */
private int currentHostID = -1;

/**
 * Add the specified URL to the workload.
 *
 * @param url
 *          The URL to be added.
 * @param source
 *          The page that contains this URL.
 * @param depth
 *          The depth of this URL.
 * @return True if the URL was added, false otherwise.
 * @throws WorkloadException
 */
public boolean add(URL url, URL source, int depth)
  throws WorkloadException
{
  boolean result = false;
  try
  {
    this.addLock.acquire();
    if (!contains(url))
    {
      String strURL = truncate(url.toString(), this.maxURLSize);
      String strHost = truncate(url.getHost(), this.maxHostSize)
          .toLowerCase();
      result = true;

      // get the host
      int hostID = getHostID(url, false);

      if (hostID == -1)
      {
        this.stmtAdd2.execute(strHost,
          Status.STATUS_WAITING, 0, 0);
        hostID = getHostID(url, true);
      }

      // need to set the current host for the first time?
      if (this.currentHostID == -1)
      {
```

```java
        this.currentHostID = hostID;
        this.currentHost = strHost;
        this.stmtSetHostStatus.execute(Status.STATUS_PROCESSING,
            this.currentHostID);
      }

      // now add workload element
      if (source != null)
      {
        int sourceID = getWorkloadID(source, true);
        this.stmtAdd.execute(hostID, strURL,
          Status.STATUS_WAITING, depth,
            computeHash(url), sourceID);
      } else
      {
        this.stmtAdd.execute(hostID, strURL,
          Status.STATUS_WAITING, depth,
            computeHash(url), 0);
      }

      this.workLatch.countDown();
    }

  } catch (InterruptedException e)
  {
  } catch (SQLException e)
  {
    throw (new WorkloadException(e));
  } finally
  {
    this.addLock.release();
  }
  return result;
}

/**
 * Clear the workload.
 *
 * @throws WorkloadException
 *           An error prevented the workload from being
 *           cleared.
 */
public void clear() throws WorkloadException
{
  this.stmtClear.execute();
  this.stmtClear2.execute();
```

```
}

public void close() throws SQLException, WorkloadException
{
  if (this.workResultSet != null)
  {
    try
    {
      this.workResultSet.close();
    } catch (Exception e)
    {
      logger.log(Level.SEVERE,
      "Error trying to close workload result set, ignoring...");
    }
    this.workResultSet = null;
  }

  for (RepeatableStatement statement : this.statements)
  {
    statement.close();
  }

  if (this.connection != null)
  {
    this.connection.close();
  }

}

/**
 * Determine if the workload contains the specified URL.
 *
 * @param url The URL to search the workload for.
 * @return True of the workload contains the specified URL.
 * @throws WorkloadException
 */
public boolean contains(URL url) throws WorkloadException
{
  try
  {
    return (getWorkloadID(url, false) != -1);
  } catch (SQLException e)
  {
    throw (new WorkloadException(e));
  }
}
```

```java
/**
 * Convert the specified String to a URL. If the string is
 * too long or has other issues, throw a
 * WorkloadException.
 *
 * @param url
 *            A String to convert into a URL.
 * @return The URL.
 * @throws WorkloadException
 *            Thrown if, The String could not be
 *            converted.
 */
public URL convertURL(String url) throws WorkloadException
{
  URL result = null;

  url = url.trim();
  if (url.length() > this.maxURLSize)
  {
    throw new WorkloadException(
        "URL size is too big, must be under "
        + this.maxURLSize + " bytes.");
  }

  try
  {
    result = new URL(url);
  } catch (MalformedURLException e)
  {
    throw new WorkloadException(e);
  }
  return result;
}


/**
 * @return the connection
 */
public Connection getConnection()
{
  return this.connection;
}
```

```java
/**
 * Get the current host.
 *
 * @return The current host.
 */
public String getCurrentHost()
{
  return this.currentHost;
}


/**
 * Get the depth of the specified URL.
 *
 * @param url
 *             The URL to get the depth of.
 * @return The depth of the specified URL.
 * @throws WorkloadException
 *             Thrown if the depth could not be found.
 */
public int getDepth(URL url) throws WorkloadException
{
  RepeatableStatement.Results rs = null;
  try
  {
    rs = this.stmtGetDepth.executeQuery(computeHash(url));
    while (rs.getResultSet().next())
    {
      String u = rs.getResultSet().getString(1);
      if (u.equals(url.toString()))
      {
        return rs.getResultSet().getInt(2);
      }
    }
    return 1;
  } catch (SQLException e)
  {
    throw (new WorkloadException(e));
  } finally
  {
    if (rs != null)
    {
      rs.close();
    }
  }
}
```

```java
/**
 * Get the source page that contains the specified URL.
 *
 * @param url
 *            The URL to seek the source for.
 * @return The source of the specified URL.
 * @throws WorkloadException
 *             Thrown if the source of the specified URL
 *             could not be found.
 */
public URL getSource(URL url) throws WorkloadException
{
  RepeatableStatement.Results rs = null;
  try
  {
    rs = this.stmtGetSource.executeQuery(computeHash(url));
    while (rs.getResultSet().next())
    {
      String u = rs.getResultSet().getString(1);
      if (u.equals(url.toString()))
      {
        return (new URL(rs.getResultSet().getString(2)));
      }
    }
    return null;
  } catch (SQLException e)
  {
    throw (new WorkloadException(e));
  } catch (MalformedURLException e)
  {
    throw (new WorkloadException(e));
  } finally
  {
    if (rs != null)
    {
      rs.close();
    }
  }
}

/**
 * Get a new URL to work on. Wait if there are no URL's
 * currently available. Return null if done with the
 * current host. The URL being returned will be marked as
 * in progress.
 *
```

```
 * @return The next URL to work on,
 * @throws WorkloadException
 *              Thrown if the next URL could not be obtained.
 */
public URL getWork() throws WorkloadException
{
  URL url = null;
  do
  {
    url = getWorkInternal();
    if (url == null)
    {
      if (workloadEmpty())
      {
        break;
      }
    }

  } while (url == null);

  return url;
}


/**
 * Setup this workload manager for the specified spider.
 *
 * @param spider
 *            The spider using this workload manager.
 * @throws WorkloadException
 *              Thrown if there is an error setting up the
 *              workload manager.
 */
public void init(Spider spider) throws WorkloadException
{
  this.addLock = new Semaphore(1);
  this.workLatch = new CountDownLatch(1);
  this.workLatch.countDown();

  this.driver = spider.getOptions().dbClass;
  this.url = spider.getOptions().dbURL;
  this.uid = spider.getOptions().dbUID;
  this.pwd = spider.getOptions().dbPWD;

  this.statements.add(this.stmtClear =
    new RepeatableStatement(this.holder.getSQLClear()));
  this.statements.add(this.stmtClear2 =
```

```
  new RepeatableStatement(this.holder.getSQLClear2()));
this.statements.add(this.stmtAdd =
  new RepeatableStatement(this.holder.getSQLAdd()));
this.statements.add(this.stmtAdd2 =
  new RepeatableStatement(this.holder.getSQLAdd2()));
this.statements.add(this.stmtGetWork =
  new RepeatableStatement(this.holder.getSQLGetWork()));
this.statements.add(this.stmtGetWork2 =
  new RepeatableStatement(this.holder.getSQLGetWork2()));
this.statements.add(this.stmtWorkloadEmpty =
  new RepeatableStatement(this.holder.getSQLWorkloadEmpty()));
this.statements.add(this.stmtSetWorkloadStatus =
  new RepeatableStatement(
    this.holder.getSQLSetWorkloadStatus()));
this.statements.add(this.stmtSetWorkloadStatus2 =
  new RepeatableStatement(
    this.holder.getSQLSetWorkloadStatus2()));
this.statements.add(this.stmtGetDepth =
  new RepeatableStatement(this.holder.getSQLGetDepth()));
this.statements.add(this.stmtGetSource =
  new RepeatableStatement(
    this.holder.getSQLGetSource()));
this.statements.add(this.stmtResume =
  new RepeatableStatement(this.holder.getSQLResume()));
this.statements.add(this.stmtResume2 =
  new RepeatableStatement(this.holder.getSQLResume2()));
this.statements.add(this.stmtGetWorkloadID =
  new RepeatableStatement(this.holder.getSQLGetWorkloadID()));
this.statements.add(this.stmtGetHostID =
  new RepeatableStatement(this.holder.getSQLGetHostID()));
this.statements.add(this.stmtGetNextHost =
  new RepeatableStatement(
    this.holder.getSQLGetNextHost()));
this.statements.add(this.stmtSetHostStatus =
  new RepeatableStatement(
    this.holder.getSQLSetHostStatus()));
this.statements.add(this.stmtGetHost =
  new RepeatableStatement(this.holder.getSQLGetHost()));

try
{
  open();

  this.maxURLSize = getColumnSize("spider_workload", "url");
  this.maxHostSize = getColumnSize("spider_host", "host");
} catch (InstantiationException e)
```

```java
    {
      throw (new WorkloadException(e));
    } catch (IllegalAccessException e)
    {
      throw (new WorkloadException(e));
    } catch (ClassNotFoundException e)
    {
      throw (new WorkloadException(e));
    } catch (SQLException e)
    {
      throw (new WorkloadException(e));
    }
}

/**
 * Mark the specified URL as error.
 *
 * @param url
 *            The URL that had an error.
 * @throws WorkloadException
 *              Thrown if the specified URL could not be
 *              marked.
 */
public void markError(URL url) throws WorkloadException
{
  try
  {
    setStatus(url, Status.STATUS_ERROR);
    this.workLatch.countDown();
  } catch (SQLException e)
  {
    throw (new WorkloadException(e));
  }
}

/**
 * Mark the specified URL as successfully processed.
 *
 * @param url
 *            The URL to mark as processed.
 * @throws WorkloadException
 *              Thrown if the specified URL could not be
 *              marked.
 */
public void markProcessed(URL url) throws WorkloadException
{
  try
```

```
    {
      setStatus(url, Status.STATUS_DONE);
      this.workLatch.countDown();
    } catch (SQLException e)
    {
      throw (new WorkloadException(e));
    }
  }


  /**
   * Move on to process the next host. This should only be
   * called after getWork returns null.
   *
   * @return The name of the next host.
   * @throws WorkloadException
   *                Thrown if the workload manager was unable to
   *                move to the next host.
   */
  public String nextHost() throws WorkloadException
  {
    if (this.currentHostID == -1)
    {
      throw new WorkloadException(
          "Attempting to obtain host before adding first URL.");
    } else
    {
      markHostProcessed(this.currentHost);
    }

    try
    {
      boolean requery = false;

      if (this.hostResultSet == null)
      {
        requery = true;
      } else
      {
        if (!this.hostResultSet.getResultSet().next())
        {
          requery = true;
        }
      }

      if (requery)
      {
```

```
      if (this.hostResultSet != null)
      {
        this.hostResultSet.close();
      }

      this.hostResultSet = this.stmtGetNextHost
          .executeQuery(Status.STATUS_WAITING);

      if (!this.hostResultSet.getResultSet().next())
      {
        return null;
      }
    }

    this.currentHostID =
      this.hostResultSet.getResultSet().getInt(1);
    this.currentHost =
      this.hostResultSet.getResultSet().getString(2);
    this.stmtSetHostStatus.execute(Status.STATUS_PROCESSING,
        this.currentHostID);
    logger.log(Level.INFO, "Moving to new host: "
      + this.currentHost);
    return this.currentHost;

  } catch (SQLException e)
  {
    throw (new WorkloadException(e));
  }

}

/**
 * Setup the workload so that it can be resumed from where
 * the last spider left the workload.
 *
 * @throws WorkloadException
 *            Thrown if we were unable to resume the
 *            processing.
 */
public void resume() throws WorkloadException
{
  RepeatableStatement.Results rs = null;

  try
  {
    rs = this.stmtResume.executeQuery();
```

```
      if (!rs.getResultSet().next())
      {
        throw (new WorkloadException(
            "Can't resume, unable to determine current host."));
      }

      this.currentHostID = rs.getResultSet().getInt(1);
      this.currentHost = getHost(this.currentHostID);
    } catch (SQLException e)
    {
      throw (new WorkloadException(e));
    } finally
    {
      if (rs != null)
      {
        rs.close();
      }
    }

    this.stmtResume2.execute();

  }


  /**
   * If there is currently no work available, then wait
   * until a new URL has been added to the workload.
   *
   * @param time
   *          The amount of time to wait.
   * @param unit
   *          What time unit is being used.
   */
  public void waitForWork(int time, TimeUnit unit)
  {
    try
    {
      this.workLatch.await(time, unit);
    } catch (InterruptedException e)
    {
      logger.info("Workload latch timed out.");
    }

  }
```

```
/**
 * Return true if there are no more workload units.
 *
 * @return Returns true if there are no more workload
 *          units.
 * @throws WorkloadException
 *              Thrown if there was an error determining if
 *              the workload is empty.
 */
public boolean workloadEmpty() throws WorkloadException
{
  RepeatableStatement.Results rs = null;

  try
  {
    rs = this.stmtWorkloadEmpty.executeQuery(
      this.currentHostID);
    if (!rs.getResultSet().next())
    {
      return true;
    }
    return (rs.getResultSet().getInt(1) < 1);
  } catch (SQLException e)
  {
    throw (new WorkloadException(e));
  } finally
  {
    if (rs != null)
    {
      rs.close();
    }
  }
}


/**
 * Compute a hash for a URL.
 *
 * @param url
 *          The URL to compute the hash for.
 * @return The hash code.
 */
private int computeHash(URL url)
{
  String str = url.toString().trim();

  int result = str.hashCode();
```

```
    result = (result % 0xffff);
    return result;
}


/**
 * Return the size of the specified column.
 *
 * @param table
 *            The table that contains the column.
 * @param column
 *            The column to get the size for.
 * @return The size of the column.
 * @throws SQLException
 *            For SQL errors.
 */
public int getColumnSize(String table, String column)
  throws SQLException
{
  ResultSet rs =
    this.connection.getMetaData().getColumns(null, null, table,
      null);
  while (rs.next())
  {

    String c = rs.getString("COLUMN_NAME");
    int size = rs.getInt("COLUMN_SIZE");
    if (c.equalsIgnoreCase(column))
    {
      return size;
    }
  }
  return -1;
}


/**
 * Get the host name associated with the specified host
 * id.
 *
 * @param hostID
 *            The host id to look up.
 * @return The name of the host.
 * @throws WorkloadException
 *            Thrown if unable to obtain the host name.
 */
private String getHost(int hostID) throws WorkloadException
{
```

```java
  RepeatableStatement.Results rs = null;

  try
  {
    rs = this.stmtGetHost.executeQuery(hostID);
    if (!rs.getResultSet().next())
    {
      throw new WorkloadException(
        "Can't find previously created host.");
    }
    return rs.getResultSet().getString(1);
  } catch (SQLException e)
  {
    throw new WorkloadException(e);
  } finally
  {
    if (rs != null)
    {
      rs.close();
    }
  }
}

/**
 * Get the id for the specified host name.
 *
 * @param host
 *            The host to lookup.
 * @param require
 *            Should an exception be thrown if the host is
 *            not located.
 * @return The id of the specified host name.
 * @throws WorkloadException
 *             Thrown if the host id is not found, and is
 *             required.
 * @throws SQLException
 *             Thrown if a SQL error occurs.
 */
private int getHostID(String host, boolean require)
  throws WorkloadException,
    SQLException
{
  RepeatableStatement.Results rs = null;

  // is this the current host?
  if (this.currentHostID != -1)
```

```
  {
    if (this.currentHost.equalsIgnoreCase(host))
    {
      return this.currentHostID;
    }
  }

  // use the database to find it
  try
  {
    rs = this.stmtGetHostID.executeQuery(host);
    if (rs.getResultSet().next())
    {
      return rs.getResultSet().getInt(1);
    }
  } finally
  {
    if (rs != null)
    {
      rs.close();
    }
  }

  if (require)
  {
    StringBuilder str = new StringBuilder();
    str.append("Failed to find previously visited Host,");
    str.append("Host=\"");
    str.append(this.url.toString());
    str.append("\".");
    throw (new WorkloadException(str.toString()));
  } else
  {
    return -1;
  }
}

/**
 * Get the ID for the given host. The host name is
 * extracted from the specified URL.
 *
 * @param url
 *            The URL that specifies the host name to
 *            lookup.
 * @param require
 *            Should an exception be thrown if the host is
```

```
 *              not located.
 * @return The id of the specified host name.
 * @throws WorkloadException
 *              Thrown if the host id is not found, and is
 *              required.
 * @throws SQLException
 *              Thrown if a SQL error occurs.
 */
private int getHostID(URL url, boolean require)
   throws SQLException,
    WorkloadException
{
  String host = url.getHost().toLowerCase();
  return getHostID(host, require);
}


/**
 * Called internally to get a work unit. This function
 * does not wait for work, rather it simply returns null.
 *
 * @return The next URL to process.
 * @throws WorkloadException
 *              Thrown if unable to obtain a URL.
 */
private URL getWorkInternal() throws WorkloadException
{
  if (this.currentHostID == -1)
  {
    throw new WorkloadException(
        "Attempting to obtain work before adding first URL.");
  }

  try
  {
    boolean requery = false;

    if (this.workResultSet == null)
    {
      requery = true;
    } else
    {
      if (!this.workResultSet.getResultSet().next())
      {
        requery = true;
      }
    }
```

```
      if (requery)
      {
        if (this.workResultSet != null)
        {
          this.workResultSet.close();
        }

        this.workResultSet = this.stmtGetWork.executeQuery(
            Status.STATUS_WAITING, this.currentHostID);

        if (!this.workResultSet.getResultSet().next())
        {
          return null;
        }
      }

      int id = this.workResultSet.getResultSet().getInt(1);
      String url = this.workResultSet.getResultSet().getString(2);

      this.stmtGetWork2.execute(Status.STATUS_PROCESSING, id);
      return new URL(url);

    } catch (SQLException e)
    {
      throw (new WorkloadException(e));
    } catch (MalformedURLException e)
    {
      throw (new WorkloadException(e));
    }
  }
  /**
   * Get the workload ID, given a URL.
   *
   * @param url
   *          The URL to look up.
   * @param require
   *          Should an exception be thrown if the workload
   *          is not located.
   * @return The ID of the workload.
   * @throws WorkloadException
   *            Thrown if the host id is not found, and is
   *            required.
   * @throws SQLException
   *            Thrown if a SQL error occurs.
   */
```

```java
private int getWorkloadID(URL url, boolean require)
  throws SQLException,
    WorkloadException
{
  int hash = 0;
  RepeatableStatement.Results rs = null;
  try
  {
    hash = computeHash(url);
    rs = this.stmtGetWorkloadID.executeQuery(hash);
    while (rs.getResultSet().next())
    {
      if (rs.getResultSet().getString(2).equals(url.toString()))
      {
        return rs.getResultSet().getInt(1);
      }
    }
  } finally
  {
    if (rs != null)
    {
      rs.close();
    }
  }

  if (require)
  {
    StringBuilder str = new StringBuilder();
    str.append(
        "Failed to find previously visited URL, hash=\"");
    str.append(hash);
    str.append("\", URL=\"");
    str.append(url.toString());
    str.append("\".");
    throw (new WorkloadException(str.toString()));
  } else
  {
    return -1;
  }
}

/**
 * Mark the specified host as processed.
 *
 * @param host
 *            The host to mark.
```

```
 * @throws WorkloadException
 *              Thrown if the host cannot be marked.
 */
private void markHostProcessed(String host)
  throws WorkloadException
{
  try
  {
    int hostID = this.getHostID(host, true);
    this.stmtSetHostStatus.execute(Status.STATUS_DONE, hostID);
  } catch (SQLException e)
  {
    throw new WorkloadException(e);
  }
}


/**
 * Open a database connection.
 *
 * @throws InstantiationException
 *              Thrown if the database driver could not be
 *              opened.
 * @throws IllegalAccessException
 *              Thrown if the database driver can not be
 *              acccessed.
 * @throws ClassNotFoundException
 *              Thrown if the wrong type of class is
 *              returned.
 * @throws WorkloadException
 *              Thrown if the database cannot be opened.
 * @throws SQLException
 *              Thrown if a SQL error occurs.
 */
private void open()
  throws InstantiationException, IllegalAccessException,
    ClassNotFoundException, SQLException, WorkloadException
{
  Class.forName(this.driver).newInstance();
  this.connection = DriverManager.getConnection(
     this.url, this.uid, this.pwd);
  for (RepeatableStatement statement : this.statements)
  {
    statement.create(this);
  }
}
```

```
/**
 * Set the status for the specified URL.
 *
 * @param url
 *            The URL to set the status for.
 * @param status
 *            What to set the status to.
 * @throws WorkloadException
 *             Thrown if the status cannot be set.
 * @throws SQLException
 *             Thrown if a SQL error occurs.
 */
private void setStatus(URL url, String status)
  throws SQLException,
    WorkloadException
{
  int id = getWorkloadID(url, true);
  this.stmtSetWorkloadStatus.execute("" + status, id);
  if (status.equalsIgnoreCase(Status.STATUS_ERROR))
  {
    this.stmtSetWorkloadStatus2.execute(
      0, 1, url.getHost().toLowerCase());
  } else if (status.equalsIgnoreCase(Status.STATUS_DONE))
  {
    this.stmtSetWorkloadStatus2.execute(1, 0,
      url.getHost().toLowerCase());
  }

}

/**
 * Truncate a string to the specified length.
 *
 * @param str
 *            The string to truncate.
 * @param length
 *            The length to truncate the string to.
 * @return The truncated string.
 */
private String truncate(String str, int length)
{
  if (str.length() < length)
  {
    return str;
  } else
  {
```

```
      return str.substring(0, length);
  }
}

/**
 * Try to open the database connection.
 *
 * @throws WorkloadException
 *             Thrown if the open fails.
 */
void tryOpen() throws WorkloadException
{
  Exception ex = null;

  logger.log(Level.SEVERE,
      "Lost connection to database, trying to reconnect.");

  for (int i = 1; i < 120; i++)
  {
    try
    {
      close();
    } catch (Exception e1)
    {
      logger.log(Level.SEVERE,
  "Failed while trying to close lost connection, ignoring...",
  e1);
    }

    ex = null;

    try
    {
      logger.log(Level.SEVERE, "Attempting database reconnect");
      open();
      logger.log(Level.SEVERE,
        "Database connection reestablished");
      break;
    } catch (Exception e)
    {
      ex = e;
      logger.log(Level.SEVERE, "Reconnect failed", ex);
    }

    if (ex != null)
    {
```

```
      try
      {
        logger.log(Level.SEVERE, "Reconnect attempt " + i
            + " failed.  Waiting to try again.");
        Thread.sleep(30000);
      } catch (InterruptedException e)
      {
      }
    }
  }

  if (ex != null)
  {
    throw (new WorkloadException(ex));
  }

}

public SQLHolder createSQLHolder()
{
  return new SQLHolder();
}

}
```

As you can see from the above listing, the **SQLWorkloadManager** class defines several instance variables. These instance variables are defined in Table 15.2.

**Table 15.2: Instance Variables of the RepeatableStatement Class**

| Instance Variable | Purpose |
| --- | --- |
| driver | The driver for the JDBC connection. |
| url | The URL for the JDBC connection. |
| addLock | Only one thread at a time is allowed to be added to the workload. |
| workLatch | Is there any work? Threads can wait on this latch when waiting for work. |
| maxURLSize | The maximum size a URL can be. Determined from the column size in the URL field of SPIDER_WORKLOAD table. |
| maxHostSize | The maximum size that a host can be. Determined from the column size in the HOST field of the SPIDER_HOST table. |
| statements | All of the RepeatableStatement objects. |
| workResultSet | Used to obtain the next URL. |
| hostResultSet | Used to obtain the next host. |
| connection | A connection to a JDBC database. |
| currentHost | The current host. |
| currentHostID | The ID of the current host. |

There are also several methods and functions that make up the **RepeatableStatement** class. These methods and functions will be discussed in the next few sections.

## Generating Hash Codes

URLs can become quite long. Sometimes they will exceed 2,000 characters. In reality, very few URLs will ever reach this length. However, since they can, they must be supported. This is why the **URL** field of the **SPIDER_WORKLOAD** table is 2,083, which is the maximum URL size supported by many web browsers.

This large field size presents a problem. The spider will often need to lookup and see if a URL has already been processed. The long URL length makes this field very difficult to index in a database. To get around this issue, we create a hash of the URL and store this into a field named **URL_HASH**. Using the hash, we can quickly narrow the search down to just a few rows. Additionally, because the hash is a number, it can very efficiently be indexed.

You may be wondering what a hash is. A hash is a very common computer programming technique where you convert a String, or other object type, to a number. Java includes support for hash all the way down to the **Object** level. The Object class contains a method called **hashCode**. The **hashCode** function returns a hash for any Java object.

A hash code is not a unique identifier and is never guaranteed to be unique. Though they are not unique, they allow us to break large sets of data down into small manageable sets that can be accessed very quickly.

To compute a hash for a URL, the **SQLWorkloadManager** class uses the **computeHash** method. The **computeHash** function relies heavily on Java's built in **hashCode** function. The **computeHash** method begins by converting the URL to a **String** and trimming it.

```
String str = url.toString().trim();
```

Next, the **hashCode** function is called to generate a hash code for the trimmed URL.

```
int result = str.hashCode();
result = (result % 0xffff);
return result;
```

The hash code is trimmed to 16-bits in length. This allows the hash code to be stored in a regular integer column type.

## Workload Synchronization

The SQL workload manager must synchronize access to the workload. There are two synchronization objects used by the **SQLWorkloadManager**. The first, named **addLock**, is defined as follows:

```
private Semaphore addLock;
```

The **addLock** semaphore is used to ensure that no two threads are added to the workload at exactly the same time. This prevents the workload from getting two or more of the same URL added. A semaphore is a synchronization object that allows a specified number of threads to simultaneously access a resource. The **addLock** resource was created to allow only one thread to access it at a time. A semaphore that allows only one at a time thread access, are sometimes called a mutex.

The second synchronization object used by the **SQLWorkloadManager**, named **workLatch**, is defined as follows:

```
private CountDownLatch workLatch;
```

The **workLatch** synchronization object allows threads to wait until a workload becomes available. A latch allows several threads to wait for an event to occur. When the event occurs, the latch allows one thread to access the resource.

## Multiple Hosts

The ability to spider multiple hosts is one of the main reasons to use the SQL workload manager. First, let me define what I mean by multiple hosts. Consider the following two URLs. These URLs are on the same host:

`http://www.httprecipes.com/index.php`

`http://www.httprecipes.com/1/index.php`

The above two URLs both specify different Internet resources; however, they are both on the same host. They both are on the host **www.httprecipes.com**.

The following two URLs are on different hosts:

`http://www.httprecipes.com/index.php`

`http://www.heatonresearch.com/index.php`

Even though both of these URLs access the file **index.php**, they are both on different hosts. The first URL is on the **www.httprecipes.com** host, and the second is on the **www.heatonresearch.com** host.

If any part of the host is different, the two hosts are considered to be different. For example, **www1.heatonresearch.com** and **www2.heatonresearch.com** are two different hosts.

To support multiple hosts, the SQL workload manager uses the **SPIDER_HOST** table. The **SPIDER_HOST** table keeps a list of all of the hosts that a spider has encountered.

The Heaton Research Spider only processes one host at a time. Once all the URLs from one host have been processed, the Heaton Research Spider moves on to the next host. Future versions of the Heaton Research Spider may add an option to mix hosts, but for now, it is one host at a time. Processing one host at a time makes it easier to work with **robots.txt** files, which are used by site owners to restrict portions of their site to spiders. You will learn more about **robots.txt** files in Chapter 16, "Well Behaved Bots".

The workload manager uses two variables to work with multiple hosts. The **currentHost** variable tracks the String value of the current host. The **currentHostID** variable tracks the table ID of the current host.

### Determining Column Sizes

The SQL workload manager scans **String** columns to determine their size. This allows URL and host names that are too long to be discarded. It is suggested that you always use a column size of 2,083 for URLs and a column size of 255 for host names. Host names can be up to 255 characters long, though they are rarely that long. However, these are only suggestions. You can set the size of these fields to any length, and the spider will adapt, and truncate as needed.

The **getColumnSize** function can be used to determine the column's size. The **getColumnSize** function begins by calling the JDBC **getColumns** function. This function will return a **ResultSet** that contains information about the specified table.

```
ResultSet rs = this.connection.getMetaData().getColumns(null,
null, table, null);
```

Next, the **getColumnSize** function loops through the results and finds the specified column.

```
while (rs.next()) {
  String c = rs.getString("COLUMN_NAME");
  int size = rs.getInt("COLUMN_SIZE");
  if (c.equalsIgnoreCase(column)) {
    return size;
  }
}
return -1;
```

If the specified column is not found, then negative one is returned.

## Summary

The **SQLWorkloadManager** allows the Heaton Research Spider to process large workloads. To use the **SQLWorkloadManager**, you must have a database with the **SPIDER_WORKLOAD** and **SPIDER_HOST** tables.

The **SQLWorkloadManager** will automatically re-establish a JDBC connection if an error occurs. Using the **RepeatableStatement** class supports this. The **RepeatableStatement** class encapsulates a **PreparedStatement**. However, unlike a **PreparedStatement**, the **RepeatableStatement** class will automatically re-establish broken connections.

Not all web sites welcome spiders and bots. You should never create a spider or bot that accesses a site in a way that is damaging to the site. You should always respect the wishes of the web site owner. Creating well behaved bots is discussed in the next chapter.

# CHAPTER 16: WELL BEHAVED BOTS

- Understanding the Ethical Use of Bots
- Understanding CAPTCHAs
- Using User-Agent Filtering
- Working with the Bot Exclusion Standard
- Implementing a Robots.txt Filter

Not all sites are welcoming, or even indifferent, to bots. Some sites actively take steps to curtail bot usage. These web sites often have good reason. Unethical bots can be a real nuisance to a web master. Some commonly unwanted BOT behaviors are:

- Posting Advertisements to BLOG Comments
- Posting Advertisements to Forums
- Registering Fake Users in Forums
- Creating Large Numbers of Web Postings
- Spamming the Referrer Logs of Web Sites
- Harvesting Email Addresses from Web Sites

You should never create a bot that performs any of these actions. It simply bogs down the Internet with a ton of useless information and annoys people using the Internet for legitimate purposes.

Although, there are exceptions, most web sites do not object to bots that simply scan for information, so long as you intend to use the information for a legal purpose. Unsolicited email, or SPAM, is becoming illegal in many parts of the world; therefore, using a spider to harvest email addresses is not something you should engage in. Furthermore, it is not something this book will teach you to do.

When programming your bot, you really have to be careful when your bot posts information to a site. Posting information to web sites is where bots and web masters most often clash. Most of the programming decisions really just come down to common sense. For example, you could create a bot that posts a link to your site on hundreds of forums. First, you should ask yourself whether the forum owners really want their systems clogged with this useless information.

Not every bot programmer will use bots ethically. Because of this, web sites are forced to take action to curtail bot usage. This chapter will cover some of the ways that web sites do this. The purpose of this chapter, is not to teach you to circumvent any of these mechanisms. Rather, this chapter makes you aware of them, so your bots always act in a well-behaved manner. The most common methods used to curtail bot usage are listed here:

- CAPTCHAs
- Bot Exclusion File
- User-Agent Filtering

This chapter will explore each of these methods.

## Using a CAPTCHA

One of the most common methods used to thwart bot access is the CAPTCHA. You have likely seen CAPTCHAs on popular web sites. A CAPTCHA displays an image of distorted text and asks the user to enter the characters displayed. Figure 16.1 shows four CAPTCHAs from popular web sites.

**Figure 16.1: Four CAPTCHAs**

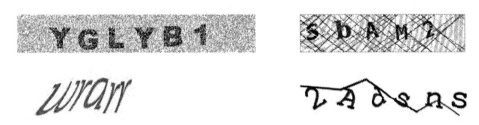

CAPTCHA is an acronym for "Completely Automated Public Turing Test to Tell Computers and Humans Apart". The term CAPTCHA is trademarked by Carnegie Mellon University. Luis von Ahn, Manuel Blum, Nicholas J. Hopper of Carnegie Mellon University, and John Langford of IBM coined the term in the year 2000. Most CAPTCHAs require that the user type the letters of a distorted image, sometimes with the addition of an obscured sequence of letters or digits, that appears on the screen.

## Origin of CAPTCHAs

The first discussion of automated tests, which distinguish humans from computers for the purpose of controlling access to web services, appears in a 1996 manuscript of Moni Naor from the Weizmann Institute of Science. Primitive CAPTCHAs seem to have been later developed in 1997 at AltaVista by Andrei Broder and his colleagues, to prevent bots from adding URLs to their search engine. The team sought to make their CAPTCHA resistance with an Optical Character Recognition (OCR) attack. The team looked at the manual to their Brother scanner, which included recommendations for improving OCR results.

These recommendations included similar typefaces, and plain backgrounds. The team created puzzles by attempting to simulate what the manual claimed would cause bad OCR. In 2000, von Ahn and Blum developed and publicized the notion of a CAPTCHA, which included any program that could distinguish humans from computers. They invented multiple examples of CAPTCHAs, including the first CAPTCHAs to be widely used (at Yahoo!).

## Accessibility Concerns

CAPTCHAs are usually based on reading text. This can present a problem for blind or visually impaired users who would like to access the protected resource. However, CAPTCHAs do not necessarily have to be visual. Any hard, artificial intelligence problem, such as speech recognition, could be used as the basis of a CAPTCHA. Some implementations of CAPTCHAs permit visually impaired users to opt for an audio CAPTCHA.

Because CAPTCHAs are designed to be unreadable by machines, common assisted technology tools, such as screen readers, cannot interpret them. Since sites may use CAPTCHAs as part of the initial registration process, or even every login, this challenge can completely block some access. In certain jurisdictions, site owners could become a target for litigation if they are using CAPTCHAs that discriminate against certain people with disabilities.

## Circumvention of CAPTCHAs

There are a number of means that unethical bot writers use to defeat CAPTCHAs. If a web master has taken the time to insert a CAPTCHA, they surely do not want bots to access their site. Although, this chapter will not demonstrate how to circumvent a CAPTCHA, it will discuss some of the methods used to circumvent a CAPTCHA, so you are aware of both sides of this "battle". Some of the more common means to circumvent CAPTCHAs are listed here:

- Optical Character Recognition (OCR)
- Cheap Human Labor
- Insecure Implementation

Optical Character Recognition is a computer process that converts images to ASCII text. This is often used for FAX documents. By using OCR, you can capture the text image of the FAX, and import it into a word processor for editing. OCR technology can also be used to circumvent a CAPTCHA. However, most modern CAPTCHAs take steps to make it very difficult for traditional OCR technology to read them.

CAPTCHAs are designed to make sure that a human is using the system. The obvious circumvention is to have a human identify hundreds of CAPTCHAs an hour in a highly automated fashion. Low-wage human workers could perform this task.

Some poorly designed CAPTCHA protection systems can be bypassed, without using OCR, simply by re-using the session ID of a known CAPTCHA image. Sometimes, part of the software generating the CAPTCHA is client-side, and the non-image-text can easily be lifted from the HTML page. As web sites become more sophisticated against bot spamming, client side CAPTCHAs are becoming very rare.

Overall CAPTCHAs are a fairly effective defense against bots. Using a CAPTCHA on a site will force the spammer, or other malicious bot programmer, to go to great lengths to access the site.

## User Agent Filtering

Some web server software allows you to exclude certain clients based on their **User-Agent**. If you are using the Apache web server, this is configured using the **.htaccess** file. For example, to exclude the **User-Agent's** of **BadBot** and **AnotherBadBot**, use the following **.htaccess** file:

```
RewriteEngine On
RewriteCond %{HTTP_USER_AGENT} ^BadBot [OR]
RewriteCond %{HTTP_USER_AGENT} ^AnotherBadBot
```

If either of these bots tries to access a URL on the sever, they will receive the following error:

```
403 Access Denied
```

Simply changing the **User-agent** name of your bot can circumvent this. Of course, this is an unethical thing to do!

User-agent filtering is generally very effective against commercial spiders that do not allow their **User-agent** to be changed.

## Robots Exclusion Standard

The robots exclusion standard, or **robots.txt** protocol, allows a web site to specify what portions of that site can be accessed by bots. The information specifying the parts that should not be accessed is specified in a file called **robots.txt** in the top-level directory of the website.

The **robots.txt** protocol was created by consensus in June 1994 by members of the robots mailing list (**robots-request@nexor.co.uk**). There is no official standards body or RFC document for this protocol. RFC, or request for comments, is a document that describes an official Internet standard.

The `robots.txt` file is simply placed at the root level of a domain where it can be viewed by a web browser. For example, to see the `robots.txt` file for Wikipedia visit the following URL:

`http://en.wikipedia.org/wiki/Robots.txt`

The Wikipedia `robots.txt` file is fairly long. The format itself is actually quite simple. The following section will describe it.

Because the `robots.txt` file is publicly accessible, it is not an effective way to hide "private" parts of your web site. Any user with a browser can quickly examine your `robots.txt` file. To make a part of your web site truly secure you must use more advanced methods than `robots.txt`. It is generally best to list a private section in `robots.txt` and to also assign a password to this part of your web site.

## Understanding the robots.txt Format

The two lines that you will most often see in a `robots.txt` file are `User-agent:` and `Disallow:`. The `Disallow` prefixed lines specify what URLs should not be accessed. The `User-agent` prefixed lines tell you which program the `Disallow` lines refer to.

As discussed in Chapter 13, you should create a `User-agent` name to identify your spider. This will allow a site to exclude your spider, if they so desire. By default the Heaton Research Spider uses Java's own `User-agent` string. Because many programs use this `User-agent` you should choose another. If a site were to exclude the Java `User-agent`, your spider would be excluded as well.

You may also see `User-agent` prefixed lines that specify a user agent of "*". This means all bots. Any instructions following a `User-agent` of "*" should be observed by all bots, including yours.

The `robots.txt Disallow` patterns are matched by simple substring comparisons, so care should be taken to make sure that patterns matching directories have the final '/' character appended. If not, all files with names starting with that substring will match, rather than just those in the directory intended.

This following `robots.txt` file allows all robots to visit all files because the wild card "*" specifies all robots:

```
User-agent: *
Disallow:
```

The following `robots.txt` is the opposite of the preceding one it blocks all bot access:

```
User-agent: *
Disallow: /
```

To block four directories on your site, use a similar **robots.txt** file.

```
User-agent: *
Disallow: /cgi-bin/
Disallow: /images/
Disallow: /tmp/
Disallow: /private/
```

If you would like to exclude a specific bot, named **BadBot**, from your **/private/** directory, use the following **robots.txt** file.

```
User-agent: BadBot
Disallow: /private/
```

The pound "#" character can be used to insert comments, such as:

```
# This is a comment
User-agent: * # match all bots
Disallow: / # keep them out
```

The wild card character can only be used with the **User-Agent** directive. The following line would be invalid:

```
Disallow: *
```

Rather, to disallow everything, simply disallow your document root, as follows:

```
Disallow: /
```

In the next section, we will see how to use a filter with the Heaton Research Spider to follow the **robots.txt** files posted on sites.

## Using Filters with the Heaton Research Spider

The Heaton Research Spider allows you to provide one or more filter classes. These filter classes instruct the spider to skip certain URLs. You can specify a filter class as part of the spider configuration file. The spider comes with one built in filter, named **RobotsFilter**. This filter scans a **robots.txt** file and instructs the spider to skip URLs that were marked as Disallowed in the **robots.txt** file.

Listing 16.1 shows a spider configuration file that specifies the **RobotsFilter**.

### Listing 16.1: Spider Configuration (Spider.conf)

```
timeout: 60000
maxDepth: -1
corePoolSize: 100
maximumPoolSize:100
```

```
keepAliveTime: 60
dbURL: jdbc:mysql://192.168.1.20/spider?user=root
dbClass: com.mysql.jdbc.Driver
workloadManager:com.heatonresearch.httprecipes.spider.workload.
sql.SQLWorkloadManager
startup: clear
filter: com.heatonresearch.httprecipes.spider.filter.RobotsFilter
```

As you can see from the above listing, the **filter** line specifies the filter. If you would like to use more than one filter, simply include more than one **filter** line.

You should always make use of the **RobotsFilter**. If a web master specifies to skip parts of their site or the entire site through the **robots.txt** file, you should honor this request. Including the **RobotsFilter** honors this file automatically.

### The Filter Interface

To create a filter class for the Heaton Research spider, that class must implement the **SpiderFilter** interface. This interface defines the two necessary functions that must be implemented to create a filter. The **SpiderFilter** interface is shown in Listing 16.2.

### Listing 16.2: The SpiderFilter Interface (SpiderFilter.java)

```java
package com.heatonresearch.httprecipes.spider.filter;

import java.io.*;
import java.net.*;

public interface SpiderFilter {
  /**
   * Check to see if the specified URL is to be excluded.
   *
   * @param url
   *            The URL to be checked.
   * @return Returns true if the URL should be excluded.
   */
  public boolean isExcluded(URL url);

  /**
   * Called when a new host is to be processed. Hosts
   * are processed one at a time.  SpiderFilter classes
   * can not be shared among hosts.
   *
   * @param host
   *            The new host.
   * @param userAgent
```

```
 *              The user agent being used by the spider. Leave
 *              null for default.
 * @throws IOException
 *              Thrown if an I/O error occurs.
 */
  public void newHost(String host, String userAgent) throws
IOException;
}
```

The first required function is named **isExcluded**. The **isExcluded** function will be called for each URL that the spider finds for the current host. If the URL is to be excluded, then a value of **true** will be returned.

The second required method is named **newHost**. The **newHost** method is called whenever the spider is processing a new host. As you will recall from Chapter 14, the spider processes one host at a time. As a result, **newHost** will be called when a new host is being processed. It will also be called when the first host is being processed. After **newHost** is called, **isExcluded** will be called for each URL found at that host. Hosts will not be over-lapped. Once **newHost** is called, you will not receive URLs from the previous host.

## Implementing a robots.txt Filter

The **RobotsFilter** class provided by the Heaton Research Spider, implements the **SpiderFilter** interface. This section will show how the **RobotsFilter** filter was implemented. The **RobotsFilter** class is shown in Listing 16.3.

### Listing 16.3: A Robots.txt Filter (RobotsFilter.java)

```
package com.heatonresearch.httprecipes.spider.filter;

import java.io.*;
import java.net.*;
import java.util.*;

public class RobotsFilter implements SpiderFilter
{
  /**
   * The full URL of the robots.txt file.
   */
  private URL robotURL;

  /**
   * A list of URL's to exclude.
   */
  private List<String> exclude = new ArrayList<String>();
```

```
/*
 * Is the parser active? It can become inactive when
 * parsing sections of the file for other user agents.
 */
private boolean active;

/*
 * The user agent string we are to use, null for default.
 */
private String userAgent;

/**
 * Returns a list of URL's to be excluded.
 *
 * @return A vector of URL's to be excluded.
 */
public List<String> getExclude()
{
  return this.exclude;
}

/**
 * Returns the full URL of the robots.txt file.
 *
 * @return The full URL of the robots.txt file.
 */

public URL getRobotFile()
{
  return this.robotURL;
}

/**
 * Check to see if the specified URL is to be excluded.
 *
 * @param url
 *            The URL to be checked.
 * @return Returns true if the URL should be excluded.
 */
public boolean isExcluded(URL url)
{
  for (String str : this.exclude)
  {
    if (url.getFile().startsWith(str))
    {
      return true;
```

```
      }
    }
    return false;
  }


  /**
   * Called when a new host is to be processed. Hosts
   * are processed one at a time.  SpiderFilter classes
   * can not be shared among hosts.
   *
   * @param host
   *            The new host.
   * @param userAgent
   *            The user agent being used by the spider. Leave
   *            null for default.
   * @throws IOException
   *            Thrown if an I/O error occurs.
   */
  public void newHost(String host, String userAgent)
    throws IOException
  {
    String str;
    this.active = false;
    this.userAgent = userAgent;

    this.robotURL = new URL("http", host, 80, "/robots.txt");

    URLConnection http = this.robotURL.openConnection();

    if (userAgent != null)
    {
      http.setRequestProperty("User-Agent", userAgent);
    }

    InputStream is = http.getInputStream();
    InputStreamReader isr = new InputStreamReader(is);
    BufferedReader r = new BufferedReader(isr);

    exclude.clear();

    try
    {
      while ((str = r.readLine()) != null)
      {

        loadLine(str);
```

```
      }
    } finally
    {
      r.close();
      isr.close();
    }
}

/**
 * Add the specified URL to the exclude list.
 * @param str The URL to add.
 */
private void add(String str)
{
  if (!this.exclude.contains(str))
  {
    this.exclude.add(str);
  }
}

/**
 * Called internally to process each line of the
 * robots.txt file.
 *
 * @param str
 *            The line that was read in.
 * @throws MalformedURLException
 *            Thrown if a bad URL is found.
 */
private void loadLine(String str) throws MalformedURLException
{
  str = str.trim();
  int i = str.indexOf(':');

  if ((str.length() == 0) || (str.charAt(0) == '#') ||
      (i == -1))
  {
    return;
  }

  String command = str.substring(0, i);
  String rest = str.substring(i + 1).trim();
  if (command.equalsIgnoreCase("User-agent"))
  {
    this.active = false;
    if (rest.equals("*"))
```

```
          {
            this.active = true;
          } else
          {
            if ((this.userAgent != null) &&
              rest.equalsIgnoreCase(this.userAgent))
            {
              this.active = true;
            }
          }
        }
      }
      if (this.active)
      {
        if (command.equalsIgnoreCase("disallow"))
        {
          if (rest.trim().length() > 0)
          {
            URL url = new URL(this.robotURL, rest);
            add(url.getFile());
          }
        }
      }
    }
  }
}
```

The **RobotsFilter** class defines four instance variables, which are listed here:

- robotURL
- exclude
- active
- userAgent

The **robotURL** variable holds the URL to the **robots.txt** file that was most recently received. Each time the **newHost** method is called, a new **robotURL** variable is constructed by concatenating the string "robots.txt" to the host name.

The **exclude** variable contains a list of the URLs that are to be excluded. This list is built each time a new host is encountered. The **exclude** list must be cleared for each new host.

The **active** variable keeps track of whether or not the loading process is actively tracking Disallow lines. The loader becomes active when a **User-agent** line matches the user agent string being used by the spider.

The **userAgent** variable holds the user agent string that the spider is using. This variable is passed into the **newHost** method.

There are also several methods and functions that make up the **RobotsFilter**. These will be discussed in the next sections.

### Processing a New Host

When a new host is about to be processed, the spider calls the **newHost** method of any filters that are in use. When the **newHost** method is called for the **RobotsFilter** class, the host is scanned for a **robots.txt** file. If one is found, it is processed.

The first action that the **newHost** method performs, is to declare a **String** which holds lines read in from the **robots.txt** file. Then it sets the **active** variable to **false**.

```
String str;
this.active = false;
this.userAgent = userAgent;
```

Next, a connection is opened to the **robots.txt** file. The **robots.txt** file is always located at the root of the host.

```
this.robotURL = new URL("http", host, 80, "/robots.txt");

URLConnection http = this.robotURL.openConnection();
```

If a user agent was specified using the **userAgent** variable, then the user agent is set for the connection. If the **userAgent** variable is **null**, then the default Java user agent will be used.

```
if (userAgent != null) {
  http.setRequestProperty("User-Agent", userAgent);
}
```

Next, a **BufferedReader** is setup to read the **robots.txt** file on a line-by-line basis.

```
InputStream is = http.getInputStream();
InputStreamReader isr = new InputStreamReader(is);
BufferedReader r = new BufferedReader(isr);
```

We are now about to begin parsing the file, so it is important to clear any previous list of excluded URLs.

```
This.exclude.clear();
```

A **while** loop is used to read each line from the **robots.txt** file. Each line read is passed onto the **loadLine** method. The **loadLine** method actually interprets the command given for each line of the **robots.txt** file.

```
try {
  while ((str = r.readLine()) != null) {
```

```
    loadLine(str);
}
```

Once complete, the streams are closed. The **close** commands are placed inside of a **finally** block to ensure that they are executed, even if an exception is thrown while reading from the **robots.txt** file.

```
} finally {
  r.close();
  isr.close();
}
```

Each line read by the **newHost** method is passed on to the **loadLine** method. This method will be discussed in the next section.

### Loading a Line from the Robots.txt File

The **loadLine** method interprets each of the lines contained in the **robots.txt** file. The **loadLine** method begins by trimming the line passed in and searching for the first occurrence of a colon (:). As you will recall from earlier in the chapter, lines in the **robots.txt** file consist of a command and a value, separated by a colon.

```
str = str.trim();
int i = str.indexOf(':');
```

If the colon is not found, the line starts with a pound sign (#) or the line is empty, then the method returns. As you will recall from earlier in the chapter, a pound sign signifies a comment line.

```
if ((str.length() == 0) || (str.charAt(0) == '#') || (i == -1)) {
  return;
}
```

Next, the line is parsed into a command, and another variable named **rest**. The **rest** variable contains whatever text occurred to the right of the colon.

```
String command = str.substring(0, i);
String rest = str.substring(i + 1).trim();
```

First, we check to see if this is a **User-agent** command.

```
if (command.equalsIgnoreCase("User-agent")) {
this.active = false;
```

If an asterisk (*) is specified as the user agent, then the program becomes "active" immediately, since this applies to all bots. Being "active" implies that the program will begin tracking **Disallow** commands.

```
if (rest.equals("*")) {
  this.active = true;
} else {
```

If an asterisk was not specified, then the user agent command must match the user agent for the spider. If they do match then the program begins actively checking for **Disallow** commands.

```
if ((this.userAgent != null) && rest.equalsIgnoreCase(this.
userAgent)) {
  this.active = true;
}
```

If we are currently active, then we need to check for additional commands.

```
if (this.active) {
```

Next, we check to see if this is a **Disallow** command. If it is a **Disallow** command, then we create a new URL from the information provided.

```
if (command.equalsIgnoreCase("disallow")) {
  if(rest.trim().length()>0) {
  URL url = new URL(this.robotURL, rest);
  add(url.getFile());
  }
}
```

At this point, the line is now parsed, and we are ready for the next line.

### Determining if a URL is to be Excluded

To determine if a URL should be excluded, the **isExcluded** function is called. If the URL should be excluded, this method will return a value of **false**. This method begins by looping through all URLs in the **exclude** list. If the specified URL matches a URL in the **exclude** list, a value of **true** is returned.

```
for (String str : this.exclude) {
  if (url.getFile().startsWith(str)) {
    return true;
  }
}
```

Return a value of **false** if the URL was not found.

```
return false;
```

Prior to adding any URL to the workload, the spider will always call this method.

## Summary

Not all sites welcome bots. This is particularly true of bots that post information to web sites. You should never create a bot that accesses web sites unethically. If a web site does not wish to be accessed with a bot, you should respect that site's wishes. Web sites use a number of means to prevent bots from accessing their site.

CAPTCHAs are a very common method for preventing bot access. CAPTCHA is an acronym for "Completely Automated Public Turing test to tell Computers and Humans Apart". A CAPTCHA displays an image and makes the user enter the text in the image. Because a bot cannot easily read the image, the bot is unable to continue.

User agent filtering is another common method for denying access to bots. Most web servers allow the web master to enter a list of user agents which identify bots that they wish to block. If any bot that is on the blocked list attempts to access the site, they will receive an HTTP error.

The Bot Exclusion Standard is another method that is commonly used to restrict bots. Web site owners can place a file, named **`robots.txt`**, in the root of their web server defining what parts of the site are disallowed for certain bots. Every bot should access this file for information about what parts of the web site to stay away from.

You now know how to create a variety of bots that can access web sites in many different ways. This chapter ends the book by showing you how to use bots ethically. How you use bots is ultimately up to you. It is our hope that you use bots to make the Internet a better place for all!

Remember, with great power, comes great responsibility.

– Uncle Ben, Spider Man, Sony Pictures 2002

# APPENDIX A: DOWNLOADING EXAMPLES

This book contains many source code examples. You do not need to retype any of these examples; they all can be downloaded from the Internet.

Simply go to the site:

`http://www.heatonresearch.com/download/`

This site will give you more information on how to download the example programs.

# APPENDIX B: SETTING UP EXAMPLES FOR MICROSOFT WINDOWS

- Installing Java
- Installing Apache Ant
- Compiling Examples
- Using Eclipse

The examples in this book require JDK 5.0 or higher. However installing JDK 6.0 or higher is recommended. The examples were tested on both versions. This appendix shows you how to download and install all of the software necessary to use these examples. This includes installing Java, installing Apache Ant, as well as how to use these examples with an IDE, such as Eclipse.

## Installing Java

The current version of Java can always be downloaded from the following site:

`http://java.sun.com/`

You should choose to download the latest version of the JDK. You do not need to download the version that includes NetBeans, unless you plan on using NetBeans.

NetBeans and Eclipse are both Integrated Development Environments (IDEs) that enhance the Java development and debugging process. Later in this appendix, there is information about using an IDE. Installation of Java occurs through a Windows installation program. You can simply accept all the installation defaults. Figure B.1 shows the installation process.

**Figure B.1: Installing Java on Windows**

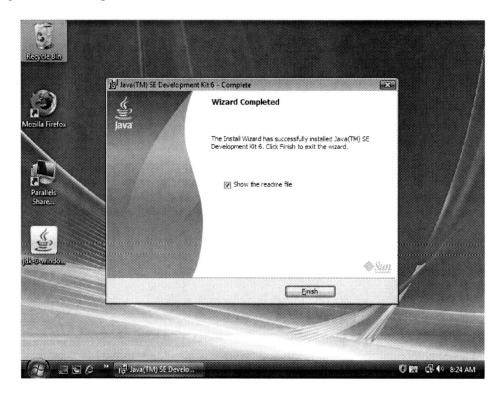

Once you have Java installed you will next need to install Apache Ant.

## Installing Apache Ant

Apache Ant is a software application used to build Java projects. This book's examples include an ant build script (**build.xml**). To compile the examples in this book, using this build script, you will need to install Apache Ant. The latest version of Apache Ant can always be found at the following URL:

**http://ant.apache.org/**

When you download Apache Ant, choose the save option, and you will obtain a ZIP file which is placed in the directory you chose to save it to. Using Windows, double click the ZIP file to examine the contents. You can then copy the folder, contained in the ZIP file, to your hard drive. The C: drive was chosen in the following example. Figure B.2 shows Apache Ant about to be copied to the C: drive.

**Figure B.2: About to Copy Apache Ant**

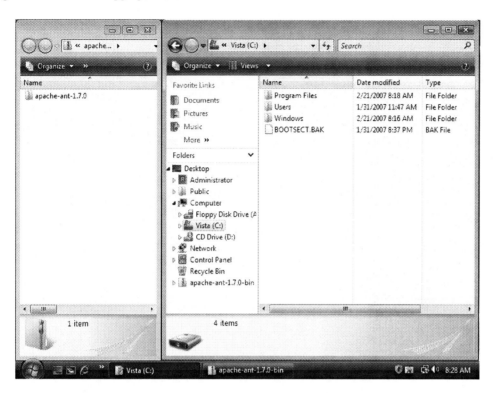

You now need to locate the BIN directory for Apache Ant. Because I copied Apache Ant to the root of my C: drive, the path to my BIN directory is as follows:

```
c:\apache-ant-1.6.5\bin\
```

Your BIN path may be different, depending on the version of Apache Ant used, or where you have copied Apache Ant. The BIN directory will always be just inside of the main Apache Ant directory. You will need to know this path for the next step.

Next, select "Control Panel" from your Windows start button. The Windows start button is the large green button on the bottom left of the screen. If your control panels are in "Category View", as seen in Figure B.3, you will need to select "Classic View".

**Figure B.3: Category View for Control Panels in Windows**

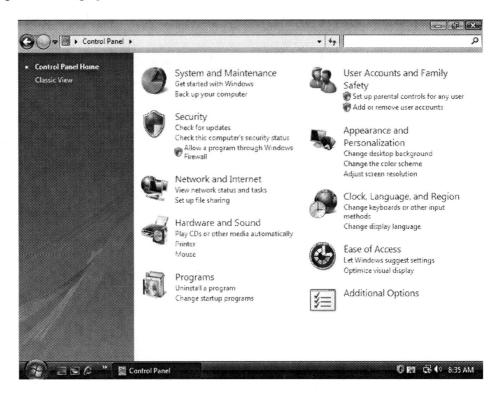

From the Classic View of the control panels double-click the "System" icon, and choose the advanced tab. You should now see Figure B.4.

**Figure B.4: Advanced Options**

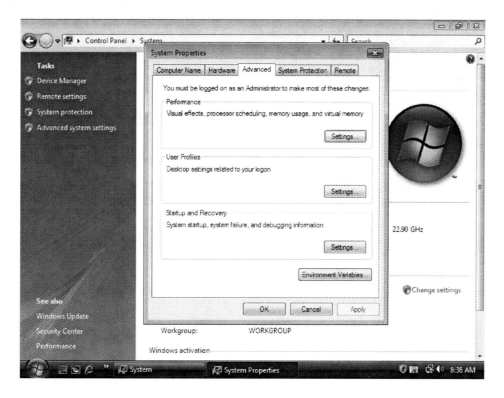

Choose "path" under "System Variables", and click "Edit". You should now see Figure B.5.

**Figure B.5: Edit the Path**

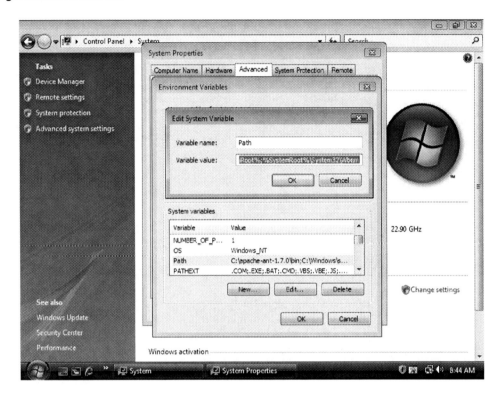

Add the path to your BIN directory to the front of the system path. Make sure you put a semicolon (;) at the end of your BIN directory's path. Semicolons separate elements of the system path. Also, be sure there are no additional spaces between elements of the system path.

You will also need to add JAVA_HOME and ANT_HOME to your "System Variables". **JAVA_HOME** should be set to the directory that Java is installed under. For my system, **JAVA_HOME** is set to:

```
C:\Program Files\Java\jdk1.6
```

You also need to set **ANT_HOME** to the directory you installed ant into. For my system **ANT_HOME** is set to:

```
C:\apache-ant-1.6.5
```

You can now test Apache Ant. Open a "Command Prompt" window and enter the command "ant". You should see ant display an error message, as seen in Figure B.6.

**Figure B.6: Testing Ant**

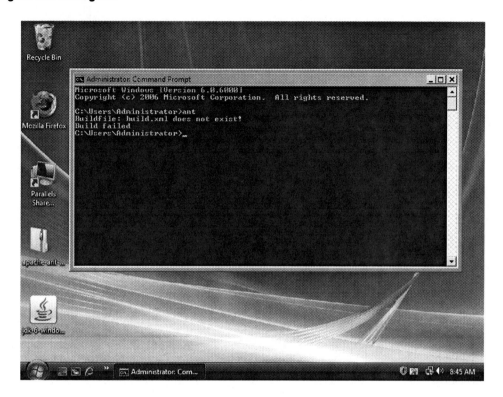

Ant was trying to run but had nothing to build! Now that Apache Ant is installed, you are ready to compile the book's examples.

## Compiling the Examples

Apache Ant is used to compile the examples from this book. The examples are contained in a directory named "HTTPRecipes". You get this directory from the ZIP file you downloaded that contains the examples. For more information on how to obtain the examples from this book, refer to Appendix A.

The examples shown here use the HTTPRecipes directory located at **c:\HTTPRecipes**. You can see the contents of this directory in Figure B.7.

## Figure B.7: The Book's Examples

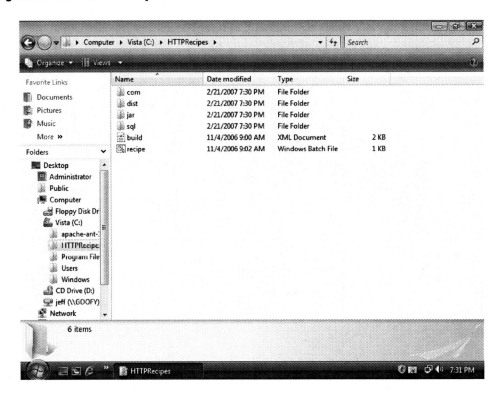

Each of these files and directories serve a specific purpose, which is listed in Table B.1.

## Table B.1: Contents of the HTTP Recipes Companion Download

| Name | Purpose |
|------|---------|
| .settings | Settings used by Eclipse. |
| com | Source code for all of the book examples. |
| dist | The distribution directory, contains the JAR file. |
| jar | Contains all of the JAR files needed to compile the examples. |
| www | Source code for the AXIS web services interface stubs. |
| .classpath | The Eclipse classpath. |
| .project | The Eclipse project file. |
| build.xml | The Apache Ant build script. |
| recipe.bat | Used to run the recipes with the correct classpath. |

To compile the book's examples, move to the **HTTPRecipes** directory and execute the following command:

```
ant
```

You will now see Figure B.8.

### Figure B.8: Successful Build

Now that you have compiled the book's examples, you are ready to execute them.

## Executing the Examples

Some of the recipes require third-party JARs to run. All of the JARs necessary to run the examples are contained in the companion download. However, these JARs must be in your **classpath** for the examples to run. To make this easier, there is a file named **recipe.bat** contained in the root directory of the **HTTPRecipes** directory. You can use it to run the examples. For example, to run the **GetCityTime** example from Chapter 3, you would use the following command:

```
recipe com.heatonresearch.httprecipes.ch3.recipe3.GetCityTime
```

Once you execute the above command, you should see Figure B.9.

**Figure B.9: Successfully Running an Example**

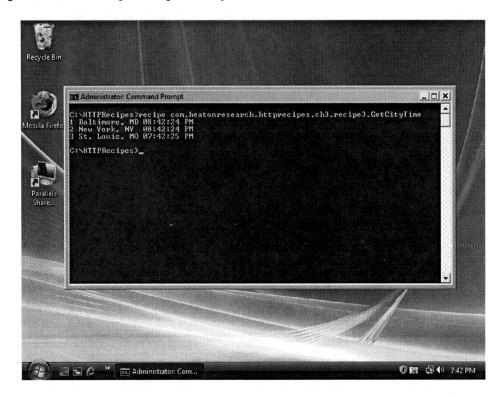

So far, you have seen how to execute the examples from the command line. The next section will show you how to use the Eclipse IDE.

## Using Eclipse

Eclipse is a very popular IDE for Java. This section shows you how to import the companion download into Eclipse. This section is not meant to serve as a general tutorial or installation guide on Eclipse.

To use Eclipse, you will have to import the companion download into Eclipse. In the Eclipse application, select the "Import" option from the "File" menu of Eclipse. From the import menu choose "Existing Projects into Workspace". Figure B.10 shows this.

**Figure B.10: Importing a Project**

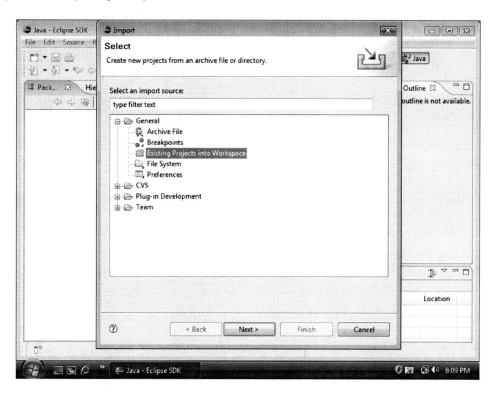

On the next screen you must choose the companion download's directory – which is the **HTTPRecipes** directory. On my machine, this is located at "c:\JavaHTTPRecipes". You can see this in Figure B.11.

**Figure B.11: Ready to Import**

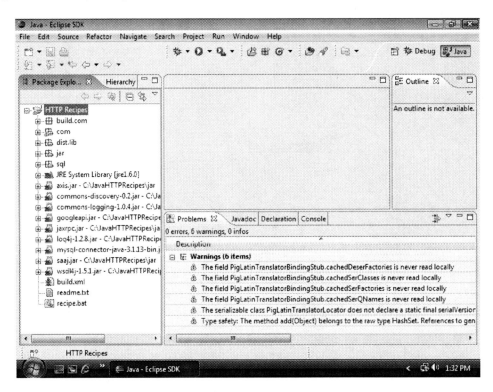

Once the companion download has been imported, you will be taken to Eclipse, but there will be some warnings. This is normal, as some of the third party web service libraries cause these. They are normal. Figure B.12 shows a successful import.

**Figure B.12: A Successful Import**

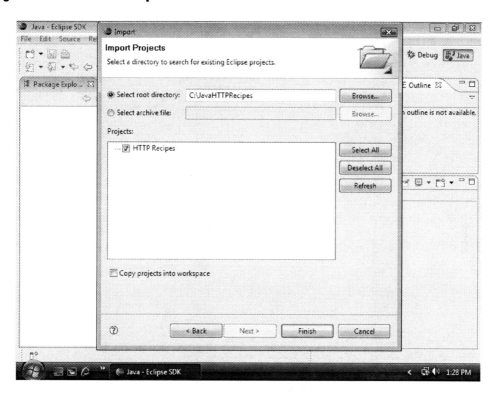

You may now run any of the examples as you normally would any project in Eclipse. You may notice a few warnings from Eclipse. These are a result of how the Axis framework generates code, these should be ignored. If you downloaded the examples to a different directory than c:\JavaHTTPRecipes you will need to reimport the JAR files from the "jar" directory. This can be done from the "Java Build Path" page of the project properties.

# APPENDIX C: SETTING UP EXAMPLES FOR MACINTOSH OSX

- Installing Java
- Installing Apache Ant
- Compiling Examples
- Using Eclipse

The examples in this book require JDK 5.0 or higher. As of the writing of this book JDK 6.0 had not been released for the Macintosh. However, if JDK 6.0 is available, you should use it. This appendix shows you how to download and install all of the software necessary to use these examples. This includes installing Java, installing Apache Ant, as well as how to use these examples with an IDE such as Eclipse.

## Installing Java

Macintosh computers obtain the latest version of Java directly from Apple. Apple has already released a version of Java that is compatible with the examples in this book. If you have kept up to date with your operating system updates, you likely already have the latest version. You can also obtain Java from Apple's Java page at:

http://www.apple.com/macosx/features/java/

To determine if you have the correct version of Java, you can open a terminal window, and issue the following command:

```
java -version
```

You should see a version of 1.5 or higher. If you do not have the correct version, visit the above URL and obtain the latest version of Java. Figure C.1 shows a terminal window with the correct version of Java.

**Figure C.1: Checking the Version of Java**

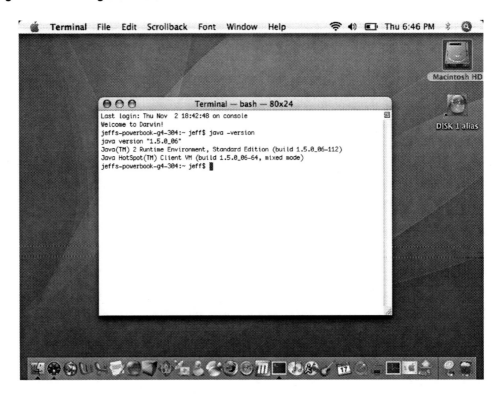

Once you have Java installed, you must install Apache Ant.

## Installing Apache Ant

Apache Ant is a software application used to build Java projects. This book's examples include an ant build script (**build.xml**). To compile the examples in this book using this build script, you will need to install Apache Ant. The latest version of Apache Ant can always be found at the following URL.

**http://ant.apache.org/**

When you download Apache Ant, you will obtain a **tar.gz** file. Using the finder, copy this file to your user directory. The rest of the install will be done from a terminal window. Open a terminal window and enter the following command:

```
sudo -s
```

This will transform you into the super user. To install ant, you must be the super user. If this is the first time that you have logged in as the super user, you will be given a brief warning. You can see this warning in Figure C.2.

## Figure C.2: About to Transform into the Super User

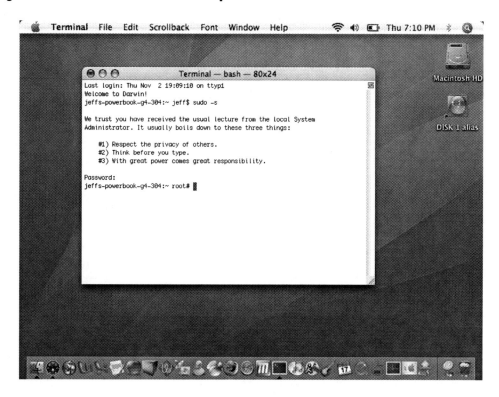

Next, we will need to create a directory to store ant in. Do this with the following command:

```
mkdir /usr/local
```

You may get an error telling you that this directory already exists. If you do get this error, simply ignore it. Now you need to move to this directory with the following command:

```
cd /usr/local
```

You are now ready to unpack the ant archive that you downloaded earlier. This is done with the following command:

```
tar zxvf ~/apache-ant-1.6.5-bin.tar.gz
```

Of course, if you downloaded a different version make sure to change the filename appropriately. If the unpack is successful, you will see dozens of files stream by on the terminal. When it is all done, your terminal will look similar to Figure C.3.

**Figure C.3: A Successful Ant Unpack**

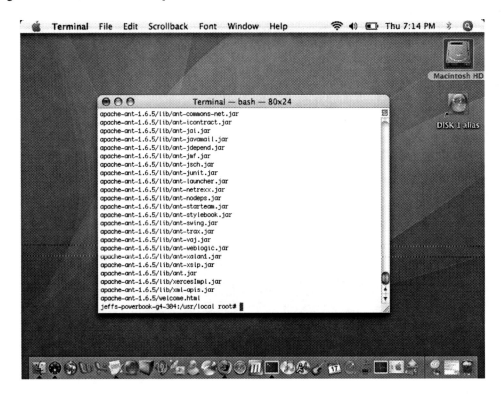

You no longer need to be the super user for the rest of this install. Enter the following to exit the super user status:

```
exit
```

You should also move back to your user directory, with the following command:

```
cd
```

Now you need to edit your profile using the **vi** editor. This will allow you to easily start the ant application. Use the following command:

```
vi .profile
```

Once inside of **vi**, move to the bottom of the file and press "i". This will put you into insert mode. Enter the following three lines at the bottom of your file. Enter them exactly as you see here. Adjust for version differences if necessary.

```
export JAVA_HOME=/Library/java/Home
export ANT_HOME=/usr/local/apache-ant-1.6.5
export PATH=${PATH}:${ANT_HOME}/bin
```

Make sure you do not erase data already in the file! This is very important! Once you enter these lines, your screen should look something like Figure C.4.

## Figure C.4: A Simple Profile

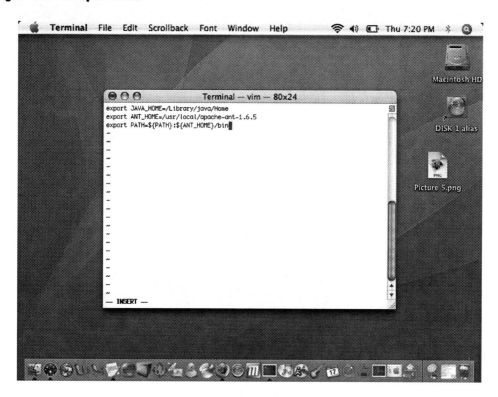

Once you have entered these lines, press the colon (:), type "wq!" and press enter. This should get you back to the command prompt. Close this terminal window and open a new one so that the changes take effect.

You can now test Apache Ant. Open a new terminal window and enter the command "ant". You should see ant display an error message, as seen in Figure C.5.

**Figure C.5: Testing Ant**

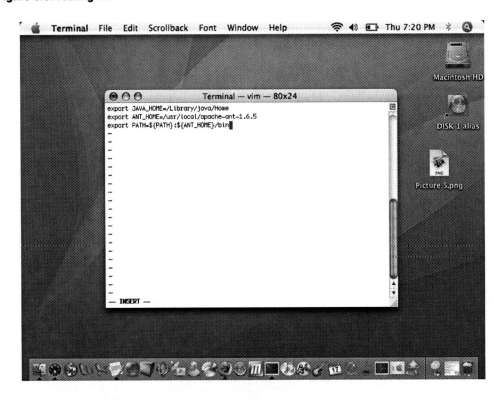

Ant could not find any files to build. That problem will be corrected as we prepare to compile the book's examples.

## Compiling the Examples

Apache Ant is used to compile the examples from this book. The examples are contained in a directory named "HTTPRecipes". You get this directory from the ZIP file you downloaded that contains the examples. For more information on how to obtain the examples from this book, refer to Appendix A.

The examples shown here are from the **HTTPRecipes** directory located on my machine at **/Users/jeff/HTTPRecipes**. You can see the contents of this directory in Figure C.6.

**Figure C.6: The Book's Examples**

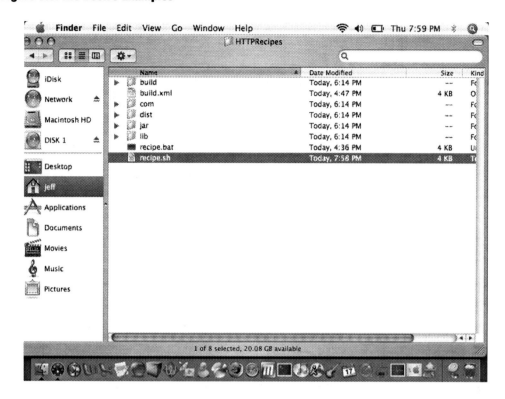

Each of these files and directories serves a specific purpose, which is listed in Table C.1.

**Table C.1: Contents of the HTTP Recipes Companion Download**

| Name | Purpose |
| --- | --- |
| .settings | Settings used by Eclipse. |
| com | Source code for all of the book examples. |
| dist | The distribution directory, contains the JAR file. |
| jar | Contains all of the JAR files needed to compile the examples. |
| www | Source code for the AXIS web services interface stubs. |
| .classpath | The Eclipse classpath. |
| .project | The Eclipse project file. |
| build.xml | The Apache Ant build script. |
| recipe.bat | Used to run the recipes with the correct classpath on Windows. |
| recipe.sh | Used to run the recipes with the correct classpath on UNIX. |

To compile the book's examples, move to the HTTPRecipes directory and execute the following command:

```
ant
```

You should now see Figure C.7.

**Figure C.7: Successful Build**

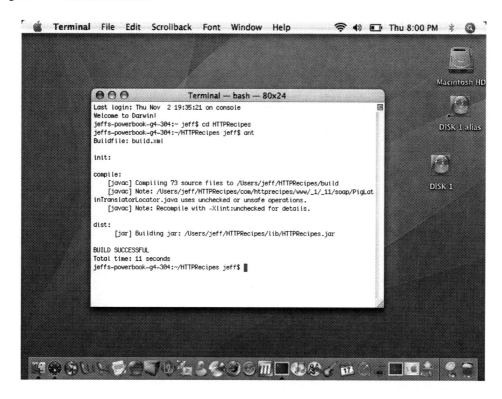

Now that you have compiled the book's examples, you are ready to execute them.

## Executing the Examples

Some of the recipes require third-party JARs to run. All of the JARs needed to run the examples are contained in the companion download. However, these JARs must be in your **classpath** for the examples to run. To make this easier, there is a file named **recipe.sh** contained in the root directory of the **HTTPRecipes** directory. You can use it to run the examples. For example, to run the **GetCityTime** example from Chapter 3, you would use the following command.

```
./recipe.sh com.heatonresearch.httprecipes.ch3.recipe3.GetCityTime
```

If you get a permissions error, you may have to enable the execution privilege on the **recipe.sh** command. To do this, execute the following command:

```
chmod +x recipe.sh
```

Once you execute the above command, you should see Figure C.8.

**Figure C.8: Successfully Running an Example on a Macintosh**

So far you have seen how to execute the examples from the command line. The next section will show you how to use the Eclipse IDE.

## Using Eclipse

Eclipse is a very popular IDE for Java. This section shows you how to import the companion download into Eclipse. This section is not meant to serve as a general tutorial or installation guide on Eclipse.

To use Eclipse, you must import the companion download into Eclipse. Inside the Eclipse application, select the "Import" option from the file menu. From the import menu choose "Existing Projects into Workspace". Figure C.9 shows this.

**Figure C.9: Importing a Project**

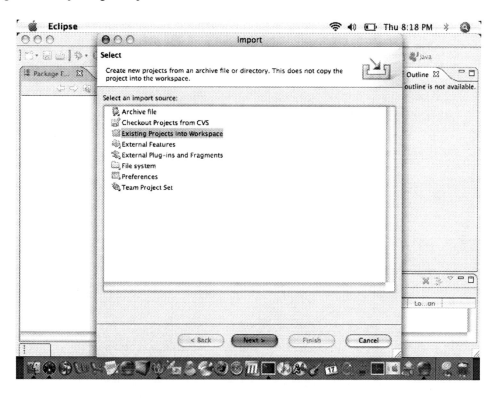

On the next screen, choose the companion download's directory. This will be something such as "/Users/jeff/HTTPRecipes". This is shown in Figure C.10.

**Figure C.10: Ready to Import**

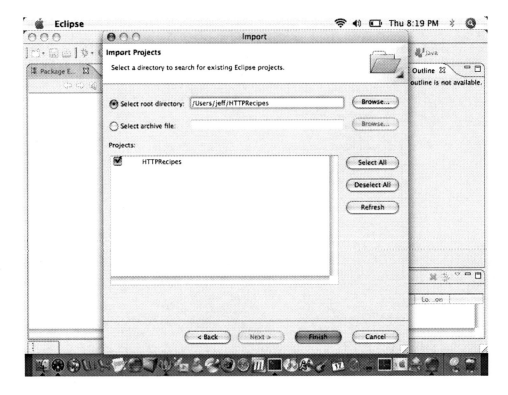

Once the companion download has been imported, you will be taken to Eclipse, but there will be some warnings. This is normal, as some of the third party web services libraries cause these. Figure C.11 shows a successful import.

**Figure C.11: A Successful Import**

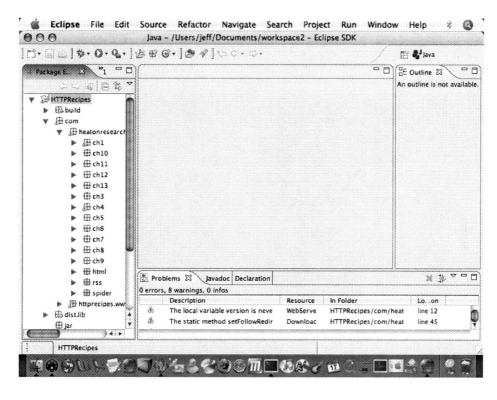

You may now run any of the examples as you normally would any project in Eclipse. You may notice a few warnings from Eclipse. These are a result of how the Axis framework generates code, these should be ignored. If you downloaded the examples to a different directory than c:\JavaHTTPRecipes you will need to reimport the JAR files from the "jar" directory. This can be done from the "Java Build Path" page of the project properties.

# APPENDIX D: SETTING UP EXAMPLES FOR UNIX TYPE SYSTEMS

- Installing Java
- Installing Apache Ant
- Compiling Examples
- Using Eclipse

The examples in this book require JDK 5.0 or higher. However installing JDK 6.0 or higher is recommended. The examples were tested on both versions. This appendix shows you how to download and install all of the software necessary to use these examples. This includes installing Java, installing Apache Ant, as well as how to use these examples with an IDE, such as Eclipse.

This appendix uses Fedora Core 5 to demonstrate how to install on UNIX type systems. Installation may vary slightly for different versions of UNIX/Linux.

## Installing Java

You can easily check the version of Java that is available on your system. Open a terminal window and enter the following command:

```
java -version
```

This will display the version information for Java. You need to have 1.5 or higher. If you do not, then you must upgrade. The current version of Java can always be downloaded from the following site:

**http://java.sun.com/**

You should choose to download the "Java SE 5 JDK". If a later version of Java is available, you may choose to download that instead. You do not need to download the version that includes NetBeans, unless you plan on using NetBeans.

You should download the JDK to your home directory. Sun Microsystems distributes JDK for Linux as a bin file that contains an RPM file. You must run the bin file to obtain the RPM file. To run the bin file, execute the following command from a terminal window inside your home directory:

```
chmod +x jdk-1_5_0_09-linux-i5860rpm.bin
```

This will give you permission to execute the bin file. If you are using a different version, remember to adjust the filename. Next, run the bin file with the following command:

```
./jdk-1_5_0_09-linux-i5860rpm.bin
```

This will display a long license agreement from Sun Microsystems, as seen in Figure D.1.

**Figure D.1: Java License Agreement**

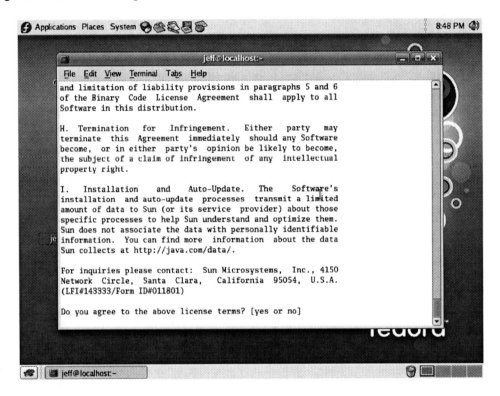

Enter "yes" for the agreement if you agree to the terms. You now have an RPM file to install. Become the super user with the following command:

```
su
```

Enter the super user password. You are now ready to install the RPM. Use the following command to install the RPM.

```
rpm -iv jdk-1_5_0_09-linux-i586.rpm
```

Once you have Java installed, install Apache Ant.

## Installing Apache Ant

Apache Ant is a software application used to build Java projects. This book's examples include an ant build script (**build.xml**). To compile the examples in this book using this build script, you will need to install Apache Ant. The latest version of Apache Ant can always be found at the following URL:

`http://ant.apache.org/`

When you download Apache Ant, you will obtain a **tar.gz** file. Using the finder, copy this file to your user directory. The rest of the install will be done from a terminal window. Open a terminal window and enter the following command:

```
su
```

This will transform you into the super user. To install ant, you must be the super user. If this is the first time that you have logged in as the super user you will be given a brief warning.

Next, we will need to create a directory to store ant in. Do this with the following command:

```
mkdir /usr/local
```

You may get an error telling you that this directory already exists. If you do get this error, simply ignore it. Now you need to move to this directory with the following command:

```
cd /usr/local
```

You are now ready to unpack the ant archive that you downloaded earlier. This is done with the following command:

```
tar zxvf /home/jeff/apache-ant-1.6.5-bin.tar.gz
```

Of course, if you downloaded a different version, make sure to change the filename appropriately. Also make sure you use your home directory. In the command above, the home directory is set for a user named "jeff". If the unpack is successful, you will see dozens of files stream by on the terminal. When it is all done, your terminal will look similar to Figure D.2.

**Figure D.2: A Successful Ant Unpack**

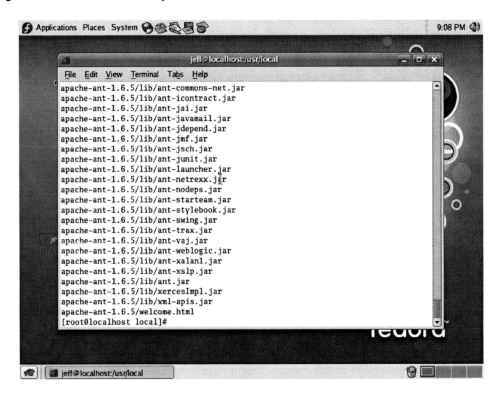

You no longer need to be the super user for the rest of this install. Enter the following to exit super user status:

```
exit
```

You should also move back to your user directory, with the following command:

```
cd
```

Now you need to edit your profile using the **vi** editor. This will allow you to easily start the ant application. Use the following command:

```
vi .bash_profile
```

Once inside of **vi**, move to the bottom of the file and press "i". This will put you into insert mode. Enter the following three lines at the bottom of your file. Enter them exactly as you see here. Adjust for version differences if necessary.

```
export JAVA_HOME=/Library/java/Home
export ANT_HOME=/usr/local/apache-ant-1.6.5
export PATH=${PATH}:${ANT_HOME}/bin
```

Make sure you do not erase data already in the file! This is very important! Once you enter these lines, your screen should look something like Figure D.3.

### Figure D.3: A Simple Profile

Once you have entered these lines, press the colon (:), type "wq!" and press enter. This should get you back to the command prompt. Close this terminal window and open a new one so that the changes take effect.

You can now test Apache Ant. Open a new terminal window and enter the command "ant". You should see ant display an error message, as seen in Figure D.4.

**Figure D.4: Testing Ant**

Ant could not find any files to build. That problem will be corrected as we prepare to compile the book's examples.

## Compiling the Examples

Apache Ant is used to compile the examples from this book. The examples are contained in a directory named "HTTPRecipes". You get this directory from the archive file you downloaded that contains the examples. For more information on how to obtain the examples from this book, refer to Appendix A.

The examples shown here are from the HTTPRecipes directory located on my machine at **/Users/jeff/HTTPRecipes**. You can see the contents of this directory in Figure D.5.

**Figure D.5: The Book's Examples**

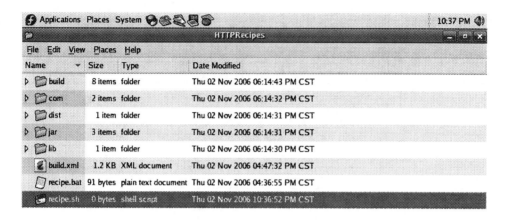

Each of these files and directories serves a specific purpose, which is listed in Table D.1.

**Table D.1: Contents of the HTTP Recipes Companion Download**

| Name | Purpose |
|------|---------|
| .settings | Settings used by Eclipse. |
| com | Source code for all of the book examples. |
| dist | The distribution directory, contains the JAR file. |
| jar | Contains all of the JAR files needed to compile the examples. |
| www | Source code for the AXIS web services interface stubs. |
| .classpath | The Eclipse classpath. |
| .project | The Eclipse project file. |
| build.xml | The Apache Ant build script. |
| recipe.bat | Used to run the recipes with the correct classpath on Windows. |
| recipe.sh | Used to run the recipes with the correct classpath on UNIX. |

To compile the book's examples, move to the HTTPRecipes directory and execute the following command:

ant

You should now see Figure D.6.

**Figure D.6: Successful Build**

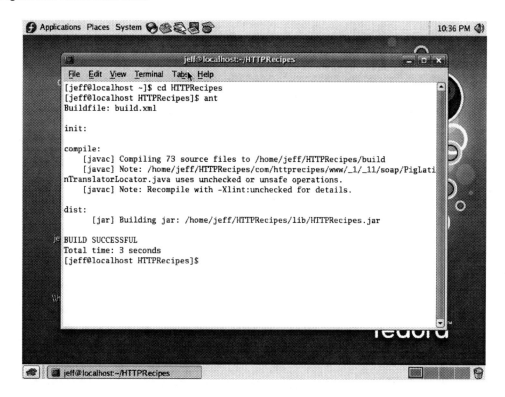

Now that you have compiled the book's examples, you are ready to execute them.

# Executing the Examples

Some of the recipes require third-party JARs to run. All of the JARs needed to run the examples are contained in the companion download. However, these JARs must be in your **classpath** for the examples to run. To make this easier, there is a file named **recipe.sh** contained in the root directory of the **HTTPRecipes** directory. You can use it to run the examples. For example, to run the **GetCityTime** example from Chapter 3, you would use the following command.

```
./recipe.sh com.heatonresearch.httprecipes.ch3.recipe3.GetCityTime
```

If you get a permissions error, you may have to enable the execution privilege on the **recipe.sh** command. To do this, execute the following command:

```
chmod +x recipe.sh
```

Once you execute the above command, you should see Figure D.7.

**Figure D.7: Successfully Running an Example on UNIX**

So far, you have seen how to execute the examples from the command line. The next two sections show you how to use a common IDE.

## Using Eclipse

Eclipse is a very popular IDE for Java. This section shows you how to import the companion download into Eclipse. This section is not meant to serve as a general tutorial or installation guide on Eclipse.

To use Eclipse you must import the companion download into Eclipse. Inside the Eclipse application, select the "Import" option from the file menu. From the import menu choose "Existing Projects into Workspace". See Figure D.8.

## Figure D.8: Importing a Project

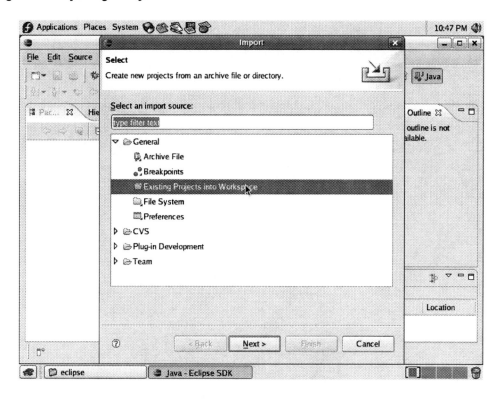

On the next screen, choose the companion download's directory. This will be something such as "/Users/jeff/HTTPRecipes". This is shown in Figure D.9.

**Figure D.9: Ready to Import**

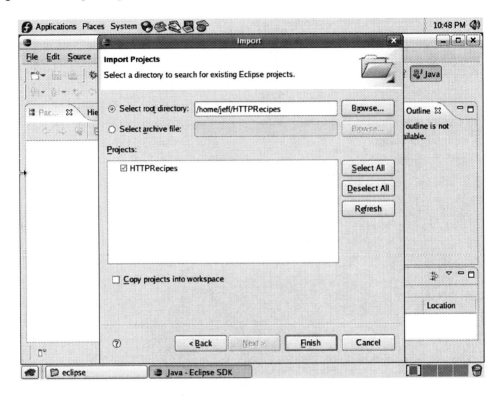

You may now run any of the examples as you normally would any project in Eclipse. You may notice a few warnings from Eclipse. These are a result of how the Axis framework generates code, these should be ignored. If you downloaded the examples to a different directory than c:\JavaHTTPRecipes you will need to reimport the JAR files from the "jar" directory. This can be done from the "Java Build Path" page of the project properties.

# APPENDIX E: USEFUL CLASSES, METHODS AND FUNCTIONS

The recipes in this book present many useful classes, methods and functions. This appendix summarizes them. This appendix also presents a list of all of the book's recipes.

## Reusable Functions and Methods

The following functions and methods were used as parts of recipes. These functions and methods would be useful in other classes and programs. Table E.1 summarizes them.

**Table E.1: Reusable Functions and Methods**

| Method/Function | Introduced in Recipe | Purpose |
|---|---|---|
| downloadPage | Recipe 3.1 | Download a URL into a string. |
| extract | Recipe 3.2 | Extract a string from a page bounded by two substrings. |
| saveBinaryPage | Recipe 3.4 | Save a downloaded page as binary. |
| downloadText | Recipe 3.5 | Download a page as text. |
| extractNoCase | Recipe 4.2 | Extract a string from a page bounded by two case-insensitive substrings. |
| downloadText | Recipe 4.3 | Download a text page and covert line endings to match the Operating System. |
| downloadBinary | Recipe 4.3 | Download a binary page. |
| addAuthHeader | Recipe 5.2 | Add the HTTP Authentication header. |
| advance | Recipe 6.1 | Advance the HTML parser to a specified tag. |
| getXMLNode | Recipe 10.2 | Extract an XML node. |
| getXMLAttribute | Recipe 10.2 | Extract an XML attribute. |

## Reusable Classes

Some examples in this book were large enough for their own class or package. Table E.2 summarizes them.

**Table E.2: Reusable Classes**

| Package/Class | Purpose |
|---|---|
| com.heatonresearch.httprecipes.ch5.recipe2. Base64OutputStream | A stream used to encode Base 64 numbers. |
| com.heatonresearch.httprecipes.html.CookieUtility | Cookie handling utilities. |
| com.heatonresearch.httprecipes.html.FormUtility | Form handling utilities. |
| com.heatonresearch.httprecipes.html.ParseHTML | An HTML parser. |
| com.heatonresearch.httprecipes.html.URLUtility | Many useful URL utilities. |
| com.heatonresearch.httprecipes.rss.RSS | Parse RSS feeds. |
| com.heatonresearch.httprecipes.spider.Spider | The Heaton Research Spider. |

# All Recipes

The following is a listing of all of the recipes in this book.

- Recipe #1.1: A Simple Web Server
- Recipe #1.2: File Based Web Server
- Recipe #2.1: Examining Cookies
- Recipe #2.2: Examining Forms
- Recipe #3.1: Downloading the Contents of a Web Page
- Recipe #3.2: Extract Simple Information from a Web Page
- Recipe #3.3: Parsing Dates and Times
- Recipe #3.4: Downloading a Binary File
- Recipe #3.5: Downloading a Text File
- Recipe #4.1: Scan URL
- Recipe #4.2: Scan for Sites
- Recipe #4.3: Download Binary or Text
- Recipe #4.4: Site Monitor
- Recipe #5.1: Is a URL HTTPS?
- Recipe #5.2: HTTP Authentication
- Recipe #6.1: Extracting Data from a Choice List
- Recipe #6.2: Extracting Data from an HTML List
- Recipe #6.3: Extracting Data from a Table
- Recipe #6.4: Extracting Data from Hyperlinks
- Recipe #6.5: Extracting Images from HTML
- Recipe #6.6: Extracting from Sub-Pages
- Recipe #6.7: Extracting from Partial-Pages
- Recipe #7.1: Using HTTP GET Forms
- Recipe #7.2: Using HTTP POST Forms
- Recipe #7.3: Using Multipart Forms to Upload
- Recipe #8.1: A Cookieless Session
- Recipe #8.2: A Cookie Based Session
- Recipe #9.1: Automatic Choice Lists

- Recipe #9.2: JavaScript Includes
- Recipe #9.3: JavaScript Forms
- Recipe #10.1: A Non-XML Based AJAX Site
- Recipe #10.2: An XML Based AJAX Site
- Recipe #11.1: Scanning for Google Links
- Recipe #11.2: Using AXIS to Access a SOAP Server
- Recipe #11.3: A Google Hybrid Bot
- Recipe #12.1: Display an RSS Feed
- Recipe #12.2: Find an RSS Feed
- Recipe #13.1: Find Broken Links
- Recipe #13.2: Downloading HTML and Images
- Recipe #13.3: Spider the World
- Recipe #13.4: Display Spider Statistics

# APPENDIX F: SETTING UP YOUR DATABASE

If you are going to use the **SQLWorkloadManager** for the Heaton Research Spider, you will need to create a proper database. Specifically, this database should have the **SPIDER_WORKLOAD** and **SPIDER_HOST** tables. This chapter shows how to create this database on a variety of database servers.

Data Definition Language (DDL) scripts contain the commands necessary to create the tables needed by the spider. DDL varies greatly from database vendor to database vendor. DDL scripts are provided in this chapter for three of the major database vendors. If you wish to use the spider on a database not listed here, you will have to develop your own DDL script based on the tables needed by the spider. Usually, you can just modify one of the scripts here as a starting point.

All of the DDL and configuration files presented in this chapter are contained on the companion download for this book.

## Setting Up MySQL

MySQL is a free database that you can obtain from the following URL:

`http://www.mysql.com`

To setup a database in MySQL, use the following DDL script in Listing F.1.

### Listing F.1: MySQL DDL Script

```
SET NAMES latin1;
SET FOREIGN_KEY_CHECKS = 0;

CREATE TABLE `spider_workload` (
`workload_id` int(10) unsigned NOT NULL auto_increment,
`host` int(10) unsigned NOT NULL,
`url` varchar(2083) NOT NULL default '',
`status` varchar(1) NOT NULL default '',
`depth` int(10) unsigned NOT NULL,
`url_hash` int(11) NOT NULL,
`source_id` int(11) NOT NULL,
PRIMARY KEY (`workload_id`),
KEY `status` (`status`),
KEY `url_hash` (`url_hash`),
```

```
KEY `host` (`host`)
) ENGINE=MyISAM AUTO_INCREMENT=189 DEFAULT CHARSET=latin1;

CREATE TABLE `spider_host` (
`host_id` int(10) unsigned NOT NULL auto_increment,
`host` varchar(255) NOT NULL default '',
`status` varchar(1) NOT NULL default '',
`urls_done` int(11) NOT NULL,
`urls_error` int(11) NOT NULL,
PRIMARY KEY (`host_id`)
) ENGINE=MyISAM AUTO_INCREMENT=19796 DEFAULT CHARSET=latin1;


SET FOREIGN_KEY_CHECKS = 1;
```

To make use of the MySQL database, you will need to make sure that the MySQL JAR file is part of your Java **classpath**. The **recipe.bat** or **recipe.sh** scripts, which can be used to run any of the recipes, automatically include the MySQL Jar. The MySQL Jar is named as follows:

```
mysql-connector-java-3.1.13-bin.jar
```

This Jar filename name will likely change slightly as new versions are introduced. You can obtain this driver (Jar file) from the MySQL web site. The following configuration file should serve as a guide for using MySQL.

### Listing F.2: Sample Spider Configuration for MySQL

```
timeout:          60000
maxDepth:         -1
userAgent:
corePoolSize:     100
maximumPoolSize:100
keepAliveTime:    60
dbURL:                    jdbc:mysql://127.0.0.1/spider
dbClass:          com.mysql.jdbc.Driver
dbUID:       user
dbPWD:       password
workloadManager:com.heatonresearch.httprecipes.spider.workload.
sql.SQLWorkloadManager
startup:          clear
filter:                   com.heatonresearch.httprecipes.spider.fil-
ter.RobotsFilter
```

## Setting Up Microsoft Access

Microsoft Access is a commercial database provided by Microsoft. To use Microsoft Access you can either use the DDL script shown in Listing F.4, or use the **spider.mdb** database that was provided with the companion download.

## Listing F.3: Microsoft Access DDL Script

```
CREATE TABLE [spider_host] (
[host_id] counter NOT NULL,
[host] varchar(255) NOT NULL,
[status] varchar(1) NOT NULL,
[urls_done] int NOT NULL,
[urls_error] int NOT NULL,
PRIMARY KEY ([host_id]),
CONSTRAINT `host` UNIQUE (`host`)
);

CREATE TABLE [spider_workload] (
[workload_id] counter NOT NULL,
[host] integer NOT NULL,
[url] varchar(255) NOT NULL,
[status] varchar(1) NOT NULL,
[depth] integer NOT NULL,
[url_hash] integer NOT NULL,
[source_id] integer NOT NULL,
PRIMARY KEY ([workload_id])
);

create index idx_status on spider_workload (status);
create index idx_url_hash on spider_workload (url_hash);
```

Java contains a built in JDBC driver that bridges to ODBC. ODBC is a database connectivity standard commonly used on Microsoft Windows. To access Microsoft Access, we will use the built in ODBC bridge. This class is named:

sun.jdbc.odbc.JdbcOdbcDriver

To use the ODBC driver to access Microsoft Access, use a URL as follows:

```
jdbc:odbc:Driver={Microsoft Access Driver (*.mdb)};DBQ=c:\spider.
mdb;DriverID=22;READONLY=false}
```

You will need to modify the above URL to contain a path to your Microsoft Access database. Listing F.4 shows a sample spider configuration file for Microsoft Access

## Listing F.4: Sample Spider Configuration for Microsoft Access

```
timeout:          60000
maxDepth:         -1
userAgent:
corePoolSize:     100
maximumPoolSize:100
keepAliveTime:    60
```

```
dbURL: jdbc:odbc:Driver={Microsoft Access Driver (*.mdb)};DBQ=c:\
spider.mdb;DriverID=22;READONLY=false}
dbClass:         sun.jdbc.odbc.JdbcOdbcDriver
workloadManager:com.heatonresearch.httprecipes.spider.workload.
sql.SQLWorkloadManager
startup:         clear
filter:                        com.heatonresearch.httprecipes.spider.fil-
ter.RobotsFilter
```

Of course, you will have to modify the above listing to include the filename and path of your database.

## Setting Up Oracle

Oracle is a commercial database product. Many companies use oracle. For more information about Oracle you should visit the following URL:

**http://www.oracle.com**

Oracle also makes a free version of their database, named Oracle Express. This free version allows developers to try the Oracle database, without having to purchase an expensive license. For more information about Oracle Express, visit the following URL:

**http://www.oracle.com/technology/products/database/xe/index.html**

The DDL script to create the tables on Oracle is shown in Listing F.5.

**Listing F.5: Oracle DDL Script**

```
-- Create SPIDER_WORKLOAD

CREATE TABLE SPIDER_WORKLOAD
(
WORKLOAD_ID INTEGER NOT NULL,
HOST INTEGER NOT NULL,
URL VARCHAR2(2083 BYTE) NOT NULL,
STATUS VARCHAR2(1 BYTE) NOT NULL,
DEPTH INTEGER NOT NULL,
URL_HASH INTEGER NOT NULL,
SOURCE_ID INTEGER NOT NULL
)
LOGGING
NOCOMPRESS
NOCACHE
NOPARALLEL
MONITORING;
```

```
CREATE INDEX IDX_STATUS ON SPIDER_WORKLOAD
(STATUS)
LOGGING
NOPARALLEL;


CREATE INDEX IDX_URL_HASH ON SPIDER_WORKLOAD
(URL_HASH)
LOGGING
NOPARALLEL;


CREATE UNIQUE INDEX PK_WORKLOAD_ID ON SPIDER_WORKLOAD
(WORKLOAD_ID)
LOGGING
NOPARALLEL;


ALTER TABLE SPIDER_WORKLOAD ADD (
CONSTRAINT PK_WORKLOAD_ID
PRIMARY KEY
(WORKLOAD_ID));

-- Create SPIDER_HOST

CREATE TABLE SPIDER_HOST
(
HOST_ID INTEGER NOT NULL,
HOST VARCHAR2(255) NOT NULL,
STATUS VARCHAR2(1 BYTE) NOT NULL,
URLS_DONE INTEGER NOT NULL,
URLS_ERROR INTEGER NOT NULL
)
LOGGING
NOCOMPRESS
NOCACHE
NOPARALLEL
MONITORING;


CREATE UNIQUE INDEX PK_HOST_ID ON SPIDER_HOST
(HOST_ID)
LOGGING
NOPARALLEL;
```

```
ALTER TABLE SPIDER_HOST ADD (
CONSTRAINT PK_HOST_ID
PRIMARY KEY
(HOST_ID));

-- Create Sequences

CREATE SEQUENCE spider_workload_seq;
CREATE SEQUENCE spider_host_seq;
```

To make use of Oracle, you will need the Oracle JDBC driver. There are several different drivers available for Oracle. Explaining all drivers is beyond the scope of this book. However, samples will be provided for the "thin" driver. This driver, along with other Oracle drivers, is contained in a Jar file that you will obtain when you set up the Oracle client. The name of this Jar file is as follows:

```
ojdbc14.jar
```

The name of the Jar file may change as new versions are released. However, you will need to add this file to the **classpath** when you run a spider session that requires Oracle. The driver that you must specify in your configuration file is as follows:

```
oracle.jdbc.driver.OracleDriver
```

Additionally, you will have to specify the database connection parameters in the database URL. This URL will look similar to the following:

```
jdbc:oracle:thin:@127.0.0.1:1532:database_name
```

A sample configuration file is shown in Listing F.6.

### Listing F.6: Sample Spider Configuration for Oracle

```
timeout:           60000
maxDepth:          -1
userAgent:
corePoolSize:      100
maximumPoolSize:100
keepAliveTime:     60
dbURL: jdbc:oracle:thin:@127.0.0.1:1532:database_name
dbClass: oracle.jdbc.driver.OracleDriver
dbUID:username
dbPWD:password
workloadManager:com.heatonresearch.httprecipes.spider.workload.
sql.oracle.OracleWorkloadManager
startup:           clear
filter:com.heatonresearch.httprecipes.spider.filter.RobotsFilter
```

You will also notice that Oracle uses a specialized workload manager. This workload manager is named:

```
com.heatonresearch.httprecipes.spider.workload.sql.oracle.Oracle-
WorkloadManager
```

This workload manager provides a few specialized SQL commands that Oracle requires.

# APPENDIX G: HTTP RESPONSE CODES

There are many different HTTP responses. This appendix lists them. This data was taken from WikiPedia (**http://www.wikipedia.org**).

## 1xx Informational

Request received, continuing process.

- 100: Continue
- 101: Switching Protocols

## 2xx Success

The action was successfully received, understood, and accepted.

- 200: OK
- 201: Created
- 202: Accepted
- 203: Non-Authoritative Information
- 204: No Content
- 205: Reset Content
- 206: Partial Content
- 207: Multi-Status

For use with XML-based responses when a number of actions could have been requested; details of the separate statuses are given in the message body.

## 3xx Redirection

The client must take additional action to complete the request.

- 300: Multiple Choices
- 301: Moved Permanently

This and all future requests should be directed to another URL.

- 302: Found

This is the most popular redirect code, but also an example of industrial practice contradicting the standard. HTTP/1.0 specification (RFC 1945) required the client to perform temporary redirect (the original describing phrase was "Moved Temporarily"), but popular browsers implemented it as a 303 See Other. Therefore, HTTP/1.1 added status codes 303 and 307 to disambiguate between the two behaviors. However, majority of Web applications and frameworks still use the 302 status code as if it were the 303.

- 303: See Other (since HTTP/1.1)

The response to the request can be found under another URL using a GET method.

- 304: Not Modified
- 305: Use Proxy (since HTTP/1.1)

Many HTTP clients (such as Mozilla and Internet Explorer) don't correctly handle responses with this status code.

- 306 is no longer used, but reserved. Was used for 'Switch Proxy'.
- 307: Temporary Redirect (since HTTP/1.1)

In this occasion, the request should be repeated with another URL, but future requests can still be directed to the original URL. In contrast to 303, the original POST request must be repeated with another POST request.

## 4xx Client Error

The request contains bad syntax or cannot be fulfilled.

- 400: Bad Request
- 401: Unauthorized

Similar to 403/Forbidden, but specifically for use when authentication is possible but has failed or not yet been provided. See basic authentication scheme and digest access authentication.

- 402: Payment Required

The original intention was that this code might be used as part of some form of digital cash/micropayment scheme, but that has never eventuated, and thus this code has never been used.

- 403: Forbidden
- 404: Not Found
- 405: Method Not Allowed
- 406: Not Acceptable
- 407: Proxy Authentication Required
- 408: Request Timeout
- 409: Conflict
- 410: Gone
- 411: Length Required
- 412: Precondition Failed
- 413: Request Entity Too Large
- 414: Request-URL Too Long
- 415: Unsupported Media Type
- 416: Requested Range Not Satisfiable
- 417: Expectation Failed
- 449: Retry With

A Microsoft extension: The request should be retried after doing the appropriate action.

## 5xx Server Error

The server failed to fulfill an apparently valid request.

- 500: Internal Server Error
- 501: Not Implemented
- 502: Bad Gateway

- 503: Service Unavailable
- 504: Gateway Timeout
- 505: HTTP Version Not Supported
- 509: Bandwidth Limit Exceeded

This status code, while used by many servers, is not an official HTTP status code.

# INDEX

## G

## H

# OTHER BOOKS FROM HEATON RESEARCH

**Introduction to Neural Networks with Java**
by Jeff Heaton
ISBN:0-9773206-0-X

Introduction to Neural Networks with Java teaches the reader to solve a variety of problems using neural networks. The reader is introduced to the open source JOONE neural engine, as well as a simple Optical Character Recognition (OCR) program, the traveling salesman problem and the feedfoward backpropagation neural network.

**Build a Computer from Scratch**
by Jeff Heaton
ISBN: 0-9773206-2-6

Building a computer is not as hard as you might think. This book shows how to select the best parts and build your very own computer. Knowing how to build your computer saves money and gets you the computer you really want. A computer you build yourself is one that YOU can always upgrade and repair.

**Java for the Beginning Programmer**
by Jeff Heaton
ISBN: 0-9773206-1-8

If you would like to learn to program in Java but have never attempted programming before, this book takes it from the beginning. This book focuses on the fundamentals of Java programming, such as loops, functions, classes and methods. Emphasis is placed on learning core programming techniques and rather than using an IDE to generate code for you.

## To purchase any of these books visit:

## http://www.heatonresearch.com/book/

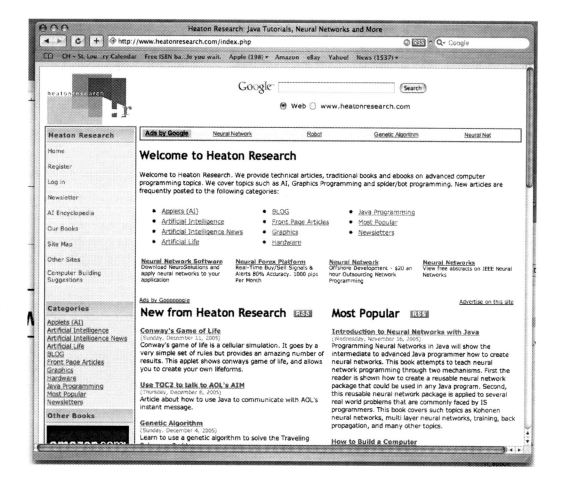

CPSIA information can be obtained at www.ICGtesting.com
235084LV00003B/34/A

9 780977 320660